D1576790

The Daily Telegraph
Book of
AIRMEN'S
OBITUARIES

The Daily Telegraph

Book of
AIRMEN'S
OBITUARIES

Written and compiled by

Edward Bishop

Bounty
Books

First published 2002
under the title *The Daily Telegraph Book of Airmen's Obituaries*
by Grub Street Publishing
Copyright © 2002 Grub Street Publishing, London
Text copyright © 2002 Telegraph Group Ltd

This edition published 2007 by Bounty Books,
a division of Octopus Publishing Group Ltd
2–4 Heron Quays, London E14 4JP

ISBN-13: 978-0-753715-31-4
ISBN-10: 0-753715-31-7

A CIP catalogue record for this book is available
from the British Library

Printed and bound in Spain

DRAMATIS PERSONNAE
(in order of appearance)

FIRST WORLD WAR VETERANS
Marshal of the RAF Sir William Dickson
Sir Frederick Tymms
Lord Balfour of Inchrye
Air Commodore H M Probyn
Archie Binding
Wing Commander Gwilym Lewis
Captain Cecil Lewis
Air Commodore "Freddie" West

FIGHTER BOYS
Wing Commander Bob Stanford Tuck
Squadron Leader J H "Ginger" Lacey
Colonel Erich Hartmann
Squadron Leader Charlton "Wag" Haw
Air Marshal Sir Peter Wykeham
Group Captain Peter Townsend
Group Captain Sir Hugh Dundas
Air Commodore Al Deere
General Adolf "Dolfo" Galland
Air Marshal Sir Denis Crowley-Milling
Group Captain W G G Duncan Smith
Wing Commander P B "Laddie" Lucas
Charles Sweeney
Wing Commander Douglas "Grubby" Grice
Group Captain Dennis "Hurricane" David
Air Vice-Marshal J E "Johnnie" Johnson
Squadron Leader Tony Bartley

THE YANKS
General Ira C Eaker
Lieutenant-Colonel Bob Johnson
Colonel "Gabby" Gabreski

BOMBER BOYS
Air Marshal Sir Harold Martin
Air Commodore Richard Kellett
Group Captain Lord Leonard Cheshire
Squadron Leader David Shannon
Sergeant Norman Jackson
Wing Commander Roderick "Babe" Learoyd
Group Captain Hamish Mahadie
Flight Lieutenant William Reid
Air Marshal Sir Peter Horsley

MARITIME AND PHOTO RECCE
Air Marshal Sir Edward Chilton
Wing Commander Mike Ensor
Flight Lieutenant Leslie Baveystock
David Beaty
Constance Babington Smith
Air Commodore Jeaffreson Greswell
Air Vice-Marshal Patrick O'Connor
Colonel Evelyn Prendergast
Marshal of the RAF Sir Denis Spotswood
Wing Commander Tony Spooner

THE GIRLS
Sheila Scott
Beatrice "Tilly" Shilling
Peggy Salaman
Monique Agazarian
Margot Gore
Air Commandant Dame Jean Conan Doyle
Elizabeth Mortimer

OPS & OPS
Wing Commander Robert Wright
Pilot Officer James "Jimmy" Wright
Group Captain Tom Gleave
Flight Lieutenant Jack Mann
Flight Lieutenant Colin "Hoppy" Hodgkinson

Wing Commander Geoffrey Page
Air Vice-Marshal "Birdie" Bird-Wilson

JOKERS IN THE PACK
Flight Sergeant William Hooper
Wing Commander Charles Samouelle
Frank Wootton
Wing Commander Bill "Sticks" Gregory
Beverley Snook
"Punch" Dickins

ESCAPERS AND EVADERS
Wing Commander Roger Maw
Flight Lieutenant Oliver Philpot
Aidan Crawley
Air Marshal Sir Harry Burton
Air Marshal Sir John Whitley
Squadron Leader Bob Nelson
Wing Commander Joe Kayll
Flight Lieutenant Jack Best
Flight Lieutenant Desmond Plunkett

CLANDESTINE
Group Captain Ron Hockey
Vera Atkins
Group Captain Hugh Verity

ROYAL CONNECTIONS
Wing Commander Jock Dalgleish
Air Commodore Sir Dennis Mitchell
Group Captain John Grindon

PLANEMAKERS
Sir Thomas Sopwith
R E Bishop
George Miles
Air Commodore Sir Frank Whittle
Hans von Ohain
Sir Arnold Hall

Dramatis Personnae

TEST PILOTS
Reggie Brie
Jeffrey Quill
Harald Penrose
Bill Bedford
Squadron Leader Frank "Spud" Murphy
Ben Gunn
Jacqueline Auriol
Wing Commander John Dowling
Air Marshal the Rev Sir Paterson Fraser
Squadron Leader Hedley Hazelden
Wing Commander Roland "Bee" Beamont

DISTINGUISHED LEADERS
Air Chief Marshal Sir Wallace "Digger" Kyle
Air Chief Marshal Sir Denis Barnett
Marshal of the RAF Sir Dermot Boyle
Air Commodore Ian Brodie
Air Chief Marshal Sir Edmund Hudleston
Marshal of the RAF Lord Elworthy
Air Chief Marshal Sir Harry Broadhurst
Air Vice-Marshal Robert Deacon-Elliott
Air Chief Marshal Sir Denis Smallwood
Air Chief Marshal Sir Frederick Rosier
Air Chief Marshal Sir Peter Fletcher
Air Marshal Sir Harold Maguire
Air Marshal Sir Kenneth Hayr

INTRODUCTION

Some fifteen years ago I was drenched and sheltering in the doorway of the former *Daily Telegraph* building in Fleet Street when David Twiston-Davies, returning from lunch, suggested I dry off in the obituaries' room and meet Hugh Montgomery-Massingberd, the obituaries' editor.

David gave Hugh a thumbnail of my writing credentials and Hugh, indicating a battered typewriter (word processors were not yet installed) put me to work on a gallant group captain for the edition. So that is how, joining the late Philip Warner and John Winton, Army and Royal Navy obituarists respectively, I completed Hugh's military team. Hugh called us his three musketeers and it stuck.

Many, many hundreds of obituaries later it has been well nigh impossible to select so comparatively few lives. The process of elimination has been painful and I have sought relief in seeking a balance between household names and lesser publicised men and women whose lives recall many aspects of last century aviation. Hence Cheshire and his fellow VCs, Peter Townsend (necessarily abbreviated), Johnnie Johnson, Bob Stanford Tuck, Adolf Galland and other fighter aces share my limited space with such lesser-known people as Tilly Shilling and Margot Gore.

Some choices, such as Wilfrid Duncan Smith, father of the Conservative Party leader, have been irresistible – partly because I composed it in circumstances which prompted the *Telegraph* to inquire whether my own obituary was to hand. I had just been put to bed at the Royal Brompton Hospital with a pulmonary embolism when I received a message that the fighter ace had died.

I was in luck. Duncan Smith's friend and fellow fighter pilot "Laddie" Lucas lived nearby. Although Laddie was none too well he kindly briefed me at my bedside. Iain Duncan Smith helped too. When Laddie died sometime afterwards I had recovered and supplied an obituary from my writing room at home.

Early on Hugh's commissions were issued with the urgency of a Battle of Britain take off. "Scramble!" instructions were passed on the phone as if to a Spitfire squadron at dispersal and our hero would lead the next morning's page. Disconcertingly, however, Hugh's radar was occasionally off beam and in wartime parlance the "gen was not pukka" resulting in abortive sorties.

I recall the occasions, for instance, when Hugh's intelligence derived from brief paid-for Court Page death notices alerted me that a highly decorated air vice-marshal and a heroic air commodore appeared to merit obituaries. Regrettably, my inquiries revealed that the "air vice-marshal" and "air commodore" were impostors who had invented their ranks and exploits.

Each had developed an elaborate fantasy. In support of his dream life the "air vice-marshal", who was a former boy scout, had faked costly mantelpiece invitations to himself – including one to Sir Winston Churchill's funeral. The "air commodore" had apparently figured in a First World War radio feature as having "bagged 12 Huns".

There was also the warrant officer to whom *The Times*, taking a lengthy and incredible death notice at face value, devoted almost half a page. I smelled a rat and dissuaded *The Daily Telegraph* from accepting a similar notice claiming more than 600 sorties over Germany and elsewhere where survival of more than 100 operational bomber sorties was exceptional. Other false claims such as two escapes, and unusually an AFM and Bar, were equally suggestive that this man who had served in the

RAF was in fact another Walter Mitty.

On the other hand many of the true life exploits and adventures of "our heroes" would test the creative talents of a fiction writer; none more that such pilots as Hugh Verity and Ron Hockey who flew moonlit missions for the Special Operations Executive and Harold "Mick" Martin and David Shannon of The Dambusters.

Having known so many of my subjects, Laddie, Verity and Hockey among them, it has been impossible not to be prejudiced in favour of including friends and acquaintances in a book the commercial size of which limits me. Yet I believe that no dispassionate selector would omit such naturals as Denis Crowley-Milling, Battle of Britain fighter pilot, escaper, and latter day Controller of the RAF Benevolent Fund and "father" of the fundraising Royal International Air Tattoo.

"Crow" can be counted among those who, leaving nothing to chance, thoughtfully suggested a briefing over lunch long, long before they died or, as with my neighbour Teddy Hudleston, many more noonday gin sessions than were strictly necessary.

Following more than forty years' association with the Guinea Pig Club and as the author of *McIndoe's Army* (Grub Street, 2001) I have not unnaturally included Tom Gleave and Geoffrey Page and other distinguished airmen whose severe burns were treated by Sir Archibald McIndoe and his team at the Royal Victoria Hospital, East Grinstead. Jackie Mann, fighter pilot with nine lives, guinea pig and airline captain, is perhaps the better remembered for his more recent notoriety as a Beirut hostage.

Generally, I have sought to link people in reasonably tidy sets of obituaries which have something in common. For instance, Constance Babington Smith, the intuitive WAAF interpreter of reconnaissance photographs appears

with other photographic reconnaissance pilots. Tony
Spooner, who planned his Malta sorties over pink gin
with the Navy, links with other RAF Coastal Command
characters.

Likewise, designers and engineers are grouped in an
endeavour to let their lives reflect something of the last
century's developments in their field. Tom Sopwith of
Sopwith Aviation and Hawkers, R E Bishop of de
Havilland who designed the Mosquito, Frank Whittle and
Hans von Ohain, his German jet opposite number, and
George Miles are among them.

Since new aircraft designs and engines require testing a
section is devoted to a number of distinguished test pilots
among whom is the magnificent Jeffrey Quill celebrated
for his pre-war work with R J Mitchell's prototype
Supermarine Spitfire and his Battle of Britain combat in
quest of improvements.

Following production testing in wartime many new
aircraft of all types were delivered to operational
squadrons from factories by women pilots wearing the
wings and uniform of the Air Transport Auxiliary which
is represented here by Monique Agazarian and other
women who flew a wide variety of aircraft types from the
latest fighters to four-engine heavy bombers.

Evaders who avoided capture and prison camp escapers
offer another opportunity to maintain my theme format.
Hence such disparate characters as Oliver Philpot of
Wooden Horse fame, Aidan Crawley, John Whitley, Jack
Best the Colditz glider man and Bob Nelson among
others who appear in this category.

Bill Hooper, one of whose cartoons adorns the jacket,
leads those I irreverently classify as the jokers in the pack.
Bill created Pilot Officer Prune whose hilarious mishaps
amused and instructed wartime aircrew wherever they
served. Charles Samouelle, the Savoy Hotel cocktail

shaker who became a desert ace, Beverley Snook, exuberant aviator of the leopardskin helmet, and "Sticks" Gregory, the dance band drummer and night fighter ace, are among those who demonstrate the diversity of talent among airmen. As I reshuffle on deadline the problems of selection continue to plague me. I regret the omission of so many who have died in the past fifteen years and merit inclusion – not least because of disappointing the many families and others who have assisted my inquiries. Those regretting the absence of Fleet Air Arm aviators must await publication of a companion volume containing the work of my late colleague John Winton.

I am particularly indebted to Air Commodore Henry Probert, his successors, Air Commodore Ian Madelin, and Sebastian Cox, heads of the Air Historical Branch, Ministry of Defence; also to past and present members of their staff, particularly Squadron Leader Peter Singleton, Group Captain Tony Stephens, and Dr Sebastian Ritchie; also to Arnold Nayler, former librarian at the Royal Aeronautical Society and Brian Riddle, his successor.

I also acknowledge the enthusiasm, care, encouragement and guidance of past and present *Daily Telegraph* obituary editors and their staff beginning with Hugh Montgomery-Massingberd and David Twiston Davies and including David Lewis Jones, Kate Summerscale, Christopher Howse, Robert Gray, George Ireland, Claudia Fitzherbert, Aurea Carpenter, Will Cohu, James Owen, Philip Ede and Katherine Ramsay.

Most of the above desk people arrived too late to take part in Hugh's hilarious obituary outings on the first of which the doors failed to close as we sailed for lunch (eventually high tea) in Boulogne but they were none the less infected by Hugh's zest and zeal. Incidentally, the story (if not the ferry) leaked, giving rise to *Private Eye's* speculation on the consequences of the loss at sea of twenty-five obituary specialists.

Finally I express my affection for and gratitude to Teresa Moore, the *Telegraph* obituary desk's Girl Friday whose good humour and general support of her family of obituarists has been essential to building the paper's reputation in the field.

EDWARD BISHOP, 2002

Editor's Note: Every effort has been made to record the actual date of death of the persons featured herein, and particular thanks go to Frank Olynyk for his help. Consequently the date appearing with the obituary is the correct date except when italicised which denotes date of appearance in the newspaper.

FIRST WORLD WAR VETERANS

MARSHAL OF THE RAF
SIR WILLIAM DICKSON
12 SEPTEMBER 1987

Marshal of The RAF Sir William Dickson, the most senior Marshal of the RAF after Prince Philip, who has died aged 88, was Chief of the Air Staff at the time of Suez and thereafter first Chief of the Defence Staff.

A skilful pilot and very much an aviator, he flew throughout his career; many a station commander was astonished to greet a Chief of the Air Staff stepping out of a jet fighter, but this was no act of showmanship on "Dickie" Dickson's part.

A quiet, modest, unassuming officer of small stature, he led by example, achieving results through quiet personal persuasion.

Such attributes were particularly valuable in 1944 when as commander of the Desert Air Force he provided the air support for Montgomery in Italy.

To these qualities he added a puckish sense of fun which was much needed during the period of defence reorganisation and consequent painful shrinking of the RAF in the late 1950s.

William Forster Dickson was born in 1898, the son of an official in the Chancery Registrar's department at the Law Courts. His mother, the former Agnes Nelson Ward, was a grand-daughter of Lord Nelson's and Lady Hamilton's offspring Horatia, whom she knew as a girl.

As a great-great grandson of Nelson it was perhaps inevitable that he should join the Royal Naval Air Service in the 1914-18 War, following education at Bowden House, Seaford, and Haileybury.

In 1918 while serving aboard the carrier *Furious* in the Grand Fleet he won the DSO for gallantry in a long distance low-level attack on a German airship station. He was also mentioned three times in despatches.

Although granted a permanent commission in the RAF after the 1918 amalgamation of the RNAS and the Royal Flying Corps, Dickson remained in naval aviation and in 1921 was awarded the Dunning Cup for his experimental flying from flight decks. The following year he received the AFC, serving later as a test pilot at the Royal Aircraft Establishment, Farnborough.

There followed a spell in the Air Ministry Directorate of Operations and Intelligence before he was posted to 56 (Fighter) Squadron and then to the RAF Staff College. Out in India from 1929 he served on the North-West Frontier and at RAF Headquarters in Delhi.

Returning home Dickson commanded RAF Hawkinge and 25 (Fighter) Squadron before joining the directing staff at the Staff College where he remained until 1938. In 1939 he took the course at the Imperial Defence College but the outbreak of war prevented its completion and he went to the Air Ministry Directorate of Plans, becoming director in 1941.

Towards the end of 1942 he became commander of 10 Group, Fighter Command, moving from there to 83 Group, 2nd Tactical Air Force until early in 1944 when he was given command of the Desert Air Force in Italy.

Dickson arrived in Italy shortly before the Battle of Cassino and led the Desert Air Force through the entire period of the Allied advance from the Gustav Line which ended in the liberation of Rome and Florence.

At the end of 1944 he was appointed Assistant Chief of the Air Staff (Policy) and in 1946 became Vice-Chief of the Air Staff, a post he held until receiving command of the Middle East Air Force in 1948. From 1950 to 1952 he was member of the Air Council for Supply and Organisation.

As Chief of the Air Staff from 1953 to 1956 Sir William played a key role in Sir Anthony Eden's decision to invade Egypt and thereafter in the conduct of operations during the Suez affair of 1956.

When some of the government's military advisers back-pedalled on previously agreed merits of such a move Dickson took a more positive line with the Prime Minister, sensing that he did not wish to hear or heed such talk.

In the event, Dickson was himself obliged to restrain the RAF at one critical point of the operation. Canberra and Lincoln bombers had taken off from Cyprus when Dickson, hearing that American civilians were being evacuated from Cairo West, ordered their return.

After serving as chairman of the Chiefs of Staff Committee from 1956 to 1959 Sir William was appointed the First Chief of the Defence Staff but did not see out his time. Early in 1959 Duncan Sandys, the Defence Minister, dropped him in favour of Mountbatten.

At the time Sir William was somewhat unfairly disparaged in Service circles as Sandys's "Man Friday", but this owed more to his quiet and unassuming manner than to the fighter pilot's tenacity that underpinned it. More to the point was Dickson's conviction, supported by that of Sir Dermot Boyle (the then Chief of the Air Staff), that a move towards missiles at the expense of manned aircraft was very much mistaken.

Off duty Dickie Dickson found great enjoyment in golf. In recent years he also devoted himself to helping and encouraging numerous causes such as the Royal Central Asian Society, the Ex-Services Mental Welfare Society, the Forces Help Society and Lord Roberts Workshops.

He was appointed OBE in 1934, CB 1942, CBE 1945, KBE 1946, KCB 1952 and GCB 1956.

He is survived by his wife Patricia, sister of the England and Middlesex cricketer Sir George ("Gubby") Allen, and a daughter. Their other daughter died in 1954.

SIR FREDERICK TYMMS
9 DECEMBER 1987

Sir Frederick Tymms, who has died aged 98, played a leading role in shaping the Empire air routes, launched civil aviation in India and more recently became an authority on the extent of law in space.

There are few aspects of international civil aviation which do not owe something to the advice and influence of Tymms, who from 1947 to 1954 served as British representative on the Council of the International Civil Aviation Organisation which he had helped to establish.

Dapper and moustached, "Freddie" Tymms was a quiet little man of great vision who achieved things with little noise but relentless work and meticulous attention to detail.

He was no mere paperpusher, though somewhat unusually for a civil servant he enjoyed action – flying, for instance, with Imperial Airways as a navigator. When landing rights for the Cairo to the Cape route were being negotiated in the late 1920s Tymms, the acknowledged architect of the African routes, penetrated the jungle in a model T Ford to inspect prospective landing grounds.

Frederick Tymms was born in South Wales in 1889 and educated at Greenhill School, Tenby. After attending extramural classes at King's College, London, he entered the Civil Service.

Although in a reserved occupation he volunteered at the outset of the 1914-18 War and won the MC as a subaltern with the 4th Battalion South Lancashire Regiment on the Somme in 1916. He then transferred to the Royal Flying Corps, flying in BE2cs and RE8s as air observer to a pilot who was to complete his career as Marshal of the Royal Air Force Sir John Slessor.

Shortly before the end of the 1914-18 War Tymms was sent to the United States to explain the technique of air artillery observation to the US Army Air Corps, returning to take the specialist navigation course at Andover. His characteristic persistence earned him a place in the new Civil Aviation Department where he built a reputation as a civil servant who achieved things.

Recognised as a rising star by Sir Sefton Brancker, the renowned civil aviation director of the period, Tymms made swift progress so that by the time Brancker died in the 1930s R101 airship disaster he was a force to be reckoned with in the developing world of international air transport.

Sir Alan Cobham and other pioneers of intercontinental flying recognised how much they owed to the technical groundwork Tymms put in on their behalf. He was always eager to leave his desk and participate – an attribute which was first apparent when he headed the air section of Sir George Binney's Arctic expedition to Spitsbergen in 1924.

The early 1930s found Tymms in India where, as director of Civil Aviation for the best part of 15 years, he fashioned the future of flying in the sub-continent. Together with young J Tata of the Bombay industrialist family – and starting with two de Havilland Fox Moths – he created Air India, serving briefly as managing director of Tata Aircraft.

In 1940 there occurred one of those rare occasions

when Tymms's determination failed. Arriving in the United States to buy aircraft for the Indian Air Force he was confronted by a signal from Lord Beaverbrook, the recently appointed Minister of Aircraft Production. "No aeroplanes for Tymms," it ordained.

Later in the war his hopes of building Mosquitos in Bombay were similarly frustrated. His service to India continued after the war until partition in 1947.

Among Tymms's legacies for civil aviation was an exhaustive redrafting of all air navigation orders; and in retirement his expertise was readily available, either through the Guild of Air Pilots and Air Navigators (of which he was Master from 1957 to 1958), individually, or through such duties as chairing the 1960 Commission of Inquiry on Civil Aviation in the West Indies.

He was appointed CIE 1935, knighted in 1941 and appointed KCIE in 1947. His wife died some years ago. There were no children.

LORD BALFOUR OF INCHRYE
22 SEPTEMBER 1988

Lord Balfour of Inchrye, who has died aged 90, was the minister on whose desk in 1940 there landed Dowding's formal confirmation of his historic verbal warning to Churchill of the dire consequences to Britain of continuing to despatch fighter aircraft to France.

Balfour was exceptionally qualified to be at the receiving end of the leader of "the Few's" written account of the day he walked into No 10 and made a dramatic plea to be permitted to conserve Fighter Command's resources for a Battle of Britain he feared was yet to come.

For Balfour was no stranger to Dowding: in 1916 as an

18-year-old Royal Flying Corps pilot he had incurred his considerable displeasure (he was later forgiven) for crashing Dowding's favourite aeroplane while delivering it to the wing he was commanding in France.

Moreover, not only had Balfour destroyed 11 enemy aircraft in the 1914-18 War and been awarded the MC and Bar for his exploits, but, uniquely for an Air Minister, he had flown the Hurricane and Spitfire before the outbreak of the 1939-45 war.

Drafted in "Stuffy" Dowding's dour, uncompromising style, the document confronting Balfour concluded: "If the Home Defence Force is drained away in desperate attempts to remedy the situation in France, defeat in France will involve the final, complete and irredeemable defeat of this country".

This was not the only crisis of that critical summer in which Balfour was a central figure.

Increasingly restive that Fighter Command's No 12 Group behind London was not wholly engaged in support of No 11 Group defending south-east England, Douglas Bader (then a squadron leader commanding No 242, a Hurricane Squadron at Coltishall), lobbied Balfour. He believed passionately that 12 Group should build Big Wing formations of three to five squadrons and sweep in from the rear.

Bader persuaded the squadron adjutant, Peter Macdonald who also happened to be MP for the Isle of Wight, to go behind Dowding's back and advocate the tactic to Balfour. Balfour then advised Macdonald to use his prerogative as an MP and take the issue to Churchill.

This he did and during the Battle of Britain's climactic week, Sept 7-15, Big Wings assembled by 12 Group were used with mixed results.

Harold Harington Balfour, the son of a colonel and a great-grandson of Field-Marshal Lord Napier of Magdala, was born in 1897 and educated at Chilverton Elms, Dover, and at the Royal Naval College, Osborne. But, after being severely beaten by the term lieutenant and a cadet captain – for losing his nerve and having to be rescued from near the top of Osborne's 70 ft mast – young Balfour did not pursue a naval career.

He joined the 60th Rifles in 1914. But frustrated, as he put it, "that limited training facilities were all jammed up", went on leave and jumped the queue by borrowing £75 from his father and paying for civilian flying lessons.

He obtained Royal Aero Club flying certificate No 1399, was attached to the RFC, and reported to Shoreham aerodrome in Sussex where he trained in a Maurice Farman Boxkite machine. An instructor crashed it, but both aviators scrambled unhurt from "a heap of wood and spars, lots of piano wire and odd bits of metal but not much else".

After advanced instruction at Gosport under the legendary pioneer airman Bob Smith-Barry, he went to France in May, 1916. During the Battle of the Somme he flew a Morane Bullet single-seat monoplane in No 60 Squadron until he squashed a finger on each hand in a collapsing deckchair and could not fly.

He returned home and when he could fly again became a test pilot at the Central Flying School, Upavon. As an instructor, he taught Billy Bishop, the Canadian VC, and Prof Lindemann – who as Lord Cherwell was to be Churchill's 1939-45 war scientific adviser.

By early 1917 Balfour was back in France and heavily engaged with No 45 Squadron, being fortunate to survive "Bloody April" in which his squadron alone lost 35 pilots and observers.

Flying the Sopwith one-and-a-half strutter – "the wings were liable to fall off at anything over 160 mph" – and later the more obliging Camel, he "went out every day to meet Richthofen's circus of Albatros fighters which could climb better and faster than we could.

"Each morning we saw his gaily coloured fleet looping, rolling and spinning well above our level and it was against these we were supposed to do offensive patrols."

Before each patrol Balfour was woken at six by his batman, "Darlars" – so called because he had been a tram driver in Darlaston – and sent off to the hangars with the stock farewell: "When you go out in the morning I often wonder if you will ever come back".

When, finally, Balfour was shot down it was from the ground. A gunner hit his engine while patrolling low during the battle of Vimy Ridge and he force-landed in a shell hole in no-man's land.

But he confounded Darlars by getting back. Out of action again, he filled in the time polishing up his technique at Gosport where Smith-Barry had now established his famous school of special flying.

On his return to France Balfour was delighted to find the squadron had been re-equipped with the Sopwith Camel.

During 1918 he experienced a significant development of aerial warfare tactics: the employment of Big Wing formations – the precedent for Bader's lobbying in 1940.

Not yet 21, Balfour was promoted major. After a brief interlude in 1919 in Baghdad as personal assistant to the Civil Commissioner in Mesopotamia, he was posted to the RAF College, Cranwell, as an instructor.

In 1923, before resigning his commission, he obtained his first glimpse of Whitehall as temporary ADC to Sir Samuel Hoare, the Air Minister. The next year he joined the *Daily Mail* as a reporter.

He was also a guinea pig in a Tory experiment for paying the expenses of young candidates in well-held Labour seats, and unsuccessfully contested Stratford, West

Ham. In 1925 he joined Whitehall Securities – a Pearson-owned company which had begun to take an interest in civil aviation and was to run a British Airways London-to-Paris route in competition with Imperial Airways.

Balfour stood for Parliament again in 1929 and won the Isle of Thanet for the Conservatives. But Parliamentary obligations did not deter him from flying "the quintessance of experience", being, in his view, "flying a perfect aeroplane on a perfect day over Salisbury."

He also enjoyed parachuting. His friends in the Commons were concerned in 1935 when he was absent for several days after landing on the back of his head at the age of 37.

One May day in 1938, he was asleep in the House of Commons library when, woken by the division bell, the chief whip told him he was wanted at No 10, adding: "You've got the devil of a job."

The job was Parliamentary Under-Secretary of State for Air; the number two to Sir Kingsley Wood, the Air Minister. As such he was busily involved with the rearmament which preceded and followed the return of the Prime Minister, Neville Chamberlain, from Munich. No appeaser himself, Balfour nevertheless welcomed the opportunity Chamberlain's mission afforded to build monoplane fighters.

In May 1940, when Churchill formed his Cabinet he brought in the Liberal, Sir Archibald Sinclair, as Air Minister, and retained Balfour in the secondary role. And so – "always the blasted bridesmaid and never the blooming bride" – he found himself at the centre of events as France fell and the Battle of Britain was fought.

These were heady days and, as an instinctive journalist, Balfour savoured the stories which he could not unleash until the peril had receded. One of his favourites concerned an astonishing field-telephone call to his office from an Army corporal speaking from Dunkirk in 1940 during the evacuation.

Routed via the Admiralty exchange, the corporal asked: "Could the RAF please send fighters to knock out a German spotting balloon directing artillery shelling". To emphasise the urgency the corporal broadcast the explosions down the line. The RAF duly obliged.

During the war he travelled extensively, touring flying schools of the Empire Air Training Scheme which he had helped to establish; and in September, 1941 he was a member of the mission to Moscow headed by Lord Beaverbrook. He clinked glasses with Stalin in a toast to "our two air forces and the common fight."

For a while, however, Balfour fell out of Beaverbrook's favour, having had the temerity but good sense to purchase three Boeing Clipper flying-boats in America without the Minister of Aircraft Production's or any governmental authority. Known thereafter as "the Balfour Boeings", Berwick, Bristol and Bangor gave splendid transatlantic service in BOAC colours.

During the war he also continued to fly, adding to his Hurricane and Spitfire experiences the Whirlwind fighter in 1941, and next year the Typhoon.

In 1944 Churchill closed Balfour's long innings at the Air Ministry and sent him to West Africa as Resident Minister.

He returned home the next year, when he went to the House of Lords, and maintained his interest in political, commercial and aviation affairs through various appointments including the presidencies of the Federation of Chambers of Commerce of the British Empire, and of the Commonwealth and Empire Industries Association. From 1955 to 1966 he was a part-time member of the board of British European Airways and chairman of BEA Helicopters from 1964 to 1966.

Throughout the postwar years Balfour maintained his interest in journalism, writing articles and publishing *Wings Over Westminster*, a sequel to his *An Airman Marches* (1935); and also *Fish, Folk and Fun*, the title of which reflected his devotion to dry fly-fishing.

He was sworn of the Privy Council in 1941 and created Baron Balfour of Inchrye in 1945.

In 1921 he married Diana, second daughter of Sir Robert Grenville Harvey, 2nd Bt. The marriage was dissolved in 1946 and a year afterwards he married Mary ("Maina"), younger sister of John Profumo.

He is survived by his wife, their daughter, and his son by his first marriage, Ian Balfour, born 1924, who now succeeds to the barony.

AIR COMMODORE
H M PROBYN
24 MARCH 1992

Air Cdre H M Probyn, who has died in Kenya aged 100, fought as a pilot in the First World War, and for most of the Second World War commanded the RAF station at Cranwell.

It was fortuitous that "Daddy" Probyn, an airman who had learned to fly in 1916 on a Maurice Farman "Pusher", should have been in charge at Cranwell when E28/39, Frank Whittle's experimental jet, made its maiden flight there on May 15 1941.

Probyn had known Whittle for a long while and had been a fervent supporter of his ideas when others doubted him. At Cranwell he gave the jet pioneer and his company, Power Jets, such help as he could, including accommodation.

He was delighted when Cranwell's long runway, clear approaches and flat open countryside were selected for Gerry Sayer's flight tests of Whittle's jet.

It astonished Probyn that this historic moment, for all the necessary secrecy, was not accorded more significance. There was no official film unit to record the event, and posterity had to make do with some shots from an unauthorised and amateurish attempt with a hand-held camera.

Probyn consoled himself that at least he had helped to organise an impromptu party in the mess. On May 21 1941, however, he had the satisfaction of welcoming Sir Archibald Sinclair, the Air Minister, and a party of officials to see the plane with the propellerless engine.

Harold Melsome Probyn was born on Dec 8 1891. In 1915 he was serving as a corporal despatch rider when he was commissioned into the Warwickshire Regiment. He subsequently transferred to the Royal Flying Corps and was posted to No 34, a BE2c Squadron on the Western Front. He later flew in 52 and 105 Squadrons, mostly in RE8s, and soon gained a reputation as a daring reconnaissance and light bombing pilot.

Towards the end of the First World War Probyn flew DH6s on anti-submarine patrols with 250 and 244 Squadrons. In 1919 he received a permanent commission in the newly formed RAF.

Between 1924 and 1928 he commanded Nos 208 and 2 Army Co-operation Squadrons in Egypt and at Manston in Kent.

In 1930 he received command of No 25, a Siskin fighter squadron based at Hawkinge on the Kent coast. Staff postings at home and in the Middle East followed.

In 1939 Probyn received a senior appointment at No 11 Group, where he helped to prepare this front-line fighter group for the Battle of Britain. In 1940 he moved to command Cranwell, where he remained until he retired in 1944.

Although he was in at the birth of the jet age, Probyn found enjoyment in old age in basic flying. He marked his 90th birthday by piloting his home-built single-seater plane in a celebration flypast.

At 92 he was still piloting a little Jodel which he had built with the help of his African cook. With its 1500cc engine, taken from a Volkswagen motor-car, it cruised at 85 mph and obtained 40 miles per gallon. Probyn spent many happy hours joy-riding from an airstrip near his home at Nyeri, north of Nairobi.

Despite his age, the only problem he encountered was the unwelcome attention of a giant buzzard which tried to attack him around Mount Kenya. Evasive tactics perfected in RFC machines confounded the bird.

As a younger man in Kenya Probyn had once sought to fly by bicycle pedal-power. After managing to get his do-it-yourself machine off the ground, he ran out of puff and that was that.

Probyn was awarded the DSO in 1917, appointed CBE 1943, CB in 1944 and thrice mentioned in despatches. He married, in 1920, Marjory Savory, who died in 1961.

ARCHIE BINDING
16 APRIL 1992

Archie Binding, who has died aged 105, was perhaps the last survivor of those Royal Naval Air Service and Royal Flying Corps airmen who crewed airships in the First World War.

He had earlier fought with the naval armoured car brigade which landed at Walfish (now Walvis) Bay in

South-West Africa and helped Gen Botha to take the German colony.

By the end of the First World War Binding had logged more than 3,000 airship hours and established himself as one of the most experienced and, as his service record stated, "capable airship engineers."

From his experience with the Navy's Coastal Airships on convoy escort and anti U-boat patrols, Binding was accustomed to the perilous practice of climbing out of the gondola cockpit high above the North Sea to service the airship's two eight-cylinder 150 hp Sunbeam engines.

"We had a lot of trouble with magneto breakdown," he recalled, "and in every flight carried a spare one. I remember having to change four magnetos in the air, and on one flight struggling home on one engine and one magneto.

"Airship flying was pretty hard work, starting every day at 4 am and lasting until sunset. We were in open cockpits and the only food for a day was Horlicks tablets."

Once, when stationed at Pulham in Norfolk, his commanding officer told him that a naval airship was drifting from the North Sea entirely out of control, as both its engines had broken down.

Binding later described how he was told "to arrange a crew and equipment, ladders, steps, scaffolding, cylinders of hydrogen and personnel for repair of airship skin and everything I thought necessary to salvage this airship.

"After a cross-country pursuit it eventually landed in a tree and I had to organise a rescue. My staff erected ladders to enable the riggers to patch up the envelope and refill it with gas to obtain lift.

"Meanwhile, I went aboard and found that both engines had failed owing to leaking radiators. I had both radiators removed and transferred to the lorry and told the driver to go to the nearest large town and to contact the best plumber to help me repair the radiators.

"I duly repaired the leads and returned to the airship and refitted the radiators, I started the engines and reported to the pilot that subject to sufficient lift he could fly back to base.

"His engineer would not take over as he had had a full day's terror, so I volunteered to take over engine control in his place.

"We duly became airborne and flew back to base with no further trouble. Although I was complimented it did not prevent my being officer of the watch. I released the crew that had had no food or rest all day and we were ready for the first watch next day."

Archer Ormond Binding was born at Clevedon, Somerset, on Dec 12 1886. His father, a builder and carrier, was one of the first carters to stable his horses in favour of steam traction lorries.

Young Archie was educated at the local National school until he was 14 and then apprenticed to Stephens & Sons, pioneers of the Stephens motor-car.

In 1907 he joined Straker Squires in Bristol and four years later teamed up with his father's engineering firm. When war was declared in 1914 he replied to a Royal Naval Air Service advertisement for engineers.

"On reporting," he recalled, "I was given a piece of steel (distorted), a hacksaw, a file and a square and told to make two sides square, which I quickly did."

After an eye test he was given the rank of petty officer engineer and directed to Victoria Station to take charge of 20 similar recruits.

On arrival at Sheerness naval barracks, Binding was told to train them himself. He knew nothing about drill, but learned the necessary movements from books and soon gained promotion to chief petty officer. His next posting was to South-West Africa. At Walvis Bay he survived a severe attack of dysentery, while his comrades "were dying like flies". On his return home, he was asked: "Where have you been? We want you for flying duties."

He was promoted warrant officer in the RNAS and then, in 1918, the Royal Flying Corps commissioned him as a second lieutenant.

His knowledge of airships was at a premium, and his reputation had been enhanced by his patented invention of a carburettor that could burn hydrogen which was otherwise wasted on airship operations.

Later Binding was involved with the rigid airships R23 and R31. R23 had a gun turret on the top of the envelope (for which Barnes Wallis carried out tests) and was used for experiments in launching a Sopwith Camel fighter slung below it.

He was awarded the Air Force Cross in 1919.

After the First World War Binding rejoined the family business. During the Second World War he worked in the production of aero-engine components and served as engineer officer with the Clevedon Fire Brigade.

He remained associated with the business until 1966, when he sold it to TRW in America.

Archie Binding was a dedicated freemason and Rotarian. Although diagnosed as having a weak heart in 1948, he survived his first wife and married again at the age of 85.

His second wife also predeceased him, as did one of the two sons of his first marriage.

WING COMMANDER
GWILYM LEWIS
17 DECEMBER 1996

Wing Commander Gwilym Lewis, who has died aged 99, was the last surviving Royal Flying Corps pilot to have flown in the first Battle of the Somme.

Nicknamed "the cherub", Lewis served with No 32 Squadron at the Front when he was 18 and became an outstanding pilot with a tally of at least 12 kills.

His flying career began in 1915. Impatient to join the RFC after leaving Marlborough, he persuaded his father to pay £100 for private flying lessons and jumped the queue.

After four hours in the cockpit (solo from the outset, mainly on a Graham White Box Kite) he was issued with a Royal Aero Club flying certificate. Thus qualified, he was accepted for pilot training and immediately posted to France with No 32 Squadron which was equipped with DH2 single-seater scout aircraft.

Looking back, he recalled dogfights as "wildly exciting", but he found deflection shooting "incredibly difficult", and felt he fell down in that respect.

His later experience of shooting pheasant and wildfowl, so he said, supported this self-criticism. "The easy shot on the tail of a diving Hun was a very different matter."

Following his first encounter, he wrote home: "It is a most extraordinary game. Better than football, yet something of the same. It is the same feeling to charge a Hun who sees you as it is to collar one of the biggest chaps in the school scrum."

Congratulations were received in the same school-boy spirit: "Our general is fearfully bucked with us," he wrote. "Out of seven Huns shot down, three belonged to No 32 . . . It is just eight weeks since we departed in a merry bunch from Netheravon to try our luck out in this land of the dead."

Gwilym Hugh Lewis was born of Welsh parents in Birmingham on Aug 5 1897. The family moved to Croydon and his father prospered in the City.

Young Gwilym was educated at Whitgift grammar school before going on to Marlborough. During the Great War his service was interrupted by surgery for appendicitis. During his absence from the Front, he received a long and welcome Christmas letter in 1916 from one of his mechanics, Cpl Charles William Dalton.

This letter was kept and greatly treasured by Lewis; he particularly valued Dalton's tribute to fellow pilots who failed to return: "Mechanics are human beings, very human sometimes, and it is awful for them to see these men, good and true gentlemen, in the true sense of the word, going off with a 'Cheerio', never to return."

In the summer of 1917, Lewis served as an instructor in Scotland and at the Central Flying School at Upavon, Wilts, where he became a flight commander.

Cross-country flights could be fun. On a practice flight with a fellow Marlburian they dropped in on their old school for lunch. On another trip he landed at Eastbourne for tea at the Grand Hotel.

Promoted captain in the autumn of 1917, Lewis joined No 40 Squadron, and its SE5s at Bruay behind Arras. In March the next year he returned from leave to find himself temporarily in command.

"At present," he wrote home, "the RFC has got its tail up, and the Hun doesn't enjoy life tremendously." With the arrival of a new commanding officer, Major Roderic Dallas, an Australian and formerly a Royal Naval Air Service commander, with a reputed score of at least 40 to his name, Lewis reverted to flight commander. But Dallas, "the admiral", or "old fool" as Lewis liked to call him, was not to survive much longer. "Too good for this world," observed Lewis.

Meanwhile, Lewis's score mounted, though he acknowledged each success dismissively: "I got on to the tail of one stupid lad who didn't seem to quite know what to do. I gave him a good deluge with both guns and he went down in flames."

After being awarded the DFC, Capt Lewis returned home on leave in July 1918, and to the Central Flying School as the senior SE5 instructor. The assistant commandant was a 21-year-old Major Jack Slessor, the future marshal of the RAF.

Following demobilisation at the start of 1919, he took his father's advice to turn down a permanent commission in the RAF, but rejected the offer of a post in is father's firm. Fearing his father would be tougher on him than on any other new employee, he accepted, at the age of 21, £240 a year from Sedgwick Collins at Lloyds.

Lewis was a pioneer of the non-marine market in America and set up a new department to handle the increase of business. By the time the Second World War broke out and Lewis found himself back in uniform, he had built it into the largest department in the company.

In 1939 he was commissioned into the RAF Volunteer Reserve as a wing commander.

From the outset he served in Winston Churchill's underground Cabinet War Room, near 10 Downing Street in Storey's Gate; Lewis's billet was next door to the prime minister's bedroom. On what he deemed to be essential occasions, it fell to Lewis to have the prime minister woken up.

During the war Lewis did his best to keep an eye on the insurance business but on his return he found that things and people at the top had changed during his absence. In 1947 he left Sedgwicks and was appointed chairman of

Arbon Langrish, where he used his experience to build up the American side.

In 1965 he sold the company to Clarksons, but retained his connection with Lloyds and in time became its oldest member.

In 1976 Lewis published *Wings Over the Somme 1916-1918*, which was reissued in 1994. Much revered in the RAF and the City, he was Life President of No 32 (the Royal) Squadron, and an honorary liveryman of the Guild of Air Pilots and Air Navigators.

Gwilym Lewis married, in 1925, Christian Robertson, who predeceased him; they had one son and two daughters. Lewis's brother, Edmund, another RFC pilot, was killed in the First World War.

CAPTAIN
CECIL LEWIS
27 JANUARY 1997

Cecil Lewis, who has died aged 98, led an astonishingly diverse life; a veteran of aerial combat over Flanders in the First World War, he was one of the first four members on the staff of the BBC, wrote 20 books and plays and founded a quasi-religious community in South Africa.

In addition he won an Oscar, lived in Tahiti, flew across Africa, and seduced literally hundreds of women. Even so, he accomplished rather less than he promised. His uncompromising zest for experience meant that he was doomed to what he described as a "weathervane life, swinging this way and that", content to taste, dabble and move on.

Cecil Arthur Lewis was born at Birkenhead on March

29 1898. His father was a Congregationalist minister whose preaching brought him a fashionable West End pulpit, from which he eloped with a rich member of his flock.

Precociously intelligent, Cecil Lewis was educated at Dulwich, University College School and Oundle, from where, in 1915, he joined the Royal Flying Corps.

A stringy beanpole of a boy, 6 ft 4 in tall, he celebrated his 18th birthday in France, and had flown only 20 hours (without any map reading, Morse or formation training), when he was posted to No 9 Squadron. He flew BE2cs and French-built Morane "Parasols" in preparation for the Somme offensive. "If ever there was an aircraft unsuited for active service," Lewis wrote, "it was the BE2c." As for the Morane, he remembered how bullets crackled through its spruce and linen frame.

On July 1 1916 Lewis saw the mile-high fountain of earth thrown up by the detonation of two mines beneath the German positions. As he related in his classic account of those experiences, *Sagittarius Rising* (1936, fifth edition 1993), the life of a pilot might be more comfortable than that of the men in the trenches, but it was no less dangerous. Life expectancy was three weeks, and in an era before parachutes a disabled plane could take five minutes to plunge 10,000 feet to earth.

Lewis had a series of narrow shaves; his wings were shot away and engine failure brought him down on the front line. Yet he survived eight months before being sent home during the winter of 1916–17 for a spell as a test pilot. He was twice mentioned in despatches and in 1916 awarded the Military Cross for "continuous bravery".

He returned to France with No 56 Squadron, equipped with the new SE5 fighters. Lewis had been specially selected to outfly and outfight Baron von Richthofen and his "Circus".

In May 1917 Lewis led the squadron over the Channel to fight the world's first mass air-battle. He recalled: "The enemy, more than double in number, greater in power, and fighting with skill and courage, gradually overpowered the British, whose machines scattered, driven down beneath the scarlet German fighters."

Lewis was one of the five in the 11-strong squadron to survive. He was also the last to see Albert Ball, VC, as the Allied ace disappeared into a cloud bank during a dog fight.

After a raid on London by 20 Gothas, Lewis and the squadron were brought back to protect the capital. The Gothas never showed up again, and Lewis enjoyed 10 days of parties before returning to France, where he managed to survive a German attack which left him with a crippled aeroplane and a bullet in the back.

He ended the war leading 152 Squadron, equipped with Sopwith Camels to be used as night fighters. At the Armistice, still only 20, he was credited with the destruction of eight enemy machines.

The experience left Lewis bitter. The war, he reflected, "deprived me of the only carefree years and washed me up ill equipped for any serious career, with a Military Cross, a Royal handshake, a £600 gratuity and, I almost forgot to say – my life."

Subsequently, as Lewis recorded in *Never Look Back* (1974), the best of several volumes of autobiography, "I should always have the opportunity to be in at the start of new things, never lead them and never remain long enough to draw any real profit."

On demobilisation Lewis and two fellow pilots formed a flying circus that toured Britain and gave joy rides in redundant Avro 504Ks. The enterprise failed to prosper, and in 1919 he joined Vickers Civil Aviation and went to Peking as flying instructor to the Chinese government.

The pilots he was teaching wore long black silk robes which concealed their hands, and small black satin hats with red buttons at the crown. Lewis's task was further complicated by there being no room for an interpreter in the aircraft.

In 1922 Lewis answered an advertisement for a job as deputy director of programmes at the BBC. There were only five applicants, and Lewis, though he knew nothing about broadcasting, was successful. He thus became the youngest of John Reith's three employees.

Versatility was essential, and Lewis found himself producing the BBC's greatest initial success, *Children's Hour*. His role as its "Uncle Caractacus" was not one that he particularly relished. From 1922 to 1926 he was Director of Programmes.

Lewis pioneered the techniques of radio drama, adapting two of Bernard Shaw's plays himself. He also organised the first simultaneous transmission of the news on the various regional stations, an event introduced by a drunk but word-perfect F E Smith.

In 1926 Lewis resigned from the BBC in typically impulsive fashion, irritated by the growth of bureaucracy and the dilution of quality necessary to a mass medium. The microphone, he wrote later, "clamoured daily to be fed. At first it was satisfied with simple fare and a little of it," but it became "a most terrible and insatiable monster".

After an abortive attempt to interest America in radio drama, he turned to writing himself, encouraged by his friend Charles Ricketts, the artist and aesthete, and by Bernard Shaw. "Your literary age I take to be about seven", observed Shaw of one effort; nevertheless he allowed Lewis to film, disastrously, *Arms and the Man*.

Lewis retreated to a villa he had built on a beautiful site above Lake Maggiore on land paid for by Ricketts. There he wrote *Sagittarius Rising*; its evocation of the thrill and beauty of flight revived his career, helped by a full-page eulogy from Shaw in the *New Statesman* in 1936.

He was then appointed the first Director of Outside Broadcasts for BBC Television, which was starting up at Alexandra Palace. Lewis quickly threw it up for a lucrative writing contract with a Hollywood studio, where his slender contribution to the script of *Pygmalion* brought him a share of an Oscar in 1938.

"For the only time in my life," he remembered, "I had more money than I could spend." He celebrated this predicament with a spell of beachcombing in Tahiti.

On the outbreak of the Second World War he rejoined the Royal Air Force. His first assignment was to test hare-brained ideas such as trailing cannon balls on cables from the hatch of a Wellington in order to intercept incoming bombers. Later he became a flying instructor, teaching his own son to fly, and served in Transport Command.

Soon after the war Lewis became powerfully influenced by the writings of the mystic Georgi Gurdjieff, who taught that man must learn to observe himself in order to wake from his living sleep.

Lewis's several attempts to explain Gurdjieff's teachings in print did not make for easy reading, but he had finally found an enthusiasm of which he did not tire. It dominated the remaining half of a hitherto directionless life, prompting him to set up a community in South Africa to preserve the philosophy against the expected Armageddon of the next war.

The venture was a failure, and Lewis returned to a routine of briefly promising openings. From 1953 to 1956 he made radio programmes promoting the United Nations, then returned to England to help launch commercial television with Associated Rediffusion. As losses mounted he was sacked, but was retained by the *Daily Mail*, which partly owned the company, to organise its Ideal Home Exhibition.

In 1966 Lewis retired to Corfu. Although he continued to write, little of his output matched the quality or panache of his early success.

He retained his attractiveness to women, and even at 95 might have passed for a spry 70. Yet he believed that Gurdjieff had cured him of conceit, and acknowledged that "a successful seducer never makes a good husband".

His non-fiction titles included *Broadcasting from Within* (1924), *The Trumpet is Mine* (1938), *Farewell to Wings* (1964), *Turn Right for Corfu* (1972), *A Way To Be* (1977), and *Gemini to Jo'burg* (1984).

He also, edited *Self Portrait: The Letters and Journals of Charles Ricketts. All My Yesterdays* (1993) was a further volume of autobiography.

As fiction Lewis wrote *Challenge to the Night* (1938), *Yesterday's Evening* (1946), *Pathfinders* (1943, revised edition 1986), *The Gospel According to Judas* (1989), and *The Dark Sands of Shambals* (1990).

Cecil Lewis married first, in Peking in 1921 (dissolved 1940) Eudoxia Horvath, daughter of the White Russian leader General Horvath; they had a son and a daughter. He married secondly in 1942 (dissolved 1950) Olga Burnett. He married his third wife, Fanny, in 1960.

AIR COMMODORE
"FREDDIE" WEST
8 JULY 1998

Air Commodore "Freddie" West, who has died aged 102, was the last surviving British VC of the 1914-1918 War.

When war broke out West was employed as a clerk in the foreign correspondence department of a Zurich bank. Deciding that fist-fights with the German clerk on the next stool were an inadequate response to the Kaiser, he returned home to London to enlist.

He began his service in the Royal Army Medical Corps, but by May 1915 he had been commissioned in the Royal Munster Fusiliers, and in November he arrived in France in charge of 20 men. In 1917, convinced that trench warfare was for rats, not men, he joined the Royal Flying Corps.

After an air-artillery spotting course at Brooklands he was posted to No 3 Squadron as an observer, then trained as a pilot and joined No 8 Squadron at Amiens, where his commanding officer, Major Trafford Leigh-Mallory, greeted his new recruits with the words: "You gentlemen are just the chickens the red German eagles are looking for."

Leigh Mallory's warning referred to the famous ace Manfred von Richthofen, the "Red Baron," and his "circus" of red painted Fokkers, whom West was soon to encounter. One Sunday in April 1918 he was patrolling the area of St Quentin-Amiens when his observer spotted three red Fokkers.

To his astonishment, West saw one of the Fokkers fall to the ground. He landed near the crashed enemy machine and was greeted by a jubilant Australian artillery officer who said: "We've had a bit of luck. Guess who we've shot down?" West inspected the dead pilot and found himself looking at the Red Baron, "quite calm in death – he might have died in bed".

He telephoned his commanding officer, who was sceptical: "Don't go and ruin our reputation by originating sensational rumours." Leigh-Mallory had later to eat his words – though the Australian gunner's claim to have bagged the Red Baron was disputed by a Canadian pilot of No 209 Squadron.

On Aug 10 of that year, flying a two-seater Armstrong F8 reconnaissance machine in the recently formed RAF, West was attacked by seven enemy aeroplanes while on hedge-hopping reconnaisance far over enemy lines. Early in the engagement one of his legs was partially severed by an explosive bullet, falling powerless into the controls and rendering the machine unmanageable.

West managed to extricate his disabled leg, regained control and, although wounded in the other leg, manoeuvred his aircraft so skilfully that his observer, Alec Haslam, was able to open fire on the enemy machines and drive them off.

In the words of the citation: "Captain West then, with rare courage and determination, brought his machine over our lines and landed safely. Exhausted by his exertions, he fainted, but on regaining consciousness insisted on writing his report."

Ferdinand "Freddie" West was born in London in 1896. After the death of his father in the Boer War, his mother, Countess Clemence de la Garde de Saignes, took him to Italy, where he became trilingual in English, French and Italian – a considerable asset in later postings as a diplomat. He was educated at the Xaverian College, Brighton, the Lycée Berchet and Genoa University, where he read international law.

After the action for which he was awarded the VC, West was treated at the London Hospital and fitted with an

artificial leg at Roehampton. Awarded £250 compensation for loss of a limb, he invested £200 in war bonds
and went off to Paris, where he paid £20 for a superior
wooden leg. Later he was made an even better one by the
Swiss tool manufacturer de Soutter, who had also lost a
leg.

Although he had been invalided out, within a year West
was back in uniform, employed as the RAF's first
diplomat at the Foreign Office – where his Navy and
Army opposite numbers also had wooden legs.

He soon returned to flying, though. He joined No 17
Squadron and was posted in 1928 as adjutant at the flying-
boat base in Malta. After commanding No 4 Squadron –
he was Douglas Bader's CO when the fighter ace lost his
legs – West returned to diplomacy in the late 1930s, when
he was appointed British air attaché to Finland, Estonia
and Latvia.

After the outbreak of the 1939-45 War he found
himself back in Amiens, commanding a wing in the Air
Component of the British Expeditionary Force; but
shortly after he was appointed air attaché in Rome, as
acting air commodore. In June 1940, when Italy came
into the war, West was ordered to Switzerland as air
attaché though he was effectively head of British air
intelligence.

He soon became a familiar figure there, limping
through the streets of Berne, followed by his White
Russian bodyguard. He engaged in a range of covert
activities, his most notable coup being the retrieval from a
crashed German aircraft of a tin box containing an
extensive card index of Luftwaffe dispositions in Italy,
which was rapturously received by the Air Ministry.

In 1946 he resigned from his post as head of the
Directorate of Foreign Liaison at the Air Ministry, joined
the J Arthur Rank Organisation and became managing

director of Eagle-Lion Distributors. Other directorships followed, including chairmanship of a betting shop group.

It was not until 1971 that West acknowledged his disability by selling his house at Sunningdale and moving into a nearby bungalow and he was still playing golf at 80. His wife, the former Winifred Leslie, died last month. He is survived by his son.

FIGHTER BOYS

WING COMMANDER
BOB STANFORD TUCK
5 MAY 1987

With 29 victories, eight enemy aircraft probably destroyed and six damaged, Bob Stanford Tuck, who has died aged 70, was one of the greatest fighter aces of the Second World War – including the Battle of Britain of 1940 – until his career was cut short over France on January 28, 1942.

Such was his reputation with the Luftwaffe that after crash-landing near Boulogne he was given a slap-up dinner by the great German fighter ace Adolf Galland, then a lieutenant colonel.

Ground gunners who had helped to shoot Tuck down were astonished that as his Spitfire crash-landed its cannon were still firing, one shell going right up the long slim barrel of a multiple 20 mm flak gun, splitting the barrel like a half-peeled banana. Patting Tuck on the back, they congratulated him repeatedly: "Goot shot, Englander goot shot".

In so doing, the German flak gunners had unwittingly nailed the secret of Stanford Tuck's success as a fighter pilot. From his schooldays at St Dunstan's preparatory school and college, Reading, he had been a keen and prize-winning rifle and pistol shot, developing an eye which made him one of the best practitioners of the fighter pilot's art of deflection shooting.

Fortunately for the RAF, Tuck's father, a First World War captain in the Queen's Royal West Surrey Regiment, had taught him to shoot and at the age of 12 he was already an "ace" rabbit and pheasant shot.

Serving in the Merchant Navy from the age of 16 as a cadet with Lamport and Holt, mostly on the South American meat run, Tuck gained his skipper's admiration for his skills in potting sharks with a Lee Enfield rifle.

But in January 1942 it was Tuck's turn to be a victim of sharp shooting before the flak gunners handed him over to Galland who also had good reason to respect the RAF ace's eye.

Based at St Omer, Galland invited Tuck to dinner with his pilots telling him, "We have met before. Last time I very nearly killed you but you saw me coming and got out of way in the nick of time."

"So that was you, was it?" Tuck replied. "I got your No 2 as he passed in front." At dinner Galland presented his guest with a bottle of whisky. They were not to meet again until after the war, when Tuck was briefed to interrogate him as a prisoner.

Thereafter a lifelong friendship developed, the pair exchanging annual visits and indulging a mutual love of hunting and shooting.

Their friendship was especially evident during the making of the feature film the *"Battle of Britain"*, when they greatly enjoyed their advisory roles on location.

Bob Stanford Tuck had never given a thought to flying until, on leave from sea, he answered an advertisement calling for RAF pilots. Accepted, he reported as an acting pilot officer on September 16, 1935. After training in Avro Tutors, he graduated to the Hawker Hart and Audax, being rated in his confidential report as "a born fighter pilot".

His shooting war began at the end of May 1940 when home-based RAF fighters, all too few of them, attempted to cover the evacuation of the British Expeditionary Force from Dunkirk. Despite great odds against him, Tuck accounted for several Me109s in this area.

Tuck's outstanding ability as a fighter pilot already recognised, he was selected for a vital experimental task.

With Wing Commander George Stainforth, a pre-war speed record holder, Tuck was selected to conduct flight trials comparing the Me109 and the Spitfire. In this vital prelude to the Battle of Britain, Tuck and Stainforth put on an amazing display for brasshats and scientists at Farnborough, taking it in turns to fly the 109 and the Spitfire. It was an experience that was to serve Tuck well as the Battle of Britain was fought over south-east England between July 10 and October 31, 1940.

It was also of immense value to Fighter Command, because the tests proved conclusively the advantage of the 109's Daimler Benz fuel injection engine against the Spitfire's Rolls-Royce Merlin carburettor, which could not cope with a sudden nose-drop from horizontal to vertical.

Perversely, Tuck was posted to command No 257 (Burma) Squadron equipped with the slower if more manoeuvrable Hawker Hurricane as the Battle of Britain reached its climax in September 1940.

It took time for him to be accepted as CO even though he had 14 official kills to his credit – 14 Swastikas stencilled on the fuselage under the cockpit of his Hurricane.

As with his friend Group Capt. Sir Douglas Bader, who was also shot down flying a Spitfire, Tuck was a great advocate of the Hurricane as a magnificent gun platform.

Tuck certainly knew. On June 21 1941 after shooting down two 109s over the sea his Hurricane IIC, badly shot up, was attacked head-on by a third 109. With no throttle and a faltering engine Tuck managed to drive off the enemy. Then he nursed the Hurricane 100 miles out from Southend to the coast. The starboard aileron dropped away and flames appeared in the cockpit. Tuck baled out – one of four occasions on which he escaped by parachute – inflated his rubber dinghy and was rescued.

By this time Tuck was not only a household name but also a wing commander at the age of 25, commanding at first three squadrons then a wing of five squadrons. The award of the DSO and three DFCs within a few months made him such a frequent figure at Buckingham Palace investitures that King George VI always had an especially warm greeting.

On the occasion of his second bar to the DFC the King told Tuck that his daughters were always asking about him.

Sadly there came the time when Tuck, brought down by ground gunners, was no longer there. It was not until after the war that the princesses and the fighter ace's admirers throughout the nation learned that he escaped in 1945 and in the last days of the Second World War had joined Russian troops fighting on the Eastern Front.

SQUADRON LEADER
J H "GINGER" LACEY
30 MAY 1989

Sqn Ldr "Ginger" Lacey, who has died aged 72, was one of the most accomplished fighter pilots in the Battle of Britain, with a score of 23 kills by the end of 1940 and a total of 28 by the end of the 1939–1945 War.

On Sept 13 1940, while still a sergeant pilot and wearing the ribbon of his first Battle of Britain DFM (a Bar followed soon after), he shot down a Heinkel 111 bomber after it had hit Buckingham Palace.

Ginger began his attack by killing the rear gunner with his first burst, before the bomber dived into cloud in the hope of shaking him off.

Another member of the Heinkel crew heaved aside his dead comrade, lined up Lacey in his sights at short range and blew away the Hurricane's radiator.

Ignoring the fire that raged through his fighter, Lacey pressed the gun button and kept firing until both the bomber's engines were ablaze and it crashed. Lacey baled out and escaped with minor burns.

It was remarkable that he managed to beat the odds of surviving as a fighter pilot from the start of the Battle of Britain in July until its last official day, Oct 31.

Though shot down or forced to land nine times, he was able to look back on it all as only the beginning of his war.

He had another narrow escape on August 30, 1940.

Ordered up with the squadron from Gravesend in the Biggin Hill sector Lacey took part in a head-on attack against 50 Heinkel 111 bombers.

His aircraft was riddled with enemy fire, and oil smeared his cockpit.

"Whoever did that," Ginger remembered thinking at the time, "was very good at deflection shooting."

This was a typical reaction from a fighter pilot who claimed that his survival owed far more to the accuracy of his shooting that to his abilities at the controls.

His engine was shot to a standstill, but rather than bale out over the Thames Lacey glided over the Isle of Sheppey and made a powerless landing at Gravesend.

It was a brilliant return, all the more appreciated for taking place in front of a unit which had filmed his take-off and could now record the 87 bullet holes in the wings and fuselage of his Hurricane.

James Harry Lacey was born at Wetherby, Yorks, on Feb 1 1917 and educated at King James Grammar School.

He joined the RAF VR in 1937 and a year later had also become a civilian flying instructor at the Yorkshire Aeroplane Club.

In May 1940 he was blooded in the desperate fighting that accompanied the Fall of France.

Three days after his arrival with 501 Squadron he shot down two enemy fighters and one bomber.

In all he bagged five enemy aircraft over France and was awarded the Croix de Guerre.

Having served as a sergeant pilot throughout 1940, Lacey was commissioned as a pilot officer in January of the next year, when he was also mentioned in despatches.

He left 501 Squadron to become an instructor, converted to Spitfires and served briefly with No 602 and as tactics officer with No 81 Group.

He also tested Hurricanes with rocket projectiles at the experimental establishment at Boscombe Down.

In 1943 he was posted to India, where his experience was invaluable in the preparation of fighter pilots for the low-level jungle dogfights which were to help the 14th Army defeat the Japanese in Burma.

In the last stages of the war Lacey took command of No 17, a Spitfire squadron, and claimed his last victim, a Japanese Oscar.

He had persuaded his pilots to shave their heads in the Gurkha fashion to instill greater confidence among the riflemen they were supporting.

After the war he remained in the Service and flew Vampire jets before becoming a fighter control specialist.

In 1963 he returned to the Far East as fighter controller at Kuching and Labuan, Borneo.

On his retirement as a squadron leader in 1967 he was saluted by Lightning jets in a flypast at RAF Topcliffe.

In civilian life he ran an air-freight business and later taught flying at an airfield near Bridlington.

COLONEL
ERICH HARTMANN
20 SEPTEMBER 1993

Colonel Erich Hartmann, the German fighter ace who has died near Stuttgart aged 71, scored the record total of 352 "victories" during the Second World War.

Such a phenomenal number may seem fanciful, but it was carefully validated. Most of it was accumulated on the Eastern Front, where the Soviet aircraft were no match for his Me 109. Nor, in general, were the opposing pilots in "Bubi" Hartmann's league.

His strike rate accelerated dramatically in the desperate Battle of Kursk on the Central Front: On July 7 1943 he destroyed seven Red Air Force aircraft above the battle.

Yet he was unquestionably an "ace of aces", as he demonstrated on the rare occasions when he encountered American aircraft. Towards the end of the war his piloting skills and marksmanship were tested against American Mustangs. In 1945 he shot down five American Mustang fighter pilots over Romania in two sorties on one day, and shortly afterwards two more over Czechoslovakia.

Hartmann ascribed his success to close combat. "My only tactics", he recalled, "were to wait until I had the chance to attack the enemy and then close in at high speed. I opened fire only when the whole windshield was black with the enemy. Then not a single shot went wild. I hit the enemy with all my guns and he went down."

Only once was he himself shot down. On Aug 20 1943 he scrambled out of his crippled Me 109 unscathed and into the hands of Soviet soldiers.

Feigning injury, he was placed on a stretcher in a truck and driven, so he was told, to find a doctor. On the way he sprang up, threw his guard against the cab and dodged shots as he scrambled through a field full of swaying sunflower stalks.

Sleeping by day and walking by night, he reached the front where he was almost shot by a German sentry who challenged him. Shortly afterwards he rejoined his fighter group, JG-52.

Erich Hartmann was born at Weissach in the former kingdom of Württemberg on April 19 1922. He spent his early boyhood in China where his father was a doctor. The family returned to Germany at a time when clandestine preparations were being made to rebuild the air force, using gliding clubs as training centres. From the age of 14, young Erich was encouraged by his mother – herself a pilot – to learn to glide.

In 1938, still only 16, he qualified as a gliding instructor. On Nov 15 1940 he joined Luftwaffe Training Regiment 10, near Königsberg in East Prussia. The next year he moved to the Air Academy School – at Gatow airfield, Berlin. On graduating he was posted to the Russian front to join 7th Squadron of JG-52, which he eventually commanded.

Fair-haired, blue-eyed and baby-faced, he was nicknamed "Bubi" and "the Blond Knight."

While his score mounted, Hartmann longed to be with his sweetheart, Ursula "Usch" Puetsch; a bleeding heart pierced by an arrow was painted on the fuselage of his aircraft.

By the time they married in 1944 he was a celebrated figure in the Third Reich. To his Knight's Cross was added a succession of Oak Leaves, Swords and finally Diamonds.

His Aryan features became a familiar sight at Hitler's "Wolf's Lair" battle headquarters.

When Hartmann was summoned to receive the Diamonds after the failed assassination attempt on Hitler of July 1944, he was told to disarm himself before entering the presence of the Führer. "No pistol", Hartmann insisted, "no Diamonds – unless I am trusted." When his point had been accepted, he duly surrendered his weapon.

On other occasions when Hitler commanded his presence, Hartmann arrived in such an inebriated state that the Nazi aides were hard put to stop him from juggling with the Führer's cap.

After flying his last operational sortie on May 8 1945 – the day the war in Europe ended – Hartmann landed on an airfield under Soviet fire after scoring his final and 352nd victory.

He then marched his group and its camp followers towards the American lines at Pisek in Czechoslovakia and surrendered to the 90th US Infantry Division.

Eight days later the Americans handed the group over to the Russians who separated women and girls and raped many of them in front of their menfolk. Most of the women were never seen again.

Hartmann was sent to Russia and imprisoned for 10 bleak years during which he suffered intense hardship until Chancellor Adenauer negotiated his repatriation in 1956. The next year he resumed with the new German air force and learned to fly jets with the Americans at Kraut Field, Luke Air Force Base, Arizona.

In 1959 he received command of a German fighter wing and was promoted colonel before his retirement.

Hartmann and his wife had a daughter.

SQUADRON LEADER
CHARLTON "WAG" HAW
27 NOVEMBER 1993

Squadron Leader "Wag" Haw, who has died aged 73, was awarded the Order of Lenin while fighting alongside the Red Air Force in the Arctic Circle.

In August 1941 Haw's squadron, No 81, was paired with No 134 in 151 Wing and sent to Arctic Russia: their orders were to protect the ports of Murmansk and Archangel and to teach Soviet pilots and ground crew how to fly and maintain Hurricanes.

Flt Sgt Haw's Hurricane and 23 others were shipped to Murmansk in the small and elderly aircraft-carrier *Argus*, from which they flew to Vaenga airfield on Aug 25.

A convoy carrying crated Hurricanes sailed on to Archangel, 400 miles to the east, as did *Llanstephan Castle*, a liner bearing some 500 wing personnel.

Fifteen aircraft were assembled at Archangel and then flown to Vaenga.

The Russians showed great affection for the Hurricanes from the outset and it was observed that they stroked the wings of their aircraft before taking off.

At first the pilots had some perilous sorties. The Rolls-Royce Merlin engine, so reliable during the Battle of Britain, proved less effective with the lower-octane Russian fuel. The British company Broquet Fuel soon corrected the problem by adding a catalyst.

The wing went on to achieve 15 confirmed kills. Haw brought down three Me 109s, which gave him the highest individual score.

In accordance with Red Air Force practice Haw was given 100 roubles (about £20) for each enemy aircraft he had destroyed.

Charlton Haw was born at York on May 8 1920. He

developed a taste for aviation at the age of 10, after a joy-ride with Sir Alan Cobham's Flying Circus.

He worked as an apprentice lithographer in Leeds until shortly before the Second World War, when he was accepted for pilot training in the RAF Volunteer Reserve.

In May 1940 Haw was posted to 504 (County of Nottingham) Hurricane squadron, an auxiliary squadron based at Wick in Scotland and giving fighter protection to the naval base at Scapa Flow.

Pre-war auxiliaries were notoriously clannish, but Haw soon made himself popular – not least through playing the piano at squadron parties.

In early September 1940 the squadron was ordered south to reinforce Fighter Command's hard-pressed 10, 11 and 12 Groups, and on September 27 Haw destroyed an Me 110 fighter before being shot down over Bristol.

Haw's flight in 504 formed the nucleus of 81 Squadron, which in July 1941 was ordered to RAF Leconfield, Yorkshire, from which it was dispatched to Russia.

On his return in December Haw was commissioned and briefly rejoined No 504; in May 1942 he was posted to No 122, a Spitfire squadron at Hornchurch, Essex.

The next February he received command of No 611, a Spitfire squadron at Biggin Hill, and in November that year of No 129, another Hornchurch-based Spitfire squadron.

In April 1944 No 129 converted to Mustangs. After covering the D-Day landings, Haw led the squadron in July and August in an offensive against flying bombs.

Finally, as leader of a wing of long-range Mustang fighters, he escorted Allied bombers on daylight raids.

After a spell at the Central Fighter Establishment he commanded No 65, a Hornet squadron, from 1946 until 1948, when he was granted a permanent commission.

He later lost his flying category because of poor

eyesight, and retired from the RAF in 1951.

For a while Haw and his first wife were the landlords of a public house in Sussex. He later ran a pet-food and boarding-kennels business at Farnham, Surrey, and in recent years made dolls' houses and toys.

In addition to the Order of Lenin, Haw was awarded the DFM in 1942 and DFC in 1944.

He is survived by his second wife and a son.

AIR MARSHAL
SIR PETER WYKEHAM
23 FEBRUARY 1995

Air Marshal Sir Peter Wykeham, who has died aged 79, commanded "The Malta Pirates", a buccaneering and exceptionally successful Mosquito intruder squadron based on Malta.

Wykeham-Barnes, as he was then known (he dropped the Barnes in 1955), had come up the hard way. He entered RAF Halton before the Second World War as an aircraft apprentice, and so excelled that he was selected for a cadetship at Cranwell.

By Christmas 1942, when he took 23 Squadron's Mosquitos to Malta by way of Algiers and Gibraltar, he had built a formidable reputation as a fighter pilot in North Africa. In their first month on the island Wykeham's Pirates flew 184 operational sorties, including 73 intruder patrols and 82 attacks on ground targets.

Wykeham and his crews allowed no respite to Italian and German airfields on Sicily and roamed the Mediterranean skies, attacking targets from Pantellaria to Naples, Taranto, Tunis and Bizerta.

Well-built and debonair, the Pirates' chief was a great intruder enthusiast. A favourite ruse of his was to panic enemy airfields at night, retire to a respectful distance and watch the flak defences pumping away at the enemy's own aircraft or at nothing at all.

Shortly after Wykeham's first DSO had been announced it was reported that the squadron commander had "damaged himself". An engineer officer jumped to the conclusion that Wykeham's Mosquito was in trouble. Aircraft were then at a premium, so he was relieved to find that Wykeham had simply torn a cartilage while exercising.

An army officer's son, Peter Guy Wykeham-Barnes was born on Sept 13 1915. After RAF Halton and Cranwell he was commissioned as a pilot officer in 1937. When war was declared he was posted to No 80, a Gladiator biplane fighter squadron defending Egypt.

When Italy entered the war in June 1940 there were only two eight-gun monoplane Hurricane fighters in the Western Desert. One was flown from airstrip to airstrip to give the Italians an impression of many. The other was flown sparingly in combat.

Wykeham had the privilege of piloting it on June 19, when he destroyed two Italian CR 42s in short order over the desert. These successes set him on the way to becoming an ace, and he eventually achieved a total score of 15.

For a spell the shortage of Hurricanes obliged him to revert to the Gladiator; even so he managed to destroy two more enemy aircraft. His Gladiator, however, was badly damaged, and he baled out, managing to trudge across the desert to British lines.

In September 1940 Wykeham was given command of 274 Squadron. The supply of Hurricanes began to improve in November, when the aircraft carrier *Furious* disembarked a first consignment at the West African port of Takoradi and they were ferried across Africa to Khartoum and on to Cairo.

He then faced the unenviable task, in command of 73 Squadron, of attempting to defend the embattled town of Tobruk. Outnumbered by superior German fighters, which had come to the rescue of the poorly performing Italians, No 73 suffered heavy losses. Wykeham was shot down again but not before he had dispatched a Ju 87 Stuka dive-bomber and an Me 109 fighter.

Although he had not fought in the Battle of Britain, Wykeham was well qualified to give the Americans the benefit of his experience after the Japanese attack on Pearl Harbor. He returned home in the spring of 1942 to command No 257, another Hurricane squadron. Command of the Malta Pirates followed soon after.

Flown back from Malta with his torn cartilage, Wykeham served as a Fighter Command staff officer until March 1944, when he went operational again as commander of 140 Wing, equipped with the Mosquito, the speedy "Wooden Wonder".

There followed a frenetic period of low-level attacks in support of the D-Day landings in Normandy and the advance through North-West Europe.

When the Danish Resistance called for the destruction of Gestapo headquarters housed in two buildings of Aarhus University in Jutland, Wykeham, by then a group captain, led 24 Mosquitos of 21,464 and 487 Squadrons in a successful low-level attack on October 31 1944.

After the war he held staff appointments at the Air Ministry until in 1948 he was recruited as a test pilot at the Aeroplane and Armament Experimental Establishment at Boscombe Down. Wykeham had a key role in the development of the Hunter and Swift fighters and also flew tests to determine the feasibility of building the Vulcan nuclear bomber.

In 1950 his advice was again sought by the Americans, and he flew many B26 bomber sorties during the Korean War. On his return to Britain he was given a succession of staff appointments both at home and in Nato. Wykeham was marked out for the top.

After commanding 38 Group from 1960 to 1962 and directing the Joint Warfare Staff at the Ministry of Defence from 1962 to 1964, Wykeham commanded the Far East Air Force until 1966, when he became Deputy Chief of Air Staff. He retired in 1969 and became a consultant in the aircraft industry.

Wykeham published *Fighter Command* (1960) and *Santos Dumos* (1962). He was elected a Fellow of the Royal Aeronautical Society in 1968 and also of the Guild of Air Pilots and Air Navigators.

He was awarded the DFC in 1940, Bar in 1941, DSO in 1943 and Bar in 1944, and the AFC in 1951. He also held the US Air Medal and was a Chevalier of the Order of Dannebrog.

He married, in 1949, Barbara Elizabeth Priestley, daughter of J B Priestley; they had two sons and a daughter.

GROUP CAPTAIN
PETER TOWNSEND
19 JUNE 1995

Group Captain Peter Townsend, the much decorated Battle of Britain fighter pilot who has died aged 80, aspired to marry Princess Margaret after the Second World War. One of seven children Peter Wooldridge Townsend was born on November 22,1914, in Burma where his father was a member of the Burma section of the Burma Civil Service.

Townsend was a baby when the family – his mother was a cousin of Hugh Gaitskell, the sometime Labour leader – returned to England. Although educating so many children was a financial strain Townsend followed his father to Haileybury where he was head of his house, swimming captain and in the XV.

When he was 14 he had a joyride in a Bristol Fighter and decided to become a pilot. In 1933 he entered the RAF College, Cranwell, where Frank Whittle who had won a place from the ranks, was a fellow student. Townsend's flying instructor was struck by his sensitivity and warned that he might put up a brilliant performance or make a complete ass of himself.

In another report Townsend was appraised as being reluctant to attempt anything that might make him noticeable and it was observed that his inner tensions induced the eczema which was to trouble him for some years.

Townsend was commissioned in 1935 and posted to No 1, a fighter squadron stationed at Tangmere near Chichester in West Sussex.

The squadron, one of the RAF's three crack interceptor units, flew the Hawker Fury biplane; direction-finding was so primitive that the pilots often followed roads and railway lines, flying low enough to read the signs.

In 1936 Townsend joined 36 Squadron in Singapore, where he was introduced to the Vickers Wildebeeste torpedo-bomber, a lumbering aircraft capable of no more than 140 mph. The squadron was wiped out when the Japanese attacked Singapore in 1942, but Townsend was not there; by 1937 his skin problems had become so acute that the doctor recommended a complete rest from flying.

On the voyage home, though, his eczema cleared up completely. He was delighted to return to flying fighters at Tangmere, this time with 43 Squadron, save that his skin immediately errupted again in protest.

To add to his woes, he was transferred to a Coastal Command bomber squadron at Tangmere. Townsend threatened to resign unless returned to 43 Squadron and to fighters. He gained his point and six months leave into the bargain. When he rejoined No 43 in September 1938 his eczema had gone for ever.

The approach of war, and the challenge of learning to fly the Hurricane, transformed Townsend. "He used to be rather aloof, going to his room at night and avoiding our games and parties," observed a fellow pilot, "but we are bringing him out of his shell. He is very shy and has no idea of his courage . . ."

On the outbreak of the Second World War, 43 Squadron was posted to Acklington, Northumberland. On February 3 1940 Townsend claimed his first victim, a Heinkel bomber. It crash-landed near Whitby – the first German aircraft to fall on English soil in the Second World War. As the Heinkel hit the ground Townsend was heard to murmur, "Poor devils, I don't think they are all dead."

He went to see the survivors in hospital; 30 years later one of them, Karl Missy, collaborated with him on *Duel of Eagles*, about the Battle of Britain.

The squadron was then posted to Wick to defend the

naval base at Scapa Flow. Townsend emerged victorious from further tussles with the Luftwaffe, but though the passion for the kill ran in him as strongly as in his fellow pilots, he found that the sight of his victims spiralling to their deaths evoked only the desire to save them.

In May 1940, after the Germans launched their attack on France, Townsend took command of 85 Squadron. During the first days of the Battle of Britain the squadron operated from Martlesham, on the North Sea coast.

On July 11 1940 Townsend was shot down while attacking a Dornier 17 over the North Sea. He parachuted into the sea, and was fortunate to be rescued by a mine-sweeper that was miles off course.

For the next few months he was continuously in action. In August, as the Battle of Britain reached its peak, 85 Squadron was moved to Debden, to the north of London, and then to Croydon. Of the 20 men Townsend took to Croydon 14 (including himself) had been shot down within 14 days, two of them twice. Yet he later recalled that "Those days of battle were the most stirring and the most wonderful I have lived."

When he was shot down over Tunbridge Wells on August 31 he received a bullet in the foot. Soon afterwards his shattered squadron was withdrawn from the front line and posted to Church Fenton, Yorkshire, where Townsend, still limping, rejoined them.

He was soon back in the South, attempting, without radar, to shoot down the bombers which were attacking London every night.

In June 1941, exhausted after 20 months of continuous flying, he was given a staff job. Its designation, Wing Commander, Night Operations, provoked some mirth after his marriage that July to Rosemary Pawle, a brigadier's daughter who lived near the airfield at Hunsdon, Hertfordshire.

Townsend returned to the fray in command of the fighter station at Drem, near Edinburgh, and flew Spitfires with 611 Squadron. Then, after a spell at Staff College at the end of 1942, he was given command of the fighter station at West Malling, Kent, until septicaemia forced him into a ground job. Townsend had been credited with 11 confirmed kills.

He was posted to training roles, first in Yorkshire and then at Montrose, Scotland. There he received a summons from Air Chief Marshal Sir Charles Portal. "If you don't find the idea particularly revolting," Portal told him, "I propose to recommend you for the job of equerry to His Majesty. The appointment will be for three months."

On Feb 16 1944 he was being conducted through the corridors of Buckingham Palace after an interview with King George VI when he encountered "two adorable-looking girls, all smiles" – Princess Elizabeth and Princess Margaret.

The well-decorated airman – Townsend had been awarded the DFC and Bar in 1940, and the DSO in 1941, as well as being mentioned in despatches – proved popular with the Royal Family, who, he later recorded, "made me feel more of a guest than an aide". He was a loyal and tactful courtier, who coped calmly with the King's occasional bouts of irascibility.

The three months' contract was extended, and in 1945 Townsend was accorded a "grace and favour" house, Adelaide Cottage, in the Home Park at Windsor Castle. When his second son was born that year the King stood godfather.

In 1949 and 1950 he entered the King's Cup air race under Princess Margaret's name on the second occasion beating the world speed record over a closed circuit.

The death of King George VI, in February 1952, and Townsend's subsequent divorce, helped to bring the couple even closer. At Windsor Castle he confessed his love. "That's exactly how I feel," he recalled Princess Margaret replying.

Townsend was appointed CVO in 1947. That year he accompanied the Royal Family on their tour of South Africa, with which he fell in love, to the point of seriously considering the possibility of starting a new life there.

After the Princess's announcement that she would not marry him Townsend returned to an earlier post in Brussels, deciding to leave the RAF and in the autumn of 1956 embarked upon a 17-month tour of the world, under contract to write articles.

After his return to Britain in March 1958 he saw Princess Margaret again, at Clarence House and at Windsor, but the consequent renewal of speculation in the press left him with a desire "to clear out once and for all".

In 1959 he married Marie-Luce Jamagne – not, he assured her, as a substitute for a lost love, but as "the ultimate", which she remained.

In 1960 they settled in Paris, and then at Clos Sainte-Gemme to the west of the city, where they built up a beautiful garden. But earning a living proved a problem; after a spell in documentary films failed to yield sufficient funds Townsend took a job with an American wine-shipping company.

That sufficed for a while but after moving to America in 1964 Townsend and his employers fell out. A brief spell with a London public relations firm led to an offer to set up an office in Paris. But after *Paris Match* published an article of his about the Battle of Britain in September 1966 he settled down to write *Duel of Eagles* (1970).

In 1968 Townsend bought a dilapidated farm, La Mare aux Oiseaux, some 30 miles south-west of Paris. His employment by Harry Saltzman to publicise the film *The Battle of Britain* (1969) helped pay to do up the property.

He also wrote about the Israeli air force for *Paris Match*.

His other books included *The Last Emperor* (1975), *Time and Chance* (an autobiography, 1978), *The Smallest Pawns in the Game* (interviews with war victims, 1979), *The Girl in the White Ship* (1981), *The Postman of Nagasaki* (about the effects of the atomic bomb, 1984) and *Duel in the Dark* (1986).

In 1993 he met Princess Margaret again at a social function and the next year was invited to Kensington Palace; he also appeared in Border Television's series The House of Windsor.

Though the title of his last book, *Nostalgia Britannica* (1994), suggested otherwise, Townsend seemed well content with his life in France and at the end of his autobiography he wrote that he would like his ashes to be scattered there.

"And if," he concluded, "the wind, the south wind on which the swallows ride, blows them on towards England, then let it be. I shall neither know nor care."

He had two sons by his first marriage, and a son and two daughters by his second.

GROUP CAPTAIN
SIR HUGH DUNDAS
10 JULY 1995

Group Captain Sir Hugh Dundas, who has died aged 74, was one of the most accomplished fighter pilots of the Second World War; he went on to successful careers in Fleet Street and in business, eventually serving as managing director and then chairman of BET.

Tall, slim and patrician in bearing, Dundas joined No 616 (South Yorkshire), an Auxiliary Air Force Spitfire squadron, as a 19-year-old pilot officer. When he encountered the enemy, over Dunkirk during the evacuation of late May 1940, he was stricken with terror.

"With sudden, sickening, stupid fear," he recalled, "I realised I was being fired on and I pulled my Spitfire round hard so that the blood was forced down from my head . . .

"Straightening out, I saw a confusion of planes diving and twisting . . . At some stage in the next few seconds the silhouette of a Messerschmitt passed across my windscreen and I fired my guns in battle for the first time – a full deflection shot which I believe was quite ineffectual . . . I was close to panic in the bewilderment and hot fear of that first dogfight."

When the Battle of Britain began in July, Dundas and his squadron were in the north on convoy patrols, and feeling rather out of it. But on Aug 15, as the Luftwaffe mounted its vaunted "Eagle Offensive", No 616 was scrambled during lunch to meet a wave of Ju-88 bombers coming in over the North Sea. Dundas destroyed one and was credited with a half share of another.

The main air battle was being fought in the tiltyard above the Channel and the South, and 616 was ordered to Kenley. On Aug 22 Dundas was shot down by Me109 fighters over Dover.

"White smoke filled the cockpit, thick and hot," he wrote, "and I could see neither the sky above nor the Channel coast 12,000 ft below. Panic and fear consumed me and I thought: 'Christ, this is the end.' Then I thought: 'Get out, you bloody fool, open the hood and get out.'"

After an immense struggle Dundas slithered along the fuselage, the ground now perilously close, and found himself falling. His parachute opened as the Spitfire exploded in a field below.

Dundas's arm and leg wounds kept him out of the

cockpit for almost a month, which to his frustration prevented him from fighting in the final and climactic phase of the Battle of Britain.

None the less in the course of the war he destroyed some eight enemy aircraft, enough to qualify him as an ace.

Hugh Spencer Lisle Dundas was born at Barnborough, Yorkshire, on July 22 1920. He was educated at Aysgarth prep school, north Yorkshire, and at Stowe.

He was articled to a firm of solicitors but − to his parents' dismay − soon insisted on joining the RAF. He failed the medical three times but in May 1939 pulled strings to join No 616. His elder brother John, who was shot down and killed in November 1940, was a weekend flier in No 609 (West Riding), another Auxiliary Air Force fighter squadron.

The Auxiliaries epitomised the popular image of Battle of Britain fighter pilots; many, according to Dundas, were "unrepentant playboys".

He rejoined No 616 in September 1940. In the mess one day "Teddy" St Aubyn, who wanted a drink, pointed at Dundas and barked: "Hey, you, Cocky, press the bell." The sobriquet stuck: St Aubyn claimed that Dundas, a 6 ft 4 in redhead, resembled "a bloody great Rhode Island Red". St Aubyn was killed in action in 1944.

In mid-September No 616 formed part of the legless ace Douglas Bader's controversial Big Wing at Duxford, near Cambridge. The squadron wintered in the comparative calm of the North, and in the spring flew south to defend Portsmouth. That summer they helped "lean into France" with fighter sweeps over the Channel.

On one sortie Dundas's Spitfire was crippled in a dogfight near Calais. He made a powerless crash-landing near Dover.

Shortly before his 20th birthday he was appointed a

flight commander in 616, and sat for the war artist
Cuthbert Orde. "I've left room for the DFC," Orde told
him. "The people I draw always seem to get it." Four days
later Dundas did.

In the autumn he was posted to No 59 Operational
Training Unit as a flight commander training Free French
pilots. To his relief, his dishevelled appearance at an
inspection by General de Gaulle, and the unruly
behaviour of his dog, earned the disfavour of his group
commander and he was posted to 610 Squadron.

Shortly afterwards, during a boisterous party in the
mess, he broke his left leg. He was promptly promoted
Squadron Leader and, leg in plaster, flew a Spitfire to take
command of No 56, the first Typhoon squadron.

At this stage the Typhoon was full of bugs, and many
pilots were being lost. But by the time of the Dieppe raid
of August 1942 the Duxford Typhoons were sufficiently
operational to take part, and on the day Dundas led 56
Squadron on a sweep.

When, that November, the Duxford Typhoons were
formed into an operational wing, Dundas was promoted
wing commander to lead it. In the New Year he was
suddenly posted to Tunisia to lead No 324, a wing of five
Spitfire squadrons.

Dundas went on to Malta, transferred the wing to Sicily
in July 1943 and, after the invasion of Italy, to an airfield
at the Salerno beachhead. In the New Year of 1944 he was
switched to staff duties in the Desert Air Force, and in
June he returned to operations with No 244 Wing.

Dundas's Spitfire was hit by flak over Arezzo. Rather
than bale out over rugged terrain he coaxed the aircraft,
its fuel running dangerously low, to an emergency landing
at Castiglione.

In November he was promoted group captain,
becoming – at 24 – almost certainly the youngest RAF

officer with that rank.

During the war Dundas became friends with Group Captain Max Aitken, son of Lord Beaverbrook; in 1948 he was appointed air correspondent for Beaverbrook Newspapers.

For a while he retained an association with the air force as commander of 601 Squadron of the re-named Royal Auxiliary Air Force. But in 1950, having been promoted within the Beaverbrook group, he stepped down.

After a succession of editorial and managerial posts including leader writer and North American correspondent for *Express* newspapers – Dundas left in 1960.

He joined Rediffusion the next year, becoming managing director in 1970. He was chairman from 1978 to 1985. Dundas oversaw the boom in colour television rentals in the early 1970s, and helped lay the foundations for the expansion of cable networks.

In 1973 he was appointed managing director of BET, then Rediffusion's parent company, of which he became deputy chairman in 1981 and chairman in 1982. He was a highly active chairman, overseeing a significant restructuring of the conglomerate to focus on service-related industries.

He was a director of Thames Television from its formation in 1968, serving as chairman from 1981 to 1987.

Dundas was a member of the Council and of the Finance & General Purposes Committee of the RAF Benevolent Fund from 1976 to 1989 and chaired the Cancer Relief Macmillan Fund from 1988 to 1991.

From 1987 to 1990 he was chairman of the Prince's Business Trust and of the Home Farm Development Trust.

In 1988 he published an account of his war experiences, *Flying Start*.

Dundas was awarded the DFC in 1941, DSO in 1944 and Bar in 1945. He was appointed CBE in 1977 and knighted in 1987. In 1969 he was Deputy Lieutenant for Surrey and in 1989 High Sheriff.

Dundas married, in 1950, Enid Rosamond Lawrence, daughter of the 1st Baron Oaksey and 3rd Baron Trevethin and sister of Lord Oaksey, the *Daily Telegraph* racing correspondent. They had a son and two daughters.

████████████████

AIR COMMODORE
AL DEERE
20 SEPTEMBER 1995

Air Commodore Al Deere, the New Zealand fighter ace who has died aged 77 was credited with shooting down 12 enemy aircraft during the Battle of Britain; he ended the Second World War with a slate of 22 confirmed kills, 10 probables and 18 enemy aircraft damaged.

Square jawed and handsome, Deere was the epitome of the dashing RAF pilot. He was uncannily well-starred, and cheated death on nine occasions when his Spitfire was shot down or forced to land. He ascribed his "nine lives" to his high standard of training and his fitness – he was a keen rugby player and boxed for the RAF.

Deere made his mark on the morning of May 23 1940, during the fall of France. While escorting a Miles Master to Calais to rescue the leader of 74 Squadron, who had been forced down, Deere shot down two Me 109 fighters. It was the beginning of an astonishing run. That afternoon Deere bagged another Me 109 over Dunkirk, and the next day he shot down an Me 110 twin-engined fighter.

The day after that he shot down two other Me 110s. But within hours he used up the first of his nine lives, when return fire from a Dornier 217 bomber over the Belgian coast forced his Spitfire down on a beach.

Deere crash-landed, and was knocked unconscious when his head struck the windscreen. His Spitfire caught fire but he came round in the nick of time and escaped. A soldier helped him to dress his wound. He found a bicycle and headed for Ostend, and then hitched a lift to Dunkirk with three British soldiers in a truck.

"I got a lift on a destroyer to Dover," he recalled, "caught a train to London, and took the Underground to Hornchurch, where I rejoined the squadron just 19 hours after taking off."

On July 9, after destroying an Me 109 he collided with another and crashed into a cornfield. Six days later, after fighting several furious actions, he was obliged to bale out at low level. He fractured a wrist, but spent only one night in hospital before returning to his squadron.

To his chagrin he was then shot down by another Spitfire. Shortly afterwards he was shot up when taking off at Hornchurch. His aircraft spun over, and he was left suspended in his harness.

By the middle of August 1940 Deere's squadron was desperately short of pilots. The replacements had no combat experience and only a few hours of training in a Hurricane or a Spitfire. The next month the squadron was so depleted that it was rested in the North.

Deere's luck persisted. He was putting a young sergeant pilot through his final combat test when the new boy flew into his tailplane. Deere's Spitfire whipped into a spiral and plummeted towards the ground; the force prevented him from baling out.

Twisting, turning and kicking, he crawled out of the cockpit, but was then blown back and caught on the stump of the tail. Not until the ground was uncomfortably close did his parachute open, and then only partly. He made a soft and smelly landing in the cesspool of a farm.

The constant threat of death made Deere's sense of humour all the more precious. Once, when Deere was returning from France, a pilot named Darling called up: "Are you all right, Deere?"

"Yes, Darling," replied Deere.

Of Irish stock, Alan Christopher Deere was born in Auckland, New Zealand, on Dec 12 1917 and educated at St Carrie's School, Wanganui. He had six brothers, five of whom served in and survived the war; two were PoWs.

Deere worked briefly as a shepherd and then as a clerk with Treadwell, Gordon, Treadwell & Haggitt, solicitors at Wanganui. But after a 10-bob flip in an aircraft he was sold on flying.

Deere's chance came when the RAF advertised in New Zealand for pilots. In 1937 he sailed for London, received a short service commission, and after training joined 54 Squadron at Hornchurch in 1938. The next year the squadron received Spitfires.

On one of his early flights Deere was overcome by anoxia while in the air, and lost consciousness. The fighter dived towards the sea and he came to just in time to pull out.

At the beginning of 1941 he had a spell as operations room controller at Catterick before joining 602 Squadron as a flight commander at Ayr in May.

On his first "scramble" – with 602 – Deere was ordered to investigate an aircraft flying west towards Glasgow; plots on the craft were intermittent and not very reliable. Deere subsequently discovered that it was in fact the Me 110 from which Rudolf Hess, deputy to Adolf Hitler, baled out over Scotland.

Deere cursed his luck. "An Me 110 unescorted was a wonderful target," he said. "With Hess aboard it was probably the prize fighter-pilot target of the war." Shortly afterwards Deere used up another "life" when his engine seized and he crash-landed on the cliff-top at the Heads of Ayr.

Deere received command of No 602 in August, and on the day of his appointment destroyed an Me 109 over Gravelines. In early 1942 he was posted to the United States to lecture on fighter tactics, and when he returned to operations in May he received command of No 403, a Canadian Spitfire squadron.

After staff duties with 13 Group, Deere completed a Staff College course and then had a short spell with 611 Squadron. In 1943 he was appointed leader of the Biggin Hill Wing.

After commanding the Fighter Wing of the Central Gunnery School, Deere joined the staff of 11 Group, and was then given command of 145 (French) Airfield at Merston. He led the wing over the D-Day Normandy invasion bridgehead on June 6 1944.

Later that month he moved with the wing to France but soon left to become Wing Commander Plans at 84 Group. In July 1945 he returned to Biggin Hill as station commander and in August, after receiving a permanent commission, took over the Polish Mustang wing. When that was disbanded he became station commander at Duxford.

Deere became assistant commandant at the RAF Staff College, Cranwell, in 1963. The next year he commanded the East Anglian Sector before joining Technical Training Command. He retired in 1967.

Passing up a better-paid job with the American aircraft company Fairchild, Deere spent the next 10 years as the RAF's civilian director of sport.

In 1959 he published *Nine Lives*.

Deere was awarded the DFC and Bar in 1940, DSO in 1943, American DFC in 1944 and the Croix de Guerre in

1944. He was appointed OBE in 1946, and from 1961 to 1964 was ADC to the Queen.

He married, in 1945, Joan Fenton; they had a son and a daughter.

GENERAL
ADOLF "DOLFO" GALLAND
9 FEBRUARY 1996

General Adolf "Dolfo" Galland, who has died aged 83, was one of the Luftwaffe's most celebrated aces with 104 "kills".

He became the youngest General der Jagdflieger (General of Fighters) in 1941 at the age of 29. In January 1945 he was dismissed following open disagreement over tactics with Hitler and Goering.

Galland saw himself in the chivalrous mantle of Manfred von Richthofen (the "Red Baron" of the First World War). Courageous in combat, Galland was fearless to the point of recklessness in his relations with his commander-in-chief Goering, and with Hitler.

When the RAF began to get the upper hand in the Battle of Britain, he infuriated Goering by asking to be re-equipped with a wing of Spitfires. Later, when summoned after his 40th kill to be invested with the Oak-leaves to his Knight's Cross, Galland incensed Hitler by asking him to order the cessation of radio disparagement of the RAF.

Galland tilted with the RAF's best, including Bob Stanford Tuck, Douglas Bader, Sailor Malan and Johnnie Johnson. He respected his adversaries, and after the war established friendships with them. Holidays on Tuck's mushroom farm were reciprocated with boar-hunting forays in Germany. The old enemies Tuck, Bader and Galland lectured together in America.

When, on Jan 28 1942, Stanford-Tuck had been brought down by ground gunners near St Omer, Galland invited him to dinner in the mess. Before Tuck was taken away as a prisoner, Galland presented him with a bottle of whisky.

Galland himself might well have become Tuck's prisoner during the Battle of Britain. On one mission, under Goering's orders to fly close escort to bomber formations, he found that the erratic wandering of the longer-range bombers had all but drained the tanks of his Me 109. Desperately short of fuel, Galland considered landing in Kent but risked the Channel crossing, crash-landing on the beach at Cap Gris Nez.

Descended from an old Huguenot family, Adolf Galland was born on March 19 1912 in Westphalia.

In 1932 he was accepted by the commercial air transport school, in Brunswick, run by Colonel Keller, a celebrated First World War pilot. His tales of bombing London determined Galland to become a military pilot. As the Versailles Treaty had prohibited service training, he was sent to Italy for a covert course. After Hitler came to power in 1933, Germany began to rearm openly, and the next year Galland became an instructor at the Schleissheim fighter pilot school in Bavaria. In 1935 he was posted to the Luftwaffe's first fighter wing, named after Richthofen.

One day, flying too low and too slow, Galland crashed, injuring his head and left eye. On another occasion he collided with a lamp-post.

With the outbreak of the Spanish Civil War, Goering took the opportunity to blood young pilots in the Condor Legion, which supported Franco. Lieutenant Galland joined a Heinkel 51 ground attack unit, rising to command a squadron.

Galland did not relish the ground attack role. In one low-level attack his aircraft was hit by rifle fire. A bullet went through a wing, another bullet buried itself in the instrument panel, and a third pierced one of his boots.

Recalled to Germany in the run-up to the invasion of Poland, Galland was frustrated to be retained in a ground attack role. But he flew some 50 He 123 sorties in the brief Polish campaign, was promoted captain and awarded the Iron Cross Second Class.

Galland badgered his superiors to have him transferred to fighters, and early in 1940 his persistence was repaid with a posting to JG 27. This came in time for the onset, on May 10, of the blitzkrieg which was to take German forces to the Channel coast.

His reputation as a fighter pilot was established when he destroyed three Belgian Hurricanes on the same day. By June 3 his score was 12.

On July 10, when the Battle of Britain began, he received the command of a Group in JG 26, based at Caffiers. A week later he was promoted major, and on August 1 – his score by now 17 – he received the Knight's Cross.

Early in 1941, the removal of his unit to Brest reduced his chances of scoring against fighters, but in the summer he returned to the Pas de Calais.

On June 21 he had shot down two Blenheim light bombers, when attacking Spitfires sent him into a crash-landing. That same afternoon he revenged himself on a Spitfire although in the process he was himself shot down and wounded. He was awarded the Swords to his Knight's Cross.

At this point Germany invaded the Soviet Union. Galland was promoted major-general and given control of fighter operations on the eastern front, in the Balkans, and in the Mediterranean and the West.

By now, with his score at 94, he had been invested personally by Hitler with the Diamonds to the Knight's Cross. Goering then told him the stones were fake and had real diamonds sent from his own jeweller.

In February 1942, Hitler, in a daring gamble, sent the warships *Scharnhorst*, *Gneisenau* and *Prince Eugen* from Brest through the Channel. He chose Galland to supervise the massive fighter cover which, coupled with bad weather, assured the success of the "Channel Dash".

Galland feared that an escalation of the RAF night bombing offensive would reveal Germany's neglect of night fighter defences. His forebodings were realised in the week following July 24 1943, when the bombing of Hamburg preceded devastating night raids on Germany.

Finally, Galland's counsel prevailed, and he swiftly moved to bolster defences with units withdrawn from other fronts. Allied night and day losses increased steeply until RAF night counter-measures and American day long-range fighter escorts began to restore the balance.

Galland then fell into disfavour. Goering accused him of disloyalty and of introducing unsound tactics. He was placed under house arrest, and had resolved to commit suicide when Hitler intervened.

Galland, though relieved of his overall command, led an elite "squadron of squadrons" (its pilots included ten holders of the Knight's Cross) equipped with the new Me 262 jet fighter. Despite heavy losses, the jets caused havoc among Allied bomber formations.

Shortly before VE Day on May 8 1945, Galland flew his last combat sortie, leading six Me 262s in a head-on attack on a formation of American B-26 Marauders.

His jet was badly damaged while attacking Mustang fighters. Forced down, Galland's aircraft dipped into a bomb crater. His injuries put an end to his fighting war.

Taken prisoner, Galland was not released until 1947. The next year he was recruited by Argentina to develop its air force.

He returned to Germany in 1955 and joined Air Lloyd, subsequently becoming its chairman. Throughout the post-war years he was much in demand as an aviation consultant.

Galland was thrice married; he is survived by his third wife, Heidi, and a son and a daughter by his second wife.

AIR MARSHAL
SIR DENIS "CROW" CROWLEY-MILLING
1 DECEMBER 1996

Air Marshal Sir Denis "Crow" Crowley-Milling, who has died aged 77, was a Second World War pilot of renown and twice escaped from occupied France – once by Hurricane and once on foot.

When the war broke out, Crowley-Milling was called up as a sergeant pilot. He had learned to fly at weekends with the RAF Volunteer Reserve while serving an apprenticeship at the Rolls-Royce aero-engine experimental unit at Derby. When France fell in 1940 his engineering apprenticeship paid the first of many dividends. Crowley-Milling found himself with the surviving Hurricanes of 242 Squadron that were stranded in France, separated from their groundcrew amid the chaos of retreat. With the help of fellow pilots, he was able to service the aircraft in which they then flew home.

As the aircraft took off for England the squadron's commander was left behind at Nantes airfield, sleeping off a heavy session. The pilots left pinned to his chest a note: "We have taken off for Tangmere. When you sober up you had better join us, because the Germans are heading this way."

Back in England, under the aggressive leadership of its new commander – the legless ace Douglas Bader – 242, essentially a Canadian squadron, was very soon plunged into the Battle of Britain.

Although Crowley-Milling had been blooded in France – almost coming to grief by mistakenly joining an enemy Me 109 fighter in formation – he learned fast.

Bader indelibly impressed his personality on the squadron and particularly on Crowley-Milling, for whom it was the beginning of a warm and close friendship.

As the fighting intensified, Crowley-Milling recalled: "I felt bloody frightened as Douglas dived us, in fairly close formation, slap into masses of bombers with fighters above. The little man inside you kept telling you that this was a dangerous game, but he was drowned by Douglas's encouragement over the radio."

On September 7 1940, Crowley-Milling took part in the action which marked the first deployment of the controversial Big Wing tactic which Bader had advocated so ardently.

This involved the assembly of between three and five squadrons, rather than relying on piecemeal attempts at interception.

Crowley-Milling remembered: "The operation saw us plunging into a great beehive over the London docks. The advantage of attacking in strength was that you broke the beehive up. I felt much happier attacking as a squadron than as a section, and with Spitfires taking on the high cover we could do that."

Before being shot down in that action Crowley-Milling destroyed an Me 110 twin-engined fighter, adding it to the He 111 bomber he had bagged on August 30.

Although he suffered head injuries, Crowley-Milling

resumed flying within days. On Sept 14 he claimed a Do 17 bomber and the next day a Me 109 fighter, part of his overall war score of at least seven "kills".

Denis Crowley-Milling was born on March 22 1919, the son of a Lancastrian solicitor. From Malvern College he joined Rolls-Royce in 1937 as a premium apprentice. While exercising his Morgan three-wheeler he visited the Cobham aerial circus. Joyrides stimulated a passion for flying.

His first wartime posting, in May 1940, was to 615, a Gladiator biplane fighter squadron in France. Brought home to convert to Hurricanes, he had only a few hours experience of the type when, on June 8 1940, 615 was ordered to Châteaudun as France fell.

After returning home on June 18 and fighting in the Battle of Britain, Crowley-Milling, long since commissioned, was posted as a flight commander in June 1941 to No 610, a Spitfire squadron in Bader's wing at Westhampnett.

On August 21, he flew his second operational sortie of the day as part of a Spitfire escort to 24 four-engined Stirling bombers briefed to bomb the steel works at Lille. Homebound, the Spitfires were engaged in a running fight with Me 109s. His engine coolant system was hit, and he forced-landed in a field near St Omer.

Crowley-Milling was put up for the night by a farmer who next morning bicycled with him to a friend's house where he was fitted out with civilian clothes over his uniform. He moved on to an MI 9 escape organisation safe house at Renty, but was at first suspected of being a German posing as an RAF pilot, and came close to being shot. But he was issued with a false identity card and on Aug 27 a St Omer shoemaker collected him by car and the next day accompanied him by train to Lille, where he joined up with a Czech sergeant pilot.

En route for Paris he was provided with new papers by the Abbé Carpentier at Abbeville. In Paris he was lodged overnight in a brothel. In the morning, assisted by Pat O'Leary's escape line, he took a train for Marseilles. There he was sheltered by Georges Rhodocanachi, a Greek doctor (whose son, Kostia, had by chance been a fellow Rolls-Royce apprentice).

Shortly afterwards Crowley-Milling was conducted on foot across the Pyrenees into Spain, where he was arrested by the Civil Guard. He was held prisoner at the Miranda concentration camp and contracted paratyphoid. He was repatriated by way of Gibraltar and was soon able to resume command of his flight in 610 Squadron.

On Aug 19 1942, Crowley-Milling flew several sorties in the costly air cover for the ill-fated Operation Jubilee assault on Dieppe.

In September he received his first squadron command. The squadron, 181, formed at Duxford, was the first to be equipped with the new Typhoon fighter-bomber.

The game was, after crossing the Channel at wavetop and climbing rapidly to 10,000 feet, to dive-bomb enemy airfields in northern France. One of his pilots, "Fish Face" Haddock, recalled: "Only a few years older than us [he was 23] he had masses of experience and made operations seem like a walk in the park."

The following summer Crowley-Milling received command of 16 Typhoon Wing until eyesight problems took him off operations. In the autumn of 1943 he joined the United States Army Air Force headquarters at High Wycombe to co-ordinate fighter operations with B-17 daylight raids.

The next year he moved to an operational requirements staff appointment at the Air Ministry where he remained until the end of the war in Europe. Dropping a rank from wing commander to squadron leader he accepted a permanent commission.

In 1947 he was posted to Egypt to command 6 Squadron, made up of Tempest fighters and then Vampire jets. It was busily operational from the Canal Zone during the Palestine troubles, jousting occasionally with Israeli Spitfires.

From 1950 to 1952 Crowley-Milling was personal staff officer to the C-in-C Fighter Command, moving on to RAF Odiham. While there he led the Meteor wing in the Coronation flypast.

Appointments followed at RAF Staff College, Fighter Command and Central Flying Establishment, and in 1962 he received command of RAF Leconfield.

In a period of fierce competition from war-decorated contemporaries, Crowley-Milling moved upwards via appointments as Air Officer Commanding Hong Kong and Air Operational Requirements Director, Ministry of Defence.

From 1967 to 1970 he was Commander RAF Staff and Principal Air Attaché in Washington. While there Crowley-Milling was responsible for setting up the arrangement under which the US Navy flies Harriers.

Returning home he took command of the RAF's tactical 38 Group, moving in 1973 to 46, its transport group, Finally, he served on the Permanent Military Deputies Committee, Central Treaty Organisation, in Turkey.

In 1975 he retired and was appointed Controller of the RAF Benevolent Fund where he had introduced the International Air Tattoo, now a popular annual fundraising event, presided over for many years by Sir Douglas Bader.

Though gravely ill, Crowley-Milling, as its vice-patron, attended its Silver Jubilee last July. Now the Royal International Air Tattoo (RIAT), it contributes significantly to the £10 million a year the fund spends on welfare.

Following Bader's death in 1982 he worked devotedly for the Bader Foundation and the RIAT's annual sponsored flying scholarship scheme to teach disabled people to fly.

He was Gentleman Usher of the Scarlet Rod of the Order of the Bath, president of the Not Forgotten Association, and in 1992 Master of the Guild of Air Pilots and Air Navigators.

Crowley-Milling was appointed CBE in 1963 and KCB in 1973. He was awarded the DFC in 1941, Bar in 1942 and DSO in 1943.

He married in 1943 Lorna Jean Jeboult (née Stuttard) whom he had known since his schooldays; they had two daughters.

GROUP CAPTAIN
W G G "SMITHY" DUNCAN SMITH
11 DECEMBER 1996

Group Captain W G G "Smithy" Duncan Smith, who has died aged 82, was the quintessential fighter pilot.

An outstanding marksman, he destroyed 19 enemy aircraft, and was awarded the DSO and Bar, and the DFC and two Bars, making him one of the RAF's most decorated fighter heroes.

Duncan Smith flew Spitfires almost throughout the Second World War, from the tail-end of the Battle of Britain in 1940 until peacetime. He was still flying them in the Malayan Emergency of the early 1950s.

As a Spitfire squadron commander and wing leader he explained to his pilots: "You do not strap yourselves in, you buckle the Spitfire on like girding on armour". He saw the aircraft as "an integral part and an extension of one's own sensitivity".

From the moment in October 1940 when he joined No 611, an Auxiliary Air Force Squadron, Duncan Smith showed himself to be a ruthless predator of enemy aircraft.

His descriptions of his exploits were rich in the phraseology of those single-minded hunters who emerged as fighter aces. After a scrap with German Me 109s over France and attacking a train at Le Treport, he noted: "We rounded off the sport by rubbing out a number of German officers while they were gardening."

Of joining up he recalled: "Most of us I believe looked forward to it in much the same way as preparing for·an important rugger or cricket match."

Yet he had no illusions. He expected "to die like many other misguided chaps, because we should never have tolerated the ineptitude of gutless politicians for so long".

In combat Duncan Smith, a convivial party man, turned hard as nails: "I rocketed down after the 109 . . . I held my fire . . . I had no intention of fouling it up . . . now I was ready to make the kill . . . I poured cannon shell into the enemy's belly . . . there was a sheet of flame . . . the 109 dived straight into the ground."

Wilfrid George Gerald Duncan Smith was born on May 28 1914 at Madras, where his father Lieutenant Colonel Wilfrid Smith was serving.

He was educated in Scotland at Nairn and Morrison's Academy, Crieff. While there he revelled in the sights of the surrounding moors and would later say that watching the golden eagles in search of prey had inspired him to fly, and to fight.

In 1933 he returned to India to begin a career as a tea planter. There he demonstrated his marksmanship when two cattle-killing tigers needed shooting.

But he was depressed, and in 1936, having qualified as

a mechanical engineer, joined the sales staff at Great Western Motors in Reading.

When war looked imminent Duncan Smith joined the Royal Air Force Volunteer Reserve. He had already started to fly when the callup came.

In October 1940, as the Battle of Britain came to an end, he was posted to No 611, stationed at Digby in Lincolnshire.

Duncan Smith began to build a reputation as a resolute fighter pilot in the New Year of 1941. Fighter Command was then mounting sweeps over France and the Low Countries, and supporting bomber formations.

In August he moved to 603 Squadron as a flight commander. He had to rest after contracting pneumonia, but by January 1942 he had returned to the celebrated Hornchurch Spitfire Wing. In the early spring he received command of 64, the first squadron to be equipped with the new and magical Spitfire IX, capable of more than 400 mph.

On August 19 1942 Duncan Smith was in the thick of the fighting above the disastrous Operation Jubilee assault on Dieppe. In the course of several sorties he shot down a Dornier 217 bomber which was attacking Allied shipping. Later that day he was hit by a Dornier gunner. Diving out of control he baled out, but lost his dinghy in the drop. Four miles off the Somme Estuary he was rescued by a British naval launch, whose skipper, seeking a souvenir, ripped off his wings and nailed them to the mast. Two days later Duncan Smith was promoted wing leader at North Weald.

Towards the end of November Duncan Smith was rested at Fighter Command's Tactics Branch, helping to introduce a School of Tactics for squadron commanders and wing leaders.

News filtering home from the Desert Air Force inspired

him "to get some sand in my shoes and sun on my back". He was offered the Luqa Wing in Malta – not quite the desert but a step in the right direction.

By the time he arrived there, the George Cross island had become a giant aircraft carrier for the invasion of Sicily, scheduled for July 1943. In the resulting operations Duncan Smith increased his score, though after one engagement he only just managed to return his badly-holed Spitfire to Malta; one hole was the size of a football.

Shortly after the invasion of Sicily he obtained his dream posting as wing leader of 244 Wing in the Desert Air Force. Just as he arrived a large force of Ju 88s pasted the wing's Lentini base, destroying or damaging some 30 Spitfires.

The day before the invasion of Italy, Duncan Smith took off on a solo mission but an engine defect led to his running out of fuel. At 2,000 ft he baled out over the sea and inflated his Mae West. To his horror there was no dinghy in the parachute pack. Nor would his rescue rockets function.

After some six hours, and at the limits of his endurance, he was picked up by an Air Sea Rescue *Walrus* amphibian, which was then attacked by enemy aircraft and badly damaged.

One bullet tore through the collar of Duncan Smith's Mae West, grazing his neck. But the *Walrus* delivered him ashore, where he purloined a Spitfire and flew barefoot back to Lentini.

At the end of November 1943 Duncan Smith received command of 324 Wing as a group captain. He led the wing as it moved – during that year's cruel winter – up to Anzio, through Rome to Tarquinia, across to the South of France, back to Florence, and over to the Rimini area.

Merlyn Rees, his operations officer and the future Labour home secretary, recalled that Duncan Smith inspired great loyalty throughout. He never fussed or interfered, and "could govern with a light rein".

At the end of the war Duncan Smith was granted a permanent commission and from 1947 commanded a wing on the North West Frontier of India.

In 1950 he moved to 60 Squadron, whose Spitfires and Vampire jet fighters supported Army and police operations in the Malayan Emergency. In this period he was the last RAF pilot to fly the Spitfire operationally.

Returning home in 1952 he completed his RAF career in station and staff appointments, including an exchange posting in America in 1954.

Duncan Smith retired from the RAF in 1960 and set up an aircraft and special products division at Triplex Safety Glass. He was particularly involved with meeting Concorde requirements.

In 1973 he again retired and spent seven years in Rome before returning to Scotland, where he wrote *Spitfire into Battle* (1981). In the late 1980s the family moved to Devon.

Apart from being a big game hunter and keen shot, Duncan Smith was a scratch amateur golfer. He won the Malayan Open in 1950.

"Smithy" Duncan Smith married, in 1946, Pamela Mary Summers, whom he met when she was appearing as a ballerina at the Opera House in Naples; they had two sons, one of whom is the Conservative MP Iain Duncan Smith,★ and two daughters.

★ Iain Duncan Smith has since become leader of the Conservative Party.

WING COMMANDER
P B "LADDIE" LUCAS
20 MARCH 1998

Wing Commander P B "Laddie" Lucas, who has died aged 82, was chiefly celebrated as a fighter pilot; he was also a Conservative MP, a successful businessman, a highly readable writer, and a champion golfer.

During the Second World War, Lucas was credited with at least six enemy aircraft destroyed – though his actual score may have been twice that number. His most remarkable achievement was in the defence of Malta during the spring of 1942.

Set between Sicily and the North African coast, the island posed a serious threat to Rommel's supply line from Europe. In March and April 1942 the Germans dropped twice the tonnage of bombs on Malta as landed on London during the worst year of the Blitz.

Lucas was sent to Malta in February 1942 and joined No 249 Squadron at Takali. Over the next four months, the three British squadrons on the island found themselves countering more than 17,000 enemy sorties; the defending aircraft were sometimes outnumbered 10 to one.

The task was initially all the more difficult as the British had to fly obsolete Hurricanes against the superior Messerschmitts of Kesselring's Sicilian-based Air Fleet 2. A measure of equilibrium was restored when Spitfire reinforcements arrived, but there was little time for inexperienced pilots to adjust to the intensity of the fighting. In April, two new squadrons landed with 46 Spitfires; the next day only seven remained operational.

Yet Lucas survived, despite several forced landings, and aged only 26 rose to command 249. His success in forging a robust and resourceful fighting unit from disparate elements meant that the squadron scored more kills than any other in defence of the island.

In July 1942, after further Spitfires had arrived and Malta had been secured, Lucas was awarded the DFC for his part in the textbook interception over St Paul's Bay of three Italian bombers, guarded by a screen of 80 Me 109s.

Lucas's force attacked unseen out of the sun, using the advantage of height and speed to cut through the opposing fighters and close with the bombers, which were rapidly dispatched. Lucas compared the exhilaration he felt to that of participating in a perfectly-worked manoeuvre on the rugby field. The comparison was just: it was with a games-player's combination of timing and aggression that Malta was held.

Percy Belgrave Lucas was born at Sandwich Bay, Kent, on September 2 1915. He early acquired the name by which he was known throughout his life; when a company of Highlanders was billeted on his parents during the Great War, the soldiers would engage his pretty nursemaid in conversation on the pretext of asking after "the wee laddie".

His father, a fine all-round sportsman, was the secretary and co-creator of Prince's golf club at Sandwich, where the smooth greens soon attracted a membership that included the Prince of Wales and Viscount Astor. Laddie, a left-hander, took up the game at the age of six, and greatly benefited from practising with such visitors as Harry Vardon and Henry Cotton. Later, when his Spitfire was hit over France, Lucas managed to coax his aircraft as far as Prince's and crash-land by the ninth green.

He was educated at Stowe, where he became an excellent games-player and where the headmaster, J F Roxburgh, exerted a powerful influence on him after the untimely death of Laddie's father.

In 1934, Lucas went up to Pembroke College,

Cambridge, to read economics. He had already given notice that he might become an outstanding golfer, having captained the England Boys' team and won the Boys' Championship in 1933. Lucas represented the University for three years, captaining the team in 1937, and enjoying some remarkable games against Oxford. In the foursomes in 1937, contested over 36 holes, Lucas and his partner found themselves nine down after 17 holes; they recovered to square the match.

Possessing both great physical strength and a determination to explore every theory on the game, Lucas also finished as the top amateur in the 1935 British Open. At 19 he found himself hailed as the finest left-handed player in the world. It was a reputation he retained for the next 25 years.

On coming down from Cambridge in 1937, Lucas put his knowledge of golf to good effect as a sports writer for the *Sunday Express*; later he commentated on the game for the BBC. On the outbreak of war, however, he volunteered for the RAF, his choice of service determined by unhappy memories of war games at school, and of a rough sea voyage to America when he was playing in the Walker Cup in 1936.

After initial training at his former Cambridge college, Lucas became one of the first pilots to learn to fly under the Empire scheme in Canada. His first posting was in 1941 to No 66 Squadron at Perranporth, Cornwall, from where he mounted strikes against shipping in the Channel. He carried into battle his family crest, painted on the side of his cockpit.

Lucas was sent to Malta early in 1942. When he returned that autumn, he was assigned as personal assistant to the Duke of Kent, but managed to send in his stead a friend, Michael Strutt, Lord Belper's son, who already knew the Duke; two weeks later both Strutt and the Duke were killed in an air-crash. Lucas was always badly afflicted by Michael Strutt's death.

After a spell on the staff at Fighter Command, Lucas returned to operations in 1943, in charge of No 616 Squadron at Ibsley, Hampshire, and then as leader of the Spitfire wing at Coltishall, Norfolk, where he quickly restored morale and was awarded the DSO. Then in 1944 he took command of No 613 (City of Manchester) Squadron, based at Cambrai, flying Mosquitoes on low-level tactical support missions and striking at the German offensive in the Ardennes.

Now a Wing Commander, Lucas won a Bar to his DSO in 1945 for making numerous attacks on enemy lines of communication, often in the teeth of appalling weather and heavy fire. He was also awarded the Croix de Guerre with Palm.

Encouraged by Lord Beaverbrook, Lucas stood for West Fulham in 1945, but failed to unseat Edith Summerskill. Lucas returned to the RAF to see out his commission and brought back from France 188 bottles of champagne in the space created by stripping the guns from his fighter. The Krug (at 12 shillings a bottle) was then drunk at his wedding in 1946 to Jill, sister of the composer John Addison and of Douglas Bader's wife, Thelma.

In the General Election of 1950, Lucas won the seat of Brentford and Chiswick, which he held for nine years. He contributed knowledgeably to aviation debates, but the pressure of supporting a young family forced him to reject Harold Macmillan's offer of a junior ministerial post. Having seen what could be achieved by working with other European airmen in the war, Lucas was frustrated by Britain's reluctance to join the Common Market. In 1959 he left politics for commerce.

From 1946 he also worked for the Greyhound Racing Association, a sports promotion company with a large property portfolio that eventually included White City and Belle Vue stadiums. He became the firm's managing director in 1957, and in 1965 its chairman.

When GRA's profits from racing dropped after off-course betting was legalised, Lucas ably expanded the uses to which its stadia were put, notably hosting Billy Graham's Crusade. However, the firm was badly hit by the property collapse in the 1970s, and by differences of opinion with their backers, the ICI Pension Fund. Lucas took early retirement in 1975.

He had always considered journalism to be his true metier, and he now began to produce a series of fluently written books that drew on his flying experiences. They included two autobiographical volumes, *Five Up* (1978) and *Winged Victory* (1995), and a study of Douglas Bader, *Flying Colours* (1981). Amiable but direct, Lucas served on many national committees, including that of the Sports Council, from 1971 to 1983.

Despite lack of time to practise, he also continued to play golf of the highest standard. He was in the British Walker Cup team in 1947 and captained it two years later. An early advocate of the larger ball, he had an excellent record in the President's Putter in the post-war years, and in 1954 played the course at Sandy Lodge wearing a blindfold; he took only 15 more strokes than par.

He was appointed CBE in 1981.

Laddie Lucas is survived by his wife and their two sons, one of whom is the night editor of *The Daily Telegraph*; another son predeceased him.

CHARLES SWEENY
20 MARCH 1999

Charles Sweeny, who has died at Bar Harbour, in Maine, aged 83, was an energetic social figure of the 1930s; the Second World War, however, proved that he also possessed drive and effectiveness.

His wedding in 1933, to Margaret Whigham, a much photographed beauty, attracted a considerable crowd to the Brompton Oratory. The daughter of George Whigham, chairman of the British and Canadian and American Celanese Corporations, she later married the 11th Duke of Argyll.

The Sweeny marriage inspired a verse in *You're the Top,* one of the hits in Cole Porter's 1934 musical *Anything Goes*:

You're the nimble tread of the feet of Fred Astaire,
You're Mussolini
You're Mrs Sweeny,
You're Camembert.

The comparisons (Astaire apart) were odorous. But when Mussolini gave way at the top to Hitler, "Charlie" Sweeny proved his mettle – despite being warned to leave Britain by Joseph Kennedy, JFK's father, who was then American ambassador in London.

"This country is finished," Kennedy told him in 1940. "It will be overrun by the Germans in a matter of weeks. All the roads will then be blocked with refugees just as they are now in France. You and your children must get out."

Sweeny judged otherwise, and although unfit for active service did a great deal for Britain in the dark days before the Americans joined the war.

As invasion threatened after the fall of France Sweeny organised the delivery of sub-machine guns, automatic rifles and armoured cars from America. By the beginning of 1941 he had equipped and trained an outfit named the 1st American Motorised Squadron as a volunteer unit in the Home Guard.

Winston Churchill was so impressed that he inspected Sweeny's private army on Horseguards Parade.

Sweeny next set himself to replace some of the fighter pilots who had been lost to the RAF in the Battle of Britain. Inspired by his uncle, Charles Sweeny, who had flown with the French Air Force in the First World War, he formed No 71, the first of the three "Eagle" squadrons, in which volunteer American airmen gave their services to RAF fighter command. Subsequently, in September 1942, they passed to the US 8th Air Force.

In 1986 Sweeny was present when Mrs Thatcher unveiled a memorial to the Eagle squadrons in Grosvenor Square.

Of Irish ancestry, Charles Sweeny was born at Scranton, Pennsylvania, on Oct 3 1909 and educated at Canterbury School, Connecticut. His grandfather had emigrated to America from Chester and made a fortune in the West; his father multiplied it in New York.

The Sweenys had a house at Le Touquet, in France, where young Charles and his brother Bobby perfected their golf. Charlie went on to Wadham College, Oxford, where he played for the University; Bobby became British amateur champion.

Exquisitely dressed, and possessed (as his wife considered) of "Irish-American Kennedy good looks", Sweeny was as much a target for columnists and photographers as his wife in the pre-war years.

The young couple entertained extravagantly. In the autumn of 1934 Sweeny hired the Embassy Club and gave a dinner dance for 150 guests, including the Prince of Wales. An unknown harmonica player, Larry Adler, provided the cabaret.

The marriage, however, eventually came apart, and was dissolved in 1947. Sweeny stayed on in London after the war. In 1939 he had worked at the City office of his father's Federated Trust and Financial Corporation; now he began to diversify into casino operations. The Earl of Lucan was one of his gambling friends.

He made three attempts to buy the Dorchester Hotel. On the last occasion the Sultan of Brunei, who had bought it for $80 million, refused Sweeny's offer of $140 million.

A heart attack in the 1970s forced Sweeny to give up golf, smoking and backgammon. He had abandoned drink as a young man after trouble with an ulcer.

Sweeny, an autobiography, was published in 1990.

There were two children from his first marriage: a son, and a daughter who married the 10th Duke of Rutland. Sweeny married secondly, in 1958, the American model Arden Snead. The marriage was dissolved in 1966.

WING COMMANDER DOUGLAS "GRUBBY" GRICE
24 MARCH 1999

Wing Commander Douglas "Grubby" Grice, who has died aged 79, destroyed sufficient enemy aircraft during the Battle of Britain to be rated an ace, and was shot down three times during the six weeks' fighting.

On August 15 1940, having already notched up some eight "kills", Grice was flying "arse-end Charlie" (rear guard) of 10 Hurricanes of No 32 Squadron, intercepting enemy raiders making for the port of Harwich. He had just reported a group of Me 110 fighters flying in a defensive circle overhead when an incendiary bullet flashed over his left wrist and into the instrument panel.

Piercing the fuel tank behind the panel, the incendiary set the Hurricane on fire. Grice was engulfed in flames and, as the fighter turned over, fell out. "I remembered my parachute drill and waited a second or two before pulling the rip cord," he recalled. "I was relieved to see land, but an offshore breeze carried me out over the sea."

Once down, having disentangled himself from the parachute rigging lines and inflated his Mae West, he waved at a trawler. Knowing that there was an air-sea rescue launch on the way, the vessel's crew did not respond.

Although Grice was unaware of it at the time, his prolonged dip in the sea was a boon: the "briney" aided the healing process of the burns Grice had suffered to the face and the wrists.

Sir Archibald McIndoe, the celebrated RAF consultant in plastic surgery, gave Grice the good news: "You're a lucky chap, because you are going to look handsome again without any help from me. I won't need a piece of your bottom for skin grafting. Thanks to you and others rescued from the sea we have discovered that a brine bath is the best treatment for a bad burns case."

Douglas Hamilton Grice was born at Wallasey, Cheshire, on June 19 1919 – the day on which Alcock and Brown made the first successful trans-Atlantic flight. Deprived by ill health of a formal education, young Douglas was tutored privately.

Subsequently, after a spell as a machine-gunner in the Artists Rifles, he was granted an RAF short service commission in December 1937. During flying training, Grice – for no obvious reason – was dubbed "Grubby", and the nickname stuck.

In September 1938, he joined No 32 Squadron,

equipped with Gloster Gauntlet biplane fighters. Not long afterwards, at Biggin Hill, he was heartened by the arrival of thoroughly modern eight-gun Hawker Hurricanes.

As France fell in the early summer of 1940, Grice, using Abbeville as a forward base, was in combat over the retreating British Expeditionary Force. On June 6, he was crossing the French coast when he saw a gaggle of Heinkel 111 bombers. But before he could engage, he was attacked by four Me 109s. "I let them get within 500 yards or so," he said, "and then did an Immelman turn – a half loop and roll off the top – so that I could meet them head on."

After shaking off the fighters, Grice attacked the German bombers, until return fire badly damaged his Hurricane and wrecked his engine. After gliding 15 miles, he belly-landed in a field near Rouen. He hitched a lift with a passing RAF padre to an airfield at Dreux, from where he was dispatched home, making a stopover on Jersey, as a passenger in a de Havilland Dragon Rapide.

Back at Biggin he learned he had been awarded a DFC.

Once operational again, Grice was briefed on the morning of June 27 to escort Bristol Blenheim bombers on a mission. On his return, he and his fellow pilot Jimmy Davies (who would later be shot down and killed) were decorated by King George VI.

On July 4, Grice was brought down for the second time. He was patrolling with 32 Squadron over Deal when he was attacked by three 109s. "There was a loud bang and the controls suddenly felt slack. I switched off and belly-landed, not far from Sandwich golf course." To his astonishment, Grice was greeted by an Army officer who had served with him as a private in the Artists Rifles.

After being shot down for the third time and recovery in hospital, Grice served briefly as a "Jim Crow" at Gravesend. This entailed observing and reporting enemy formations.

Finding that his nerve had deserted him, Grice was then invited by his namesake Group Captain Dickie Grice, Biggin Hill station commander, to return as an operations room controller.

This enabled him to further his romance with Pam Beecroft, a Biggin WAAF cypher officer, whom he married in October 1941. Following further fighter controller and staff appointments, Grice, by then a wing commander, resigned his commission in 1947.

Married and with young children, Grice served articles with the London firm of solicitors Gamlen, Bowerman & Forward. In 1951 he joined McKenna & Co, becoming a partner of the firm within a year.

Grice specialised in work for the construction industry, and counted Taylor Woodrow among his clients. He retired in 1982.

Thereafter, Grice devoted much time to his garden at Hunters Green, Chalfont St Giles. He also bought an electric organ and taught himself to play it.

In addition to winning a DFC, Grubby Grice was twice mentioned in despatches. He was appointed MBE in 1946.

He and his wife had a son and a daughter.

GROUP CAPTAIN
DENNIS "HURRICANE" DAVID
25 AUGUST 2000

Group Captain Dennis "Hurricane" David, who has died aged 82, was awarded a DFC and Bar in the space of five days during the Battle of France in 1940.

David was just 21 at the time. The awards reflected his feat of destroying at least one enemy aircraft within a few days while covering the retreat of the British Expeditionary Force, (BEF).

In the ensuing Battle of Britain, he increased his tally to 20, including five unconfirmed kills. He later fought the Japanese in South East Asia and planned operations against Javanese insurgents.

After qualifying in 1938 for a short service commission in the Royal Air Force Volunteer Reserve, David was posted in 1939 to No 87 Squadron, which was exchanging Gloster Gladiator biplanes for Hurricane fighters.

When war broke out, 87 Squadron was sent to France, one of only four Hurricane squadrons in the air component of the BEF. After experiencing the ennui of the "phoney war" in the winter of 1939-40, the squadron suddenly had to face overwhelming odds when Germany invaded the Low Countries and France. On May 10 1940, David wrote "war really starts" in his logbook.

He flew six sorties that day, and recorded his first kill, a Dornier 17 bomber (Do 17) over the Maginot Line.

The next morning he was called to defend an Army tented hospital. "We found ourselves in a scrap with 40 Junkers 87 dive bombers," he noted. He accounted for one of the 14 destroyed and, glimpsing a Do 17 nearby, sent it in flames to the ground.

A day later he set fire to a Heinkel 111 (He 111) over Lille, followed it down and saw it crash-land. Flying low over the wreck, David saw the pilot scramble out and salute him. Then the bomber blew up, killing the pilot and smearing David's windscreen with oil.

After 10 days of continuous fighting, David was now exhausted. He slept in a pigsty – all the accommodation that was available – and then was shot down. He crash-landed safely and was flown home, where his mother put him to bed. He slept for 36 hours.

William Dennis David was born on July 25 1918 in London, but spent his early childhood at Tongwynlais, a mining village near Cardiff. The family later moved back to London and he went to Surbiton County School. After his parents separated, his mother pawned her silver to make ends meet.

He left school at 14 and joined John Lovey, a wholesale clothing and footwear business run by an uncle. As war loomed, he trained with the RAFVR, flying a Blackburn B-2 biplane trainer at the London Air Park.

After the fall of France, 87 Squadron re-formed at Church Fenton, near Leeds. In July 1940, it moved to south-west England, where it was constantly in action, accounting for many enemy bombers and fighters.

David had a further taste of combat during the Battle of Britain as a flight commander with No 213 Squadron. In November he was posted to No 152 Squadron and until March 1941 flew Spitfires. At 23, he became a wing commander.

In the New Year of 1943, following a brief spell commanding No 89 Squadron in the Western Desert, flying Beaufighters, he was posted to Ceylon. He was then promoted group captain and went to the Arakan front in Burma as air adviser to 15 Indian Corps and as Senior Air Staff Officer No 224 Group. There he helped to organise the defeat of the Japanese in Burma.

David was well served by his strong physique. He also had great strength of character and sense of purpose, and had almost hypnotic powers of concentration when engaged in conversation.

After the liberation of Singapore and Malaya, he was appointed Senior Air Staff Officer, Air Headquarters, Batavia, Netherlands East Indies, during operations against Javanese insurgents.

Returning home in 1946, David was granted a

permanent commission and reverted to the rank of squadron leader. In 1949 he was posted to command a wing of de Havilland Vampire jets at Deversoir on the Suez Canal, and in Cairo enjoyed the hospitality of King Farouk.

He then had a series of Air Ministry posts which culminated in his appointment as Air Attaché in Budapest. There David was dubbed "The Light Blue Pimpernel" for his part in helping 400 Hungarians to escape after the failure of the uprising in 1956.

David had a lifelong fondness for dogs, and indulged this by purchasing a greyhound named Flash Harry. It enjoyed a measure of success and his staff at the Ministry of Defence became keen students of form in the *Greyhound Express*.

He retired from the RAF in 1967 and for a while ran a precision engineering business, Dove Enterprises. He later dabbled in property and other ventures and was in demand as a lecturer. He also advised on films such as the *Battle of Britain* (1969) and *Aces High* (1974).

David was president of the Hurricane Society and gave his time to the RAF Benevolent Fund and Royal Air Forces Association.

In his youth, he excelled at tennis and squash. He later restored antique furniture and china and wrote a memoir, *Dennis "Hurricane" David* (1999).

He was mentioned in despatches in 1942 and was awarded the AFC in 1943. He was appointed CBE in 1960. In 1991, he became a Freeman of the City of London.

He is survived by his wife, Margaret.

AIR VICE-MARSHAL
J E "JOHNNIE" JOHNSON
30 JANUARY 2001

Air Vice-Marshal J E "Johnnie" Johnson, who has died aged 85, was the top-scoring RAF fighter pilot of the Second World War; his dash, courage and flying skills were outstanding.

Johnson accounted for at least 38 enemy aircraft over Britain and occupied Europe, yet his actual score was almost certainly higher. Of the many enemy aircraft he shot down, he waived shared credits to boost the scores – and the confidence – of younger pilots.

He earned an appropriately impressive collection of decorations, including a DSO and two Bars and a DFC and Bar. This recognition contrasted starkly with the RAF's refusal before the war to approve his application to join an Auxiliary Air Force (AuxAF) squadron, or to serve in the RAF Volunteer Reserve (RAFVR).

It was only after Johnson had enlisted in the Leicestershire Yeomanry, TA, that the RAFVR reviewed his application and accepted him for pilot training. But for the delay, Johnson might well have been ready for action at the beginning of the Battle of Britain on July 10 1940. As it was, his late entry and a badly set collarbone fracture meant that he did not open his score until the New Year of 1941.

When, subsequently, in the summer of 1941, Fighter Command launched a series of aggressive cross-Channel sweeps, the airmanship and combat skills exhibited by Johnson as a member of No 616, South Yorkshire's AuxAF Spitfire squadron, were recognised by Douglas Bader, then leading his celebrated Spitfire wing from Tangmere at the foot of the South Downs.

Bader paid Johnson the compliment of inviting him to

fly in his own section, and the two men struck up a lifelong friendship. On August 9, during the wing's operation in support of a bomber attack on Gosnay, near Lille, Johnson was present when the legless Bader was brought down and taken prisoner.

Of that day, Johnson recalled how the amiable banter of his groundcrew relieved the tension as they strapped him in at Westhampnett airfield, a satellite of Tangmere. He remembered, too, how "the usual cockpit smell, that strange mixture of dope [varnish], fine mineral oil, gun oil and high octane assailing the nostrils" was "vaguely comforting".

He tightened his helmet strap, swung the rudder with his feet on the pedals, wiggled the stick, thought about Lille and Me 109s and switched on his gunsight. "In a slanting climb we cross Beachy Head and steer for the French coast. Bader rocks his wings, we level out for the climb, slide out of our tight formation and adopt wider battle formations at 25,000 ft."

Over the Pas de Calais, the wing encountered a swarm of Me 109s. "We fan out alongside Bader. There are four 109s with others on either side. Before opening fire I have a swift glance to either side. For the first time I see Bader in the air, firing at a 109. My 109 pulls into a steep climb, I hang on and knock a few pieces from his starboard wing."

Spotting a solitary Messerschmitt, Johnson dropped below, to take aim with his cannon at the unarmoured underside of the aircraft. Moments later a plume of thick black smoke marked the end of the 109.

In July 1942, when his score had already reached double figures, Johnson received command of No 610 (County of Chester), an AuxAF Spitfire squadron based at Ludham, hard by Hickling Broad in Norfolk. The next month, on August 19, 610 flew with New Zealander

Jamie Jameson's No 12 Group Spitfire wing in the air battle over Dieppe, in support of the disastrous Dieppe Raid.

"Over Dieppe," Jameson recalled, "the wing was immediately bounced by a hundred FW 190s and a few Me 109s. I heard Johnson effing and blinding as he broke 610 into a fierce attack. I was hard at it dodging 190s, but I found time to speak sharply to Johnson about his foul language."

Johnson flew four sorties over Dieppe, adding to his tally of "kills". But he was always the first to acknowledge his debt to his groundcrew. "My life depended on my rigger Arthur Radcliffe and my fitter, Fred Burton," he wrote. "They strapped me in, waved me off and welcomed me back – and whenever I was successful they were as pleased as me."

James Edgar Johnson was born at Barrow-upon-Soar, near Loughborough, Leicestershire on March 9 1915. He was educated at Loughborough School and Nottingham University, where in 1937 he qualified as a civil engineer.

Aged 17, he bought a BSA 12-bore shotgun for £1 down and nine similar monthly payments. Rabbits fetched a shilling each, and he reckoned that if he could average two rabbits from three shots he would pay for the gun.

He became adept at deflection shooting on the ground and, graduating to wildfowling on the Lincolnshire marshes, adapted the skill to bring down widgeon, pintail and teal. "The principles of deflection shooting against wildfowl and aeroplanes," he would reflect, "were exactly the same, except that aeroplanes could sometimes return your fire. The best fighter pilots were usually outdoor men who had shot game and wildfowl."

Johnson also learned to ride at an early age; and he enjoyed his Yeomanry service – though after seeing

Spitfires and Hurricanes on a visit, on horseback, to Wittering, he declared that he would "rather fight in one of those than on the back of this bloody horse".

When the RAFVR expanded, he seized his chance and began training as a sergeant pilot, and was mobilised as war came. In August 1940 he joined No 19, a Spitfire squadron, but with the Battle of Britain raging over England the squadron was too pressed to train new pilots. In early September he moved to No 616, but was then hospitalised to have his fracture reset. He returned to the squadron in December.

Following command of No 610, in March 1943 Johnson was posted to lead the Canadian fighter wing at Kenley. Before long, Syd Ford, commanding No 403 Squadron, laid a pair of blue Canadian shoulder flashes on Johnson's desk. "The boys would like you to wear these," said Ford. "After all, we're a Canadian wing and we've got to convert you. Better start now."

Attacking ground targets and acting as escorts to US Eighth Air Force Fortress bomber formations, Johnson's Canadians produced ever increasing scores – in addition to Johnson's 14 kills and five shared between April and September. When Johnson left the squadron to rest from operations, his send-off party was such that the wing was stood down the next day.

Such was Johnson's reputation with the Canadians that when, early in 1944, the Royal Canadian Air Force formed No 144 Wing of three squadrons at Digby, in Lincolnshire, they insisted Johnson command it.

At the D-Day landings on June 6 1944, Johnson led the wing four times over the Normandy beaches. Thereafter, from a base near St Croix-sur-Mer, he and his men saw much action, and he himself had soon notched up his 28th kill, an FW 190 shot down over the Normandy bocage.

On the ground, Johnson got about on a horse he had found abandoned by the Germans. In the mess, dissatisfied with field rations, he brightened up meals with airlifts of bread, tomatoes, lobster and stout supplied by the wing's favourite Chichester landlord.

In April 1945, Johnson was promoted group captain and given command of No 125 Wing, equipped with the latest Griffon-engined Spitfire XIVs. After VE Day, on May 8, he led the wing to Denmark.

In the course of the war, he had never been shot down and had only once been hit by an enemy fighter, over France in August 1944.

After Denmark, he was posted to Germany in command of No 124 Wing. In 1947, having reverted to the substantive rank of wing commander (the price of peace and a permanent commission), he was sent to Canada to attend the RCAF staff college at Toronto.

The next year he went on exchange to the US Air Force, and in 1950-51 he served with the Americans in Korea, before returning to Germany to command RAF Wildenrath until 1954.

In 1957, once more in the rank of group captain, Johnson was transferred to the world of bombers, as Commander of the new Victor V-bomber station at Cottesmore, Rutland. He relished the opportunities to imbue bomber crews with fighter philosophy and to fly their powerful jet aircraft – and also to hunt with the Cottesmore and to hold hunt balls in the officers' mess.

After promotion to air commodore and a spell as Senior Air Staff Officer at Bomber Command's No 3 Group, at Mildenhall, Suffolk, he received (on promotion to air vice-marshal) his final command – Middle East Air Forces, Aden. Johnson rated the latter command "the best air vice-marshal's job in the Air Force".

After retirement from the RAF in 1965, he sat on

company boards in Britain, Canada and South Africa. He also launched, and until 1989 ran, the Johnnie Johnson Housing Trust, providing housing and care for the elderly, the disabled, and vulnerable young people and families. Today the trust manages more than 4,000 houses and flats.

He wrote several readable books, notably *Wing Leader* (1956), a wartime autobiography, and *Full Circle* (1964). With his friend and fellow ace Wing Commander PB "Laddie" Lucas, he wrote *Glorious Summer* (1990); *Courage in the Skies* (1992); and *Winged Victory* (1995).

In addition to the decorations mentioned already he was awarded an American DFC, Air Medal, and Legion of Merit, and the Belgian Croix de Guerre and Order of Leopold.

He was appointed CBE in 1960 and CB in 1965. He became a Deputy Lieutenant for Leicester in 1967, and was appointed to the Légion d'honneur in 1988.

Johnnie Johnson married, in 1942, Pauline Ingate; they had two sons.

SQUADRON LEADER
TONY BARTLEY
6 APRIL 2001

Squadron Leader Tony Bartley, who has died aged 82, was an RAF Spitfire fighter ace who was awarded the DFC after scoring eight victories against enemy aircraft in the Battle of Britain during the summer and autumn of 1940.

The following summer, Bartley was attached to Vickers-Supermarine as a production test pilot, and made a significant contribution to the development of the Spitfire. Among the weaknesses that Bartley identified was the inadequacy of the Spitfire's rear-ward view during combat. But improving this would have required a major alteration in the geometry of the rear fuselage, which was made impossible by production pressures in 1941. Also, large one-piece perspex canopies had not yet been developed, and it was not until 1944 that Bartley's recommendations were put into effect with a later Mark of Spitfires.

Anthony Charles Bartley was born on March 28 1919 at Dacca in India. His father, Sir Charles Bartley, was an Irish barrister who served as a judge in the Calcutta High Court.

Bartley was educated at Stowe and in 1939 joined the RAF on a short service commission. He was posted to No 92 (East India) Squadron in November 1939, as it was forming at Tangmere in Sussex with the fighter version of the twin-engine Bristol Blenheim.

After the Blenheims had been replaced by Spitfires in March 1940, Bartley fought over Dunkirk during the fall of France and evacuation of the British Expeditionary Force.

In March 1941 he was posted as flight commander to No 74 Squadron at Manston, on the Kent coast. But he was soon a flying instructor at No 56 and No 53 Operational Training Units (OTU), before moving on to Vickers-Supermarine in July. During this time he performed the acrobatics for the film *The First of The Few* (1942) which chronicled the life of the Spitfire's designer, R J Mitchell, played by Leslie Howard.

At Vickers-Supermarine, Bartley forged a fruitful relationship with Jeffrey Quill, who had been the second pilot to fly Mitchell's prototype and was now senior test pilot. Quill particularly welcomed Bartley's combat experience of the Spitfire's early 20 mm cannon installations, which had proved problematic.

Once, Quill refused to provide Bartley with a Spitfire to return to Worthy Down, Hants, from a party at Heston airfield in London; Quill was horrified to discover that

Bartley, large though he was, had instead crammed into the confined cockpit of a Spitfire with another bulky officer, putting both their lives and the aircraft at risk.

When, in the New Year of 1942, Bartley returned to operations with No 65 Squadron – receiving command in May – he knew from his experience at Vickers-Supermarine that some of his Spitfires were dangerously unstable. He immediately telephoned Quill and reported an incident involving Group Captain John Peel, his station commander at Debden in Essex. Peel had inadvertently applied so much "G" when pulling out from a dive that he had collapsed and hit his head on the control stick.

Quill visited Bartley, flew the Spitfire, and declared it unfit for the flight line of an operational squadron. After further tests, he found several more of the No 65's Spitfires to be unstable and they were duly modified.

In August 1942, Bartley received command of No 111 Squadron and led it to North Africa during the November Operation Torch landings. He shot down several enemy fighters over Tunisia, including at least three Me 109s.

In January 1943, Bartley hitched a ride home in a four-engine American Liberator bomber which lost two engines and crash-landed in Wales. Bartley was not injured, and on his return was awarded a Bar to his DFC. In February of that year, he was posted to Headquarters No 83 Group in the new Tactical Air Force forming within Fighter Command.

After training squadrons in ground attack and Army support for the forthcoming invasion of Normandy, Bartley attended the US Command and General Staff College at Fort Leavenworth, Kansas, and taught at the School of Air Tactics at Orlando, Florida.

This proved useful when, on his return, he became liaison officer with the 70th Fighter Wing of the US 9th Air Force, moving on, in October 1944, to Transport

Command to set up staging posts in Europe. When the war ended in Europe in May 1945, Bartley volunteered for service against the Japanese and in July 1945 established a transport staging post in the Palau Islands.

The Pacific and Far East war ended within weeks and Bartley fixed a lift home in a Douglas Dakota which was returning for an overhaul. He was released from the service and in 1946 returned to Vickers-Armstrong as a test pilot and sales executive.

But Bartley's marriage the next year to the actress Deborah Kerr brought a change of direction and he moved to Hollywood. After studying film production with MGM, he formed European American Productions and wrote and produced television films for Fireside Theatre, MCA and Douglas Fairbanks Presents.

Bartley later joined CBS Films where he was responsible for European sales and production. Among the programmes he wrote and produced was *Assignment Foreign Legion*, starring Merle Oberon.

Bartley then joined Associated Rediffusion, the early independent television company, serving as head of the international division and assistant general manager until 1965, when he moved to Canada to represent Global Television and write a history of Canada for the Canada Broadcasting Company.

In the late 1960s Bartley was appointed director of the Caribbean Broadcasting Corporation in Barbados, and in 1971 he moved to Ireland where he formed Intercontinental Telefilms and continued to write and develop television programmes. His autobiography, *Smoke Trails in the Sky*, was published in 1984.

His marriage to Deborah Kerr was dissolved in 1958. They had two daughters. He married secondly, in 1965, Victoria Mann. They also had two daughters.

THE YANKS

GENERAL
IRA C EAKER
6 AUGUST 1987

Gen Ira C Eaker, who has died aged 91, was the American Air Force's Texan tough, cigar-smoking bomber commander who shared the single-minded 1939-45 war bombing philosophy of "Bomber" Harris, which has earned them both recent criticism.

In some respects the United States Army Air Force's equivalent of "Blood, and Guts" Patton, Eaker believed in leading from the front. He wrote; "Great leaders in the air and on the ground do not send men. They lead them." He practised what he preached.

Impatient for action on Aug 17, 1942, Eaker took part in the first American daylight raid over Europe, flying a B-17 Fortress appropriately named "Yankee Doodle". The target was the railway yards at Rouen in northern France.

From this small beginning there developed the crescendo of day and night strategic bombing orchestrated respectively by Eaker, first as Commanding General of the US 8th Air Force's VIII Bomber Command and later in command of the 8th Air Force, and Harris, RAF Bomber Command's leader.

Partners in their single-minded determination to destroy Germany's will and war effort, the two bomber leaders were firm friends, a relationship fostered by Harris's welcome to Eaker as his guest at his home, Springfield, near High Wycombe, for several months after Eaker's arrival in England in February, 1942.

Inviting Eaker from the outset to his staff discussions and as an observer at Bomber Command operational planning meetings, Harris nourished and advertised the friendship.

"We're so close," he would joke, "that Gen Eaker kisses my wife when he leaves for the office in the morning and kisses her again at night."

Somewhat characteristically, on Eaker's safe return from the Rouen raid, Harris signalled him: "Yankee Doodle certainly went to town and can stick another well deserved feather in his cap."

Their friendship did not, however, deter Harris from querying the American's belief in daylight bombing, though Harris loyally supported him.

Nevertheless, in the face of mounting losses, there were increasing calls for Eaker to switch to night bombing. When the question was raised in January 1943 at the Casablanca summit of Allied leaders, Eaker flew in and succeeded in scotching it.

By the autumn of that year the awful truth was dawning. Bombing results by Eaker's crews were found to have been over-estimated and his Flying Fortresses were becoming increasingly vulnerable to improving enemy air defences.

Whatever might have been the case earlier, the concept of daylight bombing was no longer valid without heavy long-range fighter support.

By 1944, however, Eaker had succeeded Air Chief Marshal Sir Arthur Tedder, as he then was, as C-in-C Mediterranean Allied Air Forces. His Air Force was based in Italy and he continued the strategic bombing offensive against Germany and the Balkans.

In June, 1944, he flew the first bombing raid from Italy to Germany using the Soviet Union as the eastern end of the mission.

Eaker was also responsible for planning the bombing of the monastery at Monte Cassino and in August, 1944, he was Air Commander of "Operation Dragoon" the Allied invasion of southern France.

Born in Texas, Ira Clarence Eaker entered the United States Army in 1917, beginning his career as an infantry officer. Transferring to the Air Corps he became a pilot in 1918. In 1929, he was part of a team which set a world endurance record of 151 hours aloft using air refuelling.

During the inter-war years he studied at several universities, including that of Southern California, where he received a degree in journalism. He became well-known as a writer and speaker on topics relating to air power.

Eaker collaborated with Gen "Hap" Arnold who was head of the US Army Air Forces throughout the 1939-45 war, in writing three books: *This Flying Game* (1936), *Winged Warfare* (1941), and *Army Flyer* (1942).

During the course of his career, Eaker was decorated with the Silver Star and Distinguished Flying Cross among other US military awards and also held decorations from Britain, France, the Soviet Union, Italy, Poland, Yugoslavia, Brazil, Chile and Peru.

In addition he was appointed an honorary KBE in 1943 and KCB in 1945.

After his retirement in 1947, Eaker entered industry serving as a corporate officer with the Hughes companies. Making use of his earlier journalistic training he wrote a syndicated newspaper column for 18 years.

LIEUTENANT-COLONEL
BOB JOHNSON
27 DECEMBER 1998

Lieutenant-Colonel Bob Johnson, who has died aged 78, was the joint top scoring American fighter pilot in Europe during the Second World War; his tally of 28 confirmed kills was equalled only by Francis Gabreski.

Flying P-47D Thunderbolts with the 61st and 62nd squadrons of the US 56th Fighter Group, Johnson led a charmed life during the costly campaign to protect Flying Fortress and Liberator bombers as they made daylight raids on Germany.

Johnson owed his survival as much to his aircraft as to his aerial skill. Known as "The Jug" – short for juggernaut, because of its size and sturdy build – the single-engined Thunderbolt could take heavy punishment.

Following a typically bruising encounter with German FW 190 fighters, Johnson stopped counting after finding more than 100 holes and tears in the propeller, nose, fuselage and wings, of his aircraft.

As he walked away from the Thunderbolt, Johnson also counted his blessings. One 20 mm cannon shell had exploded in the cockpit next to his left hand. Others had mangled the cockpit frame and jammed the canopy.

Only then did Johnson realise why the canopy would not slide back when he had earlier contemplated baling out.

Such punishment, if not always so extreme, was commonplace among American fighter squadrons supporting the Eighth Air Force's daytime assaults on Berlin, which complemented Bomber Command's night offensives.

When, on March 6 1944, the Americans mounted their first heavy daylight attack on the German capital, Johnson was already a flight commander in the 61st Squadron of Colonel Hubert Zemke's celebrated "Wolfpack".

At the briefing, Johnson learned that as his commanding officer Gabreski was away, he was to lead 35 Thunderbolts – half of the 56th Fighter Group – in support of 800 Fortress and Liberator heavy bombers.

Shortly after 10 am, Johnson took off from his base at Halesworth, Suffolk, in his red-nosed Thunderbolt, which he had dubbed "All Hell". Over the Dutch coast, the first wave of bombers came into view, formed into tightly packed "boxes" of 30 Fortresses each.

Johnson had his fighters fly close to the boxes. Then he spotted the gaggles of enemy fighters. Johnson yelled: "Watch those monkeys ahead. Hell, they're Focke-Wulfs!"

The Thunderbolts jettisoned their long-range fuel tanks, spread out, and wheeled into position to turn in on the enemy fighters. As they did so, the bombers' gunners opened fire indiscriminately.

In the ensuing melée, Johnson's Thunderbolts were overwhelmed by three formations of FW 190s and Me 109s, each containing 30 to 40 aircraft. Johnson later recalled the sky being filled with parachutes.

After seeing a Flying Fortress cut in half and watching some 30 others plunge to earth, he took consolation in destroying an FW 190. After a diving chase, he destroyed another, and climbed again.

Spotting a lone Fortress being savaged by six enemy fighters, he threw his Thunderbolt into the attack, forcing the enemy pilots to break off and dive.

Johnson followed one Me 109 down until, with his fuel rapidly diminishing, he turned and headed for home.

Although this first daylight raid on Berlin was rated a success, the Eighth Air Force had lost 69 bombers, 11 fighters and almost 700 men. But lessons were learned, and Johnson's recommendations of ways to reduce losses were eventually taken up by all American fighter groups.

Robert Samuel Johnson was born at Lawton, Oklahoma, on February 21 1920. His father was a car mechanic. In 1941, after graduating as an engineer from Cameron Junior College, he joined the US Army.

The next year he qualified as a pilot at Kelly Field, Texas, and was commissioned. In the New Year of 1943 he was assigned to the 61st Fighter Squadron, stationed at Horsham St Faith, near Norwich.

At the outset of his operational career, on cross-Channel fighter sweeps and bomber support missions, Johnson did not endear himself to his superiors. He was sharply reprimanded for separating from his flight and going off to seek glory for himself.

But he learned from experience and was already an acknowledged ace with 18 kills when the attacks on Berlin began in 1944. On March 8, he shot down two 109s, and on March 15 he claimed three enemy fighters in one day – two 190s and a 109.

In June 1944 Johnson returned home and, flying a Thunderbolt, made a public relations tour of America, promoting the purchase of government bonds. After the war he joined the Thunderbolt's manufacturers, Republic Aviation.

In 1958 he published *Thunderbolt!* (with Martin Caidin). Johnson was awarded the American DSC, the DFC with eight clusters, the Silver Star, the Purple Heart, Air Medal with four clusters, and the British DFC.

COLONEL
"GABBY" GABRESKI
31 JANUARY 2002

Colonel "Gabby" Gabreski, who has died aged 83, was America's greatest surviving ace; during the Second World War he achieved a total 31 "kills", and added six and half during the Korean War.

When the Japanese attacked Pearl Harbor on December 7 1941, Gabreski had just joined his first operational unit of the US Air Force in Hawaii. Although he managed to take off from Wheeler Field in a Curtiss P-36 fighter, he was too late to challenge the departing raiders.

The son of Polish immigrant parents, he was keen to avenge Germany's seizure of Poland, so he made his way to London. Here, after meeting a Polish pilot at the Embassy Club, he was invited to join No 315, one of the RAF's Polish fighter squadrons. This he did, with the blessing of the American authorities, and he was soon escorting bombers in a Spitfire IX. He flew aggressive cross-Channel sweeps until February 1943, when he rejoined the US Eighth Air Force and flew with the 61st Squadron in Hub Zemke's 56th Fighter Group.

After the Spitfire, Gabreski found the P-47 Thunderbolt fighter, with its big radial engine and 40 ft wingspan, a cumbersome beast. However, he soon mastered its powerful turbocharger and outstanding roll. He was promoted major and given command of the squadron.

On December 11 1943, Gabreski led 16 Thunderbolts among 200 fighters which were escorting B-17 Flying Fortresses in an attack on Emden. As they joined the bomber force over northern Holland, they found the bombers already under attack from 40 rocket-firing Me 110s. Several bombers were shot down, despite their desperate efforts to keep formation. But the scene changed as Gabreski and his men hurled themselves at the 110s. In one dive, Gabreski shot down one enemy aircraft, his pilots accounting for the other two.

By now perilously low on fuel, Gabreski was making for home when a lone Me 109, a far more formidable adversary than a 110, surprised him. Its pilot shot away a rudder pedal in Gabreski's plane and part of one of his flying boots, and so damaged the Thunderbolt's engine that it began to falter. With stringent fuel economy, Gabreski just made it to the coastal emergency landing ground at Manston, Kent.

Over the ensuing weeks Gabreski increased his score to 28, sometimes destroying two or three enemy aircraft in a day. Eventually, in the summer of 1944, after completing 193 operational sorties, he was offered a trip home. He was about to board a transport for America when, anxious not to miss that morning's mission, he obtained permission for "just one more". He was making a second run to strafe enemy aircraft parked on an airfield when he went in so low that his Thunderbolt's propeller hit rising ground and he crash-landed.

Helped by a Polish forced-labourer, he evaded capture for five days until he was picked up and sent to Stalag Luft 1 as a prisoner of war. He returned home in 1945.

Francis Gabreski was born at Oil City, Pennsylvania on January 28 1919. As a pre-medical student at the University of Notre Dame, he began taking flying lessons with the Army Air Corps. A difficult pupil, he narrowly escaped being rejected.

The US Air Force sent him to Maxwell Airfield for advanced training, but he was almost failed again after fainting at the morning parade. Although he confessed that he had fallen victim to a hangover, he was retained. Gabreski was commissioned as a second lieutenant in

March 1941, and posted to the 45th fighter squadron of the 15th Fighter Group at Hawaii's Wheeler Air Base. He was shaving when he heard the first explosions at Pearl Harbor.

After the war, Gabreski worked in flight testing and in fighter units before being assigned as commander of the 51st Fighter Wing. During the Korean War, he helped to develop tactics for jet fighters. Between July 1951 and April 1952, in a F-86 Sabre jet, he shot down six MiG-15s, and shared another. Gabreski later worked in the aviation industry, ultimately switching to railways and becoming president of Long Island Rail Road. He wrote an autobiography, *Gabby: A Fighter Pilot's Life*.

He married Catherine Cochrane, whom he met at Pearl Harbor; they had three sons and six daughters.

BOMBER BOYS

AIR MARSHAL
SIR HAROLD MARTIN
3 NOVEMBER 1988

Air Marshal Sir Harold Martin, who has died aged 70, was a fearless and brilliant low-level bomber ace who took part in the celebrated attack on the Möhne and Eder dams in May, 1943 – immortalised in the film *The Dambusters*.

Later the Australian-born "Mickey" Martin established another reputation as a master of Mosquito aircraft night-intruder operations over enemy airfields in Europe and in low-level marking for heavy bomber attacks.

The exceptional effectiveness of his career as an operational pilot was recognised in multiple awards, bringing his tally of decorations to a remarkable DSO and Bar, DFC and two Bars and AFC.

By the spring of 1943, when he joined No 617, the "Dambuster" squadron of four-engine Lancaster bombers, Martin had already been blooded in No 455, an Australian Hampden bomber squadron and No 50 squadron of Lancasters.

But it was in 617 that his outstanding skills in low-level attack reached their apogee. Group Capt Leonard Cheshire, at one time his commander in 617, said yesterday: "It was only when I met him that I realised all I had to learn. I learned everything I knew of the low flying game from Mick.

"He was the ideal wartime operational pilot. He had superb temperament, was quite fearless and innovative in his thinking. He was meticulous in his flying discipline and never did make a mistake."

Indeed Martin was punctilious to the point of personally polishing every inch of his perspex cockpit canopy.

When Martin joined 617 in March, 1943, his commanding officer was Wg Cdr Guy Gibson, whom he had met beforehand at Buckingham Palace when Gibson was there for a DSO and Martin for his first DFC; they had swapped notes on low flying.

On the night of the dambusting raid Martin was in Formation 1, detailed to go for the Möhne dam. As he arrived over the target area Bob Hay, his bomb aimer, seeing the 100 ft-thick reinforced concrete, exclaimed: "God, can we break that?"

As he went in, Martin tracked head on for the middle of the dam between its towers as they stood out in the moonlight. Then the flak gunners spotted him and concentrated a curtain of fire where he must pass – between the towers.

"Bomb gone", reported Hay as he released the Barnes Wallis-designed bouncing bomb – the one that skipped the water as in the child's–game of Ducks and Drakes – and in that moment two shells hit the Lancaster's starboard wing, one exploding in an inner fuel tank.

But Martin was lucky: the tank was empty. At that stage the dam seemed to be still there.

Then, shortly afterwards, Gibson heard Martin shout: "Hell, it's gone. It's gone. Look at it for Christ's sake!"

After this raid Martin was ordered to report to the Royal Australian Air Force in London for an interview for the Australian press. Encountering a dark, attractive Australian girl called Wendy – she was the daughter of the Melbourne artist Ida Outhwaite – he lost interest in the required official "line-shoot" and asked his interviewer to lunch. Shortly afterwards they were married.

Harold Brownlow Morgan Martin was born in 1918

and seemed destined to follow his father into the medical profession.

After attending Randwick High School for Boys, Sydney Grammar School and Lyndfield College, he had various adventures in England, including a spell as a gentleman-rider.

On the outbreak of the 1939-45 War he joined the Cavalry Division of the Australian Army before switching to the RAF in 1940 and being commissioned into the Royal Air Force Volunteer Reserve the following year.

In the autumn of 1941 Martin began his low-flying apprenticeship in 455 Squadron, One night his Hampden was so low over Kassel that he hit a balloon cable.

Had the cable not been carried away and dangled from his wing, his career would have ended there and then. He eventually cleared the cable by diving to 50 ft and getting it caught in a tree. On the night of the 1,000 bomber raid on Cologne in May, 1942, Martin, in a 50 Squadron Lancaster, had another lucky let off.

He was awarded his first DFC in this period after a particularly hair-raising exploit in which his Hampden was hit in many places, one engine catching fire.

Martin had commanded 617 temporarily before Cheshire took over, along with the squadron's newly-minted motto: *Apres Moi Le Deluge*. Cheshire had voluntarily dropped from group captain to wing commander for the privilege and soon he and Martin were making a formidable team.

In February, 1944 Cheshire marked the Gnome – Gnome-Rhone engines factory at Limoges from a height of 200 ft, supported by Martin and the rest of 617, then demolished the works with extraordinary accuracy.

In operations against V-weapon sites in France, Martin acted as master or deputy master-bomber. During an attack on a vital rail viaduct at Antheor, in Italy, Martin literally flew down the side of a mountain to mark the target at low level. In this attack his bomb aimer, Bob Hay, was killed by a cannon shell which struck his forehead.

During June, 1944 Martin moved into the equally perilous business of low-level night-intruding with No 515 Squadron of Mosquitos and developed a speciality for baiting flak gunners to draw their fire.

Cheshire said that Martin had an innate sense for turning up at the right place at the right time. Once, after their ways had parted from 617, Cheshire broke silence over the Rhine to inquire about the weather.

Out of the blue and a Mosquito came Martin's voice. "What the hell are you doing?" Cheshire asked.

Back came the characteristic "Sticking my neck out for you types." And he was, beating up a night-fighter airfield to protect the bombers.

After the war Martin flew Transport Command Stirlings and Yorks and in 1947, in a Mosquito, set a London to Cape Town record for which he was awarded the Britannia Trophy and his AFC. The next year, flying a Mosquito, he nursed six RAF Vampire jets in the first jet crossing of the Atlantic.

Less at home in the peacetime air force, he nevertheless climbed through a succession of staff appointments and a post as air attaché in Tel Aviv to a number of commands. He was Air Officer Commanding No 38 Group, Air Support Command from 1967 to 1970; C-in-C RAF Germany and Commander Nato 2nd Tactical Air Force from 1970 to 1973; and air member for personnel, Ministry of Defence, until he retired in 1974. He then held posts with Hawker Siddeley until 1979.

Martin retained his love of the Turf and owned a racehorse called Amber Call shortly after the war. He also enjoyed polo, as well as pottery and painting, relishing his membership of the Chelsea Arts Club.

Martin, who was appointed CB in 1968 and KCB in 1971, is survived by his wife and two daughters.

━━━━━━━━━

AIR COMMODORE
RICHARD KELLETT
8 JANUARY 1990

Air Commodore Richard Kellett, who has died aged 84, accomplished in 1938 the then remarkable feat of flying 7,158.95 miles non-stop from Egypt to Australia in just over 48 hours before going on to further distinction as an RAF bomber pilot in the 1939-45 War.

His record-setting flight, from Nov 5 to 7, was linked to his wartime exploits in that it took place in a Vickers Wellesley bomber whose geodetic construction led to Barnes Wallis's design of the Wellington – mainstay of Bomber Command at the outset of the war.

Almost exactly a year later Kellett was appointed to command 149 Wellington Bomber Squadron and led a succession of perilous daylight raids on heavily defended German naval targets at Wilhelmshaven and Kiel in the weeks before the first Christmas of the war.

Briefed to attack enemy warships, Kellett regularly led formations of up to 24 Wellingtons from three squadrons out to sea over East Anglia. The target area of the Heligoland Bight was known as "the Hornet's Nest" because it was alive with flak and fighters.

On one such operation only ten of 22 Wellingtons which had reached Heligoland returned and of these three were so grievously damaged that they crash-landed before reaching base. Nevertheless formations led by Kellett accounted for numbers of swarming enemy fighters, on one raid claiming a bag of 12 Me 109 and 110 fighters. He was awarded the DFC in 1940.

In the autumn of 1942 Kellett was a group captain "driving a desk" in North Africa when he decided to take part in a raid on Tobruk. But he was shot down and taken prisoner.

His powers of leadership became greatly appreciated behind the wire of Stalag Luft III, the PoW camp at Sagan and he was a Senior British Officer there at the time of the celebrated Wooden Horse escape based on the Trojan epic.

But he counted the highlight of his time as a "Kriegie" when a golf club arrived in a parcel. A ball was improvised, an 18 "hole" course laid out, though holes were of necessity tree trunks or washing lines.

The son of an Anglo-Irish Surgeon Rear-Admiral, Richard Kellett was born at Plymouth on Oct 24 1905 and educated at Bedford School. He opted for a career in the RAF rather than the Navy after being told that Cranwell cadets were given a motor-bicycle to assist their training.

In the late 1920s while serving in Iraq he force-landed in the desert and was saved by a fellow pilot from capture by hostile tribesmen who were advancing on the rescuing aircraft as it took off.

In 1936 Kellett had the unusual experience of being seconded to the Imperial Japanese Army to advise on engineering for the Japanese Air Force, his services being recognised by the Emperor with the Order of the Sacred Treasure of Japan.

He returned home in 1937 to command No 148, a Wellesley squadron. Next year, as an unassuming regular officer, he was surprised to find himself featuring in world headlines when, as leader of the RAF's Long Range Development Unit, he piloted one of two Wellesley bombers to complete the then sensational non-stop flight from Ismailia in Egypt to Australia.

To meet every eventuality on the flight Kellett had thoughtfully packed a dinner jacket. Among those taking part in an ecstatic reception at Darwin was Dorothy Abbott, daughter of the Administrator of the Northern Territories whom he married two years later when she was 19.

His feat was recognised with awards of the AFC in 1939 and the Royal Aero Club's Britannia Trophy. He was appointed CBE in 1943.

After the war he returned to the Middle East in charge of training, but his health had suffered and in 1946 he retired on medical grounds.

He then settled in Rhodesia and later moved to South Africa, where he worked as a factory manager until returning to Britain in 1965. He bought a boat with the intention of pottering around the Mediterranean with his second wife, the former Kitty Buchanan (née Broome), but on arriving in Majorca they decided to stay put.

GROUP CAPTAIN
LORD CHESHIRE, VC
31 JULY 1992

Lord Cheshire, VC, who has died aged 74, was the bomber ace who witnessed the second atom bomb attack on Japan in 1945 and devoted the rest of his life to Christian care of the sick and the needy.

His Victoria Cross was not awarded, as is more usual, for a specific act of supreme valour. Of 51 airmen VCs, he was one of just five – four in the 1914–18 War – thus honoured for an extended period of operational flying and outstanding qualities. He completed 103 bombing sorties.

That an airman so honoured in war should in middle age have been awarded the Order of Merit and created a life peer for humanitarian services must be an unmatched achievement.

When, in 1943, at the early age of 25, Cheshire was promoted group captain – the equivalent of an RN captain or Army colonel – he was the youngest RAF officer to achieve such high rank.

When he was subsequently appointed to drive a desk in command of a Bomber Command station, he had already beaten the actuarial odds of survival by a wide margin. But administration and the constrictions of a brass hat palled and he gladly accepted a reduction to wing commander when offered command of the already legendary Dambusters squadron, No 617.

Bomber Harris's "old lags" of No 617 had gone through a bad patch since Wing Commander Guy Gibson, VC, had handed over to Squadron Leader George Holden. Holden had been killed and until Cheshire arrived in September 1943, Squadron Leader Micky Martin (later Air Marshal Sir Harold Martin) was temporarily in command.

Tall, thin, dark, sensitive and introspective, cool and calculating in the air, Cheshire had little in common with the more outgoing, dashing Gibson. In his first days with the squadron he even failed to notice the little WAAF sitting at the wheel of a shooting brake outside his office until she knocked on his door and explained that she was his driver. Not thinking he rated a car, he had been walking everywhere.

But Cheshire possessed the quiet, thoughtful determination required to restore the morale and talent of a squadron which had suffered from an anti-climax after its glorious moment.

This duty discharged, his health declined. The long and

sustained operational career and the trauma of observing, describing and reflecting on the atomic blast had taken their toll. RAF doctors diagnosed psycho-neurosis and he left the service at his own request in the New Year of 1946.

Three years later Cheshire stumbled into his long and eventually debilitating vocation of caring for the ailing and afflicted, irrespective of race or creed.

It all began with an impulsive offer to take a terminally ill man into his own home. "I didn't know about nursing, but whatever I could provide was better than nothing."

All too soon he was to learn, rather more painfully, about nursing as a patient in Midhurst Sanatorium, where he was admitted in 1952 with tuberculosis. Two years later he re-emerged, physically and mentally prepared to take on the world.

Geoffrey Leonard Cheshire was born at Chester on September 7 1917. His father was Geoffrey Cheshire, Professor of Law and Bursar at Exeter College, Oxford.

Young Geoffrey was educated at the Dragon School, Oxford, and Stowe, and took a law degree at Merton College, Oxford.

Oxford provided no portent of the serious, caring and deeply religious Cheshire of international renown. As an undergraduate he drove fast motor-cars, drank to excess and enjoyed a succession of blondes. "I had little aim in life," he admitted later, "other than my own pleasure and profit – both of which I pursued with relentless determination."

He switched from driving to flying, through membership of the University Air Squadron. In 1937 he went solo in an Avro Tutor and was commissioned as a pilot officer in the RAFVR that October.

He put his wings up in December 1939, and on June 6 1940 joined No 102, a Whitley bomber squadron at

Driffield, Yorkshire. As second pilot to a New Zealand skipper, he learned diligently. Blindfolded, he groped round his Whitley, making sure he could find anything he needed in the dark.

As Cheshire raided a range of targets, including Berlin, Kiel, Essen, Duisberg, Bremen and Cologne, his painstaking preparation paid off. On the night of November 12–13 1940, he was over Wesseling seeking a target. Cloud frustrated him for almost an hour and he switched to an alternative, the railway yards at nearby Cologne.

He made his run, opened the bomb doors, and at that moment shrapnel detonated the flare he was about to drop. Ten feet of the fuselage ripped away and filled the rear of the plane with flames and smoke as he fought to regain control.

As the rest of the crew fought to put out the fire, Cheshire coaxed the wrecked Whitley home against an 8 mph headwind. He was awarded an immediate DSO.

It was rare for such a junior officer – he was still only a flying officer – to receive a DSO ahead of the more liberally awarded DFC, which he gained in March 1941. This was followed almost immediately by a Bar to the DSO "for outstanding leadership and skill on operations" and promotion to flight lieutenant.

Meanwhile that New Year he had completed his first tour of operations, volunteered for a second tour, and been posted to No 35 Squadron at Linton-on-Ouse, the first unit to be equipped with Halifax four-engined bombers.

In the early spring of 1941 he was detached for North Atlantic ferry work, a posting which effectively rested him in New York, where the bright lights and welter of hospitality re-activated the old hedonism.

Cheshire tumbled into the glamorous company of the film star Constance Binney, 16 years his senior. In the roaring Twenties she had taken up the mantle of Mary Pickford. Now, following a mad, whirlwind romance, she married her bomber hero. It was a disaster and did not last. The marriage does not appear in Cheshire's *Who's Who* entry.

A return to operations in October 1941 proved therapeutic. He completed his second tour and was rested from January 1942, as flying instructor at No 1652 Heavy Conversion Unit at Marston Moor. Even so, he escaped occasionally from the tedium of circuits and bumps to fly operationally and took part in Bomber Harris's first 1,000-bomber raid on Cologne.

He then began his third tour in command of No 76, a Halifax squadron at Linton-on-Ouse. It was the squadron in which his pilot brother, Christopher, had been shot down over Berlin in 1941, and taken prisoner.

Meanwhile Cheshire had received a second Bar to his DSO, and command as a group captain of the station at Marston Moor. He returned to operations with the prestigious command of No 617. Though delighted to lead the Dambusters he was dismayed that the squadron, celebrated for its low-level flying skills, was now expected to conform to the general policy of high-level bombing.

After four months of relentless high-level training, on the night of February 8-9 1944, Cheshire and his Lancaster crews were ordered to destroy the Gnome-Rhone Factory at Limoges in France. On no account were workers' dwellings to be harmed.

Cheshire, skilled at low-level attack, knew that for all the prevailing high-level policy he could best mark the target from 200 ft. He went in above the rooftops. The factory crumbled. The workers were spared.

This success encouraged him to pursue the cause of low-level marking in the speedy Mosquito, and he wangled one for his personal use. His tactics, marking for

617, led to the destruction of so many war factories that Harris and his bomber barons finally nodded approval.

The squadron received three more Mossies, and on the night of April 24–25 marked targets in Munich for an attack by 260 bombers. The range was extreme for the Mosquito, and running the fuel tanks dry was a risk. Cheshire, accompanied by Dave Shannon of dams fame and two others, survived heavy flak between Augsburg and Munich, where they dived their Mossies to 700 ft and marked targets spot on.

It is a popular misconception that Nagasaki, his final wartime experience, turned him to Catholicism and good works. As a professional bomber pilot, he was more distressed at the time by the inaccuracy of the US air crew, who missed the target by two miles, than by the atomic blast. Nor did Nagasaki persuade him to join CND – he came to support the nuclear deterrent in time.

After the war he returned to a large empty house near Liss, in Hampshire, where he took in an old soldier, Arthur Dykes, who was dying of cancer. After him there was a 93-year-old woman, whom he gently washed every day.

While the old soldier, a lapsed Catholic, lay dying, Cheshire watched him regain his faith. "It was so simple and serene and sure," he said later, "it made a deep impression on me."

He was searching "frantically for direction". He had failed to find it in the Church of England and on Christmas Eve 1948 was received into the Roman Catholic Church.

In 1959 he married a fellow Catholic, Sue Ryder (later Baroness Ryder of Warsaw), founder of the renowned charity shops and homes. In the meantime his Catholicism and an earlier pilgrimage to Lourdes had led him to another interest, the Turin Shroud, of whose British branch he became president.

In the meantime the Leonard Cheshire Foundation Homes – established at the prompting of his friend Sir Alfred (later Lord) Denning – were steadily multiplying. Eventually there were more than 270 in 51 countries.

In 1989 Cheshire launched the World War Memorial Fund for Disaster Relief. He was also co-founder of the Ryder-Cheshire Mission for the Relief of Suffering. His publications included *Bomber Pilot* (1943), *The Face of Victory* (1961) and *The Light of Many Suns* (1985).

Cheshire was awarded the Order of Merit in 1981, and created Baron Cheshire in 1991. He had a son and a daughter by his second wife.

SQUADRON LEADER
DAVID SHANNON
8 APRIL 1993

David Shannon, one of the Second World War's most decorated bomber pilots who has died aged 70, was a veteran of the legendary "Dambusters" Raid on the industrial Ruhr led by Wing Commander Guy Gibson.

The Australian-born Shannon, who won two DSOs and two DFCs, had the distinction of completing three tours of bomber operations against heavily defended targets in Germany and Occupied Europe.

It was on the evening of May 16 1943 that the crews of 617 Squadron sat down to an egg supper at RAF Scampton, Lincs, before taking off on the dambusting mission.

Shannon, a 20-year-old with a mop of fair hair and a luxuriant moustache, engaged in the customary badinage about who would get whose bacon and egg the next morning if they failed to return.

At 9.47 pm Shannon's girlfriend, Anne Fowler, a Station WAAF waved him off. Jack Buckley, his air gunner, a Yorkshireman much older than most of the crew, reduced the tension as they climbed aboard the Lancaster bomber by asking: "Have you cleaned your teeth, David?"

Shannon flew in Guy Gibson's leading wave. Their target was the Möhne dam, and possibly the Eder too.

At the moment Gibson called Shannon to make his attack on the Möhne, "Mick" (later Air Marshal Sir Harold) Martin, another Australian, yelled: "Hell! It's gone! It's gone! Look at it, for Christ's sake!" And it had. So Gibson told Shannon: "Skip it".

At the Eder dam, fog shrouded the area. Shannon dived into the darkness between two 1,000-ft high surrounding ridges – perilously, and yet not steeply enough. Four further dives were as unsuccessful.

Finally, plunging into the blackness of the valley, he released the spherical bouncing bomb which Dr (later Sir) Barnes Wallis had devised. Water heaved up over the parapet of the dam.

Only Les Knight, another young Australian, had a bomb left. Shannon advised: "Come in down moon and dive".

The bomb was spot on. Gibson saw the dam well open and unleash some 200 million tons of water. It was daylight on May 17 when Shannon and the other survivors of the raid (56 were missing from the 133 who had set off) returned to the bacon-and-eggs breakfast which developed into a party.

That night Shannon proposed to Anne Fowler who agreed to marry him, providing he removed the moustache. The whiskers went.

Ten days later, on Shannon's 21st birthday, King George VI visited the squadron. "You seem a very well preserved 21", the King told him. "You must have a party tonight."

When chided in the small hours by a senior officer for

being drunk, Shannon replied: "Sir, if so, it's by Royal Command".

The son of Howard Shannon, MP, chairman of the South Australia Farmers' Union, David John Shannon was born at Unley near Adelaide on May 27 1922 and educated at the local high school. He began his career in insurance before joining the Royal Australian Air Force in 1940 and training to be a pilot.

Soon after his arrival in Britain, Shannon's bomber career nearly ended before it began when one of a Whitley bomber's two engines cut out immediately after his first solo take-off.

His first operational posting was to 106 Squadron, commanded by Guy Gibson. Flying Manchesters and Lancasters, he took part in "Bomber" Harris's 1,000-bomber raids. Shannon was awarded his first DFC after 36 operational sorties.

When Wing Commander Gibson was asked to form 617 Squadron for a special role, he picked four of his 106 Squadron crews, including Shannon's.

Although the Dambusters Raid was the crowning event in Shannon's war, it was but one of a succession of bomber operations. His low-level expertise led to a successful period as a Mosquito target-marker.

Shannon also distinguished himself in the costly raid on the Dortmund-Ems canal in September 1943. Other special targets were attacked under the command of Leonard Cheshire.

At one breakfast, Cheshire remarked on the "beautiful sunset" the night before. "I'm not interested in beautiful sunsets", said Shannon, "only in beautiful sunrises".

Towards the end of the war Shannon was given the rank of Wing Commander and a quieter appointment. He did not relish this and asked to revert to Squadron Leader.

After the war, at Cheshire's suggestion, Shannon briefly

ran a flower shop in Mayfair. Then he joined Royal Dutch Shell, for which company he travelled extensively. He became a director of subsidiaries in Colombia and Kenya.

Subsequently, in the 1960s, he was a chicken-farmer in Suffolk and bred Welsh mountain ponies before returning to the oil world.

Latterly he was engaged on preparations for the commemoration of the 50th anniversary of the Dambusters Raid.

After his first wife's death, Shannon married secondly, Mrs Eyke Taylor. He had a daughter by his first marriage.

SERGEANT
NORMAN JACKSON
26 MARCH 1994

Norman Jackson, who has died aged 74, was one of 10 Lancaster aircrew awarded the Victoria Cross during the Second World War and the first RAF flight engineer to be so honoured: he won his decoration for an exploit described in the citation as "almost incredible".

By April 1944 Jackson had flown 30 missions and was a "tour expired" flight engineer with the rank of sergeant in 106 Squadron. Although not obliged to fly, he volunteered to accompany his crew, who still had operational sorties to complete.

On the night of April 26, shortly after receiving news of the birth of his youngest son, Jackson took off for a raid on Schweinfurt.

The Lancaster dropped its bombs over the target but was then lacerated by canon-fire from a Focke-Wulf 190; a fire erupted on the upper surface of the starboard wing, adjacent to a fuel tank.

Jackson, despite being wounded by shell splinters in the right leg and shoulders, immediately tackled the potentially catastrophic blaze. Pushing a small fire extinguisher inside his jacket, he clipped on his parachute pack and jettisoned the escape hatch above the pilot's head. With the Lancaster still flying at 22,000 ft and 200 mph, he climbed on to the top of the fuselage and began to inch towards the blazing wing.

Almost immediately his parachute opened and the canopy and rigging spilled back into the cockpit. The pilot, bomb aimer and navigator gathered the parachute together and held on to the rigging lines, paying them out as Jackson crawled aft. But he slipped and fell from the fuselage on to the starboard wing.

He held on by grasping an air intake on the leading edge. The extinguisher fell from his jacket and was lost; the flames burned Jackson severely. Then the Germans strafed the Lancaster once more. Jackson was hit, lost his grip and was sucked through the fire and off the trailing edge of the wing, dragging his parachute behind him.

For a while Jackson hung in the slipstream; then his surviving comrades released the parachute and he fell towards earth, his canopy in flames. The remaining crew baled out; four landed safely, but the captain and rear gunner perished with the aircraft.

Jackson's parachute canopy was two-thirds burned and he was fortunate to sustain only a broken leg on landing; but his right eye was closed through burns, and his hands were horribly burned and useless.

At daybreak he crawled towards a village on his knees and elbows. He knocked on the door of a cottage, whose occupant spat at him and shouted: "Churchill gangster!" The man was then pushed aside by his two beautiful daughters, who bathed Jackson's wounds. "I was lying there like a lord," recalled Jackson. "I began to think I was pretty lucky."

After 10 months in hospital he was sent to a prison camp. He made two attempts to escape; the second time he succeeded in penetrating the German lines, and met the Americans near Munich.

The citation for his VC pointed out that, even had he been able to extinguish the fire, there was little prospect of his regaining the cockpit: he had undertaken an act of unquestionable heroism.

"It was my job as flight engineer to get the rest of the crew out of trouble," recalled Jackson. "I was the most experienced member of the crew, and they all looked to me to do something."

He was decorated by George VI at Buckingham Palace. Jackson's mother was delighted: "The only other outstanding thing he ever did," she told reporters, "was to ride in a procession through Twickenham on the smallest bicycle ever made."

Norman Cyril Jackson was born in Ealing on April 8 1919. When a few weeks old he was adopted by a family named Gunter; the same family adopted another boy, Geoffrey Oliver Hartley, who was later awarded the George Cross while serving with the police in Malaya but was eventually killed by bandits.

Jackson qualified as a fitter and turner and on the outbreak of war was in a reserved occupation. None the less he volunteered for the RAF and enlisted as a Classified Fitter IIE (engines).

He was posted to No 95, a Sunderland Flying Boat Squadron at Freetown, Sierra Leone. This was a ground crew job, but Jackson applied to train as a flight engineer in bombers. "I don't know why," he recalled "because I wanted to live!"

In July 1943 he joined 106 Squadron, then at Syerston, as a sergeant. In November the squadron moved to Metheringham.

After the war Jackson worked as a travelling salesmen for Haig whisky. He overcame the handicap of permanently scarred hands, and with the help of a friend built a house for himself and his family – his own adoption made him a passionate family man.

He was periodically haunted by nightmares of his brush with death, and confessed to bouts of melancholy. But he reflected that he was more fortunate than many of his compatriots, who had either perished or had struggled to adjust to civilian life. He rarely spoke of his VC.

The war left him deeply religious: "Nobody prayed harder than I did before we took off and after we landed," he recalled. "So did all the rest of them, though nobody mentioned it."

Jackson was married and had six children.

WING COMMANDER
RODERICK "BABE" LEAROYD
24 JANUARY 1996

Wing Commander Roderick "Babe" Learoyd, who has died aged 82, was awarded the Victoria Cross after bombing an aqueduct carrying the Dortmund-Ems canal over the River Ems, north of Munster, on the night of Aug 12 1940.

This was an exceedingly dangerous mission. The canal was an architectural showpiece and a main artery for water-borne industrial traffic. Each bank was lined with anti-aircraft batteries and Learoyd was flying a lumbering Handley Page Hampden.

Four other Hampdens had attacked earlier that night. Two of them had been shot down, and the German gunners and searchlight operators had adjusted their aim to perfection.

Coming in off a shallow dive, Learoyd levelled out at 50 ft. By the light of a half-moon he saw he was over a fork in the canal where it branched into two aqueducts. He asked Sergeant John Lewis, his bomb aimer, to guide him in. But the aircraft was soon caught in the searchlights and Learoyd whose bulk had earned him the sobriquet "Babe" had to duck below the windscreen and fly on his instruments, while his two air gunners opened up on the searchlights on either side.

Machine gun bullets hammered into the Hampden's belly and in quick succession two ack-ack shells tore through the bomber's starboard wing. Learoyd held course to Lewis's directions, until the bomb aimer had released the load. One bomb, fused for 10 minutes delay, landed near the bank of the aqueduct.

When Lewis at last shouted: "OK. Finish!" Learoyd heaved the aircraft into a steep turn, away from the guns. The Hampden was by then covered in oil leaking from the hydraulics and the wing landing flaps were drooping. Fortunately, the wing fuel tanks were intact; the crew found something else to cheer about when they discovered that one of their carrier pigeons had laid an egg.

With remarkable composure, Learoyd coaxed the Hampden back to base, arriving at Scampton shortly after 2 am. He circled the airfield waiting for daylight, and eventually made a belly-landing at about 5 am. When he inspected the damage, he saw that his lucky Pinocchio emblem painted on the left side of the cockpit had survived.

Whether Learoyd or another Hampden caused the damage is uncertain, but the canal was rendered unusable for 10 days, with consequences for the German preparations for the invasion of Britain.

Learoyd's citation ran: "The high courage, skill and determination which this officer had invariably displayed on many occasions in the face of the enemy, set an example which is unsurpassed." His VC was the first of 19 to be awarded to Bomber Command air crew during the war.

Roderick Alastair Brook Learoyd, was born at Folkestone on Feb 5, 1913. He was educated at Hydneye House, a preparatory school near Hastings in Sussex, and Wellington before the Chelsea College of Aeronautical Engineering.

For a while he drifted, trying his hands at fruit farming in Argentina and motor engineering. In 1936 he was granted a short service commission in the RAF, and the same year joined 49 Squadron, flying Hawker Hind light bomber bi-planes. When the Hampden was introduced in 1938, No 49 was the first squadron to receive the twin-engined, all-metal, monoplane bomber.

Learoyd was operational from the first day of the war, when he carried out a reconnaissance over the North Sea.

After winning the VC, Learoyd had a stint as personal assistant to Air Chief Marshal Sir Robert Brooke-Popham. In February 1941 he received command of No 83, and that June was appointed Wing Commander (Flying) at No 14 Operational Training Unit, Cottesmore.

Shortly before Christmas, he took command of No 44 at Waddington – the first operational squadron equipped with the four-engined Avro Lancaster.

During this command, one of Learoyd's flight commanders, Squadron Leader John Nettleton, led the low-level daylight attack on the MAN diesel works at Augsburg in April 1942, for which he was awarded the VC.

In May 1942, Learoyd moved to No 25 Operational Training Unit, Finningley. From 1943 he held a series of staff appointments, including a spell in RAF Public Relations. Though he was a modest man, he was prevailed upon to make a number of morale-boosting appearances at civil and military gatherings, aircraft and munition factories and RAF stations.

Learoyd had postings to Operational Training Units 107 and 109 and in May 1945 was sent to No 48 Squadron, flying Douglas Dakotas.

After four weeks, he joined No 1314, a Flight of Dakotas based at Accra in West Africa. The next year he returned to Britain. In the autumn of 1946 he was demobilised and placed on the reserve with the rank of wing commander.

Learoyd's good humour and easy manner made him an excellent conveyor of VIPs and he was employed for three years by the civil aviation authorities in Malaya, as a personal pilot to colonial governors.

In 1950, he left the tropics to enter the tractor and road construction business. Three years later he was appointed export sales manager at the Austin Motor Company, where he remained for the rest of his working life.

GROUP CAPTAIN
HAMISH MAHADDIE
16 JANUARY 1997

Group Captain Hamish Mahaddie, the much decorated bomber ace who has died aged 85, was given the task of poaching crack crews from Bomber Command to serve in the RAF's Pathfinder Force.

Mahaddie had an irrepressible spirit which earned him the DSO, DFC, AFC and Czech Military Cross within 32 days, early in 1943. He later added a Bar to the AFC.

On his 45th sortie, in 1943, captaining "C Charlie", a four-engined Halifax of 7 Squadron, he was making a bombing run over Cologne when a Ju 88 night fighter pumped 174 cannon shells into his bomber. The Halifax went into a dive until Mahaddie managed to achieve "control of sorts", as he put it.

"In retrospect," he recalled years afterwards, "Bob Pointer, the mid-upper gunner seems to have assumed the role of what the Navy calls a Battle Control (Damage) Officer. Not only was Bob moving about the aircraft in verbal touch with all the crew, providing medical aid to the badly wounded wireless operator, but he was also assuring the rear gunner that things were under control forward.

"The flight engineer had effected an excellent jury-rig connecting the aileron cables across the entire wing area. The rear gunner flashed his emergency light to warn me we were about to have a visit from a fighter. My ham-fisted response sadly severed the flight engineer's makeshift repair before I sought cloud cover. Happily this was soon repaired.

"Tommy, the navigator, who had lost all navigational aids, had only an astro compass for help. Nevertheless we made a good landfall some five miles south of track on the French coast."

Back at base Mahaddie discovered that his seat-type parachute had stopped a cannon shell. The wireless operator's middle two fingers had been severed by a shell and Bob Pointer had collected a shell splinter in the right buttock.

Fifty years later, writing in *So Many* (the RAF Benevolent Fund's tribute to bomber aircrew), Mahaddie reflected on this example of aircrew teamwork: "Without a command from the captain, each crew member somehow found a task that was essential to the well-being of the whole aircraft and brought C Charlie back to base."

Such teamwork influenced Mahaddie's selection of

Pathfinders when in the New Year of 1943 he was designated Group Training Inspector by Air Vice-Marshal Don Bennett, the leader of the Pathfinder Force.

Mahaddie applied himself to the job with such ruthless efficiency that he became known to Bomber Harris and his staff as "Bennett's horsethief". Mahaddie poached those aircrew that his experience told him would have the daring and accuracy to pinpoint and illuminate heavily defended targets.

Mahaddie, who in little more than two years of war had been promoted from sergeant to group captain, did once meet his match as a talent scout. Studying form at the Black Boy, a Nottingham pub frequented by aircrew, he came across Wing Commander Guy Gibson on a similar mission for 617, the squadron he was to lead on the Dambusters raid.

Security was such that not even Mahaddie knew of the future VC's virtual carte blanche over the choice of crews, though he sensed something was up when Gibson poached Dave Shannon, the low-level attack specialist from under his nose at RAF Warboys, the Pathfinders' training base.

Thomas Gilbert Mahaddie was born at Leith on March 19 1911. His father had been a drummer boy in the Gordon Highlanders. The "Hamish", by which he was known, is thought to have originated in Iraq where he rode a horse of that name.

After leaving school at 13 Mahaddie worked for an Edinburgh grocer. But, after reading a Boy Scout magazine article extolling Trenchard's RAF Halton apprenticeships, he applied for one. Mahaddie was one of 305 boys who in 1928 formed the 17th entry at Halton. There, he said, he "got four meals a day, which I never did at home".

Following postings as a rigger to the RAF College,

Cranwell, and to Iraq, he was accepted there for pilot training. When Sergeant Mahaddie returned home, he joined 77 Squadron, flying Whitleys.

When war broke out, Mahaddie flew some leaflet dropping missions. Feeling that the official message was too mealy-mouthed he would add his own robust sentiments. Of this period he commented: "We may have been the best flying club in the world but we were untrained, amateurish and grossly incompetent".

In 1944 Mahaddie was seconded to the US Army 8th Air Force to brief it on Pathfinder techniques. His final wartime sortie was to fly with 60 Lancasters to repatriate RAF PoWs from Lubeck.

After the war he commanded a transport wing in Germany, and the flying wing at Binbrook, Lincolnshire, where he also captained the crew responsible for trials of the Canberra, the RAF's first jet bomber. He left the Service in 1959 and worked as an electronics consultant to the Armed Forces.

Known for his Scots banter and trademark bowler hat, he became revered as an adviser for film companies. With his persuasive ebullience, he worked wonders in obtaining vintage aircraft. His name appears on the credits of 14 films including *633 Squadron* and *The Battle of Britain*, for which he assembled 131 aircraft. In 1989 he published *Hamish, the Memoirs of Group Captain T G Mahaddie*.

Mahaddie was twice married and twice widowed. He leaves two sons by his first marriage.

FLIGHT LIEUTENANT WILLIAM REID

28 NOVEMBER 2001

Flight Lieutenant William Reid, who has died aged 79, won a Victoria Cross in 1943 for his heroism on a bombing expedition to Germany.

On the night of November 3 1943, Reid was serving with 61 Squadron as captain of a Lancaster bomber on the way to Düsseldorf when it was attacked by a Messerschmitt 110 nightfighter as it crossed the Dutch coast. His windscreen was shattered, the plane's gun turrets, steering mechanism and cockpit were badly damaged, and Reid himself sustained serious injuries to his head, shoulders and hands. The plane dived 200 ft before he managed to regain control.

Saying nothing about his injuries, Reid called his crew on the intercom for a damage report and proposed that they forge ahead regardless. As the Lancaster continued on its mission, it was soon attacked again, this time by a Focke-Wulf 190, which raked the plane with gunfire, killing Reid's navigator, fatally wounding the wireless operator and knocking out the oxygen system. Reid sustained further injuries to his right arm, but still refused to turn from his target.

Sustained by bottled oxygen from a portable supply administered by his flight engineer, Sergeant J W Norris, Reid pressed on for another 50 minutes. He memorised the course to his target and continued in such a normal manner that the bomb aimer, cut off from the cockpit by the failure of the plane's communications system, had no idea his captain was injured. After reaching Düsseldorf, he released his bombs right over the centre of the target – a ball bearing factory – then set course for home.

Semi-conscious at times, freezing cold because of his

broken windscreen, and half blinded by blood from a head wound which kept streaming into his eyes, Reid, assisted by flight engineer Norris, somehow kept the plane in the air despite heavy anti-aircraft fire over the Dutch coast and the physical effort required to hold the control column steady.

As they crossed the North Sea, all four engines cut out and the plane went into a spin. Luckily Norris remembered in the nick of time that he had forgotten to change over the petrol cocks to a full tank, and swiftly rectified the fault.

Eventually they managed to find their way home, taking their bearings from the Pole Star and the moon. As he came into land at their base, Reid had to use an emergency pressure bottle to hand-pump the undercarriage down, and this exertion and the aircraft's descent into warmer air reopened his wounds. As the Lancaster touched down, the undercarriage collapsed along the runway for 60 yards before coming to a halt.

His citation read: "Wounded in two attacks, without oxygen, suffering severely from cold, his navigator dead, his wireless operator fatally wounded, his aircraft crippled and helpless, Flight Lieutenant Reid showed superb courage and leadership in penetrating a further 200 miles into enemy territory to attack one of the most strongly defended targets in Germany, every additional mile increasing the hazards of the long and perilous journey home. This tenacity and devotion to duty were beyond praise."

William Reid was born at Baillieston, Glasgow, on December 12, 1921, the son of a blacksmith. He was educated at Coatbridge Secondary School and studied metallurgy for a time, but then applied to join the RAF.

After training in Canada, he received his wings and a commission in June 1942, then trained on twin-engined

Airspeed Oxfords at Little Rissington before moving to an OTU at North Luffenham. There, his skill as a pilot led to his being selected as an instructor, flying Wellington bombers, albeit with the promise of a posting to a Lancaster unit.

The posting did not materialise until July 1943, when he was sent to 1654 Conversion Unit, Wigsley, near Newark, where he flew his first operational mission as second pilot, in a Lancaster of 9 Squadron, in a raid on Mönchengladbach.

In September he was posted to 61 Squadron at Syerston, Newark, to commence Lancaster bombing operations, and flew seven sorties to various German cities before the raid on Düsseldorf.

After a period in hospital, Reid went to C Flight 617 ("Dambuster") Squadron at Woodhall Spa in January 1944 and flew sorties to various targets in France.

In July 1944, 617 Squadron was linked with 9 Squadron for a "Tall-boy" deep penetration bomb attack on a V-bomb storage dump at Rilly-la-Montagne, near Rheims. As Reid released his bomb over the target at 12,000 ft, he felt his aircraft shudder under the impact of a bomb dropped by another Lancaster 6,000 ft above. The bomb ploughed through his plane's fuselage, severing all control cables and fatally weakening its structure, and Reid gave the orders to bale out.

As members of his crew scrambled out, the plane went into a dive, pinning Reid to his seat. Reaching overhead, he managed to release the escape hatch panel and struggled out just as the Lancaster broke in two. He landed heavily by parachute, breaking his arm in the fall.

Within an hour he was captured by a German patrol and taken prisoner. After various transfers, he ended the war in Luckenwalde PoW camp, west of Berlin.

Reid left the RAF in 1946 and resumed his studies, first

at Glasgow University and later at the West of Scotland Agricultural College. After graduating, he went on a travelling scholarship for six months, studying agriculture in India, Australia, New Zealand, America and Canada.

In 1950, he became an agricultural adviser to the MacRobert Trust, Douneside. From 1959 to his retirement in 1981, he was an adviser to a firm of animal feed manufacturers.

Reid took a deep interest in ex-servicemen's associations; he was a member of the GC and VC Association and honorary vice-president of the Aircrew Association. He was president of the Aircrew Association's Tay branch and its Scottish Saltire branch, and president of the Royal British Legion Scotland (Crieff) branch.

He always made light of his wartime achievements: "I don't think I was a hero." he said; "I don't think of myself as a brave man. We were young. All we wanted was to get our tour over and done with."

When he married Violet Gallagher in 1952, he did not tell her of his VC. She was, he confessed, "a wee bit impressed" when she found out. She and their son and daughter survive him.

AIR MARSHAL
SIR PETER HORSLEY
20 DECEMBER 2001

Air Marshal Sir Peter Horsley, who has died aged 80, began as a deck boy on a cargo boat to Malaya before a successful career in the RAF and on the staff of the Queen and Prince Philip.

Despite the apparent respectability of his air force career – which he ended as Deputy C-in-C, Strike Command –

and his service at court – first as equerry to Princess Elizabeth and the Duke of Edinburgh, then, after George VI's death, as equerry to the new Queen and finally, to Prince Philip – Horsley's rise was far from conventional.

Beresford Peter Torrington Horsley was born on March 26 1921, the youngest of seven children. His father, the head of a prosperous West Hartlepool family business, had lost much of his fortune in the 1922 crash and shot himself. Peter's mother also died when he was a child. It was, he later recalled, "a miserable start".

He was educated at the Dragon School, Oxford, and Wellington College. Horsley felt himself at odds with the system there, and shortly after his 18th birthday, abandoned his position as a prefect (the actor Christopher Lee was one of his fags), "sold" his room at auction and obtained an interview with Alfred Holt, a Blue Funnel director.

Holt, whose children had been at prep school with Horsley, was sympathetic, and employed him as deck boy in TSS (Twin Screw Ship) *Cyclops*, bound for the Far East. When it docked at the Malayan island of Penang, Horsley heard that war had been declared and immediately obtained a transfer to *Menelaus*, another Blue Funnel vessel, which was homeward bound.

Menelaus was provided with a Japanese gun dating from 1917 and Horsley sailed home as gun trainer and deck boy. Under war regulations he was now a member of the Merchant Navy and officially unable to join the RAF, an ambition he had long cherished. He deserted.

After biding his time in the Home Guard, Horsley's gamble paid off when he was called to the Aircrew Reception Centre at Uxbridge, Middlesex. On his arrival there, however, Horsley was dismayed to be informed that only the air gunner category was available.

He accepted it and then lobbied his family's solicitor, by

then an Air Ministry staff officer, to pull strings, so that he could be re-mustered as pilot under training. Horsley did so well that after receiving his wings he was commissioned and posted immediately to the flying school at RAF Cranwell as an instructor.

Horsley, to his chagrin, was posted to a flying training school at Penfold, Alberta. Finally, in 1943, he was sent to a de Havilland Mosquito conversion unit at Greenwood, New Brunswick.

There Horsley fell in love with Phyllis Phinney, a Canadian psychology student at Arcadia University, and also teamed up with Frank "Bambi" Gunn, who became his operational navigator. Towards the end of that year, Horsley, accompanied by Bambi, crossed the Atlantic on the *Queen Mary*.

Horsley joined No 21, a Mosquito night intruder squadron, based at Hunsdon, Hertfordshire, as part of Group Captain Pickard's No 140 Wing. Most of Horsley's operations were flown at night against airfields and night fighters. "This type of intrusion involved groping our way across Europe at low level using whatever navigational clues were available," he recalled.

"Once the bombs were gone, Mosquitoes were coned in searchlights and sprayed with exploding shells and tracer. The aircraft, bucking with freedom from its load, would be thrown into an escape route, throttles fully open, jinking and weaving as close to the ground as one dared."

Horsley noted that attacks on V-1 flying bomb sites required flying just above the crest of the waves to the French coast and as low as 50 ft above the target. Tight discipline was essential to avoid being blown up by the bombs of the aircraft in front.

All the while Horsley flew with Bambi Gunn. On D-Day, June 6 1944, and for some time afterwards the pair flew two or three cross-Channel sorties each night. They relied on benzedrine to stay awake, and resorted to naval rum to get some sleep.

Horsley was eventually shot down by anti-aircraft fire and his plane began to fall, burning, into the sea off Cherbourg. Horsley yelled to his navigator: "Bale out Bambi, bale out!" before pushing himself out and, after scrabbling for the D-ring of his parachute, finally floating towards the sea.

"The shock of the cold water and the first choking mouthful of sea water woke me to the stark reality of the situation," said Horsley. He managed to inflate his "Mae West" and it brought him to the surface, where, after a frightening struggle to free himself from the parachute, he was able to inflate his minuscule rubber dinghy. It floated upside down and, after a Herculean effort, Horsley climbed across its base. At daybreak Horsley managed to right the dinghy and sit in a pool of sea water and blood from a flak wound he had sustained. After three days, during which a storm capsized the dinghy, he was picked up by an Air Sea Rescue high speed launch.

As Horsley began to recover he was convinced he had hovered between this world and the next. He also believed that he had received messages from two officers he knew to be dead and from Bambi who, as he learned later, had died. These experiences engendered a future interest in the supernatural. As he recuperated at a naval sick quarters, Horsley was tormented by the memory of waves breaking over him. One night Bambi appeared in his dreams, his face lit by flames, and said: "I forgot my parachute, Peter."

Horsley was soon moved to the RAF rehabilitation centre at Loughborough, where he recalled fondly a Belgian nurse who countered an horrific shivering attack by undressing, joining him in bed and warming him with her body.

As his health improved Horsley fell in with a rowdy gang of aircrew with whom, returning from a pub crawl, he splashed naked in a fountain. He was expelled, and then attempted to return to No 140 Wing. When this was thwarted, he dodged a request to attend a medical board and obtained the consolation of a posting to 2nd Tactical Air Force's communications squadron in France.

After returning home in 1947, Horsley joined No 23 Training Group where he was posted to the Central Flying School. After accepting a permanent commission, Horsley was posted in 1948 as adjutant at the Oxford University Air Squadron. In July 1949, he was promoted to squadron leader and appointed equerry to Princess Elizabeth and Prince Philip. On February 6 1952 he became equerry to the Queen and, from 1953 until 1956, equerry to the Duke of Edinburgh.

At first, Horsley was expected to carry out normal RAF duties as commander of No 29, a Meteor IX jet night fighter squadron at Tangmere in Sussex, in tandem with Palace duties. In 1953 the problem was resolved when Horsley was invited to join Prince Philip's staff full time. In this period Horsley also pushed forward arrangements for Prince Philip to learn to fly.

He also became interested in Unidentified Flying Objects and began a prolonged investigation into the more credible reports of sightings. Horsley concluded that whereas the majority could be eliminated by natural occurrences, there were some RAF and British Overseas Airways sightings which defied explanation.

Although his service career had been interrupted by seven years at court, in the late 1950s and early 1960s Horsley became a senior instructor at the RAF Flying College, Manby, Lincs, and commanded the fighter station at RAF Wattisham, Suffolk. Posted from Suffolk to Cyprus as group captain responsible for Near East Air Force

(NEAF) operations, Horsley received command there of the Cold War bomber base at RAF Akrotiri.

Upon his return home he attended the Imperial Defence College and moved on to the Joint Warfare Establishment at Old Sarum, Wilts, before becoming assistant chief of air staff (operations) in the rank of air vice-marshal. Horsley found this first experience of – as he put it – "Whitehall's bureaucracy and political jungle" a shock.

Even so, he coped with issues which included the overthrow of the Libyan king and seizure of the RAF airfield at El Adem, a revolt in Jordan, the Soviet invasion of Hungary and Spain's closure of the Gibraltar border. From 1971, Horsley was commander of No 1 Group's nuclear deterrent bomber force. After two years he became Deputy C–in–C, Strike Command, where he remained until retirement in 1975.

Horsley, who had a lifelong interest in stamp collecting, was then appointed chairman of Robson Lowe, the stamp auction house. For a time he also realised a childhood dream by serving as managing director of Stanley Gibbons, the philately business. Other directorships included ML Holdings, a defence related company, National Printing Ink, Osprey Aviation and Horsley Holdings.

Horsley's business commitments inevitably involved travel. In 1986 he was driving to a meeting at Plymouth, Devon, when on a straight dual carrriageway his BMW swung, hit the central reservation, crossed into the opposite carriageway and collided with an approaching car whose occupant was killed.

As he began to recover from serious injuries, Horsley sought to discover how the accident occurred. His inquiries suggested to him that the SAS or some other secret agency was keen to hush up the affair, particularly concerning the Army major who had died in the other car.

Horsley later became convinced that his car had been followed by a Volvo from which it had been controlled by radio and made to crash. He thought it possible that the accident had been contrived by assassins hired to avenge the death of four sons of a Gulf sheikh, who had died at the hands of British troops in a South Yemen ambush.

Horsley came to believe that assassins might have entered the BMW after the accident and removed the radio equipment they had installed. Certainly, when the police examined the car, they found nothing amiss.

A fluent and readable writer, Horsley published an autobiography, *Sounds From Another Room* (1997), which recounted his experiences of planes, princes and the paranormal.

In retirement, Horsley enjoyed country life in Hampshire, golf, fishing, the pub and village activities.

Horsley was appointed KCB in 1974. He was awarded the Croix de Guerre in 1944 and AFC in 1945, and appointed CBE in 1964 and LVO in 1956.

Horsley married, first, Phyllis Phinney, by whom he had a son and a daughter. After the marriage was dissolved in 1976 he married Ann Mackinnon (née Crwys-Williams).

MARITIME AND PHOTO RECCE

AIR MARSHAL
SIR EDWARD CHILTON
4 AUGUST 1992

Air Marshal Sir Edward Chilton, a former leader of Coastal Command who has died aged 85, was one of the RAF's most distinguished maritime specialists.

As station commander at RAF Chivenor, north Devon, in 1943, he played a crucial role in helping to turn the tide against Admiral Dönitz's U-boats in the Battle of the Atlantic. Day and night his squadrons, committed to the Battle of the Bay, harassed the U-boats which were sailing from and to Biscay bases on the French Atlantic coast.

Then, as the Allies planned the invasion of Normandy in 1944, he was posted to a key operations appointment at Coastal Command's No 19 Group headquarters at Plymouth. There his experience of aerial anti-submarine warfare contributed significantly to the RAF's part in frustrating U-boat attempts to disrupt landings.

"Chilly" Chilton's success in 19 Group can be attributed as much to the diplomatic skill with which he handled naval colleagues in the combined naval and air force operations room, as to his maritime expertise.

His nickname gave a misleading impression of *froideur*. He was in fact a most warm-hearted officer, who understood that being accepted by the senior service was essential in an environment where the average admiral's idea of co-operation with the RAF was "Do as I say".

Chilton's consuming interest in matters maritime had been fired early in his career when, from 1927 to 1930, he flew as a test pilot with the elite flying-boat development unit at Felixstowe (the Felixstowe flyers were a law unto themselves, and became known in the RAF as the flying boat union).

Chilton, renowned for his intellectual approach to service matters, was much influenced by the pioneer flying-boat experiments of Wg Cdr John Cyril Porte. He wrote a biographical sketch of Porte, who had died shortly after the end of the First World War from pulmonary tuberculosis contracted in submarines.

In the course of his research, Chilton discovered a paper on "The Aeroplane in Use Against Submarines", which Porte had submitted in 1912 to an Admiralty committee investigating measures of defence against submarines.

Chilton was appalled that Porte's principles for anti-submarine warfare from the air as laid out in the paper had not been followed up by the Admiralty, nor even passed on to the RAF after its creation in 1918 from a merger of the Royal Naval Air Service and the Royal Flying Corps. In autumn 1991, during an RAF Historical Society seminar at the RAF Staff College, Bracknell, Chilton was still contending that the services would have been much better equipped to tackle the U-boat threat at the outset of the Second World War if Porte's paper had not been shelved.

Charles Edward Chilton was born on Nov 1 1906 and educated at Portsmouth Grammar School and the RAF College, Cranwell, where he was commissioned in 1926.

After courses at Calshot, he was posted to Felixstowe where he specialised in navigation. In 1931 he joined No 209, a flying-boat squadron and flew the biplane Blackburn Iris, then the largest aircraft of the RAF.

In 1933 Chilton, while working as a navigation instructor at the Central Flying School, published a prescient paper in the RAF *Quarterly*, in which he called attention to the similarities between the role of the fireship of the Middle Ages and the 17th century, and that of the destroyer and the torpedo bomber in modern times.

He issued a warning – to no avail – that there were likely to be problems with the torpedo bomber at the moment of release, when it would be an easy target for the enemy's guns. He also anticipated the then unthinkable demise of the destroyer.

In 1935 Chilton visited South Africa as an exchange officer, and two years later returned home to serve on the navigation staff at Bomber Command.

In 1940 he was posted to the operational requirements staff at the Air Ministry, and next year joined the training staff at Flying Training Command.

After the Battle of the Atlantic and the Normandy invasion, he was transferred to a senior administrative appointment in South-East Asia and from there to posts in Malaya and Ceylon.

From 1952 to 1953 Chilton was air officer commanding in Gibraltar, and then became assistant chief air staff (policy). In 1957, after further staff appointments, he was posted to Malta as air officer commanding and deputy commander-in-chief, Allied Forces Mediterranean.

Two years later he took over at Coastal Command, and also assumed responsibility for the associated Nato appointments in the South Atlantic, the Channel and the North Sea.

It was a source of much satisfaction that he was able to complete his career at the head of the maritime arm which he had served with such distinction in the Second World War.

"Chilly" Chilton's long experience made him the right man to take the maritime chair at a time when the RAF was successfully fighting off an attempt by Earl Mountbatten, then Chief of the Defence Staff, to take

Coastal Command's aircraft away from it.

Chilton was appointed CBE in 1945, CB in 1951 and KBE in 1959. In 1960, as a Master Navigator, he was particularly delighted to represent the RAF in Portugal at celebrations to commemorate the fifth centenary of Prince Henry the Navigator, the founder of Portuguese maritime power.

On his retirement from the RAF he joined IBM (Rentals) as a consultant and director, serving there until 1978. In the meantime he kept up his interest in navigation as a Fellow and sometime Vice-President of the Royal Institute of Navigation.

He enjoyed sailing, fishing and country walking. He was also a prolific writer of letters to *The Daily Telegraph*. His repertoire ranged from points of national defence to the plight of war widows in an age of excessively generous welfare handouts.

Chilton married first, in 1929, Betty Ursula, who died in 1963; they had a son. He married secondly, in 1964, Joyce Cornforth.

WING COMMANDER MICK ENSOR
27 DECEMBER 1994

Wing Commander Mick Ensor, who has died aged 72, was one of RAF Coastal Command's most decorated pilots: at 23 he had accounted for at least two German U-boats and been awarded the DSO and DFC (both with Bar).

Several of Ensor's most outstanding successes took place with 500 Squadron in the western Mediterranean during Operation Torch, the Anglo-American invasion of Vichy-

French North Africa in late 1942.

On Nov 15 Ensor was flying a Lockheed Hudson when he sighted *U-259* off Algiers. He dived to intercept, levelled out at 50 ft and straddled the U–boat with depth charges.

An enormous explosion on the deck blew in the Hudson's floor, shattered Ensor's windscreen, knocked him unconscious and lifted the aircraft to 600 ft. When Ensor came round the aircraft had dropped into a dive, but he managed to prevent it plunging into the sea. The wings had bent upwards, the elevator had been blown off and the rudders seemed set to go as well. He had no alternative but to coax the aircraft high enough for the crew to bale out.

At 3,000 ft the weight of the navigator as he entered the nose to find his parachute sent the crippled aircraft into another dive. A hasty retreat towards the tail enabled Ensor to resume level flying at 200 ft.

When he had climbed again to 1,000 ft one of his two engines stopped and the aircraft began to dive and spin. Ensor immediately ordered the crew to jump, and was himself the last man out.

Only one of his three crew survived: one hit the fuselage and dropped unconscious into the sea, and another's parachute failed to open. The two survivors were picked up by naval sloops.

Michael Ensor was born at Rangiora, New Zealand, on Jan 5 1922 and educated at St Andrew's, Christchurch.

He was accepted for a short service commission in the RAF before the outbreak of the Second World War, but his entry was deferred. In July 1940 he took the option of training as a pilot in the Royal New Zealand Air Force.

Late the next year he joined the Auxiliary Air Force's 500 Squadron, which was based at Bircham Newton and was in the process of exchanging Bristol Blenheims for Hudsons. He saw action early in 1942.

After attacking three enemy ships in the Heligoland area off the coast of Germany, and hitting one of them, Ensor was approaching the mouth of the Elbe at 100 ft when his Hudson hit a rock in the sea and bounced upwards.

The starboard engine had been damaged, and Ensor switched it off. His airspeed indicator and radio were also out of action, and over Holland he found that his gyro compass was 180° out.

Intense anti-aircraft fire forced him to hedge-hop, and his navigator dropped into the nose to guide him through trees, buildings and flak. "It was as though someone was spraying sparks at us," Ensor recalled.

Finding his way out to sea, he encountered a heavy snowstorm. He was down to 30 minutes' fuel when he glimpsed land and decided to put down wherever he was. He made a lucky belly-landing in a field sown with anti-invasion obstructions. On his return to base Ensor learned that crew and aircraft were listed as "missing". He was awarded the DFC.

In April 1942 Ensor moved with the squadron to Stornoway in the Hebrides to fly Atlantic anti-submarine patrols. He mounted several attacks on U-boats, but damage and sinkings were unconfirmed.

On November 13 Ensor's Squadron Commander, Wing Commander Denis Spotswood (later Sir Denis, Marshal of the RAF) surprised the surfaced *U-595* north of Oran. Spotswood's depth charges disabled the submarine, but the U-boat's gunners returned fire. His Hudson sustained damage and was forced to withdraw.

Two more Hudsons took up the attack and were also hit. Then Ensor followed up and, flying in the face of persistent gunfire, dropped his charges across the U-boat. The U-boat's captain ceded the day and ran his craft aground.

After Operation Torch, Ensor was posted home to Coastal Command HQ at Northwood, producing papers on anti-submarine tactics. But he was 21, and staff work did not appeal.

In August 1943 Ensor joined No 224 as a flight commander under Wing Commander A E Clouston, also a New Zealander. Equipped with four-engined Consolidated Liberators and based at St Eval in Cornwall, the squadron was in the front line of the RAF's war against U-boats in the Battle of the Atlantic.

Ensor was again in the thick of the action: on one sortie he seriously damaged a U-boat; on another the damage inflicted on his Liberator by a German submarine's gunners was so heavy that he was lucky to make the long fight home. He was then given command of the squadron.

On May 5 1945 – three days before VE Day – Ensor sank a U-boat off Denmark. It was his last wartime mission. In all he had made a remarkable 114 operational sorties.

After the war he chose to continue with a service career. He disliked desk jobs, and flew as much as permitted.

With his next squadron, No 206, Ensor captained an Avro York on 200 trips during the Berlin Airlift. In 1949 he was seconded to the US Navy and flew as an aircraft captain in the Pacific during the Korean War.

On his return to Britain in 1952 he received command of No 217, a maritime reconnaissance squadron based once again at St Eval.

He later converted to jets and in 1958 was appointed chief flying instructor at the Maritime Training Unit at Kinloss in Scotland. After a course at the Armed Forces Staff College at Norfolk, Virginia, Ensor had appointments at the Air Ministry and on Malta.

He retired in 1965, and two years later set up a business in New Zealand.

Ensor was awarded the DFC and Bar and DSO in 1942, Bar to his DSO in 1943 and AFC in 1952.

He married, in 1945, Patience, daughter of Sir Colin Coote, a former editor of *The Daily Telegraph*. She died in 1975; they had four sons.

FLIGHT LIEUTENANT
LESLIE "BAVEY" BAVEYSTOCK
18 AUGUST 1997

Flight Lieutenant Leslie "Bavey" Baveystock, who has died in New Zealand aged 82, sank two U-boats in 1944; he had earlier been involved in an action in which a comrade won the VC.

In 1942 he had been shot down while taking part in the raid on Cologne by 1,000 bombers on the night of May 30–31. Baveystock was able to bale out, evade capture and return to his squadron within six weeks. The pilot of his aeroplane was awarded a posthumous VC.

Baveystock's own decorations during the war were the DFM (in Bomber Command), and (after his transfer to Coastal Command as a flying boat pilot) the DSO, DFC and Bar.

He claimed his first U-boat on the night of the D-Day landings, June 6–7 1944. Baveystock was on patrol at the controls of a Sunderland flying boat belonging to 201 Squadron in Coastal Command. Among the German craft attempting to enter the Channel from the Western Approaches was *U-955*. Baveystock sighted the U-boat and immediately decided to attack.

He knew the engagement was going to be perilous. He illuminated the surfaced submarine with flares and attacked through a hail of gunfire. At 75 ft, he dropped six depth charges, two of which exploded on either side of the U-boat's hull and sent it to the bottom.

Elated, Baveystock returned to base at Pembroke Dock. But he then learned that his father had died in London, and he was granted immediate compassionate leave. In his absence his flight commander Squadron Leader "Babe" Ruth skippered Baveystock's Sunderland and crew on the next sortie. They never returned.

On August 18 that year, Baveystock was patrolling with a new crew when nature called, and Brian Landers, his second pilot, took over the skipper's seat. As Baveystock reached the flying boat's lavatory, Landers spotted a wake on the port bow and sounded the morse "S" submarine alarm. When Baveystock reappeared, he was still pulling up his trousers. He took over, dropped depth charges and despatched *U-107*, his second U-boat of the summer.

The two successes might have seemed simple, but they were the product of countless searches over the Atlantic, each lasting 12 or 13 hours. These exercises required endless patience but they allowed Baveystock to build up maritime expertise. In the course of these patrols he had also succeeded in sinking the *Alsterufer*, a German armed blockade runner, north-west of the Azores.

Leslie Harold Baveystock was born on November 5 1914 in Finchley, north London, where he was educated at Christ's College. At the age of 16 he entered his father's furniture-making business.

Baveystock enlisted in 1940, trained in Canada, and in April 1942 was posted as a flight sergeant to No 50 Squadron at Skellingthorpe, Lincolnshire. There he was second pilot in a twin-engined Avro Manchester bomber which had seen better days. To his dismay he found the aircraft was patched all over, as a result of flak, and lacked its mid upper gun-turret. But so determined was Bomber Harris to send out the RAF's first 1,000-bomber force, that on the night of May 30–31 Baveystock and his rickety aircraft took off for Cologne. Baveystock's one regret then was that the raid prevented him from meeting his wife during a short leave he had manoeuvred.

All went well over Germany until, on the return flight after the bombing of Cologne, Baveystock's Manchester was coned by searchlights and hit by flak. His skipper, Pilot Officer Leslie Manser, went into a dive. The port engine was on fire.

Flying on one engine was particularly difficult because the elevators had been badly damaged. Baveystock and his fellows jettisoned everything they could. Even so, Manser was losing control of the bomber but said calmly: "Put on parachutes" – and then, "Good luck. Jump, jump, jump."

Baveystock recalled: "There was no counting to ten, as we were so low." He splashed into a Belgian marsh. Before long he found Stanley King, the second wireless operator, and then Bob Horsley, the first wireless operator. Manser had been killed.

Fortunately Baveystock and the others were taken under the wing of members of MI9, the invasion and escape organisation, and made their way to freedom along the celebrated Comet Line escape route, all the way through France towards the Spanish border. They, together with a Canadian pilot they had picked up on the way, were escorted by the celebrated Dédée de Jongh, then only 25.

After reaching St Jean de Luz, the last railway station before Spain, Baveystock and party were told how best to cross the Pyrenees by Florentino Goicoechea, a Basque smuggler who led many such expeditions.

On June 13 Baveystock reached San Sebastian; from there the British consulate forwarded him to the Embassy in Madrid. Remarkably, the entire crew apart from Manser and Richard Barnes, the navigator (who had been captured) were now together again and sent on to Gibraltar.

On arriving home on July 12 in the troop ship *Nakunda* Baveystock reported: "It is to Pilot Officer Manser's coolness and courage that the rest of the crew owe their lives." Manser was awarded an almost immediate posthumous Victoria Cross.

In the aftermath of their escape, several Comet Line members were shot, or sent to concentration camps, where some died. Dédée de Jongh, after making 36 trips over the Pyrenees and back, was imprisoned for a year before being moved to a concentration camp. She survived the war and was awarded the George Medal; she later went to Africa to look after lepers.

Baveystock, after his time with Coastal Command, was released from the RAF at the end of 1945. He emigrated to New Zealand where he farmed and was in business.

Leslie Baveystock married, in 1938, Elizabeth Lynas Caddie; they had a son and a daughter.

DAVID BEATY
4 DECEMBER 1999

David Beaty, who has died aged 80, won a DFC and Bar as a wartime U-boat hunter with the RAF; he later became a BOAC airline captain and drew on his flying experiences to write readable and authentic adventure fiction.

Beaty had recently helped to pioneer civil air-to-air refuelling and the opening of BOAC's post-war transatlantic service when in 1949 Wernher Laurie published his novel *The Take Off*, which he had begun while in the RAF. William Morrow, the New York publisher, was so impressed that he took Beaty to Claridge's and offered him the equivalent of a BOAC captain's salary for two years if he wrote full time.

The result was a steady flow of some 26 works of fiction and non-fiction, the majority of which – beginning with *The Heart of the Storm* – were published in London by Secker & Warburg. Reviewers soon sensed Beaty's near obsessional interest in pilot trauma.

Beaty's talent for strong, skilful storytelling based on his personal experience and flying expertise was particularly potent in *Cone of Silence* (1959), a story about a jet pilot who had once been found guilty of pilot error. The book questioned whether the pilot had received the wrong flying instructions – a recurring theme in Beaty's works – and became a feature film starring George Sanders.

Beaty's interest in the subject of alleged pilot error prompted him in 1966 to enter University College, London, to study psychology. Having been awarded his MPhil, he published *The Human Factor in Aircraft Accidents* (1969) which postulated that pilots were only human and subject to the same frailties as others.

It followed, Beaty argued, that aircraft manufacturers should take such aspects of the human condition into account when designing and building aircraft; and that civil and military operators should allow for such factors.

Although the book encountered considerable opposition from the aircraft industry and some pilots, Beaty persevered with his theme. Recognising as time passed that technology had improved safety, he re-wrote *Human Factor* and published *The Naked Pilot* in 1991.

In 1992 he was appointed MBE for services to aviation.

In the 20-year interim, Beaty, while maintaining his flow of fiction, made the occasional foray into the real world. As a Foreign Office official from 1968 to 1973, he was involved with overseas aid and established the Centre for Education Development Overseas.

Arthur David Beaty was born on March 28 1919 in Ceylon, where his parents were Methodist missionaries. He was educated at Kingswood School, Bath, and at Merton, Oxford, where as editor of *Cherwell* he was a colleague of Iris Murdoch's.

Beaty enlisted in 1939 and was commissioned as a pilot officer in the RAFVR in 1941, when he joined No 201, a Short Sunderland flying-boat Coastal Command squadron stationed at Castle Archdale in Northern Ireland.

After a spell with No 221, a Vickers Wellington squadron based at Reykjavik, Iceland, he flew Wellingtons from Malta with a maritime special duties flight.

On the night of January 23-24 1942, Beaty's reconnaissance resulted in the sinking off Benghazi, North Africa, of the Italian merchantman *Victoria*, the pearl of the Italian merchant fleet which was supplying Axis forces in North Africa.

Subsequently, Beaty captained a B-17 Flying Fortress of No 206 Squadron ranging the Atlantic from the Azores. In the early hours of March 13 1944, he attacked the surfaced *U-575* which had been damaged earlier at the hands of a Vickers Wellington. Going in at dawn, Beaty, his front and mid-upper gunners blazing away, pressed home his attack in the face of heavy flak and straddled the Type VIIC enemy submarine with four depth charges.

After the explosions, *U-575* appeared stationary on the surface and then, leaving two tell-tale oil patches, submerged stem first with bows at a steep angle. Subsequently, a second Fortress reported that the slick had formed an arrowhead, indicating slow passage under water.

Shortly afterwards, two American destroyers and a Canadian frigate arrived on the scene. Assailed by a combination of their fire and attack by an American carrier aircraft, the crippled U-boat sank. It was a useful victory: commanded by Oberleutnant Wolfgang Boehmer – who was picked out of the water – *U-575* had sunk 11 ships, including the corvette *Asphodel*. Beaty was awarded the DFC.

In the New Year of 1945, he received a Bar to his DFC after captaining a Consolidated Liberator which was badly damaged in an attack on five U-boats escorted by a destroyer in the Skagerrak. After losing one of his four engines and sustaining a damaged port aileron, a heavily holed fuselage and wing, Beaty was ordering his seven-man crew to bale out when a parachute accidentally opened inside the aircraft. Against great odds, he coaxed his aeroplane home.

Beaty, if not relishing the drama of such situations, certainly recognised their plot value as he began to write. After joining BOAC following release from the service in 1946, he welcomed the additional airline experience gained on 200 Atlantic crossings.

Nor, as with *Human Factor*, did he restrict such insider knowledge to fiction. In *The Water Jump* (1976), he supported his fascination with flying the Atlantic with a highly original and instructive history of a challenge which had "attracted lunatics and would-be suicides and had a strange fascination for women".

Beaty's authoress wife Betty, whom he had met when she was a wartime WAAF equipment officer and married in 1948, was also acquainted with cabin life. In her husband's BOAC days she was a British European Airways stewardess. They had three daughters.

Although he had consciously flown with Coastal Command, preferring to "fight uniformed men", Beaty retained an enormous respect and admiration for Bomber Command crews. Recognising that they had sustained the

RAF's heaviest losses, he published in 1995 *Light Perpetual*, an assembly of memorial windows to aviators, many of which inevitably featured bomber casualties.

The remainder of Beaty's output included: *Leave of Leisure* (1959), *Call Me Captain* (1959), *Village of Stars* (1960), *The Wind off the Sea* (1962), *The Siren Song* (1964), *Milk and Honey* (1964), *The Gun Garden* (1965), *Sword of Honour* (1965), *The Temple Tree* (1973), *Electric Train* (1975), *Excellency* (1977), *The White Sea Bird* (1979), *Strange Encounters* (1982), *Wings of the Morning* (1982), *The Stick* (1984), *The Blood Brothers* (1987), *Eagles* (1990) and *Ghost of the Eighth Attack* (1998).

Beaty was elected Member of the Royal Aeronautical Society in 1981.

CONSTANCE BABINGTON SMITH
31 JULY 2000

Constance Babington Smith, who has died aged 87, made the first identification from a photograph of a German V1 flying bomb at Peenemunde in 1943; as a result, the RAF carried out raids which reduced the damage done to Britain by Germany's new airborne weapons.

She was working as a photographic interpreter in the Allied Photographic Intelligence Unit, and in April 1943 had been briefed by the Air Ministry to be on the lookout for a long-range gun, remotely controlled rocket aircraft and "some sort of tube out of which a rocket could be squirted".

Peenemunde was the site of a German research station on the Baltic. Allied photographic reconnaissance from the air had indicated unusual activities there, possibly the construction of earthworks for testing rockets. In June

1943, one of Constance Babington Smith's fellow interpreters, André Kenny, made the first identification of two V2 long-range rockets lying horizontally on road vehicles at Peenemunde.

At the same time, Constance Babington Smith was briefed to look out for "anything queer". Examining a photograph taken on June 23 she spotted "four little tail-less aeroplanes taking the air" which "looked queer enough to satisfy anybody". What she had seen, it turned out, were four Me 163 liquid rocket fighters. But V2 long-range rockets were identified from photographs of Peenemunde for the first time that month.

On November 13 1943, she was asked to look out for aircraft at Peenemunde which might be pilotless. Her search was under way when on November 28 a de Havilland Mosquito, piloted by Squadron Leader John Merifield returned with a sensational photograph.

As Flight Officer Constance Babington Smith studied it through her stereoscope, she identified a ramp holding a tiny cruciform shape on rails. Her discovery, together with the subsequent examination of many thousands of photographs of other possible launch sites and storage depots, indicated that a flying bomb offensive was being prepared on the other side of the Channel.

The bombing of the launch sites was given urgent priority, under the codename "Crossbow". Constance Babington Smith had the task of providing photographic material to assist targeting by Bomber Command and its Pathfinder Force, and at the end of 1943 Allied air forces flattened launch sites in France.

But by the spring of 1944 the Germans had built less obvious emplacements in the Pas de Calais and in June Hitler unleashed the V1 assault on London and the south of England. The V2s began to fall on London in September.

In the meantime, Constance Babington Smith had been pursuing another vital brief – watching out for new types of aircraft, especially jets. "Keeping an eye on Peenemunde," she said, "was a minor task compared to the everlasting watch for new German aircraft."

When Group Captain Frank Whittle, inventor of the jet engine, paid her a visit, he was much impressed by what she had found – notably the Me 163, He 280 and Me 262 – and was rather enamoured of this unusual WAAF officer.

Constance Babington Smith learned later that Whittle was subjected to much leg-pulling about the interest he showed in her, especially when he made inquiries about the scent she used – which he learned was Guerlain's *L'Heure Bleue*. She wore the scent, she said, to counteract the masculinity of her uniform.

After the war, Constance Babington Smith settled down to the life of a writer. She published an account of her wartime experiences, a book about test pilots, several volumes of letters by her cousin Dame Rose Macaulay, and a clutch of well received biographies.

Constance Babington Smith was born on October 15 1912, one of the five daughters – and four sons – of Henry (later Sir Henry) Babington Smith and his wife Lady Elizabeth (née Bruce), daughter of the 9th Earl of Elgin – grandson of the Lord Elgin who acquired the Parthenon marbles.

Constance's father had been private secretary to George Goschen, the Conservative Chancellor of the Exchequer, in 1891–92. After a further period of work in the Treasury, he was appointed in 1894 private secretary to Lord Elgin, the new Viceroy of India. He married Lord Elgin's daughter in 1898.

Constance was brought up mainly at Chinthurst, a house designed by Edwin Lutyens at Wonersh, near Guildford. There she was educated by governesses and tutors, before being sent to live for a few months with a French family at Versailles.

During the 1930s, she led a busy social life in London and worked for the fashionable milliner Aage Thaarup. Already fascinated by aeronautical matters, she also wrote articles for *The Aeroplane* magazine.

Having been commissioned as a section officer in the WAAF in December 1940, she was asked to set up an aircraft interpretation section for the RAF's photographic reconnaissance unit at Heston airfield.

In 1941 she moved with the unit to Danesfield, a mock Tudor mansion on the Thames between Marlow and Henley which during the war became RAF Medmenham. While her brother Bernard, a mathematician, was working there on the interpretation of night-time photographs, Constance was soon entrusted with the responsibility of searching for secret weapons.

Constance Babington Smith was mentioned in despatches in 1942 and was appointed MBE in 1945. In the summer of 1945, she was sent to America to assist in photographic interpretation for the Pacific War, and she was awarded the US Legion of Merit in 1946.

Having been demobilised in America, she stayed on for a time working as a researcher for *Life* magazine, in particular for their series on Churchill. She returned to Britain in the late 1940s and soon afterwards settled in Cambridge, where in due course she was granted dining rights at Churchill College.

Her first book, *Evidence in Camera*, a fascinating record of wartime photographic intelligence and her part in it, was published in 1958. No problem, she explained, had been regarded as too difficult to solve; the interpreters had set out to discover every secret a photograph might contain.

Geologists, geographers, archaeologists, mathematicians,

explorers, botanists, map-makers and a host of others were drafted in to interpret huge quantities of photographs. During the preparations for the Normandy landings, for instance, as many as seven million prints a month were being turned out for examination.

Constance Babington Smith's second book, *Testing Time: a Study of Man and Machine in the Test Flying Era*, appeared in 1961. The book charts the development of the test pilot's role from the days of Roe and Sopwith, and conveys the excitement and danger of test flying that attracted such adventurers as Sir Henry Tizard and Sir Geoffrey de Havilland – and even Lord Cherwell, who took flying lessons in a dark suit and wing collar.

Next, she turned to editing the letters of her cousin Rose Macaulay, producing three volumes in succession: *Letters to a Friend from Rose Macaulay, 1950-52* (1961); *Last Letters to a Friend from Rose Macaulay, 1952-58* (1962); and *Letters to a Sister from Rose Macaulay* (1964).

Having returned to aeronautical matters with *Amy Johnson* (1967), she published three further biographies: *Rose Macaulay* (1972); *John Masefield: a Life* (1976); and *Iulia de Beausobre* (1983).

The last book was an account of the remarkable life of the Russian emigré who married the historian Sir Lewis Namier. Her last substantial project bore fruit in *Champion of Homeopathy: the Life of Margery Blackie* (1986).

Brought up in the Church of England, Constance Babington Smith became interested in Orthodoxy as a result of her friendship with Iulia de Beausobre, and in 1972 she joined the Greek Orthodox Church. She learned modern Greek and paid regular visits to Greece, making many good friends there.

Never forgetting the part played by the de Havilland Mosquito in wartime photographic reconnaissance, and of the debt owed to the Mosquito crews, Constance

Babington Smith was a founder director of the Mosquito Memorial Appeal Fund – now the de Havilland Museum Trust – which preserved the prototype Mosquito at Salisbury Hall, St Albans. She was always modest about her own part in the war.

She never married.

AIR COMMODORE
JEAFFRESON GRESWELL
19 NOVEMBER 2000

Air Commodore Jeaffreson Greswell, who has died aged 84, was the first pilot during the Second World War to use the Leigh Light, a powerful airborne torch, to illuminate enemy submarines during night attacks.

In 1941, Greswell had been posted to the Coastal Command Development Unit, where he came into contact with Wing Commander Humphrey de Vere Leigh, who had hunted U-boats in the First World War.

Greswell was much impressed by Leigh and by the light that he had designed to mount in the gun position of a Wellington. Early trials were successful and in the New Year of 1942, Greswell was selected to command No 1471 Flight based at RAF Chivenor, in north Devon, to introduce the light operationally.

On the night of June 3-4 1942, Greswell took off from Chivenor in a twin-engine Vickers Wellington bomber of No 172 Squadron. In the Bay of Biscay, he lit up and then depth-charged the Italian submarine *Luigi Torelli*.

Greswell's first approach to the *Luigi Torelli* was frustrated by an incorrect altimeter setting, which meant that his co-pilot, Flying Officer A W R Trigg, was unable to level the beam at the enemy.

After the altimeter was reset, Greswell took the Wellington to 50 ft above the sea and attacked from the starboard beam, dropping two Torpex-filled depth charges either side of the submarine.

The charges' fuses were supposed to explode at a depth of 25 feet, but they proved defective and the explosions occurred at a greater depth. Even so the submarine's steering gear and compass system were badly damaged, forcing its captain Count Augusto Migliorani to seek refuge in Spanish waters.

He could not believe his luck when 10 minutes after his attack on the *Luigi Torelli*, his torch found a second Italian submarine, *Morosini*. Having already expended his depth charges he went in at 50 feet and attacked with machine gun fire.

Morosini failed to return from its patrol, but disappointingly for Greswell and his crew, its loss was not ascribed to their attack. As for the *Luigi Torelli*, though damaged, it ended its war running supplies to the Far East. The Japanese scuttled her in August 1945.

Though neither submarine had been sunk by his action, Greswell had demonstrated the potential of the Leigh Light and this enabled Air Chief Marshal Sir Philip Joubert, Coastal's commander-in-chief, to obtain early delivery of Leigh Light Wellingtons. Greswell's mission also provided valuable lessons for the future, the most vital being that the attack aircraft's altimeter should always be set correctly.

For his actions in attacking the two submarines, Greswell was awarded the DFC.

Jeaffreson Herbert Greswell was born on July 28 1916, at Ashtead, Surrey, and educated at Repton. In 1935 he joined the RAF on a short service commission and in 1937 joined No 217, an anti-submarine squadron.

After the outbreak of war in 1939, he began flying anti-submarine patrols over the Western Approaches in an operationally obsolescent twin-engine Avro Anson.

Following his exploit in 1942 over the Bay of Biscay with the Leigh Light, Greswell joined the staff at Coastal Command headquarters. In December he went to the United States to liaise with anti-submarine staff and promote the Leigh Light concept.

After returning home in the spring of 1943, Greswell served briefly at Coastal's No 19 Group and in June received command of No 179, a Wellington Leigh Light squadron based at Gibraltar.

The aim of his squadron was to combat the U-boats that were threatening Allied shipping off North Africa and passing through the Straits of Gibraltar. Greswell took part in Operation Swamp which sought to concentrate anti-submarine aircraft wherever a U-boat preyed, and to co-operate with naval anti-submarine vessels.

In the New Year of 1944 Greswell took part in a typical Swamp sortie. At midnight, he approached *U-343*, commanded by Oberleutnant Wolfgang Rahn, and released his depth charges at 100 feet.

His crew observed explosions on the far side of the surfaced U-boat and level with the conning tower. A fellow 179 pilot, Flying Officer W F McDavidson, flew into heavy flak from the U-boat as he was releasing his depth charges, and his Wellington fell blazing into the sea. But Greswell and McDavidson had between them so damaged the U-boat it was unable to dive. It was subsequently sunk by the naval armed trawler *Mull*.

After almost a year with 179, Greswell was posted in April 1944 to Coastal Command headquarters, moving on in July to Coastal's No 18 Group. In July 1945 he returned as a member of the command's air staff.

There followed a spell in the Far East where in 1946 he liaised with the British Pacific Fleet at Hong Kong and the next year served at Air Command South East Asia (ACSEA) headquarters. As memories of Coastal's contribution receded, Greswell was concerned lest its vital role in defeating the U-boats be forgotten.

Happily his appointment in 1949 to the staff of the Joint Anti-Submarine School provided an opportunity to press home the mutual benefits of co-operation between the RAF and the Navy.

Greswell was appointed to the staff of the RAF Flying College, Manby, in 1952. In 1954 he moved to the Ministry of Defence as the RAF representative on the joint planning staff team which drew up plans for the 1956 Suez operation.

Greswell later maintained that these papers had been disregarded by the politicians, with the result that the Navy was denied the tactical air cover it needed.

From 1957 to 1959, Greswell was station commander at RAF Kinloss. Later he was standing group representative on the Nato council in Paris. In the four years before his retirement in 1968 he was commandant of the Royal Observer Corps, steering the volunteer organisation through the shoals of change.

He was fond of croquet and gardening during his retirement near Ringwood in the New Forest.

In addition to his DFC, he was awarded a DSO in 1944 and was also mentioned in Despatches. He was appointed OBE in 1946, CBE in 1962, and CB in 1967.

He married, in 1939, Gwyneth Hayes, who survives him, with a son and two of their three daughters.

AIR VICE-MARSHAL
PATRICK O'CONNOR

10 APRIL 2001

Air Vice-Marshal Patrick O'Connor, who has died aged 86, was from the 1950s among the RAF's first specialists in neuro-psychiatry; earlier, in 1944, he had saved the life of John Cruickshank following the action in which the latter had won the VC.

In August 1944, a stricken Catalina flying boat ran up on the beach at Sullom Voe, Coastal Command's base in the Shetland Islands, where O'Connor was station medical officer.

As he boarded the aircraft, he immediately realised that only a blood transfusion on the spot would give its pilot, Cruickshank, any chance of survival. Using such limited equipment as he had available, including a chamber pot, O'Connor stabilised the wounded man sufficiently to move him to hospital.

Only then did O'Connor appreciate the full extent of Cruickshank's 72 separate injuries, mainly in his legs and chest. Nor did O'Connor learn the story of the action in which Cruickshank had been engaged until the award of the VC came through some time later.

Cruickshank had been on an Atlantic patrol when he encountered a U-boat on the surface. He tried to drop depth charges, but these failed to release so he came around for a second run.

This time they were released successfully and sank the submarine, but not before one of its shells had hit the Catalina, killing the navigator and badly wounding other crew members, including the co-pilot and Cruickshank himself.

For six hours Cruickshank, bleeding profusely and lapsing in and out of consciousness, coaxed the flying boat back to the Shetlands, reaching Sullom Voe two hours before dawn. All the while he refused to accept any morphia to ease his pain, lest it affect his judgement.

Fearing that the damaged craft would sink on landing, Cruickshank circled around the base until there was sufficient light to land the Catalina in the shallows and run her up on a beach, where shortly afterwards he was found by O'Connor.

Patrick Joseph O'Connor, the son of a farmer, was born on August 21 1914, at Straffan, Co Kildare, Ireland.

He was educated at Roscrea College and at university in Dublin. After a brief period working as house surgeon at Scunthorpe District Hospital, he received an emergency commission in 1940 and was posted to RAF Coastal Command's No 18 Group. He served at a number of stations before arriving at Sullum Voe in May 1944.

In the last months of the war he was sent out to the Middle East, serving in Persia and Egypt before moving to Greece and Habbaniyah, Iraq, where he was senior medical officer with the Iraqi Levies.

Having decided to stay in the RAF, O'Connor returned to Britain in 1947 and had a series of postings, including RAF Hospital, Halton, Buckinghamshire, where from 1955 he specialised in neuro-psychiatry.

O'Connor soon built a considerable reputation in this field. In 1957 he moved to the RAF's Central Medical Establishment and in 1964 was appointed consultant adviser in neurology and psychiatry to the RAF. He developed a particular expertise in the treatment of alcoholism and phobias among RAF personnel. He was appointed Air Commodore in 1966, and Air Vice-Marshal in 1971.

O'Connor retired in 1978, but was then appointed civil consultant in psychiatry to the RAF. For 20 years he was also a consultant in neurology and psychiatry to the Civil

Aviation Authority and to British Airways. He developed a busy private practice in Harley Street and continued to work into his eighties.

O'Connor was mentioned in dispatches in 1941. He was appointed OBE in 1943 and CB in 1976. He had a wide knowledge of antiques, and enjoyed gardening.

He married, in 1946, Elsie Craven. They had a son and two daughters; another daughter predeceased him. John Cruickshank was the RAF's last surviving VC.

COLONEL
EVELYN PRENDERGAST
30 JUNE 2001

Colonel Evelyn Prendergast, who has died aged 83, flew perilous low observation sorties over the Normandy battlefields in an unarmed Auster, a slow and fragile American two-seater cabin aeroplane popular with weekend club fliers.

As a 25-year-old gunner officer commanding No 659 Air Observation Post (AOP) Squadron, Prendergast was fortunate to survive heavy ground fire from a formidable German dual purpose 88 mm gun.

After flying hedge-hopping missions in July 1944 to report enemy tank and troop movements during the battle for Caen inland from the beaches, Prendergast was awarded the DFC.

The citation was signed by General Montgomery, commanding 21st Army Group, who commended him for continuing a particular patrol under heavy fire and returning with "most valuable information". Monty concluded: "His conduct throughout has been an inspiration to those serving under him."

Prendergast went on to cover the fighting for the Falaise Gap. Later he was approaching Paris, which he believed to have been liberated, when the tanks of a Panzer division concentrated their fire on him.

Forced to crash-land, he delivered his wounded passenger for treatment (the two-to-three seat Auster was also a communications runabout) and informed Paris-bound Free French tanks in the van of the Allied advance on the capital of enemy positions.

Evelyn David Vereker Prendergast was born in London on February 19 1918, during a Zeppelin air raid. He was the grandson of General Sir Harry Prendergast VC, whose Burma Field Force deposed King Thebaw in Mandalay in 1885.

Educated at Wellington and the Royal Military Academy, Woolwich, Prendergast was commissioned into the Royal Artillery in 1938. In the New Year of 1940 he joined the British Expeditionary Force in France with 1st Heavy Regiment RA and when France fell was evacuated from Dunkirk.

In the summer of 1940, as Britain awaited the expected invasion and the Battle of Britain was fought overhead, Prendergast was accepted for pilot training. In 1943 he received command of No 659 AOP Squadron when it was formed at Firbank, York.

He led the squadron to Normandy shortly after the D-Day landings on June 6 1944. During the subsequent advance through north-west Europe, Prendergast's reports of enemy positions just ahead of Allied troops, armour and artillery were of immense value.

After the war Prendergast took the first Long Gunnery Staff Course before being posted overseas to instruct at the Indian School of Artillery, Deolali. Returning by rail from a spot of fishing in Kashmir, he took over the train when the driver abandoned his cab and announced that he was going home to Pakistan. It was Independence Day (August 15 1947), and the driver was terrified of being caught up in the turmoil of partition.

Although Prendergast was in mufti and armed only with his fishing rod, he set about organising the resumption of the marooned passengers' journey and conveyed them to safety.

Prendergast attended Staff College in 1949 and afterwards was posted to Malaya, where he was ambushed on a jungle patrol, and shot in the elbow in a friendly-fire incident.

In the 1950s he served in Germany, returning to command 95 Amphibious Observation Regiment at Poole in Dorset. He was then posted to the School of Artillery at Larkhill as General Staff Officer 1 (GS01), Tactics, and as chief instructor in gunnery from 1967 to 1970.

Prendergast also oversaw the introduction of the 105 mm light gun and the beginning of trials of the 155 mm SH70. From 1970 he worked on the analysis of defence operations.

After writing a paper for the Nugent Committee on the use of Ministry of Defence land – it resulted in the introduction of an MOD conservation officer – he retired in 1973 to the Blackmore Vale in Dorset, where he relished the opportunity to devote himself to countryside pursuits.

Prendergast had since boyhood been interested in fishing, shooting, gardening and natural history; he now became chairman of the Dorset Bird Club and a member of the council of the Dorset Natural History and Archaeological Society.

These activities were more than a mere interest. Prendergast immersed himself in detailed research, the results of which were published by the Archaeological

Society. First they brought out his history of the Abbotsbury duck decoy; this was followed in 1983 by his observations on the decline of the black grouse in Dorset.

Prendergast also did much field work for surveys co-ordinated by the British Trust for Ornithology (BTO), and in 1983 he co-authored *The Birds of Dorset*. He was also a BTO ringer and set up a migration ringing post at Chapman's Pool on the Purbeck shore. In addition, in the course of several winters Prendergast ringed more fieldfares in his orchard than were caught and ringed throughout the rest of the country.

In the wider world he edited *The Adjutant*, the journal of the Army Bird Watching Society, and was an elected member of the British Ornithological Union.

In the 1990s Prendergast extended his bird-ringing activities to Africa, organising expeditions to Madagascar and Gambia which provided him with material for contributions to *Ordonatologica*, an international journal.

Prendergast did not confine his studies to birds. In Dorset he surveyed fern distribution and scoured village gardens in his neighbourhood for mistletoe. Dragonflies were another interest. On a stretch of Ministry of Defence land he discovered and investigated a population of southern damselfly, and in 1991 he published *The Dragonflies of Dorset*.

Much respected as a gunner officer and in the world of wildlife, Prendergast was a popular host whose garden was much admired. His potent and memorable elderflower wine was a feature of his hospitality.

He married first, in 1949, Phyllis St Leger Boxwell who died in 1978; they had two sons. In 1985 he married Mary Daubeney.

MARSHAL OF THE RAF
SIR DENIS SPOTSWOOD
11 NOVEMBER 2001

Marshal of The RAF Sir Denis Spotswood, who has died aged 85, was responsible for many developments in the post-war evolution of the RAF; in earlier days, he was a great flying-boat enthusiast, and a successful U-boat hunter with Coastal Command.

In the 1970s, as Chief of the Air Staff, Spotswood nursed the RAF through a testing period of consolidation. His masterly handling of the introduction and operational employment of a new generation of aircraft, notably the Phantom, Harrier, Buccaneer, Nimrod and Hercules, was among the most noteworthy of his achievements.

He also negotiated arrangements with Germany and Italy for the joint provision of the Tornado multi-role combat aircraft, and brought the RAF into line with Britain's new defence effort centred on Nato commitments.

Spotswood had first come to notice in November 1942, when he led No 500, an Auxiliary Air Force Squadron equipped with twin-engine Lockheed Hudsons, in support of the Torch landings in North Africa. On November 14, he caught *U-595* on the surface north of Oran and attacked. His depth charges lifted the enemy submarine out of the water, and he followed up with two strafing runs.

The U-boat's gunners none the less crippled Spotswood's Hudson, and forced him to break off the attack. But his action enabled another Hudson crew in his squadron to further damage *U-595*, forcing her skipper to beach her on the desert shore where American troops captured the survivors.

Denis Frank Spotswood was born on September 26

1916 and educated at Kingston Grammar School, Surrey. Aiming for a career in journalism he joined the *London Evening Standard* in 1932. Three years later he was rowing on the Thames with his friend Arthur Scarf (later awarded a posthumous VC after the Japanese invasion of Malaya), when the two decided to join the RAF.

Too old to seek a cadetship at the RAF College, Cranwell, Spotswood was granted a short service commission in March 1936, and within six months had been awarded his wings. Posted to No 201, a Saro London Squadron, in 1937, Spotswood was detached to the flying-boat experimental station at Felixstowe to assist Robert Watson-Watt on the development of Radio Direction Finding.

Infected with the enthusiasm of the flying-boat fanatics he met, Spotswood contrived a posting to No 209 Squadron, which was equipped with the Short Singapore and later the Supermarine Stranraer and Saro Lerwick. Spotswood's love affair with flying boats was further enhanced by the chance to fly the second Short Sunderland to enter operational service.

The outbreak of war in 1939 brought the somewhat risky routine of piloting Lerwicks on patrols over the Western Approaches. The Lerwick had a deservedly poor reputation, though Spotswood, keen to fly anything capable of taking off from and landing on water, was prepared to overlook its failings, even its unpleasant handling characteristics. In April 1941, No 209 was re-equipped with the US Navy's Consolidated Catalina.

After two years of operational flying, he was sent to Canada to collect a Catalina and ferry it across the Atlantic. But, as no Catalina was available, he brought back a Hudson instead – and as a result was posted to a Hudson Operational Training Unit as an instructor. Coming to the notice of Air Chief Marshal Sir Philip Joubert, head of

Coastal Command, Spotswood received command of No 500 Squadron. It was an inspirational posting: under Spotswood the squadron sank at least four of the 22 U-boats it attacked during their time covering Torch and in subsequent operations from North African bases.

Although this period marked the end of Spotswood's wartime operational flying, his prolonged maritime experience put him at a premium as a staff officer and from April 1943 he worked in the Air Ministry's directorate of Air Tactics. That summer, he attended a short war staff course and was then sent out to the Far East, where he joined an Anglo-American planning team under Admiral Lord Louis Mountbatten, Supreme Allied Commander, South East Asia Command.

As Mountbatten and General "Uncle Bill" Slim prepared for the push through Burma, Spotswood accompanied Mountbatten on some of his morale-boosting visits to troops in the jungle. Soon he became Mountbatten's senior RAF planner, and was thus partly responsible for the RAF's vital contribution to the success of the jungle campaign. Following the re-occupation of Singapore, Spotswood devoted himself to the welfare of Allied PoWs and civilian internees who had suffered at the hands of the Japanese. He returned home in time for Christmas 1945. He had by then been awarded a DFC (1942) and a DSO (1943).

Spotswood's operational and staff successes had made him an obvious candidate for a permanent commission, which he was now offered and accepted readily. Moreover, his clear mind equipped him perfectly for his next posting as a member of the directing staff at the RAF College, where he prepared wartime officers for peacetime duties.

In some respects, Spotswood was also preparing himself for his next move: from 1948, he commanded the de Havilland Mosquito night fighter stations at Horsham St

Faith and Coltishall in Norfolk. Bringing Nos 23, 141 and 264 Squadrons to readiness in face of the growing Soviet threat, he flew as often as his duties as station commander permitted.

After two years, Spotswood joined the directing staff at the Imperial Defence College, a clear indication that he was on the way up. He qualified as a jet pilot, before in 1952 taking up a US Air Force exchange post as chief of the tactical operations plans branch at the Pentagon.

Although it seemed a backward step, Spotswood was in no way dismayed at returning to Britain in 1954 for a second tour in command of a fighter station, at Linton-on-Ouse, Yorkshire. But it was to be his last such command before he was reclaimed, towards the end of 1956, for staff duties as deputy director of plans during the turbulent period arising from the Sandys Defence Review.

Spotswood was much relieved to say goodbye to Whitehall when, in mid-1958, he was appointed Commandant of the RAF College, an exceptional privilege for a former short service commission officer who had not held Cranwell cadetship. Being an outsider helped him to identify needs and to introduce necessary changes. The latter included making provision for cadets to take external degrees, and educating technical cadets alongside Cranwell's traditional flight cadets.

Following this pleasant interlude, in 1961 Spotswood was plunged into the intricacies of Nato planning at Supreme Allied Headquarters Europe as assistant chief of staff in the air defence division. Afterwards, he chaired a group studying the RAF's future frontline requirements and was later gratified that much of his report was adopted, including recommendations which led to the creation of Strike Command.

In the summer of 1964 when aircraft of the RAF's nuclear deterrent V-bomber force were frequently being brought to a state of quick reaction alert, Spotswood received command of Bomber Command's No 3 Group, comprising Vickers Valiant and Handley Page Victor squadrons and with additional air-to-air refuelling duties.

The next year, he received his first high-level post when he was appointed Commander-in-Chief RAF Germany and leader of the 2nd Tactical Air Force. Here he had not only to cope with the Soviet threat, but also to manage politically-imposed economies, to prevent erosion of the infrastructure and also to keep the RAF in good standing with the American and other Nato air forces.

In 1968, Spotswood took charge of the recently formed Strike Command whose creation he had advocated. Three years later, on April 1 1971 – the anniversary of the amalgamation in 1918 of the Royal Naval Air Service (RNAS) and the Royal Flying Corps (RFC) to form the RAF – he reached the top of the Service as Chief of the Air Staff.

In 1974, when he retired as CAS and was appointed Marshal of the RAF, Spotswood was content that the RAF, despite reductions, remained a force to be proud of and that he had strengthened its influence in Nato.

Spotswood was now appointed vice-chairman of Rolls-Royce, a post he held for six years, and went on to hold numerous board appointments. He was president of the Society of Aerospace Companies in 1978-79.

Outside industry, he was chairman of the Royal Star and Garter Home (1981-85) and of the Trustees of the RAF Museum (1974-80). He was a life vice-president of the RAF Benevolent Fund. He was elected a Fellow of the Royal Aeronautical Society in 1975.

He was appointed CBE in 1946, CB in 1961, KCB in 1966, and GCB in 1971.

He married, in 1942 Ann Child; they had a son.

WING COMMANDER
TONY SPOONER
29 JANUARY 2002

Wing Commander Tony Spooner, who has died aged 85, was an outstanding pilot and navigator whose expertise was in the location and destruction by night of enemy shipping during the Second World War.

As captain of a special duties Vickers Wellington, Spooner operated from Malta. He arrived there in the autumn of 1941 accompanied by Bronco and Harpic, his pair of frisky mongrel puppies. His modified bomber had radar which, though rudimentary, nonetheless improved the chances of identifying enemy ships sailing under cover of darkness. His aircraft, bristling with an array of air-to-surface vessel (ASV) aerials, was known in England as a "Stickleback"; on Malta, for reasons Spooner never discovered, it became known as a "Goofington".

Although Spooner was only a recently commissioned 25-year-old pilot officer, he established an early and highly unusual rapport with both Air Vice-Marshal Hugh Pughe Lloyd, Malta's Air Officer Commanding (AOC), and Captain W G Agnew, leader of Force K, the Navy's scourge of Axis shipping.

The fact was that both Lloyd and Agnew recognised Spooner's buccaneering qualities, and his piloting and navigational skills. Agnew, at Lloyd's instigation, invited Spooner to tea in *Aurora*, one of Force K's two light cruisers, and sought his assistance in sinking ships supplying the Axis armies in North Africa.

Spooner's early night sorties showed promise, and Lloyd promoted him to flight lieutenant. Within six weeks Spooner's surveillance had enabled Force K to sink many enemy ships, virtually preventing supplies reaching Rommel and his Afrika Korps at a time when they were perilously close to Egypt. Spooner's technique was to drop parachute flares which silhouetted the enemy vessels, while the two light cruisers and two destroyers of Force K remained concealed in the dark.

Meanwhile, the Fleet Air Arm also benefited from his reconnaissance, as night-flying Swordfish and Albacore torpedo-bombers from Malta located and attacked enemy shipping.

So closely did Spooner work with the Navy that he received the great compliment of an official signal ordering him to attend the operations room at 11 am daily for a pink gin.

This cosy relationship continued until Force K was subsumed into a larger unit. Then, in early 1942, Spooner succumbed to the stress of frequent night operations and the enemy's relentless daytime air attacks; Lloyd ordered him to rest. Shortly afterwards Spooner was awarded the DFC. The citation paid tribute to his "persistence against great odds", and to his "exceptional skill and determination".

Neither did the Navy ignore Spooner's contribution, inviting him to a splendid lunch at which they overlooked his speech – delivered after much port had been consumed – advocating the takeover of the Fleet Air Arm by Coastal Command.

Anthony Spooner was born in London on November 26 1916, and educated at Charterhouse. He began working for an insurance company in Worthing, Sussex, for £10 a month, but was already finding this tedious when he fell in with the young bloods at Shoreham Flying Club; they inspired him to obtain a commercial pilot's licence. He was accepted as a pupil at Brooklands Flying Club, near Weybridge in Surrey in October 1937. Spooner also broadened his training by joining the Royal Air Force Volunteer Reserve (RAFVR) as a sergeant.

In 1938, after gaining his commercial licence and an instructor's certificate, he was employed by Liverpool Flying Club at Speke and joined the government's Civil Air Guard programme to train pilot volunteers.

After the outbreak of war, Spooner was commissioned as a pilot officer. In 1940 he was posted to No 221, a Wellington operational squadron at Bircham Newton, near the Wash.

As Spooner arrived, the squadron was being equipped with ASV radar in preparation for a move to Northern Ireland, and then to Iceland for Atlantic patrols. His next posting was to Malta.

On his return from the Mediterranean, he took charge of a unit training Wellington crews to drop torpedoes, until he was posted as a flight commander in No 53, a Consolidated Liberator squadron. He immediately fell in love with the four-engine Liberator and admired its ability to lose two engines yet remain airborne. Another bonus was its very effective U-boat-hunting ASV radar, much more advanced than on his earlier Wellington. On an early sortie, Spooner's Liberator was bounced by five Me 110 fighters which damaged two engines, killed one air gunner, and wounded another. The Liberator and the dead man were replaced the same day.

In 1944 Spooner's "high degree of skill and courage" was recognised with a DSO. The citation added that, on one night sortie, Squadron Leader Spooner had attacked two U-boats, releasing depth charges over both of them in the same run. Shortly afterwards, he had located and attacked two more.

After the war Spooner was a pilot with the British Overseas Airways Corporation (BOAC, later British Airways). He also became active in the British Airline Pilots' Association (BALPA), being twice elected chairman.

In 1956 he became honorary secretary of the International Federation of Airline Pilots' Associations (FALPA). Four years later he began to fly BOAC's Boeing 707s on transatlantic and round-the-world routes.

In retirement, Spooner devoted himself to golf and bridge, at which he was a double national master. He also published a number of books, including an autobiography, *In Full Flight*.

He married, in 1939, Anne Hunt, who survives him with their two sons and a daughter.

THE GIRLS

SHEILA SCOTT
20 OCTOBER 1988

Sheila Scott, who has died aged 61, became an international heroine in 1966 when she was the first European woman to fly solo around the world.

As an official of the National Aeronautics and Space Administration noted at the time: "Sheila Scott belongs in the company of Lindbergh and Earhart and Saint Exupery."

A tense, fragile blonde and an inveterately nervous smoker, Scott decided to become a pilot in 1959. Stretched out among a group of flaked-out friends recovering from a heavy party, she announced to no-one in particular that she was going to learn to fly. Within a year she had a private pilot's licence.

Gripped by flying-fever, she bought herself a former RAF de Havilland Tiger Moth, modified with an enclosed cockpit and painted blue with silver wings. She christened it Myth, equipped it for air racing and set about winning trophies.

Scott had found her vocation. She coveted a commercial licence, and was shattered when she was turned down on grounds of imperfect eyesight. But in 1961 she visited America, where doctors said that her sight was adequate and she gained a commercial licence as a ferry pilot. Eventually British doctors reversed their decision, and she went on to qualify for a variety of aircraft, ranging from helicopters to seaplanes.

But the excitement of competitive flying proved too alluring; Scott compared it to taking a drug: "You cannot have it once without wanting to recapture it again and again." In 1964 she abandoned commercial work, sold Myth, hired a single-engine Piper Comanche 400, Myth Sun Pip, and hurled herself at 15 European light aircraft records: she broke the lot within 36 hours.

Ready to take on the world, Scott took off from London Airport in a Piper Comanche 260, christened Myth Too on May 18 1966. It was a nightmare. Her radio worked only intermittently; bureaucratic jacks-in-office frustrated her arrivals and departures; navigational and electrical equipment went haywire; the weather opposed her. Beset by difficulty and fatigue she became feverish and contracted dysentery.

Yet she flew on, covering almost 32,000 miles in 189 flying hours. Just before take-off Myth Too had taxied to the statue of Alcock and Brown, the British Atlantic pioneer fliers, and Scott had touched it for luck. At her lowest moments she consoled herself by talking to Buck Tooth, – a toy rabbit talisman which sat on her cabin fuel tank.

Her achievement won her the award she always valued most, the American Harmon trophy for the year's most outstanding women pilot. She also picked up among other awards and accolades the Silver Award of Merit of the Guild of Air Pilots and Air Navigators of which she was the first woman recipient.

It took nothing away from her performance that two years earlier an American, Jerrie Mock, has been the first woman to fly solo around the world. Scott went on to take many other records, and to write two books about her adventures, *I must Fly* (1968) and *On Top of the World* (1973) before ill-health cut back her activities.

Sheila Christine Scott was born at Worcester in 1927 and educated locally at the Alison Ottley School. She was rebellious and came close to expulsion; but, having volunteered to train as a nurse at Haslar, the naval hospital at Portsmouth, she responded well to the discipline which helped to form her determined character.

At the same time, though, trysts with amorous midshipmen and the uncertainties of life in a wartime port instilled in her an urgent desire to live for the moment, however dangerously. Immediately after the 1939-45 War this took the form of acting in small film parts and in repertory.

Ever restless, Scott went on to experiment with modelling, writing and dress designing. Her self-imposed absence of security took its toll, and she sought serenity in Buddhism, among other things, before finding her true metier and surrendering to "a lonely impulse of delight".

Hungry for new adventure after flying the world, Scott found herself short of funds. By chance she fell in with Ken Wood, the food-mixer manufacturer, who was about to open a factory in South Africa and he agreed to back her. She took the Cape Town record in July 1967 and reversed the process back to London the same month.

In 1969 she broke the North Atlantic east-to-west direct crossing record, and the same year set still more world records, including those for London to Kenya and South Africa and South Africa to London. In December she survived desperate troubles as one of three solo fliers taking part in an England to Australia air race.

On the principle that long-distance flying was the elixir which kept her alive she went on to fly twice more around the world and in 1971 made the first solo light aircraft flight over the North Pole — probably the most testing flight of her career. Her main unfulfilled ambition was to fly over the South Pole; but in 1972 it was ended when Mythre was wrecked by hurricane Agnes in Pennsylvania.

Always needing money to maintain her flying "high", Scott never recovered financially. She ended her days living alone in a one bedroom basement flat in Pimlico on little more than a state pension – though recently this was augmented by a fund raised by Peter Cadbury, the businessman and former pilot in the Fleet Air Arm.

In the aviation world Scott was widely clubbable, being co-founder and first governor of the British section of Ninety-Nines Inc, the International Association of Licensed Women Pilots. She was also the first British member of Whirly Girls, the association of the first 100 women helicopter pilots in the world. Balloons and airships also interested her and she helped to found the British Balloon and Airships Club.

Aviation awards were heaped upon her, among them the Brabazon of Tara awards in 1965, 1967, and 1968 for outstanding achievement by a woman pilot, the Royal Aero Club's Britannia Trophy in 1968 and its Gold Medal in 1972. She was appointed OBE in 1968.

Scott married in 1945 but the marriage only lasted five years and she never remarried.

BEATRICE "TILLY" SHILLING
18 APRIL 1990

Beatrice "Tilly" Shilling, who has died aged 81, was not only a notable aero engineer, responsible for remedying a defect in the Rolls-Royce Merlin engine during the Second World War, but also a renowned racing motorcyclist.

In the 1930s she stormed round the Brooklands circuit and was awarded a coveted Gold Star for lapping the track at more than 100 mph on her Norton 500.

"Tilly" Shilling was once described by a fellow scientist as "a flaming pathfinder of women's lib"; she always rejected any suggestion that as a woman she might be inferior to a man in technical and scientific fields.

In 1940, when Hurricane and Spitfire pilots encountered a life-or-death carburettor problem, she was already a highly regarded scientist at the Royal Aircraft Establishment at Farnborough.

The problem which landed on her desk in the carburation department was this: pilots were obliged to turn on their backs in combat to dive because the "negative-G" of simply putting the nose down resulted in starving the engine, causing it to splutter or cut out.

This was a critical defect since the Daimler-Benz engine powering enemy Me 109s permitted Luftwaffe pilots to perform the manoeuvre unhindered. Miss Shilling came up with a simple stop-gap device – which cost less, as it happened, than a shilling.

Nicknamed "Miss Shilling's Orifice", it was a metal disc about the size of an old threepenny bit, with a small hole in the middle. It was brazed into the fighter's fuel pipe, and when the pilot accelerated in a dive the disc stopped even momentary starvation of the Merlin engine. By March 1941 Miss Shilling's Orifice had been installed throughout Fighter Command, sufficing until replaced by an improved carburettor.

A butcher's daughter, Beatrice Shilling was born at Waterlooville, Hants, on March 8 1909 and after working as an electrician and electrical linesman she took an engineering degree at Manchester University.

In the 1930s she was recruited as a scientific officer by the RAE and began on a small salary doing fairly menial work. Even as a senior member of that establishment she was renowned for rolling up her sleeves and getting her hands dirty – shopworkers respected the fact that she could braze a butt joint between two pieces of copper with the skill of a fitter.

When she married George Naylor, whom she had met at aerodynamics night-school classes, colleagues presented her with a set of stocks and dies. It was said that she turned her own wedding ring on a lathe in stainless steel.

After the war she shone in charge of investigations at Farnborough – such as a probe into aquaplaning by aircraft taking off or landing on wet runways. These occurrences raised particular public alarm when an Elizabethan airliner crashed on take-off in slush at Munich, killing most of the Manchester United football team.

Her investigation of the related problems included conducting a series of trials for the Engineering Physics Department to assess braking performance on an experimental high-friction runway surface in conditions of heavy rain. She summoned a convoy of bowsers to spray water on the concrete, while a wingless naval Scimitar ran up engines as if for take-off.

Miss Shilling shared her passion for speed on wheels with her husband, and visitors to their home were astonished by the variety of motor-cycle parts scattered around. In the 1950s she successfully raced her 1935 Lagonda Rapier at Silverstone, her skilful engine-tuning producing a speed of more than 100 mph.

She also participated in sportscar racing at Goodwood, and another of her pastimes was pistol shooting.

Miss Shilling was appointed OBE in 1948 and retired in 1969, after 36 years at Farnborough. She is survived by her husband.

PEGGY SALAMAN
12 SEPTEMBER 1990

Peggy Salaman, the aviatrix who has died in Arizona aged 82, became an international celebrity while still a bright "Young Thing" when she beat the London to Cape Town light aeroplane record, picking up a couple of lion cubs on the way.

On October 30 1931 – with a "Cheerio, Mummy, I'm determined to do or die and, believe me, I'm going to do" – Miss Salaman waved her mother good-bye and flew off into the night from the Channel coast airfield at Lympne in Kent.

Peggy Salaman's flight captured the imagination of the press; here was "The Girl With Everything Money Could Buy Who Had Got Bored With It All". Such details as the fact that she had packed an evening gown for Cape Town – and that she had brought along packets of chewing gum to seal any petrol tank leaks – were lovingly chronicled.

Five days, six hours and 40 minutes after she left Lympne she landed in Cape Town accompanied by Gordon Store, her South African navigator and fellow pilot. Her time knocked more than a day off the previous record of Lt-Cdr Glen Kidston, who that spring had completed the journey in six days and 10 hours.

But, taking into account the fragility of the little single-engined de Havilland Puss Moth, it was an even greater achievement than the figures indicate. Kidston had flown a heavier and more powerful Lockheed Vega – in effect, a Mini compared with a Rolls.

Indeed the Moth was hardly more than a standard flying club machine, maximum speed 125 mph. There was, however, an additional fuel tank and a metal propellor to add about 5 mph to the speed. Navigation lights were fitted but there was no radio.

The Moth, which she called the Good Hope, was a present from her mother. It was dressed in a livery of Navy blue with a pale blue stripe – "Like the perambulator I had for her as a baby," said her mother.

The daughter of a businessman and property developer, Peggy Louise Salaman was born in London in 1907 and educated at Queen's College, Harley Street, and Bentley Priory (which, in 1940, was to become Dowding's HQ during the Battle of Britain).

Finished in Paris, she did a London Season before, in pursuit of her passionate determination to fly, taking lessons at Hanworth with Capt Finley, a former RFC pilot.

She obtained an 'A' licence, and in July 1931 she entered the Moth in the King's Cup air race, where – accompanied by Lt Geoffrey Rodd as her pilot – she won the prize for the fastest machine.

That October, as she headed for Le Bourget in Paris on the first leg of her epic flight, Miss Salaman's only sartorial concession to aviation was a helmet. The rest of her attire in the cockpit comprised grey flannel trousers and a white sweater.

A pith helmet and shorts were packed with the ball gown for the tropics. With Store navigating, she flew the old "Red Route" of the British Empire.

After Rome and Athens came Juba, where she was much taken by a pair of lion cubs. She duly bought the cuddly young creatures for £25 and named them Juba and Joker; they were bottle-fed on board as the Good Hope progressed towards Entebbe.

Then it was on to Bulawayo, but the combination of nightfall and a hilly area urged caution, and she landed in wild bush country between Abercorn and Broken Hill, Northern Rhodesia.

Came the dawn and take-off was found to be

impossible until a strip had been prepared. Fortunately Store had armed himself with a machete and she had a revolver. Together they felled some young trees. An elephant trench was filled with earth to clear a runway.

Airborne again, Store, as she recalled, "threaded his way through Africa as easily as a taxi-man in London".

In the last stages of the adventure Miss Salaman left the 18-day-old cubs at Kimberley to be sent on by train. They had become too much of a handful.

On arriving at Cape Town and hearing that she had broken the record, she trilled: "How perfectly lovely!" She added: "We could have got here much earlier, but we slowed to 90 mph over gorgeous mountains and admired the magnificent scenery."

Afterwards she was told the Moth was now unfit to fly. Store stayed on in South Africa, but she sailed home with the lion cubs in the liner *Warwick Castle*.

At sea she heard that the celebrated aviator Jim Mollison, already chasing her record, had crashed in Egypt. She cabled to him: "Hard lines. You missed our luck."

Back in London she returned to the family in Cambridge Square, Bayswater. The cubs resided in the cloakroom, but as they grew the maids complained.

Not only were they considered potentially dangerous but there were disagreeable odours – despite unsparing applications of *eau de cologne* – and ineradicable scratches on the parquet floor. Bertram Mills came to the rescue but he was unable to tame them for his circus; eventually the lions, by now renamed Romeo and Juliet, were housed in a private zoo.

Subsequently she gained a commercial licence in America, where she entered a Los Angeles Air Derby and finished 42nd out of 80.

During the 1939-45 War she served in the WAAF, as a

plotter, and then in the Wrens. Afterwards she helped to look after displaced children at a camp in Brittany.

Miss Salaman was married briefly to Denis Flanders, the architectural and landscape artist.

During a visit to America in the 1950s she met her second husband, Walter Bell, an electrical engineer and airman with two private aircraft.

Flying around America together, they landed one day at Phoenix, Arizona, and were so enchanted with it that they bought a house in the adobe style and settled there.

███████████████

MONIQUE AGAZARIAN
3 MARCH 1993

Monique Agazarian, who has died aged 72, flew Spitfire and Hurricane fighters – as well as more than 20 other varieties of RAF and Fleet Air Arm aircraft – during the Second World War.

"Aggie" was one of a small elite of intrepid women pilots to wear the wings and uniform of the Air Transport Auxiliary ferry organisation. One of her contemporaries was Amy Johnson, the pre-war record breaker, who died after baling out over the Thames estuary.

One of the few women taught to fly with the ATA – the majority held peacetime licences – Agazarian was pretty "green" when first confronted with a Spitfire.

"I had been on leave," she recalled, "so when they asked me when I came back whether I had done my cockpit checks I thought they would not let me fly if I told the truth. So I said 'yes'.

"You had to be quick taking off in a Spitfire because they 'cooked' if they sat on the ground too long. So I just pointed it in the right direction and went."

Just after take-off, being unaccustomed to the cockpit layout, she caught her gauntlet in the prop control-lever and put it into course pitch. But she managed to recover "and had a glorious time".

"Spitfires really were delightful to fly," she enthused. "You just thought what you wanted to do and it did it.

"The first time I rolled I was quite nervous. But it turned over so sweetly. You really were part of the machine."

The 1st Lord Beaverbrook, then Minister of Aircraft Production, so valued "Aggie" and her fellow pilots that he gave them a pass, stating: "This pilot can authorise his or her own flights."

At the end of the war Agazarian interpreted this as permission for a low-level wing-tip "beat-up" of her mother's Knightsbridge home in a naval Seafire. That final fling typified Agazarian's irrepressible spirit. After resuming her studies on her return to civilian life, she went on to participate in a number of successful civil aviation business ventures.

The daughter of an Armenian born businessman, Monique Agazarian was born in Surrey on July 17 1920. When she was three her French mother bought a 1914–18 War Sopwith Pup for £5 at a Croydon auction and installed it at the bottom of the family garden.

The much-loved "toy" exerted a lasting influence on the Agazarian children.

One brother, Noel, fought with 609 Squadron in the Battle of Britain and was credited with $11\frac{1}{2}$ victories before he was killed in the Middle East in 1941. His Spitfire is displayed at the Imperial War Museum.

Another brother, Jack, was seconded from the RAF to the clandestine Special Operations Executive. Parachuted into France to help the Resistance, he was captured, tortured and executed. A third brother, Levon, flew fighters.

Young Monique was educated at the Convent of the Sacred Heart, Roehampton, before going to a Paris finishing school. Early in the war she helped nurse Sir Archibald McIndoe's "Guinea Pigs" (burned aircrew-patients) at the Queen Victoria Hospital, East Grinstead. She was also attached to the RAF at Uxbridge.

Determined to fly like her brothers – despite being below the ATA's height requirement of 5 ft 5 in – she wangled her way through the medical, and learned to fly on Magisters.

When the ATA ferry organisation was stood down at the end of the war she ran a Malcolm Club at RAF Gutersloh in Germany and took a commercial B-licence.

Island Services, a passenger charter which also flew flowers from the Scilly Islands, employed her as office manager. Soon she was flying Proctor charters and joyrides from Croydon and the Scillies.

After the company acquired its first Dragon Rapide, she flew the Jersey route too.

By 1948 she was managing director of Island Services' London operation. The next year she married Ray Rendall, a former RAF pilot whom she had recruited to fly for the firm. In that period she took IAS into joyriding, operating from Northolt and Heathrow. This proved a popular family treat and inspired some children to become pilots. Flights ranged from 10s to £1.15s for a view of London's dockland.

In 1950, by now chairman of Island Air Services (as the company had become), Agazarian launched weekend gambling jaunts to Deauville, extending the £4 return service to La Baule and Le Touquet.

The same year she piloted the IAS Rapide G-ALB Pickles III in the King's Cup air race, but a port engine oil leak forced her to retire on the final leg.

Joyriding flourished at Heathrow until it was curtailed

because of the ever-increasing amount of airline traffic. Towards the end of the 1950s she moved to Ramsgate Aerodrome in Kent, but it proved to be too distant from the market.

IAS was wound up and Agazarian briefly joined Air Links, before taking up residence in Lebanon.

In 1973 she returned home and took a part-time job with Air Training Services, the first private company to operate a jet simulator.

When she took the business over in 1976 she worked out of the Piccadilly Hotel with the slogan "Fly Down Piccadilly".

Later based at Wycombe Air Park, Booker, Bucks, she established a flight simulator and ground training centre between the Red Baron restaurant and control tower.

She continued to commute to Booker from Knightsbridge in her battered Peugeot ("Ben Hur") until she sold the business in October 1992.

In 1988 she published *Instrument Flying and Background to the Instrument and IMC Ratings*.

Her marriage to Rendall was dissolved in 1973. They had three daughters.

MARGOT GORE

20 AUGUST 1996

Margot Gore, who has died aged 80, commanded a busy ferry pool of the Air Transport Auxiliary during the Second World War.

Even among the ATA's legendary galaxy of intrepid women pilots, Gore stood out.

An unflappable character, she had a wise head beyond her years and a delightful sense of humour – these natural qualities of leadership brought her control of No 15 Ferry Pool at Hamble on Southampton Water in September 1941 in the senior rank of commandant.

Her team of some 30 women pilots – and a host of engineers, drivers, cooks and operations staff in support held Gore in great respect. As a pilot she set them a high standard of airmanship.

She was probably the first woman to pilot a Boeing Flying Fortress and handled the bomber superbly – never more so than on the day she astonished Hamble by passing low over a hangar and landing on the tiny grass airfield.

Ferrying many types of new and repaired military aircraft between factories and operational airfields – often without radio – could be perilous in wartime Britain. Once, in the heavily defended area of Southampton and Portsmouth, she was approaching Eastleigh in a Hudson bomber when an entire balloon barrage began to rise from the ground and enmesh her. Cables missed her by inches.

Margot Wyndham Gore was born at Worthing on January 24, 1913. She spent some of her childhood foxhunting in Ireland.

She began her working life as a stenographer at Smithfield Market, and saved up for flying lessons in the Civil Air Guard. When war came she was a flying instructor at Romford.

Afterwards she taught at the West London Flying Club and, together with her wartime colleague Joan Nayler, joined the WAAF Volunteer Reserve on its formation.

It was characteristic of Gore's determination that she decided to sit the School Certificate in her late thirties, in order to prepare for her studies as an osteopath.

She went on to win the London School of Osteopathy's gold medal and to become chairman of the British School of osteopathy.

Margot Gore was an accomplished golfer and ladies' captain of the Huntercombe Golf Club. She was appointed MBE in 1945.

━━━━━━━━━━

AIR COMMANDANT
DAME JEAN CONAN DOYLE
19 NOVEMBER 1997

Air Commandant Dame Jean Conan Doyle, who has died aged 84, was Director of the Women's Royal Air Force from 1963 to 1966.

During the Battle of Britain of 1940 she served in one of the RAF's most secret intelligence units. Following a spell earlier that summer at RAF Fighter Command's frontline No 11 Group headquarters, she was posted to the Air Ministry's experimental station at Cheadle, Staffordshire.

Cheadle was the centre of a new chain of wireless telegraphy (W/T) stations known as the Y Service, and Jean Conan Doyle was involved in the interception of Luftwaffe W/T traffic between German bombers, reconnaissance aircraft and their controllers.

At Y Service's branch at Kingsdown, Kent, she was also involved with the interception and translation of enemy fighter aircraft R/T (radio telephony) transmissions, reporting to Fighter Command's sector stations.

Jean Lena Annette Conan Doyle was born at Crowborough, Sussex, on December 21 1912, the daughter of Sir Arthur Conan Doyle and his second wife Jean Leckie. His first wife, Louise, had died of tuberculosis.

Jean Conan Doyle's earliest memories were dominated by her father's industry as a writer and, as she grew up, by what seemed to be the all-pervading presence of his celebrated character, Sherlock Holmes. She recalled her father writing in pen and ink, the nib scratching non-stop across sheet after sheet, and then listening at the lunch table while he read his morning's work aloud.

This she enjoyed; of Sir Arthur's children – Jean had two brothers – she was the bookish one, and the only one allowed into his study when he was at work. Yet outdoors, and using the name Billy (to avoid confusion with her mother Jean), she accepted a tomboy role with her brothers in the cricket nets.

She was only 17, and barely out of Granville School, Eastbourne, when her father died in 1930. By then she had seen much of the world as his travelling companion on lecture tours of Europe, the United States, South America, Canada, South Africa and Australia.

In 1938, with the prospect of war, Jean Conan Doyle joined No 46 (County of Sussex) RAF Company, attached to the ATS (there was as yet no Women's Auxiliary Air Force). Having enlisted as an Aircraft-woman, 2nd Class, she was in March 1940 commissioned as an assistant section officer. After serving at No 60 Group and 11 Group, she joined Y Service, and was then posted to No 63 Wireless Unit, Bomber Command's No 9 Group HQ, Fighter Command HQ, and RAF Northern Ireland.

Jean Conan Doyle embarked on her post-war career with No 28 Group, moving to the Bückeburg Air HQ of the British Forces of Occupation in 1947, where she was senior WRAF officer.

In the early 1950s she held appointments at RAF Technical Training Command, as Deputy Director of WRAF Personnel, and then in the Inspector General's department. In 1956 she received command of the WRAF Officer Cadet Training Unit at Hawkinge, in Kent.

Three years later Jean Conan Doyle was appointed Inspector General of the WRAF, a troubleshooting post which involved a lot of travel and suited her outgoing personality. She was always willing to help and was a good listener, with plenty of time for everyone.

Frustrated by the wastage of WRAF officers and airwomen through marriage within the Service, she began to make a practice of asking new wives to remain. At first this caused some confusion, but married couples soon became the norm.

Following posts at the Air Ministry, and as Chief WRAF Administrative Officer, Technical Training Command, Jean Conan Doyle was in 1963 appointed Director of the WRAF. She retired in 1966.

After the death of her brother Adrian in 1971, she devoted much of her time to protecting her father's copyrights. These ran out in 1980, the 50th anniversary of Sir Arthur's death, but have since been revived under European arrangements. American rules entitle the estate to 70 years' copyright. Thus Jean Conan Doyle continued to hunt for unauthorised publication.

As she became more involved with the legacy of her father's affairs, she came to sympathise with Sir Arthur's exasperation over the daily inescapability of reference to Sherlock Holmes. She knew exactly, she once said, how her father felt when he pushed Holmes off the Reichenbach Falls. Yet she prized her father's copy of the Holmes adventure *A Study in Scarlet.*

Whenever she spotted an attempt by a writer or filmmaker to stray from her father's intentions, she would fire off a letter. She was not pleased by the film *The Seven Per Cent Solution* (1976) in which Nicol Williamson, playing Holmes, sought psychiatric help from Freud. Nor did she approve of posters for a film of *Brigadier Gerard* which displayed two naked girls, claiming that it would have offended her father.

But she applauded Jeremy Brett for his cold and unemotional characterisation of Holmes in the stage play *The Secret of Sherlock Holmes*, and later in the television series.

Jean Conan Doyle was an Honorary ADC to the Queen from 1963 to 1966, a governor of the Royal Star and Garter Home from 1968 to 1982, and a member of the Council of the Officers' Pension Society from 1970 to 1975 (vice-president from 1981 to 1988). She was a member of the Committee of the Not Forgotten Association from 1975 to 1991, serving as president from 1981 to 1991.

She received the Air Efficiency Award in 1949 and was appointed OBE in 1948, and DBE in 1963.

In 1965, aged 53, she married Air Vice-Marshal Sir Geoffrey Bromet, who was then 73. After his death in 1983 she reverted to her maiden name.

ELIZABETH MORTIMER
26 AUGUST 1997

Elizabeth Mortimer, who has died aged 85, won the Military Medal during the Luftwaffe's sustained assault on Biggin Hill, Kent, the celebrated sector station for RAF Fighter Command in the Battle of Britain.

On Sunday, August 18 1940, Elizabeth Mortimer, serving as a sergeant in the Women's Auxiliary Air Force, was manning the switchboard in the airfield armoury when a heavy raid began.

The raid hit a nearby Bofors anti-aircraft gun, with loss of life, damaged motor transport sheds, pockmarked the airfield with craters and littered it with unexploded bombs. But Elizabeth Mortimer stayed at her post.

As accurate bombing intensified, she ignored the danger, calmly continuing to relay essential messages to defence positions.

Then, before the All Clear had sounded, she picked up a bundle of red flags and ran all over the airfield marking each unexploded bomb, thus helping Hurricane and Spitfire pilots returning from combat to land safely.

As she continued to mark danger spots, a bomb exploded nearby, badly winding her. But after recovering she carried on planting the flags; at one point an officer ordered her to stop, but once his back was turned she resumed.

Elizabeth Mortimer was the first WAAF to win a Military Medal, and one of three to be awarded the medal at Biggin Hill during the summer of 1940. Her citation noted that she had "displayed exceptional courage and coolness which had a great moral effect on all those with whom she came in contact."

Joan Eugenie Mortimer, always known as Elizabeth, was born on June 2 1912. She was called up as a clerk three days before the outbreak of war on Sept 3 1939. After serving in the armoury at Hendon, her Squadron – No 601 (County of London)- was moved to Biggin Hill.

Determined to remain with the squadron, along with her friend Betty Dobell, Elizabeth Mortimer had asked for a transfer but did not wait for approval. The two WAAFs drove through the night to Biggin and were reunited with 601. It was six weeks before their Hendon commanding officer discovered where they were.

Following the bombing of Biggin Hill, it was discovered that Elizabeth Mortimer had sustained serious damage to her ears. Eventually she was discharged with a disability pension.

After the war, she worked as a child minder and in

other domestic jobs to help support her widowed mother at their Stowmarket home.

During the Battle of Britain, Elizabeth Mortimer had become engaged to a fighter pilot. But he was killed and she never married.

OPS & OPS

WING COMMANDER
ROBERT WRIGHT
27 JANUARY 1992

Bob Wright, who has died aged 85, was a Hollywood scriptwriter in the 1930s, but no imaginary adventure could have been more dramatic than his experiences during the Second World War.

Newly returned from California, Wright was plucked from the radar filter room at Fighter Command's HQ at Bentley Priory in Middlesex by Sir Hugh Dowding, the leader of "the Few", to be his personal assistant.

Throughout the most critical weeks of the Battle of Britain in the summer and autumn of 1940 Wright was at Dowding's side, or sitting as watchdog by his door. He dealt with all the Fighter chief's paperwork, and controlled calls to the solitary telephone on his desk.

When eventually "Stuffy" Dowding decided to break silence on his direction of the air battle, he selected Wright as the medium. In a foreword to Wright's *Dowding and the Battle of Britain* (1969), the Air Chief Marshal described the author as "someone who I felt understood and shared, with discretion, my views on my career in the Royal Air Force."

After the war Wright devoted himself to seeking to set right what he described as "the grave injustice done Lord Downing in November 1940", when the victor of the Battle of Britain was virtually dismissed.

Such was Dowding's regard for Wright (then a flight lieutenant) that he commended him to his successor, Sir Sholto Douglas. Wright went on to serve Douglas at home and in the Middle East, and also served Sir Keith

Park in Cairo. But, although approaching 40, Wright escaped from his desk to fly as a night-fighter radar navigator.

A naval engineer's son, Robert Charles Wright was born at Portsmouth on September 3 1906. He spent some of his childhood in South Africa before moving with his family to Australia, where he was educated at Scotch College, Melbourne.

He was rejected by the Air Force in Australia on the grounds of poor eyesight and in 1926 he joined the *Wellington Evening Post* in New Zealand as a reporter.

Then in the early 1930s, he went out to California where he studied at Stanford University, worked for a spell in a bookshop in San Francisco and tried his luck in Hollywood where he obtained freelance script assignments for films and radio.

On the outbreak of war in 1939 Wright returned to Britain. He was commissioned into the RAFVR and posted to Fighter Command HQ.

Sholto Douglas, on inheriting Wright as his personal assistant from Dowding, quickly warmed to this "Anglo-South African-Australian-New Zealand-Californian", who had "an independence of mind and a rather prickly dislike of red tape" in tune with his own outlook.

He never did discover, however, just how Wright despite his age, and being medically categorised "permanently unfit for flying" succeeded in wangling himself into "Cat's Eyes" Cunningham's 604 Squadron of Beaufighters, in the autumn of 1941.

Wright's pilot, George McLannahan, and fellow members of the air crew knew him affectionately as "the Old Boy".

After Wright, temporarily serving with another squadron, had helped to cover the North Africa "Torch" landings, Douglas ordered the Old Boy to return to his desk. But Wright managed to persuade Park – whom he had also served as personal assistant – to post him home from the Middle East to rejoin Cunningham. "Cat's Eyes" was now commanding No 85, a Mosquito long-range night-fighter squadron, escorting bombers over Germany.

In November 1944 Wright was returning to base in Norfolk, when his Mosquito crashed while landing. The pilot was killed but Wright, grievously burned, was courageously rescued by Tom Woodhead, a member of his ground crew.

Wright was transferred from hospital at Ely to the Queen Victoria Hospital, East Grinstead, where he was repaired by Sir Archibald McIndoe, the plastic surgeon, and welcomed by fellow patients as a member of the "Guinea Pig Club". Hardly had Wright left McIndoe's care, however, when a V2 rocket landed 50 yards away from his home in Kent, and he was back in hospital.

Deciding that enough was enough, Douglas – by now leading Coastal Command at its Northwood Headquarters – sent a motor-car for his former personal assistant. Douglas told Wright in no uncertain terms that while Wright had his deepest sympathy, he really had stuck his neck out and asked for trouble.

Douglas took Wright with him to his next appointment in Germany and when Douglas succeeded Montgomery as military governor of the British Zone, Wright stayed on as a personal staff officer.

A typical incident of the Wright-Douglas partnership was when Wright told his chief that he had been offered a trip to America and Douglas replied: "Why can't I go too? I've never been to America, and you know my father lives there."

So Wright fixed it with Maj-Gen Bob Harper of the US Army Air Force and off they flew in Harper's B-17 Flying Fortress. Their escapades in California and other points west became known as their "Lost Three Weeks".

It was a welcome break before Wright's attendance at the Nuremberg war crimes trials, where he had the – as he termed it – distressing experience of coming face to face with Goering.

After being released as a wing commander in 1947, Wright returned to screen writing at Elstree Studios and then established himself as an author. First he collaborated with C F Rawnsley for *Night Fighter* (1957), a bestseller which told the story of Rawnsley's brilliant night-skies partnership with "Cat's Eyes" Cunningham.

Then Wright collaborated with Marshal of the RAF Lord Douglas of Kirtleside (as Sholto Douglas had become) on two autobiographical volumes, describing the great airman's service in both World Wars: *Years of Combat* (1963) and *Years of Command* (1966).

Later Wright embarked upon a history of the RAF, an ambitious project sadly defeated by a series of heart attacks, and by increasing disability from spondylitis, which developed after his wartime crash.

Wright rejected Douglas's offers to submit his name for an honour. He is survived by his wife, Margaret, a son and three daughters.

PILOT OFFICER
JAMES "JIMMY" WRIGHT
12 FEBRUARY 1993

Jimmy Wright, who has died aged 70, was a grievously burned and blinded RAF film cameraman of the Second World War; his example inspired countless other disabled and handicapped servicemen.

For seven years Wright was a patient of Sir Archibald McIndoe, the plastic surgeon, as one of his "Guinea Pigs" at the Queen Victoria Hospital, East Grinstead. Subsequently Wright astonished even that most optimistic and supportive of surgeons by launching a film production company.

Although terribly burned and left with only partial use of his hands, Jimmy Wright was determined to follow the example of his father, Ernest ("Jim") Wright, a Royal Flying Corps fighter pilot in the First World War who had gone on to become a distinguished newsreel war correspondent.

In 1944 King George VI decorated both father and son at the same Buckingham Palace investiture with a MBE and DFC respectively.

Jimmy Wright had been commissioned into the RAF as a pilot officer in 1942. He qualified as an air gunner so that he could fly as aircrew, although he was an RAF Film Unit cameraman. While flying with No 223, a Baltimore bomber squadron, he had two lucky escapes before the crash which was to deliver him into McIndoe's hands.

First, his aircraft was hit by enemy fire over mountains in central Italy. He was not wearing a parachute at the time and after struggling into a harness, discovered, as he fell to earth, that he had put it on the wrong way round. He grabbed the rip cord in the nick of time. On the second occasion he was rescued after an American ship had been hit by an aerial torpedo in the Mediterranean.

Wright was taking off in a Marauder, from the captured Italian naval base at Taranto, when the reconnaissance bomber crashed. The flames disfigured him beyond recognition.

Although he was just alive, an Army warrant officer included Wright's name in a casualty signal in the certainty that within hours he would be dead.

As it happened, his father was in the Mediterranean theatre as a war correspondent and flew over to investigate. Jim Wright found his son alive but massively drugged.

Wright Senior's experience of morphia in the 1914–18 War convinced him that such doses would kill his son. He seized a syringe from a nurse and dashed it to the floor. He then arranged for Jimmy Wright to be freighted home – "bandaged from head to foot like a mummy and packed between two aero-engines in a Liberator", as Edward Bishop put it in his history of *The Guinea Pig Club*, and subsequently *McIndoe's Army*.

James Ernest Frederick Wright was born on August 18 1922 and educated at Denham Lodge School and the Regent Street Polytechnic. After a brief spell in a bank he joined Technicolor in 1940 at Harmondsworth as a trainee in the camera department. At one stage he carried equipment for Freddie Young, the celebrated film cameraman.

At the age of 18 Wright was rejected for RAF aircrew because of poor sight, but in 1942 he was admitted through "the back door", as a cameraman wearing an air gunner's brevet. He reported to the RAF Film Unit at Pinewood Studios, where at first he could not understand why "airmen" failed to salute him – until he discovered they were film extras.

Soon he was accompanying bomber operations over

France and the Low Countries, before being posted to the Desert Air Force.

On his arrival at the "Sty" (as members of the Guinea Pig Club, McIndoe's aircrew patients, called the Queen Victoria Hospital), Wright recognised the voice of the anaesthetist, Dr Russell Davies, officiating at the first of his many operations. When he was at Technicolor Wright had filmed the wounds of six of Davies's early wartime burns patients.

Now Wright was a Guinea Pig himself, at the outset of a long odyssey of pain, rehabilitation and resettlement which culminated in years of endeavour on behalf of others.

In the normal course of events he might not have expected to work again. Yet in 1952 he founded Anglo-Scottish Films at Shepperton Studios. It proved a testing period for a sightless man. One night he returned home to find that the manservant looking after him had stolen much of his property.

But he persevered to produce films for the Central Office of Information and businesses, as well as commercials for cinema and television. In 1961 he set up Film City Productions, which became renowned for its special effects studio. Cinexsa Film Productions followed.

When Granada Television's *Searchlight* current affairs programme needed outside assistance, Wright provided personnel, particularly for overseas locations. He also filmed Bob Hope shows for General Motors.

In 1967 Wright married Jan Jessey, who worked tirelessly alongside him. As a "St Dunstaner" himself Wright did not stint his efforts for the blind. From 1977 he ran the *Spelthorne Talking News*, a local report service for the blind and other handicapped people. In September 1990 he parascended across the Channel from Ramsgate to Dunkirk in aid of the RAF Benevolent Fund's Battle of Britain 50th anniversary appeal. He was accompanied by two fellow members of the Guinea Pig Club, Les Wilkins (who had lost both hands in 1944) and Des O'Connell.

In 1991 Wright produced *Sight by Touch*, a video for the Braille Authority. Wright was appointed OBE in 1980 and received a BAFTA award in 1981. He was on the Court of the Royal School of the Blind, Leatherhead, and the committee of the Julie Andrews Appeal to fight arterial disease.

Irrepressibly cheerful, Jimmy Wright was great company. He was invariably first at breakfast and almost last to bed at the Guinea Pig annual reunions known as "Lost Weekends".

He is survived by his wife and two sons.

GROUP CAPTAIN TOM GLEAVE
12 JUNE 1993

Group Captain Tom Gleave, who has died aged 84, was a gallant fighter pilot in the Battle of Britain, in which he was grievously burned.

Shot down in flames over Kent at the height of the battle in the summer of 1940, Gleave became one of the first "Guinea Pigs" – burns patients of Sir Archibald McIndoe, the RAF's celebrated wartime consultant in plastic surgery, at the Queen Victoria Hospital in East Grinstead.

Gleave had arrived there suffering from "standard Hurricane burns", to face, hands, arms and legs. McIndoe ("the Maestro" as Guinea Pigs called him) immediately set about growing him a new nose.

Gleave's seniority, as a regular squadron leader and

"elderly" fighter pilot of 32, assured him the office of Chief Guinea Pig for life.

For more than half a century he inspired the club's fund-raising and welfare activities, ever mindful of the needs of surviving members as they entered old age.

The years of aftercare were the legacy of the spirit fostered in Ward 3, where McIndoe introduced a regime quite alien to the lie-to-attention, standby-your-beds attitude that had prevailed until then.

Visitors to Ward 3 often retreated in horror. This was not because of the appalling nature of the Guinea Pigs' injuries, or the grotesque disfigurement of rhinoplasty patients growing new noses from other parts of their bodies, but rather the discovery of beer barrels in the ward, and regular "grogging parties" at weekends.

A German cannon shell had ignited the right fuel tank of Gleave's Hurricane as he attacked a formation of bombers over Kent; the fire engulfed him rapidly. He felt for the revolver which he wore in the cockpit as a last resort.

His clothes were on fire, the skin of his hands and wrists blistering in white bubbles and the flames licking at his legs, but he rejected the option of suicide and struggled to escape, only to be thwarted by his oxygen tube, which refused to disconnect.

Clawing off the helmet to which it was attached, he opened the canopy. Then an explosion ejected him more suddenly and forcefully than he would have wished.

Having landed by parachute near the fighter station at Biggin Hill, Gleave was taken to Orpington Hospital. He came round from an emergency operation to find himself not in but under a bed. There was an air raid, and he could hear the noise of the bombs.

Shortly afterwards his wife arrived. Confronted by her husband bandaged like a mummy with slits for his eyes (the lids were burnt) she asked him: "What on earth have you been doing with yourself?"

"I had a row with a German," replied Gleave. His answer later became the title of his short book about his wartime experience.

Thomas Percy Gleave was born on Sept 6 1908 and educated at Westminster High School and Liverpool Collegiate School.

He joined the Sefton Tanning Company in 1924, and four years later earned a pilot's "A" licence at the Liverpool and Merseyside Flying Club. Later that year he went to Canada, where he worked for a tannery. On his return home in 1930 he was commissioned into the RAF.

Passed out as an "exceptional pilot" in 1931 – and subsequently as an "exceptional fighter pilot" – Gleave was soon a member of the RAF's aerobatic team.

In 1933 he determined to enter the record books with a flight to Ceylon, but was obliged to crash-land his aircraft in mountainous Turkish terrain. The next year he qualified as a flying instructor. After several postings as an instructor he joined Bomber Command on New Year's Day 1939.

When war broke out Gleave agitated for a fighter squadron, until eventually his wish was granted. He commanded 253, a Hurricane squadron, from June to August 1940, when he handed over to Squadron Leader H M Starr. After Starr was killed on Aug 31 Gleave resumed command.

Before Gleave was himself shot down his official score was "one confirmed and four probable": postwar investigation raised this to five Me 109s on August 30 and a Ju 88 on August 31.

Fighter Command's preferred policy during the Battle of Britain was for Spitfires to tackle the escorting 109s, while Hurricanes took on the bombers. For a Hurricane pilot to destroy a 109 was in itself an achievement, but to bag five in one day was astonishing.

The action in which Gleave shot down his 109s would have been sufficient, had confirmation been available, to rate him an official ace and at the least DFC. Gleave was promoted wing commander while he was lying in bed at the Royal Victoria. Partially repaired by the Maestro, he was restored to non-operational flying in August 1941; a pale patch on his forehead indicated the provenance of his new nose.

Operationally fit by October, he was given brief command of the fighter station at Northolt before taking over Manston, the frontline airfield on the Kent coast.

From there, on February 12 1942, he dispatched six Swordfish biplane torpedo bombers of the Fleet Air Arm's 825 Squadron on their ill-fated attempt to sink the battle-cruisers *Scharnhorst* and *Gneisenau* and the cruiser *Prinz Eugen* as they made their "Channel Dash". All six Swordfish were shot down in the Channel.

Convinced that circumstances had obliged him to send his men on a suicide mission, Gleave stood alone at the end of the runway and saluted each Swordfish as it took off.

Before leaving Manston in September 1942 Gleave pleaded for a long, wide runway of concrete or tarmac to save the crippled and short-of-fuel bombers which, having struggled across the Channel, were unable to reach their bases. Gleave's runway is still maintained for emergency military and civilian landings.

Gleave next joined the planning staff of "Operation Round Up" (later "Overlord"), the proposed invasion of Normandy. This entailed a promotion to Group Captain Air Plans, Allied Expeditionary Air Force. For his vital contribution to the invasion Gleave received the CBE and the US Legion of Merit (later changed for the Bronze Star).

From October 1 1944 until July 15 1945 he was General Eisenhower's Head of Air Plans at Supreme Headquarters Allied Expeditionary Force.

After VE Day Gleave returned to the "Sty" for further repairs. He later served as Senior Air Staff Officer, RAF Delegation to France, from 1945 to 1947.

After further staff appointments at home he underwent more plastic surgery at East Grinstead, and was invalided out of the RAF in 1953.

Thereafter Gleave joined the historical section of the Cabinet Office, where he was engaged on official histories of the Second World War. He spent more than 30 years on the task, mainly as a member of the Mediterranean and Middle East team.

He was elected a fellow of the Royal Historical Society, and was air historian and deputy chairman of the Battle of Britain Fighter Association. He also served the Blond McIndoe Centre for Medical Research and the East Grinstead Trust.

Gleave was twice mentioned in despatches, received the French Legion of Honour and Croix de Guerre, and was awarded the wings of the Polish and French air forces.

He married and had a son (who died in a canoeing accident in Canada) and a daughter.

FLIGHT LIEUTENANT
JACK MANN
11 NOVEMBER 1995

Jackie Mann, who has died at Nicosia aged 81, first showed his mettle as a Spitfire pilot in the Second World War; and his spirit was still undaunted nearly half a century later, when he was taken hostage in Beirut.

Jack Mann was born at Northampton on June 11 1914, and educated at St James's School before training as an aircraft engineer at Phillips and Powis of Reading.

His passion for aviation led him to volunteer for flying training, and by 1940 he was a sergeant pilot in No 64, a Spitfire squadron in Fighter Command. Later he served with 92 Squadron.

Mann relished the ebb and flow of fighting over southern England in the Battle of Britain, and set about the enemy with reckless bravado. Six times the Spitfire he was flying was hit; six times he succeeded in crash-landing his crippled aircraft.

His horror of baling out derived from the time when he had circled protectively above a colleague who had ejected, and watched helplessly as the man's burning body dropped out of the harness 1,000 feet from the ground.

On one occasion Mann's Spitfire was hit by 15 cannon shells over the Channel. He managed to make it back to land, though the starboard wing fell off on impact and killed two sheep.

Convinced that he had landed in occupied France, Mann beat out his burning clothing and returned to the cockpit to obtain his parachute which he threw into a ditch. His hope was that the Germans would fail to find it and deduce that he had baled out miles away.

Starting off through fields, Mann approached a farmhouse where he encountered an elderly woman who commiserated with him on his "horrible motor-cycle accident" and mounted her bicycle in search of a doctor. He was in Kent.

It is said that, on the fourth occasion that Mann's Spitfire was hit, his family arrived at the hospital with a coffin to collect the remains. They were told he had already returned to his squadron.

Mann's closest shave came in March 1941 when a bullet in the petrol tank set his plane ablaze as he was flying over the French coast. Rather than bring the Spitfire down in occupied France and become a prisoner of war, he determined to coax the aircraft back to England – notwithstanding the flames which were roasting his cheeks and forehead.

He crashed in a field but managed to get clear before the Spitfire exploded. Subsequently he underwent prolonged plastic surgery as one of Sir Archibald McIndoe's "Guinea Pigs" at the Queen Victoria Hospital, East Grinstead.

It was at this time that he met Sunnie, who was born Dilys Pritchard. They were married at Chiswick Registry office in 1943.

While Mann was in hospital he was awarded the DFM. When he recovered the RAF thought in terms of a ground posting in India, until Sunnie intervened with McIndoe. "Take him off flying," she warned, "and he'll blow up."

So, Mann became a night-fighter pilot and instructor before leaving the RAF at the end of the war as a flight lieutenant.

Afterwards the Manns moved to Beirut where Jackie was for more than 10 years a pilot for Middle East Airlines, while Sunnie worked as a stewardess. Mann resolutely refused to learn Arabic or French, and insisted on eating only British food. "I'm a bacon and egg man," he said.

Later, he became manager of the Pickwick Club in Beirut, while Sunnie concentrated on her horses. They were a disputatious couple, who spent a considerable time apart. Nevertheless, after an Israeli shell had accounted for Mrs Mann's horses in 1981, and the Pickwick Club had been closed by a bomb in 1983, they lived together in a flat which cost £1.50 a month.

In spite of the alarming deterioration of the situation in Beirut, the Manns refused to budge. They were often trapped between the ever-shifting front lines, and spent days at a time in underground shelters. Sometimes there was no water, sometimes no power, while the threat of bombing and kidnapping was ever present.

By 1989 they were the only British couple left, naively convinced that they were too old and frail to present a target to the hostage takers. This calculation was disproved on May 12 1989, when Jackie Mann failed to return from his daily trip to the bank.

He had been bundled into a car by members of an organisation which styled itself the Union of Palestine Refugees. In September 1989 reports circulated that Mann was dead, but Sunnie, mindful of his talent for survival in the Second World War, never despaired.

Aged 74 when taken hostage, Jackie Mann was held in solitary confinement throughout the entire period of his incarceration, and frequently chained. "They treated me as if I were some sort of goat," he later recalled, "and hit me on the head if I was in any way recalcitrant, which happened several times a day." He kept his spirits up by incanting "Bugger off, you bastards."

His guards would hold a gun to his head, then pull the trigger to reveal it was unloaded. One of their leaders offered his release if he submitted to homosexual rape. "I can force you, you know." "I'd rather you didn't," Mann replied.

His glasses were lost, which denied him the solace of reading; he resorted to endless games of patience. Although he was given regular meals his dislike of Arab food remained insurmountable and he lost three stone. After 865 days in captivity Mann was finally released in Damascus on September 24 1991, in response to Israel's liberation of 51 Shi'ite Moslem prisoners and the handing over of the bodies of nine Lebanese guerrillas two weeks earlier.

When Mann, weak but cheerful, landed in Britain at RAF Lyneham, a Spitfire greeted him with a victory roll. But he was not tempted to live in Britain, – "not on your life, too bloody cold".

The Manns moved to Cyprus, where they assured reporters that they were still squabbling. In 1992 they published *Yours To The End*, a memoir which showed some animus against Lady Thatcher for having refused to countenance a deal for the release of hostages. Sunnie Mann died on Nov 30 1992, aged 79; they had no children.

Mann was appointed CBE in 1992.

FLIGHT LIEUTENANT
COLIN "HOPPY" HODGKINSON
13 SEPTEMBER 1996

Colin "Hoppy" Hodgkinson, who has died aged 76, lost both his legs learning to fly, but, inspired by the example of the legless fighter ace Douglas Bader, became an accomplished fighter pilot in the RAF.

Although he called himself "the poor man's Bader", Hodgkinson had no cause to cast himself as an understudy. Such was his courage that he succeeded despite bouts of claustrophobia and an admitted fear of flying and combat.

He also had a horror of being forced to ditch in the Channel and stuffed his hollow legs with ping-pong balls, hoping that they would help to keep him afloat. Once, at 30,000 ft, he took violent evasive action before realising that what he had taken to be a clatter of gunfire was the noise of ping-pong balls exploding at that altitude.

But his self-doubt was masked by the bluff, boisterous bonhomie that characterised not only his wartime career as a fighter pilot but also his postwar success in the competitive world of advertising and public relations.

Hodgkinson was already beginning to be talked about as "a second Bader" when he joined No 611 Squadron in June 1943. He flew Spitfires from Coltishall, Norfolk, under Wing Commander "Laddie" Lucas, the hero of the Battle of Malta.

One August morning Hodgkinson was part of an escort to 36 American B-26 bombers in an attack on Bernay airfield near Evreux, north-west of Paris. The wing was turning for home when more than 50 FW 190s appeared up-sun. The Luftwaffe fighter pilots fell upon the Spitfires.

Lucas turned 611's Spitfires into the attack. There was a furious mêlée in which the squadron fought all the way back to the coast.

Hodgkinson, remembering his father teaching him to shoot on the family's Somerset estate, shouted: "Swing with it" and, making a well-judged beam-into-quarter attack, picked off a 190 and sent it spinning earthwards just as it was fastening onto Lucas's tail.

Lucas recalled: "It was an uncommonly quick and accurate piece of shooting. Hodgkinson contributed handsomely to a total of five 190s destroyed against two Spitfires lost.

"In 12 rough and eventful minutes Hodgkinson had demonstrated that, despite his massive disability, he could match his skills against the best that Adolf Galland and his Jagdeschwader 26 had to offer."

It was Hodgkinson's second "kill". Earlier he had shot down a FW 190 just off the end of Brighton pier.

Colin Gerald Shaw Hodgkinson was born at Wells, Somerset, on February 11 1920. His father had been awarded the MC and Bar as a Royal Flying Corps pilot in the First World War, and was to serve as an intelligence wing commander in the Second World War.

Hodgkinson's earliest memories of his father were of a powerful man in hunting pink. As he learned later, he was an outstanding Master of Foxhounds with the Mendip, a big-game hunter and a fine shot.

Soon in the saddle himself, the squire's son followed his father's country pursuits until, being judged difficult and unruly, he was condemned to the harsh discipline of a cadetship at the Nautical College, Pangbourne.

In the summer of 1938 Hodgkinson spent an idyllic holiday riding with the French Cavalry School at Saumur, in the Loire, before being accepted for pilot training as a midshipman in the Fleet Air Arm.

After training aboard the aircraft carrier *Courageous*, he had gone solo and completed 20 hours in a Tiger Moth biplane trainer when he collided with another aircraft.

At the time, accompanied by his instructor, Hodgkinson was practising blind flying on instruments with a hood over his head. The Tiger crashed from 800 ft at Gravesend, killing the instructor and so grievously injuring Hodgkinson that his legs were amputated.

During a long period in hospital he encountered Sir Archibald McIndoe, who invited him to his celebrated wartime RAF plastic surgery unit at the Queen Victoria Hospital, East Grinstead, for some work on his face.

Although he was a naval type, Hodgkinson was welcomed into McIndoe's Guinea Pig Club brotherhood of burned airmen. Such was their spirit that he determined to emulate Bader and to fly again.

He set his heart on flying Spitfires and by the autumn of 1942 had wheedled his way out of the Navy and into the RAF as a pilot officer.

He was briefly with 131, a Spitfire squadron, before moving on in the new year, successively to Number 610 and 501 Squadrons. He learned his trade by flying sweeps over occupied France.

The following March he was promoted flying officer and in June joined 611, then in the famous Biggin Hill wing. After his August bomber escort exploit over France, Hodgkinson returned to 501 as a flight commander.

In November, during a high altitude weather reconnaissance his oxygen supply failed, and he crashed into a French field. Badly mangled and minus one of his tin legs, he was rescued from the blazing Spitfire by two farm workers.

He would be reunited with them in 1983, when they presented him with a part of his aircraft's propeller. He had not seen them since being stretchered away en route for a prisoner of war camp via a railway station where his guards abandoned him for some hours in a lavatory while they sheltered from air-raids.

After 10 months Flight Lieutenant Hodgkinson was repatriated, being deemed of no further use to his country. Yet such was his irrepressible spirit, that after being mended again by McIndoe, he resumed flying, ending the war with a ferry unit at Filton, Bristol.

This gave, as he was to admit, the opportunity of indulging in some pocket-money smuggling, trading such "contraband" as nylons, utility cloth, tea and coffee for cases of brandy among other "imports". Once, he said, he carried gold in his tin legs.

Although he was released from the service in 1946,

Hodgkinson returned in 1949 as a weekend flyer. He became a jet pilot and flew Vampires with 501 and 604 squadrons of the Royal Auxiliary Air Force until the early 1950s.

Civilian life presented fresh challenges, and he plunged enthusiastically into the postwar regeneration of advertising and public relations. From the agency Erwin Wasey he moved into PR, learned the ropes and broke away to establish Colin Hodgkinson Associates.

With the drive and press-on spirit he carried over from fighter days, Hodgkinson prospered, and attracted a mix of prestigious and solid industrial accounts.

He also tried politics, standing as a Conservative in the safe Labour seat of South West Islington in the 1955 General Election. He made an impressive debut and rediscovered his youthful boxing skills in a punch-up with Labour supporters.

Articulate and a fluent writer, Hodgkinson was briefly air correspondent with the fledgling ITN. In 1957 he published *Best Foot Forward*, an entertaining account of his life until then.

Ten years ago he moved permanently to his holiday home in the Dordogne.

He married first June Hunter, a former fashion model; they had a daughter. After her death he married Georgina, a Frenchwoman, who survives him.

WING COMMANDER GEOFFREY PAGE

3 AUGUST 2000

Wing Commander Geoffrey Page, who has died aged 80, endured more than 40 plastic surgery operations after being badly burned during the Battle of Britain, but returned to duty to command a squadron and, with a one-armed colleague, later destroyed six enemy aircraft in 10 minutes.

In July 1940, Page was serving with No 56, a Hurricane squadron, and claimed three German bombers in 10 days in the middle of the month. Barely out of his teens Page was sensitive and imaginative, and in a letter at the time wrote: "It fascinates me beyond belief to see my bullets striking home and then to see the Hun blowing up before me. It also makes me feel sick.

"Where are we going and how will it all end? I feel as if I'm selling my soul to the devil. I need someone to talk to who isn't tied up in this legalised murder."

As the air battle wore on over south-east England, fatigue slowed reactions, and the stress of frequent sorties frayed nerves. On August 17, Page was scrambled to intercept a gaggle of Dornier bombers off the Kent coast but, as he recalled, "drowning in fear, fatigue and nervous exhaustion", he was shot down over Epple Bay and had to bale out of a cockpit ablaze with burning fuel.

He subsequently underwent many painful operations to repair his face and rebuild his crippled hands. These were carried out at the Queen Victoria Hospital, East Grinstead, by Sir Archibald McIndoe, the renowned plastic surgeon, and each taxed Page's mental fortitude to the limit. "Days and nights followed each other in slow agonising shuffle," he remembered.

McIndoe made no bones about the fact that those

passing through Ward 3 – the converted First World War Army hut which served as the hospital's annexe for McIndoe's patients – were "guinea pigs" and in 1941, after a hard night's drinking, the Guinea Pig Club was born.

Page was elected to the committee and recorded the minutes of the first meeting. "The objects of the club," these began, "are to promote good fellowship among, and to maintain contact with, approved frequenters of Queen Victoria Cottage Hospital."

After the war, McIndoe ensured that the club continued to provide medical treatment, and help with jobs for the "pigs", and that the bonds forged in wartime were re-cemented each year at a weekend in East Grinstead.

Despite his operations, Page was determined to return to the fray, and using all his considerable charm, eventually persuaded the authorities that he could control an aircraft with his damaged fingers.

Early in 1943 he flew briefly with No 132, a Spitfire squadron based at Hornchurch, Essex, and then in North Africa. But the hot sun there proved incompatible with his grafted skin, and he was posted instead to the Air Fighting Development Unit at Wittering, Huntingdonshire.

There he was teamed with Squadron Leader James MacLachlan, a one-armed New Zealand fighter ace with a DSO and a DFC and two Bars. Together they put a wide variety of Allied aircraft through their paces. Page's courage and flying skills quickly earned him the respect of all at the base.

On June 29 1943, he and MacLachlan decided to undertake some practical evaluation of the American P-51 Mustang, a long-range fighter ideally suited to dayime strafing of enemy airfields. With MacLachlan's artificial arm clamped to the throttle lever of his aeroplane, the pair raced over to Paris, where between them they accounted for six enemy aircraft in 10 minutes.

"After that, the journey home was uneventful," Page recalled, "A kindly rainstorm hid us as we slipped safely over the coast for base and a large tankard of frothing beer." Page's tally further boosted a score which by the end of the war was to total at least 17 aircraft. It brought him a DFC in 1943, a Bar to it in 1944, and a DSO later that same year.

Alan Geoffrey Page was born at Boxmoor, Hertfordshire, on May 16 1920 and went to Dean Close, Cheltenham, and London University. He wanted to become a pilot, but was warned off by his uncle Sir Frederick Handley Page, the aircraft manufacturer, who said that pilots were two a penny.

Somewhat reluctantly, Page studied engineering, but seized the opportunity to learn to fly with the University Air Squadron. On the outbreak of hostilities in 1939 he was called up for pilot training at RAF Cranwell, where he was rated "exceptional".

Early in 1944, Page assumed command of No 132 Squadron, and led it in the run–up to the invasion of Normandy. Shortly afterwards, he received command of No 125, a fighter wing comprising four squadrons and operating from seized airfields in France. He was still only 24.

In September, Page was attacking ground targets near the Arnhem bridgehead when he was wounded by anti–aircraft fire and forced to crash-land. He fractured a bone in his back and was returned to hospital. It was the end of his war.

In the New Year of 1945, he was sent on a lecture tour of America. There he met his wife, Pauline, daughter of the actor Nigel Bruce, who played Dr Watson to Basil Rathbone in many Sherlock Holmes films. The couple were married in 1946.

In the spring of 1945, Page underwent further surgery before being attached to Vickers-Armstrongs as a test pilot. He then commanded No 64, a Hornet squadron, and in 1947 was appointed personal assistant to the senior RAF officer at the UN military staff commission in New York.

The next year he left the RAF to join Vickers-Armstrongs as a sales executive and later established himself in Switzerland as an international aviation consultant. He was also active in the Battle of Britain Fighter Pilots Association, and was the moving force behind the creation, in 1993, of the Battle of Britain memorial, sited on the cliffs near Dover.

He published, in 1981, *Tale of a Guinea Pig*, republished last year as *Shot Down In Flames*.

Geoffrey Page was appointed OBE in 1995. He also held the Order of Orange Nassau.

He is survived by his wife, and by two sons and a daughter.

AIR VICE-MARSHAL "BIRDIE" BIRD-WILSON
29 DECEMBER 2000

Air Vice-Marshal "Birdie" Bird-Wilson, who has died aged 81, overcame terrible burns from an air crash to take part with great distinction in the Battle of Britain; after shooting down six enemy aircraft in the summer of 1940 he became the 40th victim of the Luftwaffe ace Adolf Galland.

Raked by the guns of Galland's Me 109, Bird-Wilson's Hurricane fell blazing into the Thames. "I knew I'd been hit," he recalled. "Flames came into the cockpit, the hood perspex was all gone. I pulled the hood back and leaped out. Two of my section orbited round me. I was burned, but picked up by a naval motor torpedo boat."

Although still carrying shrapnel from this encounter in his head, Bird-Wilson went on to destroy a further five enemy aircraft during the war. Bird-Wilson's war record was the more remarkable for his having recovered from a crash shortly after the outbreak of war.

He was piloting a B A Swallow, a light civilian aeroplane being used for communications service, when he crashed in foul weather at Cranwell. He was fortunate to survive the accident, in which his passenger, a fellow pilot, was killed.

Treated for serious burns at the Queen Victoria Hospital, East Grinstead, Bird-Wilson was among the earliest aircrew "guinea pig" patients of the plastic surgeon Sir Archibald McIndoe. For some months he walked around without a nose. But, he recalled, "my fighter pilot friends accepted me and so did my girlfriend. They were not put off by this embarrassing sight." On its foundation he was welcomed into the East Grinstead pioneers' Guinea Pig Club.

Periodically he returned to East Grinstead, where eventually McIndoe offered him the nose of his choice. By April 1940 his face was restored and he quickly returned to fly a Hurricane operationally. He helped cover the Allied retreat in France in May and June 1940. At the last opportunity, he flew home from Brittany via the Channel Islands.

Later, reflecting on events in 1940, he marvelled at his survival. "I was still only 20. We'd lost a lot of the older chaps in France. We hadn't the experience of the German pilots like Galland who'd fought in the Spanish Civil War.

"So we'd fly around in pre-war Hendon pageant formations. The RAF hadn't had a Spain, nor the intelligence to learn from the tactics it produced. It hadn't kept pace with German thinking and the Gallands of the Luftwaffe.

"Once during the Battle of Britain when we lost a CO he was replaced by an intelligence officer from behind a desk at the Air Ministry. He brought the idea with him that you should attack head on. He tried out this tactic and regrettably it did not work. We found his shirt in Weymouth harbour."

Bird-Wilson retained a vivid memory of attacking formations of more than 100 enemy aircraft as one of a force of only 12 Hurricanes. "Your throat dried up as you got nearer," he remembered. "I don't believe any man who said he wasn't afraid."

When the Battle of Britain ended that autumn it shocked Bird-Wilson that "there was hardly anybody left of the pilots who started out with me. All one's friends had gone.

"I had no qualms about admitting to nightmares. Sleeping at dispersal near my Hurricane I would often wake from a very frightening dream of flying at night. I would be sitting up in bed and sweating like a pig."

Harold Arthur Cooper Bird-Wilson was born on November 20 1919, son of a Bengal tea-planter. He was sent to a boarding school in England at the age of four and a half while his parents remained in India. His reaction was to build a protective shield round himself and develop early self-reliance. He went on to Liverpool College, and was commissioned in the Royal Air Force in 1937.

Bird-Wilson was still only 18 when he joined No 17 Squadron in August 1938. At first he learned his fighter skills in the squadron's biplane, the Gloster Gauntlet. In June 1939, the squadron was re-equipped with Hawker Hurricanes, a change which allowed Bird-Wilson just 10 weeks to convert to the far speedier, modern monoplane eight-gun fighters.

After the Battle of Britain, he spent two periods in 1941 as an instructor and then in command of a training squadron at No 56 Operational Training Unit. In between he served with No 254 Squadron, flying Spitfires in offensive sweeps over northern France. The next year, he received his first two squadron commands, Nos 152 and 66 Squadrons. These gave air cover to convoys and escorted day bombers over France.

In 1943 Bird-Wilson began a brilliant period as a leader of aggressive fighter wings. Rested in the New Year of 1944, he attended a command and general staff course at Fort Leavenworth, Kansas.

In April he was again in the thick of it with No 83 Group. First he led the Spitfire wing at Harrowbeer in Devon and then a Mustang wing at Bentwaters in Suffolk. He shot down his last enemy aircraft (a much-advanced model of the Me 109 which had set his Hurricane on fire in 1940) while escorting daylight raids in support of the invasion of Normandy.

Moving onto jets before the end of the war he received command in 1945 of No 1335, the RAF's first jet conversion unit. This led in 1946 to command of the Central Flying Establishment's air fighting development squadron. In 1948 he was posted to the Middle East operations staff.

The next year, Air Chief Marshal Sir John Baker, Middle East Air Force Commander-in-Chief, appointed him as his personal staff officer.

Further Central Flying Establishment posts followed from 1952 to 1954, when he joined the British Joint Services Mission in Washington. He was at the Air Ministry from 1961 to 1963, then commanded the Central Flying School, and in 1965 was appointed air officer commanding Hong Kong.

He was at the Ministry of Technology from 1967 to 1970, when he received command of No 23, a training group. He retired in 1974.

He devoted the next 10 years to bringing his great operational research and staff experience to bear on Britain's aerospace responsibilities in Saudi Arabia.

Bird-Wilson was awarded a DFC in 1940, a Bar to it in 1943, a DSO in 1945, an AFC in 1946 and Bar in 1955. He was appointed CBE in 1952, and was also awarded a Dutch DFC and a Czechoslovak Medal of Merit.

He married first, in 1942, Audrey Wallace. She died in 1991; they had a son and a daughter. He married secondly, in 1994, Margaret McGillivray Butler.

JOKERS IN THE PACK

FLIGHT SERGEANT
WILLIAM HOOPER
14 OCTOBER 1996

Bill Hooper, who has died aged 80, created the cartoon character Pilot Officer Prune, a bungling buffoon, whose escapades demonstrated to airmen in the Second World War precisely how not to behave, thereby saving many lives.

"Fatuously exuberant yet permanently bone-headed," was Hooper's description of the hugely successful character, Percy Prune. "He invariably made a muck of everything he set out to do and yet survived to make another."

Prune was first conceived as an RAF training aid by the *Punch* contributor "A A" (Anthony Armstrong Willis), but was brought to life, and made completely credible, by Hooper's drawings. All air crew could readily recognise, and chuckle at, the silly ass pilot who always got it wrong.

Prune's idiocies, relayed to the RAF through its training manual *Tee-Emm*, were thought so instructive that the Free French Air Force adopted and adapted him as "Aspirant Praline". Overseas editions of *Tee-Emm* conveyed tales of Prune to the Far East and the Dominions; the Americans also followed his adventures avidly. During the war he was as famous as any ace.

Such was his appeal that for some years the fictional Pilot Officer Prune had his own office at the Air Ministry, with his name on the door, his hat and clobber on the desk and his own telephone extension.

When some believers began to doubt his existence because he was never promoted, Prune was court-martialled, as well he might be for his many transgressions, and remained a mere Pilot Officer.

Although Hooper drew him initially as a No 11 Group Fighter Command pilot – top button always undone in true Battle of Britain style – Prune, for training purposes, was posted variously to Bomber and other Commands – so that their silly asses would also benefit from his prangs.

But it was as a spotted-scarved fighter boy that Prune is best remembered, sketched by Hooper and shouting his immortal line, "I leave my top button undone because I haven't got one. It was shot off in a dog fight." He was also known for his stabs at pithy wisdom: "You can't make an omelette without spilling milk," he once observed.

When *Tee-Emm* was wound up after the war it had published 60 issues in five volumes of Prunery. It was not the end of Percy Prune who went on to appear in commercial publications.

William John Hooper was born on August 21 1916, the son of a micro-engineer. He was educated at Eddington, a boarding school at Herne in Kent, where he was whacked on his drawing hand for doodling aide-memoires in his exercise books. Going on to Imperial College, London, he left without qualification and was employed as an unpaid laboratory assistant to Dr Francis Camps in his Windsor Forest clinic.

He then found employment as a bodyguard to a jeweller in Ireland. Tiring of this, he took to the road, tramping the Irish lanes and keeping himself by drawing favourite horses and dogs of families he encountered on his travels.

At the outbreak of war Hooper volunteered to train as an air gunner but was re-mustered as a general duties clerk. Posted as an aircraftman to No 54 Fighter Squadron, his observation of its pilots during the Battle of Britain in 1940 gave him the inspiration for Prune and the aircraftman Plonk.

Posted to Catterick when the squadron was rested, Hooper's new CO, Squadron Leader R F Boyd, asked him to illustrate an advisory booklet, *Forget Me Nots For Fighters.* This led to an invitation to meet Flight Lieutenant Anthony Armstrong Willis at the Air Ministry. Over lunch at a Holborn restaurant Hooper sketched Prune on a starched white napkin and suggested Plonk as Prune's mechanic.

In time, Hooper, never more than a flight sergeant, joined Willis in London where he camouflaged his non-commissioned status by wearing a blazer with black Royal Australian Air Force buttons, an RAFVR tie, dark grey flannels and highly polished black shoes.

Becoming known as "that Prune bloke" but sometimes taken for a boffin, Hooper, with his special Air Ministry pass had universal access to RAF stations.

After demobilisation Hooper moved into Fleet Street contributing cartoons to various newspapers and spending some time as the *Sunday Chronicle*'s political cartoonist.

Television took him up and he worked for the BBC graphics department and appeared in children's and other programmes.

He also drew for the National Coal Board, creating Davy Lump, a Pruneesque miner, as his contribution towards reducing pit accidents.

As well as *Forget Me Nots For Fighters*, Hooper's publications include: *Behind the Spitfires* and *You Can't Laugh It Off* (as "Raff"); *Plonk's Party*, *Whiskers Will Not Be Worn*, *Prune's Progress*, *Nice Types* and *Goodbye Nice Types* (as Raff, with Armstrong Willis); *The Odd Facts Of Life* and *The Passing of Pilot Officer Prune* (as Bill Hooper); *Clangers* (as Bill Hooper, with Colonel Dickinson); and *The Bucks and Bawds of London Town* (as K de Barn). In 1991 he published his last book, *Pilot Officer Prune's Picture Parade.*

Hooper, happily ensconced in a studio set up for him at Princess Marina House, the RAF Benevolent Fund's veterans home at Rustington, West Sussex since 1993, was working until the end.

His wife, Nöelle Lang, wartime WAAF and the model for Prune's girlfriend, Winsum, predeceased him. They had a son John, the Rome correspondent of the *Guardian*.

———

WING COMMANDER
CHARLES "SAMMY" SAMOUELLE
MARCH 1997

Wing Commander Charles "Sammy" Samouelle, who has died aged 77, was a desert air ace; he won an immediate DFC and Bar within the same week in 1942.

Samouelle joined the RAF in August 1940 straight from the Savoy Hotel, where he had graduated from bell-boy to apprentice cocktail fixer.

After receiving his wings in Canada, he returned to Britain as a sergeant pilot to No 92 Squadron, flying Spitfire Vcs from Biggin Hill, the celebrated Kent fighter station. In the New Year of 1942, shortly after he had been commissioned as a pilot officer, Samouelle was posted with the squadron to the Middle East.

Fighter aces almost invariably emerged from the ranks of quick-eyed pilots whose peace-time country pursuits had developed their shooting skills. Samouelle proved that a cocktail-shaker could also make an air ace.

Samouelle accumulated a tally of at least 11 enemy aircraft shot down and one destroyed on the ground – and many more if some credited as probables or damaged are included.

Most of his victories were achieved in 1942, during the

critical defence of El Alamein, and the fighter sweeps, bomber-escort missions and subsequent pursuit of the Axis armies in North Africa.

Living conditions on makeshift desert landing grounds were desperate at the best of times, but Samouelle, perhaps making use of his training at the Savoy, came to be acknowledged as one who made life a little more tolerable.

Charles James Samouelle was born at Islington on February 2 1920 and educated locally at Acland Central School. After leaving at 16 he found a job at the Savoy Hotel. At 17 he married a girl of 18, and by the time he enlisted at 20 they had started a family.

Following his exploits in the Desert Air Force, Samouelle returned home to a public relations post at the Air Ministry. His charm and ability to get on with people served him well on the factory liaison circuit. He toured Britain boosting the morale of war workers – a real live fighter ace reminding them how vital their contribution was to aircrew.

Samouelle also resumed his association with Henry Cradock, sometime world champion cocktail-fixer, who had moved from the Savoy to the Dorchester, where Samouelle's friends never quite understood why drinks were on the house.

When, in the autumn of 1944, Samouelle returned to operations, he flew as a flight commander in No 41, a Spitfire XIV Squadron of 125 Wing, 2nd Tactical Air Force (second TAF) in Belgium. Subsequently, he commanded No 130 Squadron in the same wing. Ian Smith, the future Prime Minister of Rhodesia, was one of his pilots.

In this period Samouelle made further "kills" and enhanced his reputation as a fighter pilot and leader. Attacking a German airfield at Rheine, he was observed so low that hangar guns were firing down on him.

After VE Day in May 1945, the squadron deployed to Norway, where Samouelle, using his catering and carpentry skills, built a bar and transformed a stark mess into a home from home.

In August that year his public relations flair was re-employed on secondment to the National Savings Committee, on behalf of which he teamed up with the actress Deborah Kerr and other celebrities for personal appearances.

At the end of the war Samouelle returned briefly to civilian life. In the face of food rationing and catering restrictions he went back to the RAF.

While serving in No 99, a York Transport Command squadron, Samouelle took part in the Berlin Airlift of 1948–49. He went on to be a flying instructor, and in 1952 was given command of the Meteor Training squadron at Finningley.

Routine command and staff appointments followed until 1975, when he retired and joined the training staff of British Steel. A serious injury obliged him to leave in 1980.

Ever a handyman, Samouelle built desks for his children as they grew up, and furniture for his home. Carpentry and electronic wizardry – he kept up with technological advances – brought him much enjoyment over the years.

Samouelle was appointed OBE in 1971. His wife, Elsie Mary Protheroe, predeceased him. He leaves a son and three daughters.

FRANK WOOTTON
21 APRIL 1998

Frank Wootton, who has died aged 83, was a distinguished, if unofficial, war artist whose work in Normandy and Burma helped to establish him as Britain's leading aviation painter.

Wootton arrived in Normandy shortly after the D-Day landings. He had enlisted in the RAF in 1940 but, although he had previously undertaken commissions for the Service, his dexterity was assessed only in terms of his potential as an aircraft fitter.

He had already had an application to become an official war artist turned down by Sir Kenneth Clark, the chairman of the War Artists Advisory Committee. Clark was said to have been put out by a failure to consult him when Wootton had been asked to record scenes at Biggin Hill during the Battle of Britain.

After courses at an RAF technical training school, Wootton hoped to be posted to an operational station; but his commanding officer, aware of his drawing skills, kept him on to produce training manuals and lecture diagrams.

Wootton's plight then came to the attention of Air Chief Marshal Sir Trafford Leigh-Mallory, former commander of No 12 Group during the Battle of Britain, who was now leading the Normandy invasion air force.

He recruited Wootton to record the conflict and, as he was not an official war artist, provided him with suitable badges and a pass as an RAF artist. This gave him more freedom of movement than that permitted to official artists.

Wootton first painted abandoned gliders at Pegasus Bridge, near Caen, before being attached to No 35 Photographic Reconnaissance Wing. He was recording a Mustang undergoing maintenance when enemy shrapnel ripped the canvas on his easel. Wootton glued a patch on the canvas before completing the painting.

Once the Allies were well-established in North West Europe, Leigh-Mallory was ordered to South East Asia, whereupon he invited Wootton to "fly out with me and paint the jungle". Wootton flew home from Antwerp to prepare for the Far East, but his aircraft was shot down (Wootton was asleep at the time) over the Channel. He was picked up by an Air Sea Rescue launch.

Shortly afterwards, Wootton was about to fly out to Asia with Leigh-Mallory in the Air Chief Marshal's personal Avro York transport when he realised that he needed more time to put together materials suitable for the jungle climate. The transport left without him, and crashed in the French Alps, killing Leigh-Mallory and all on board.

Wootton eventually arrived in India in the New Year of 1945. He was assigned to Nos 355 and 356 Liberator Bomber Squadrons, stationed at Salbani, north west of Calcutta. He spent six months covering different aspects of attacks on Japanese positions as far away as Rangoon, before moving on to fighter units.

Among the moments he committed to canvas was that when a Mosquito crew spotted a roof-top message that had been written by British prisoners-of-war: "Japs gone. RAF extract digit."

On one of his trips into the jungle, Wootton became lost while seeking a bridge which had been destroyed by the RAF; he came upon the home of a local Burmese chieftain, and reciprocated his hospitality by drawing his host's daughter and baby.

The man was so delighted that he sent for a chest of jewels and invited Wootton to take his pick. Wootton politely declined, but four large sapphires were pressed into his hand.

Frank Anthony Albert Wootton was born on July 30

1914 at Milford, Hampshire. At the age of 14, he won a scholarship to Eastbourne College of Art, and two years later spent a year travelling around Germany, sketching and even painting murals in a castle.

He then began work in London as a commercial artist, cycling home to his family at weekends on a bicycle he had built himself.

Later, he worked for Shell's advertising agency and, having gone freelance, received his first commission from de Havilland to paint the company's new Moth Minor. Thereafter, he received a steady stream of work from aircraft manufacturers, both in Britain and America, until war intervened.

After VJ Day, Wootton returned home and, though technically still in the RAF, was allowed to travel to Persia to record the Anglo-Iranian Oil Company's search for oil. He then resumed his freelance career, which flourished as he received commissions from BOAC, and the aircraft and motor industries.

In the mid-1960s, stimulated by the encouragement he had earlier received from Sir Alfred Munnings (who had admired an equestrian study by Wootton at the Royal Academy), he began to devote time to painting horses. "You'll find the real money in horses," Munnings had told him.

The critics praised Wootton's paintings as being in the tradition of Stubbs, and Wootton held several successful exhibitions of equestrian pictures. His sensitive approach to landscape and the play of light was matched by faultless draughtsmanship and complete command of painting technique.

But aviation remained his first love, and in 1983 he was invited to stage the first exhibition at the new National Air and Space Museum in Washington, DC. Wootton worked flat out to produce new subjects, while at the same time urging the RAF, museums, companies and clubs to lend earlier pictures of his for the show.

The exhibition of 57 paintings ran for a year, and then transferred to the Air Museum at Oshkosh, Wisconsin, for a further six months. Wootton was later commissioned by King Ibn Saud to design the interior of his personal Comet.

Wootton published a number of books, including *The Landscape Painting of Frank Wootton* (1989) and *Frank Wootton, 50 Years of Aviation Art* (1992). He was the Founding President of the Guild of Aviation Artists.

At a dinner to mark the presentation by him of a painting of the Royal Review of Bomber Command at RAF Marham in 1956, Wootton encountered his former commanding officer. Wootton recalled the advice the man had given him in 1943: "Play your cards right lad, and you might make a good living on the pier."

Frank Wootton was appointed OBE in 1995.

His first marriage was dissolved and in 1958 he married Virginia (Jinny) Ann Cawthorne. They had a son and a daughter.

WING COMMANDER
BILL "STICKS" GREGORY
9 OCTOBER 2001

Wing Commander Bill "Sticks" Gregory, who has died aged 87, was Air Interception (AI) radar operator to the Second World War night fighter ace Wing Commander Bob Braham.

Gregory's superb radar skills helped Braham to destroy 29 German aircraft in the night skies over Britain and occupied Europe – a tally which was among the highest of any wartime RAF fighter pilot, flying by day or night.

The two men were first paired when Gregory, then a flight sergeant, stood in temporarily for Braham's usual radar operator, a Canadian named Ross. Braham was soon noting Gregory's "cheerfulness", and rating him "far above average in the AI business". When Ross was rested, Gregory began to partner Braham regularly.

Their first combat took place in early July 1941. Flying in a twin-engine Bristol Beaufighter of No 29 Squadron over a moonlit Thames Estuary, Gregory called to Braham: "Contact dead ahead and at 2,000 yards."

As Braham went into a gentle dive to close the range and to get below a Ju 88 bomber, the enemy opened fire. When Gregory urged Braham to open up, Braham said calmly: "No, not yet. We must get closer to make sure of him." Despite heavy fire from the Ju 88, Braham continued to delay firing, until with three short bursts he sent the bomber blazing down into the Thames.

Later that year, after a brief detachment in Scotland to assist No 141 Squadron convert from obsolescent Boulton Paul single-engine Defiants to Beaufighters, Braham and Gregory returned to No 29 at West Malling in Kent.

Early in 1942, Gregory was commissioned a pilot officer – a promotion for which Braham had been pressing – and he and Braham were posted as instructors to No 51, a night fighter Operational Training Unit at Cranfield.

Keen to return to operations, in early June the two men slipped away for an unofficial weekend visit to their old squadron, No 29, in Kent. During a night sortie, Gregory positioned Braham to attack a Do 217 bomber. Braham soon set it alight, and it dived into the sea off Sandwich.

Bad weather then caused them to divert to Manston, on the Kent coast. With fog rolling in from the sea, Braham overshot and crash-landed in a ploughed field. The crash truck crew were astonished to see Gregory and his pilot emerge in one piece.

William James Gregory, the son of a builder, was born on November 23 1913 at Hartlepool, where he attended the Lister Sealy School. Before the war, he worked for his father as a plasterer, and was drummer in the Debroy Somers Band earning the nickname "Sticks".

He enlisted in the RAF soon after the outbreak of war, and in May 1940 was posted to No 29 Squadron as a wireless operator/air gunner. Subsequently, he was redesignated observer/radio operator and then radar operator.

Before teaming up with Braham, Gregory had a nasty experience when he and his pilot were, as he noted in his logbook, "scrambled to intercept Huns raiding Liverpool". They were about to shoot down a Do 17 when their Beaufighter was hit in the starboard wing by "friendly" anti-aircraft fire.

Having baled out at 16,000 feet, Gregory landed on the roof of Lime Street station – and as he climbed down to the ground rail passengers mistook him for a German airman and roughed him up.

After the mishap at Manston, Gregory and Braham returned to No 29 Squadron where Braham became a flight commander. In December 1942 Braham, aged only 22, received command of No 141 Squadron at Ford on the south coast; Gregory, at 29 the old man of the team, stayed with him.

One moonlit night, Gregory and most of the squadron aircrew were having a party at Worthing, on the Sussex coast, when they heard enemy aeroplanes overhead. Racing back to their airfield they took off in their waiting Beaufighter.

Gregory brought the aircraft to within visual range of a Do 217 bomber, flying at 15,000 feet. There was an exchange of fire in which Braham, having rather enjoyed himself at the party, opened up at too long a range.

Gregory's caustic comments quickly sobered Braham up, and in four long bursts he sent the Dornier diving ablaze into the sea.

Early in 1943 the squadron moved west to Predannack, near the Lizard Point in Cornwall, mainly for night training. Visiting Fighter Command, Braham urged the use of AI night fighters in support of the bomber offensive over occupied Europe, in which heavy losses were being incurred. Although his proposal was not accepted at this stage, he won approval for moonlight attacks on rail and road traffic on the Brest peninsula.

At the end of April 1943 Braham and Gregory led No 141 Squadron to Wittering, near Stamford, Lincolnshire. Their aircraft were now fitted with "Serrate", a radar device which enabled Gregory and his fellow operators to home in on enemy fighter transmissions from a distance of up to 100 miles.

This was an ideal aid in Gregory's new night-intruding role, and after he and Braham had exchanged their Beaufighter for a de Havilland Mosquito equipped with Serrate, the two men went into action in support of Sir Arthur Harris's bomber formations.

One night, flying over Cologne, they were attacked by two enemy night fighters, one of which shot out their port engine, obliging them to make a perilous return back to base. Another night, supporting a raid over Mannheim, Gregory logged "a hell of a dogfight". In a 25-minute battle, they destroyed one German aircraft – an Me 110 fighter – and drove off another.

In March 1944, Gregory, by now highly experienced, joined the night operations staff at No 2 Group, 2nd Tactical Air Force (2nd TAF) headquarters, where Braham had preceded him.

Such was his and Braham's hunger for action that from time to time they would slip away from their desks to freelance on sorties over Europe with various Mosquito squadrons. On one daylight sortie, they destroyed an He 177 heavy bomber which was circling Châteaudun airfield in France at 1,000 feet. Caught in a stream of fire from their Mosquito's nose guns, the bomber, Gregory recalled, "reared up like a wounded animal, winged over on its back and dived vertically into the ground".

On May 12 1944, Gregory and Braham – truanting again from the operations room – had just taken part in the destruction of a Fw 190 fighter off the Danish coast when an Me 109 fighter struck. Short of fuel, and further damaged by anti-aircraft fire, Braham coaxed the stricken aircraft towards home until he had to ditch 70 miles off the Norfolk coast, where they were rescued by two minesweepers.

Shortly after that, the team broke up. Braham was shot down and ended the war as a prisoner; Gregory continued staff duties. While Braham accumulated three DSOs, three DFCs and an AFC in the course of his wartime service, Gregory was awarded a DSO, two DFCs, an AFC and a DFM.

At the end of the war, Gregory accepted a permanent commission specialising in navigation and fighter control. He received the Air Efficiency Award in 1946, and after commanding RAF Wartling, in East Sussex, retired in 1964.

Thereafter, until final retirement, he worked as an estate agent at Eastbourne. He was a member of Cooden Beach golf club and, having retained his drumming skills, played with a local band. Later in life, so as to be near his daughter, he moved to Camberley, Surrey, where golf, bowls and darts – he was known as "The Demon" – brought him much enjoyment.

Bill Gregory married, in 1942, Jean Atkinson; they had a daughter.

BEVERLEY ("BEV") SNOOK
12 OCTOBER 2001

Beverley ("Bev") Snook, who has died aged 72, was a former chairman of the Royal Aero Club and an air racing competitor so exuberant that he might have been described as accident-prone.

In 1961 Snook was piloting one of his two Mark IX Spitfires in the London to Cardiff air race when the fighter caught fire after landing at Exeter airport. He explained afterwards: "I had taxied for nearly a mile when the plane suddenly exploded and burst into flames. Fortunately, I was able to jump out." He escaped with only cuts and bruises.

Tales of Snook's misadventures were legion. On one occasion he was flying low, close to the rocky Isle of Man coastline, when a seagull hurtled into the cabin. At the end of another air race he finished upside down in a de Havilland Tiger Moth biplane after being flipped over by a crosswind on landing.

There was also the occasion on which he sought to impress a "date" by taking her up in his diminutive Aeronca-C3 runabout light aircraft, sometimes described as a "flying bathtub". When the propeller fell off, Snook was obliged to land at a nearby RAF station. The journey continued by train, with Snook holding the propeller in one hand and the young lady, Pauline Goodson, in the other. Far from being put off by this experience, she married him shortly afterwards.

In the mid 1950s, when he was only 26, Snook flew solo from England to Australia, piloting a single-engine Percival Proctor. He was lucky to survive monsoon storms while crossing a mountain range in Thailand. The plane was, he recalled, "tossed about like a cork" and the torrential rain stripped it of paint.

Such exploits caused Snook to enliven the post-war club and commercial flying scene. In his early career he was readily identifiable at aviation events by his flamboyant leopardskin flying helmet, reputed to have been owned by Mrs Elliott-Lynn, a pre-war sporting pilot. The helmet had been presented to Snook by Col Rupert "Mossy" Preston, secretary-general of the Royal Aero Club.

Beverley John Snook was born on June 28 1929, and educated at the City of London School and Westminster College. As an Air Training Corps cadet in wartime he obtained joyrides with the US 8th Air Force.

Snook had hoped to fly with the RAF, but this ambition was thwarted by medical problems. Afterwards he obtained a private pilot's licence which enabled him to indulge the pleasure he found in sports flying and air racing.

After the war, Snook worked for the aircraft brokers R K Dundas, suppliers of commercial and sporting aircraft, before joining Aerocontacts as overseas sales manager. In 1956 he launched Trans Global, a group of aviation companies trading in aircraft and spares, becoming chairman and managing director.

As his business career developed Snook became increasingly involved in the Royal Aero Club of the United Kingdom which he chaired from 1982 to 1986.

Through his various offices in the club Snook fostered sports flying and flew regularly in Britain's domestic national air races. Although he never won the King's Cup (the top annual Royal Aero Club air racing award) his racing career was certainly colourful. On one occasion, racing a Tiger Moth and wearing his famous leopardskin helmet, Snook miscalculated his dive across the finish and ended up in the Tiger's wreckage some way short of the line. His efforts to drag bits of the Tiger across the line failed to satisfy the judges.

However, in 1966 he had partial consolation for his lack of success in the King's Cup when he came second; and some years later he had the great satisfaction of watching his son Nicholas win the event.

Snook did win, in 1959, the Grosvenor Trophy, and in 1965 he took the John Morgan Challenge Trophy. Becoming chief steward at Royal Aero Club meetings after doctors had stopped him taking part, Snook remained a flamboyant figure on airfields where his white Rolls-Royce announced his presence and Pauline presided over the refreshments.

Snook was a founder member of the Vintage Aeroplane Club in 1951; co-founder of the Tiger Club in 1956; chairman of the private aviation parliamentary committee (1982-84); and vice-president of the Guild of Aviation Artists from 1983. He was also a Fellow of the Royal Aeronautical Society and a Liveryman of the Guild of Air Pilots and Air Navigators.

He was appointed OBE in 1985.

Snook married Pauline Goodson in 1956. They had two sons.

"PUNCH" DICKINS
3 AUGUST 1995

"Punch" Dickins, who has died aged 96, was a celebrated bush pilot responsible for opening up air routes in north-west Canada.

Until the 1920s large parts of the dominion's northern regions were inaccessible for much of each year. But Dickins and his fellow airmen created regular links with the south, opening up land for commercial development and, in the process, making aircraft a familiar sight to

Eskimos who had never seen a car or a train.

He joined the newly formed Western Canada Airways in 1927 and for the next decade his elegant figure – in goggles, fur jacket, high boots and enormous mittens – was internationally recognised. He made a series of pioneering flights over more than a million previously uncharted miles, and earned such nicknames as "The Snow Eagle" and "Canada's Sky Explorer".

Dickins made the first flight across the unmapped Barren Lands of the North-West Territories and flew the first aircraft on the prairie air-mail circuit from Winnipeg to Regina, Calgary and Edmonton and back to Winnipeg. In 1929 he became the first pilot to fly the 2,000 mile length of the Mackenzie River from Edmonton to Aklavik on the Arctic Ocean, and also made the first landing at the Great Bear Lake, where his passenger, the prospector, Gilbert LaBine, started the first uranium mine.

Cautious and skilful Dickins disliked the roistering life favoured by some of his colleagues; he was also well-endowed with luck. The only time he ran out of petrol in the north, he landed on the banks of the Slave River without a radio and was considering building a raft when a steamer pulled into view. The skipper shouted that yes, they had some aircraft fuel aboard, adding that it was for "some chap called Dickins who thinks he is going to fly in here next winter".

In 1930 Dickins became superintendent at Edmonton of the Mackenzie River District of Canadian Airways, and five years later carried out a successful air survey to photograph blind spots on the Yukon-Northwest Territories border. He was then made assistant to the president of Canadian Pacific.

After the Battle of Britain in 1940 Lord Beaverbrook, the Canadian-born British Minister of Aircraft

Production, asked Dickins to become operations manager of Atfero, an air ferry organisation which flew American-built bombers across the Atlantic to the RAF.

Dickins demonstrated outstanding organisational ability at an international level, and he built up transatlantic deliveries to 150 aircraft a month before the organisation was turned over to RAF Ferry Command in 1942.

Dickins then became general manager of Canadian Pacific Airlines, with a brief to amalgamate a number of small and scattered airlines into one network. At the same time he oversaw the management of six flying schools, which produced 12,000 aircrew in Canada as part of the British Commonwealth Air Training Plan.

Clennell Haggerston Dickins was born at Portage la Prairie, Manitoba, on January 12 1899, and became known as "Punch" because his elder brother could not manage his first name.

The family moved to Edmonton, Alberta, when he was eight, and he attended the local university for a year before enlisting in the 196th Western Universities Infantry Battalion in 1917.

After its removal to Bramshott, Surrey, he transferred first to the Royal Flying Corps as a pilot and then to its successor, the RAF. Dickins was posted to No 211, a bomber and reconnaissance squadron equipped with DH4s and DH9s which was operating over Flanders.

Although seven victories were attributed to him in the course of some 79 sorties, he claimed, with characteristic modesty, that this was because his observer was an excellent gunner. He was awarded the DFC in 1918.

After the war Dickins worked briefly for General Motors, and then joined the Canadian Air Force; he became one of the RCAF's first officers on its creation in 1924. He carried out high-altitude experimental fighter flights at Edmonton and flew forest patrols from High

River, Alberta, as well as making aerial photographic surveys of northern Saskatchewan and Alberta.

The federal government's creation of Trans Canada Airways meant that Canadian Pacific's growth was restricted after the Second World War, and in 1947 Dickins became vice-president in charge of sales for the de Havilland Aircraft Company of Canada. For his last 20 years in business he played an important part in marketing the twin-engine Otter and the five-seater Beaver, still a standard for northern flying.

In 1973 Dickins was named a member of Canada's Aviation Hall of Fame. "Despite adversity," read his citation, "he dramatised to the world the value of the bush plane, and his total contribution to the brilliance of Canada's air age can be measured not only by the regard in which he is held by his peers, but by the nation as a whole."

Dickins was appointed OBE in 1936 and OC in 1968.

He had three children with his wife, Connie, who wrote *I Married a Bush Pilot* (1981).

ESCAPERS AND EVADERS

WING COMMANDER
ROGER MAW
19 AUGUST 1992

Wing Commander Roger Maw, who has died aged 86, designed and built the wooden vaulting horse (the "Trojan Horse") which made possible one of the most daring prisoner-of-war escapes.

Without Maw's skills – and the tools he so craftily concealed from the camp's guards – Flight Lieutenants Eric Williams and Oliver Philpot and Lieutenant Codner of the Royal Artilery could never have made the "home run" from Stalag Luft III in Lower Silesia.

Their inspiration was the epic tale of Troy. First they built a vaulting horse, then recruited keep-fit fanatics for ceaseless exercise, tunnelling all the while from under the horse to the camp perimeter. Finally they concealed themselves inside the horse and wriggled their way to freedom.

That was the splendid conception. But it had to be sold to the handymen of the camp. The prisoners' theatre boasted an excellent carpenter, but he did not want to know. His tools were, he explained, "on parole" for the dramatic productions so essential to morale.

"Why not go along and see 'Wings' Maw?" he suggested. "He's got a few tools, and he'll lend a hand."

A small man with a large moustache, Maw received the plotters in the casual wear he had been shot down in. His Egyptian sandals, pink socks, bright yellow shirt, large red neckerchief and worn grey flannel trousers hardly befitted the former Commander of No 108, a bomber squadron operating against targets in Libya and Greece.

If asked he would explain his gear: "Thought I'd dress like a foreigner, then I shouldn't be noticed if I had to bale out. But I must have dressed as the wrong sort of foreigner, because I was arrested quite soon."

Maw inhabited a small room at the end of block 64 – the privilege of a wing commander. It was crammed with tins of string, nuts, bolts, bits of glass and paint. There were also strands of wire, bedboards, pieces of broken-down stove and the remains of a wooden bicycle he had tried to make.

His *pièce de resistance* was the fake tools, laid out to bamboozle the German "ferrets", as the PoWs called guards set to discover escape plots. His real tools – sharp and useful – were hidden behind the walls.

When Maw's wooden horse was ready it stood 4 ft 6 ins high. The base covered an area of 5 ft x 3 ft, and the sides were made of plywood sheets from Red Cross packing cases, stolen from the German store.

Eric Williams later published *The Wooden Horse*, a best-selling account of the escape, which became the basis for film and television productions.

Son of a Lincolnshire landowner, who farmed at Cleatham Hall, Kirton Lindsey, Roger Hargreaves Maw was born on June 24 1906 and educated at Westerleigh School, St Leonards on Sea, and Oundle. He learned to fly as an RAF reservist, and in 1927 joined his first squadron, No 503, flying Fairey Fawn biplane light day bombers. In the early 1930s he served in Nos 9,101 and 57 Bomber Squadrons, then spent three years with No 39 in India.

On his return to Britain in 1936 Maw joined No 18. The next year he moved to No 105, an Audax Squadron, and then became an instructor at No 3 Flying Training School. After staff appointments in Nos 20 and 23 Groups in 1940, he joined No 142 in 1941; later that year he was given command of No 12, another Wellington squadron.

In the spring of 1942 he took command of No 108 in the Western Desert. Heavy losses were incurred as the Desert Air Force battered the Libyan port of Tobruk.

Maw came up with a plan which entailed delaying the attack until the whole force had assembled near Tobruk, then going in simultaneously from every possible angle, to disorient and swamp the defences.

But in August 1942 Maw's aircraft was shot down. He baled out and, with a badly injured leg, crawled towards German lines.

Released from the RAF at the end of the war in Europe, he made wooden toys for a time, then settled at a farm at Welton Cliff, Lincs.

Maw was awarded the DFC in 1941.

He married, in 1937, Janet Thornton; they had a son and two daughters.

FLIGHT LIEUTENANT
OLIVER PHILPOT
6 MAY 1993

Oliver Philpot, who has died aged 80, was one of three prisoners of war to escape from Stalag Luft III, in an episode later celebrated by the film *The Wooden Horse*.

The escape from the prison camp at Sagan, Silesia, in 1943 was based on the ruse of placing a hollow wooden vaulting horse some 100 ft from the camp wire.

At the outset Flt Lt Eric Williams, whose idea was inspired by the Trojan Horse, and Lt R M C Codner, Royal Artillery, wedged themselves inside the horse, sank a shaft and began to dig a tunnel. Fellow prisoners staged a keep-fit exhibition which duped their German guards for months.

The operation began on July 8 1943, but Flt Lt Oliver Philpot later joined as third man. Day after day, as PoWs vaulted for two or three hours at a stretch, Philpot toiled at his share of the tunnelling.

Then, at 1 pm on Oct 29, Codner was sealed into the tunnel. After the evening parade, at which the count was falsified, Williams and Philpot were carried out inside the horse. At 5 pm they too were sealed in.

Philpot and his comrades waited until it was almost dark and then emerged some 12 ins short of the target spot, to find themselves right in the sentry's path. Fortunately the night patrol was late.

Clad in black clothes and face masks, the party made its way into a wood, where it split up: Codner and Williams headed for Stettin, while Philpot plumped for the longer trip to Danzig.

Posing as a Norwegian quisling, Philpot prayed he would not meet any genuine Norwegians as he did not speak the language. His cover story was that he was a margarine executive (his own peacetime occupation) on exchange from Norway to Berlin.

He carried a small suitcase containing shaving gear and wore a black Homburg, an RAF officer's greatcoat and gloves, new shoes, a pair of Fleet Air Arm officer's trousers and a black civilian jacket.

He chewed on a pipe, as an excuse for slurring his speech, and for good measure he sported a Hitler moustache.

He bought a rail ticket at Sagan and travelled to Frankfurt-on-Oder. The next morning he caught the slow train to Kustrin, where he joined the Konigsberg Express, went to sleep sitting on his suitcase in a third-class gangway, fell off and exclaimed "Damn!" But his fellow passengers simply laughed.

Challenged by a plain-clothes policeman on the train,

Philpot fobbed him off with an identity card which displayed the mug shot of a fellow officer. He changed at Dirschau and boarded a fast train to Danzig.

It was 23 hours since he had broken ground at Sagan. He treated himself to a glass of beer in the station refreshment room, took a tram to recce the docks and returned to an hotel near the station, where he was obliged to share a room.

The next morning Philpot took a ferry trip in the harbour, where he noticed a Swedish ship loading coal. Later that evening he climbed up a mooring cable and wriggled on to the deck.

After lying low for a while he crawled to a door leading to a galley, drank the hot chocolate he found simmering there and stowed away in a coal bunker.

Next morning (November 2) the ship put to sea. Having waited until the craft was well clear of Danzig, Philpot revealed himself and was invited by the captain to be a guest for the remainder of the voyage.

The ship docked at midnight on November 3 at Sodertalje, where Philpot spent a night in a police cell. The next day he walked into the British Legation at Stockholm, where repatriation was arranged. Williams and Codner also scored a "home run" by way of Sweden.

The son of a lighting engineer from London, Oliver Lawrence Spurling Philpot was born in Vancouver, British Columbia, on March 6 1913 and educated at Radley and Worcester College, Oxford, where he learned to fly with the University Air Squadron.

In 1934 he joined Unilever as a management trainee and two years later was appointed assistant commercial secretary in the company's Home Margarine Executive.

He reported for full-time service in the RAF in August 1939 and was posted to 42 Squadron as a pilot officer. This Coastal Command unit was equipped with the obsolete

Wildebeeste torpedo bomber.

In June 1940 the squadron converted to Bristol Beauforts and saw action in the Norwegian campaign. On one sortie Philpot pressed home an attack on Christiansand in Norway after his Beaufort had been badly shot up. With his crew dead or dying, he managed to fly back to Leuchars in Scotland, where he made a belly landing.

On December 11 1941 his Beaufort was hit by a German flakship while attacking a freighter at the centre of a merchant convoy. He ditched the Beaufort, which broke in two. Philpot and his crew clambered into a dinghy and were adrift for two nights before being picked up by the enemy.

After the "Wooden Horse" escape he was debriefed by MI9, the escape organisation, and did not return to operations. In 1944 he was appointed a senior scientific officer at the Air Ministry.

On demobilisation in 1946 he joined the Maypole Dairy Co; two years later he was appointed chairman of Trufood. In 1950 he became office manager at Unilever House, and the next year moved to T Walls & Son as general manager.

Subsequently he was a director of Arthur Woollacott & Rappings; chairman and managing director of the Spirella Co of Great Britain; managing director of Benesta (later Aluminium) Foils.

In 1962 he joined Union International and from its head office ran eight companies. From 1965 to 1967 he was deputy chairman and chief executive of Fropax Eskimo Food, later Findus. Finally, from 1974 to 1978, Philpot was managing director of Remploy.

In his spare time he gave unstinting service to various charities. He was chairman of the RAF Escaping Society, and served on the National Advisory Council on

Employment for Disabled People. He was also overseas administrator for Help the Aged, a member of the general advisory council of the IBA and a manager of the St Bride Foundation Institute.

In 1950 Philpot published *Stolen Journey*. He listed his recreations as "political activity including canvassing, sculling Boat Race course and return (No 452 in Head of the River Race for Scullers, 1986), talking, idling, listening to sermons, reading *Financial Times* and obituaries in *Lancet*".

Philpot was awarded the DFC in 1941 and MC in 1944.

His first marriage, by which he had a son and two daughters, was dissolved in 1951. He married secondly, in 1954, Rosl Widhalm; they had a son and a daughter.

AIDAN CRAWLEY
3 NOVEMBER 1993

Aidan Crawley, who has died aged 85, was a man of legendary dash and talent — brilliant cricketer, crusading journalist, gallant pilot, daring PoW escaper, minister in Clement Attlee's Labour government, influential figure in television, Conservative MP and well-reviewed author.

The son of Canon A S Crawley, a canon of St George's Chapel, Windsor, and Chaplain to King George V, Aidan Merivale Crawley was born on April 10 1908. He was educated at Harrow and Trinity College, Oxford.

It was as a cricketer that Crawley first made his mark. He was one of the very few players to appear in "Lord's Week" (Eton *v* Harrow; Oxford *v* Cambridge) for seven years running, in his case from 1924 to 1930.

From early boyhood there was a panache about his

batting, even if his temperament scarcely matched his natural skill. But as he matured his high promise was increasingly fulfilled.

In 1928 he made a record total of 1,137 runs for Oxford University, including five hundreds. Next year, driving straight to the Wellingborough ground from a Commem Ball, Crawley hit 10 sixes and 22 fours in an innings against Northamptonshire.

With his high backlift, full follow-through, and rackets-player's wrist, he was a classic striker of the ball. Batting for the Gentlemen at the Pavilion End at Lord's he straight drove "Tich" Freeman over the "free seats" (now the Compton-Edrich Stand) into the nursery ground – a very rare achievement.

After his undergraduate days he appeared occasionally for Kent, and was once 12th man for England. But he had already developed too busy a life to play regular county cricket.

Crawley had been going to North Borneo for Unilever when an offer from Esmond Harmsworth (son of the 1st Viscount Rothermere) diverted him into journalism. He joined the *Daily Mail* on October 5, 1930, and was immediately plunged in at the deep end with coverage of the R101 crash in France.

In 1932 he gained a lobby ticket for the House of Commons, although he continued with other assignments both at home and abroad. The conditions he witnessed as a reporter on the *Swansea Evening Post* led him towards socialism.

Yet he also immensely enjoyed his position as the *Mail's* hunting correspondent. Crawley hunted with no fewer than 66 packs of hounds.

In 1933 Esmond Harmsworth invited him on a world tour. In the long bar of the Raffles Hotel in Singapore Crawley met a distraught theatrical producer who complained that his junior lead had run off with the harbourmaster's daughter. He took over the part, and went on with the company to Shanghai, before returning via Hollywood and New York.

Back home, Crawley abandoned journalism to chance his arm in documentary films. He completed a successful series on the Holy Land and the Middle East for schools.

In 1936 Crawley, uneasy about developments in Europe, joined the Auxiliary Air Force, and after qualifying as a pilot was attached to No 601 (County of London Squadron).

Tall and handsome in the jutting-jawed style of a Percy Westerman hero, Crawley seemed perfectly cast in the role of fighter pilot. But he became frustrated when, during the first winter of the war, he was required only to fly night patrols over the Channel.

In April 1940 he was dispatched to Turkey, overtly as an assistant air attaché, in fact as a member of the Balkan Intelligence Service. He also operated in Yugoslavia and Bulgaria; and was smuggled out of Sofia when the Germans arrived in March 1941.

Subsequently Crawley joined 73, a Hurricane fighter Squadron in Egypt. On July 7 1941 he took off from Sidi Haneish, in the North African desert, with instructions to give cover to barges which were supplying besieged Tobruk, and to strafe enemy positions.

Shot down by machine-gun fire, he crash-landed amid a company of enemy troops. The Germans flew him to Salonika, and then put him on a train for Vienna. Crawley whiled away the journey with a copy of *Berlin Illustrierte*, in which he was astonished to see a photograph of himself, described as an explosives expert and a dangerous member of the British Secret Service.

Subsequently Crawley made a remarkable escape from Oflag XXIB, in Schubin, a small market town some 150 miles west of Warsaw.

He left camp through a tunnel which began in a cesspool. Clad in plus-fours made out of a blanket, he found shelter with a Polish family before journeying on by bus and train. His papers served to convince officials that he was a Sudeten German schoolteacher on his way to Berlin.

Two fellow-escapers were also to become well-known: Anthony Barber, the future Tory Chancellor, and Robert Kee, the author and broadcaster. In Berlin Crawley ran into Kee when they were both shaving in a public lavatory; they had to pretend not to recognise each other. Crawley then caught a train to Munich, where he took refuge from an RAF raid in an underground shelter. There he found much merriment and *bonhomie*: his companions cursed the bomber crews and tucked into food and wine which they gladly shared with him.

But on his next train, to Switzerland, he was rumbled near Innsbruck. His papers still passed muster; it was extreme exhaustion that gave him away. He was returned to Schubin and then sent to Stalag Luft III, 80 miles south-east of Berlin.

Crawley was appointed information officer of the escape committee and camp interpreter. In the latter role he was obliged to convey to Group Captain Wallis, the senior British officer, that 50 officers had been shot after the celebrated "Great Escape".

Crawley himself escaped several more times, but was always recaptured. He began to assemble material for an account of the various attempts to get out of Germany, taking it with him as the British prisoners were marched through the ice and snow of the east European winter. Such was the genesis of his book, *Escape from Germany*, published in an abbreviated version (for security reasons) in 1956, and in full by HMSO in 1985.

At the 1945 general election Crawley won Buckingham, for which he had been adopted before the war, for Labour. He became parliamentary private secretary to successive Secretaries of State for the Colonies, and in 1950 was appointed Parliamentary Under-Secretary of State for Air.

But in the 1951 general election he narrowly lost his Buckingham seat. He went back to making documentary films, but now for television. His *Americans at Home* series was judged so successful that the BBC offered him a programme called *Viewfinder*, which dealt with current affairs at home and abroad.

In 1955 Crawley was appointed the first editor-in-chief of Independent Television News. The new operation made the BBC seem absurdly amateurish and old-fashioned; within a year, however, he was back making television documentaries for the BBC. He also appeared on *Panorama*.

His reputation in international affairs was such that in 1960 he was appointed a member of the Monckton Commission on the Federation of Rhodesia and Nyasaland. In 1961 he was back with independent television, as editor of Associated Rediffusion Intertel features.

Meanwhile, in 1957, Crawley had left the Labour Party. In 1962 he won a tight by-election in the Conservative cause in West Derbyshire. He took his seat to booing from the Labour benches; in compensation he received a personal letter of congratulation from the Prime Minister, Harold Macmillan.

But his warnings about Communist infiltration of the unions were ignored, and promotion appeared elusive. His second parliamentary career ended in 1967 at the behest of London Weekend Television, which had appointed him chairman.

Crawley was a skilled political lobbyist, but unfortunately London Weekend concentrated harder on gaining the franchise than on what to do with it. In 1971, after Rupert Murdoch had intervened to prevent economic disaster, Crawley exchanged the chairmanship for the presidency of the company.

As the first chairman of the National Cricket Association from 1968 to 1975, Crawley was deeply involved with the administration of cricket below first-class level. In 1971 he was the instigator, in collaboration with the *Cricketer*, of the National Village Championship, now an annual event. His career in cricket was crowned by the presidency of MCC in 1973.

Crawley's *De Gaulle* (1969) was a notably fair and accurate biography; *The Rise of Western Germany 1945-7* was a readable account of the transition from Nazi ruin to democratic prosperity; and *Leap Before You Look* (1988) was an autobiography that eschewed special pleading.

He was appointed MBE in 1946.

Aidan Crawley married, in 1945, the American author and journalist Virginia Cowles, who was killed in a car crash in 1983. They had two sons, Andrew and Randall, both killed in an aircraft crash in 1988, and a daughter, Harriet.

AIR MARSHAL
SIR HARRY BURTON
29 NOVEMBER 1993

Air Marshal Sir Harry Burton, who has died aged 74, was the first RAF prisoner of war to make the "home run" after escaping from Germany.

In September 1940, Burton was captain of a Wellington bomber in 149 Squadron, briefed to drop incendiaries on targets in the Black Forest. On the flight home the bomber was hit by anti-aircraft fire. Burton ordered the crew to bale out. He remained aboard to destroy secret equipment, and escaped just in time.

Burton landed in a Belgian swamp, where he hid his parachute and darkened his uniform buttons with mud. In the morning, his wings concealed by a scarf, he attempted to pass himself off as a Belgian worker.

Rumbled, he was dispatched to Stalag Luft I at Barth on the Baltic, where the escape committee put him in charge of maps. During that winter some 50 escape attempts were made. A tunnel on which Burton had worked was discovered, and he was given 10 days' solitary confinement.

Having loosened the cell bars, on his fifth night he climbed out and made for the main gates. He had with him a small map, two bars of chocolate and a table knife. He burrowed under one gate, crawled over the second, climbed a 10-foot wire, avoided the Alsatians whose patrol times he had memorised, and escaped in the early hours of May 27 1941.

When day broke Burton rested in woods. At nightfall he followed a railway line to the coast; he knew that a ferry to Sweden was due to leave that next afternoon. He hid beneath a rail freight car, with his back on an axle and his feet and shoulders thrust against supporting bars.

When shunting began the axle rotated, and he had to heave himself up until the car stopped.

He was imprisoned on his arrival in Sweden, but the Air Ministry confirmed his identity from London, and he was flown home.

Harry Burton was born on May 2 1919 and educated at Glasgow High School. Granted a short service commission in 1937, he received a permanent one just as the war was ending in 1945.

He was a bomber pilot from the outset, serving first in 215 Squadron; in September 1940, shortly before he was shot down, he was posted to No 149.

After his escape Burton joined the operations staff of 41 Group, before moving for similar duties to RAF Transport Command. In January 1945 he was given command of No 238, flying Dakotas in Burma in support of the British 14th Army. The next year Burton returned to Transport Command. In 1950, after a stint at the School of Land–Air Warfare at Old Sarum, he was posted to the Indian Defence Services Staff College.

From 1953 to 1955 he was Wing Commander, Flying, at RAF Benson. Two years later he became Station Commander at Weston Zoyland.

After commanding the bomber base at RAF Scampton in Lincolnshire, in 1960 he was appointed deputy commander of a force of three Vulcans, which in 1962 showed the flag over the Commonwealth and Empire Games at Perth.

In the early 1960s he was Senior Air Staff Officer at 3 Group Bomber Command and Air Executive to the Deputy Nuclear Affairs, SHAPE. In 1967 he received command of 23 Group. His last appointment was Commander-in-Chief, RAF Air Support Command. When the body of the Duke of Windsor was flown home for burial in 1972, Burton accompanied the coffin in an

RAF VC10. He retired in 1973.

For the past 17 years he was chairman of the board of management of Princess Marina House, the RAF Benevolent Fund's home, where he inspired the development of a new north wing. A former navigator arrived there in a wheelchair and asked if a bomber chap called Burton was around. He was Duncan McFarlane, who had been with Burton when their Wellington was shot down. They had not seen each other for 47 years.

Burton was awarded the DSO in 1941, appointed MBE in 1943, CBE in 1963, CB in 1970 and KCB in 1971.

He married first, in 1945, Jean Dobie, who died in 1987; they had a son and a daughter. He married secondly, in 1988, Sandra Robertson (née McGlashan).

AIR MARSHAL
SIR JOHN WHITLEY
26 DECEMBER 1997

Air Marshal Sir John Whitley, who has died aged 92, served in RAF Bomber Command during the Second World War and made a remarkable escape from Occupied France.

In April 1943, Whitley was a group captain and commander of the bomber station at Linton-on-Ouse. As a station commander, he was supposed to refrain from active participation in bomber operations, but on the night of April 10 he was flying as second pilot of a Halifax bomber of No 76 Squadron when it was attacked by an Me 110 fighter. The Halifax's fuel tanks caught fire and the crew was ordered to bale out.

As Whitley dropped through the escape hatch, part of his equipment became caught and he found himself suspended a foot below the fuselage, dangling in the slipstream. He then noticed that his parachute pack was only half-attached to his harness.

He was trying to remedy this when the object on which he was caught gave way and he went hurtling into free fall. Fortunately, when his parachute opened it held him, and he landed at Hirson, on the Franco-Belgian border.

As Whitley was leaving the aircraft, he had grabbed a haversack that contained his home-made escape kit, packed for just such an emergency. From it he extracted civilian clothing and a razor. He then proceeded to shave off his large moustache, which might otherwise have betrayed him as an RAF officer.

After walking a few miles, he found food and shelter in a farmhouse; in return he presented the farmer's wife with his gold and onyx RAF cufflinks. Whitley was then driven to Leuze, where he was hidden for three weeks until passed on to an escape organisation, which reunited him with the only other two survivors of his crew.

He used a lull in the escape time-table to undertake some light intelligence work, making notes on a new German radar station in the area before cycling on to a country inn for refreshment.

Whitley began his run for home on May 4 when, with a bomber wireless operator, Sergeant Laws, he was sent by train to Paris.

There they were passed to an escape-line helper named Fouquerel, who had been butler to Lord Dudley at La Touquet. His apartment was teeming with escapers, but Fouquerel explained the presence of so many young men to the concierge by passing himself off as a specialist in venereal disease whose patients required residential treatment. Fouquerel was later arrested and shot.

Whitley now received new travel documents and

assumed the identity of one M Bidet, a baker with business in St Jean-de-Luz; Sergeant Laws became a hairdresser. On the evening of May 8 the pair began a rail journey to Bayonne, where they picked up bicycles and an escape courier.

Pedalling past Biarritz, Whitley was horrified to be admonished by his escort in English; his cycling style, complained the courier, was much too straight-backed and obviously that of an Englishman. Whitley obediently began to hunch himself low over the handlebars.

At St Jean-de-Luz, Whitley met Spanish guides who led him to a farmhouse where he was handed over to the professional smuggler Florentino Goicoechea. He led the party stumbling over the Pyrenees by night, pausing occasionally to revive himself from brandy bottles he had stashed in bushes along the route. At 4 am the escapers crossed into Spain.

The next morning Whitley and Laws were driven to a rendezvous with the second secretary of the British Embassy, who took them into Madrid (and to a bullfight). From there they went to Gibraltar, and on May 24 Whitley was flown home by a Dakota; had he taken the next flight he would have been shot down.

John René Whitley was born on September 7 1905 at Devonport, where his father, an engineer, was building the Admiralty Dockyard. He spent the next part of his childhood in Chile, where his father constructed a railway.

John's mother died of blackwater fever when he was four, and for the next five years he was cared for by relations in Boulogne. During the First World War, John's father was taken prisoner in Iraq, but he too managed to escape.

John was sent to Haileybury, where he excelled at games but did not shine academically. On leaving school, he joined a firm of City timber merchants as an office boy, escaping the tedium of its routine by working as a fireman on a locomotive during the General Strike in 1926.

When he returned to the City, a friend told him about the adventures his brother – a pilot – had had during the strike, when the RAF took over from the Royal Mail. So Whitley joined the service and was awarded his wings in 1927, despite having a tetchy flying instructor who would pull out the joystick and use it to beat his pupils about the head.

Whitley was posted to No7 Squadron at Worthy Down, near Winchester, and survived two near-fatal crashes early in his career. In 1931 he hitched a lift from Farnborough in the tail gunner's cockpit of a Virginia bomber, which hit airfield buildings as it came in to land.

Whitley's cockpit finished up on the station commander's car as he was driving to lunch. The pilot, second pilot and wireless operator were killed; Whitley got away with a minor neck injury.

The next summer, Whitley was a passenger in a bomber when engine trouble obliged him and the pilot to bale out at only 800 ft. The pilot was killed but Whitley escaped with a sprained ankle.

In 1932 Whitley was posted to India, where he served with the bomber transport flight at Lahore and piloted the Viceroy.

Whitley was awarded the AFC in 1937, and in 1939 was posted to No 24 Communications Squadron, where he piloted both Chamberlain and Churchill.

In May 1940 he was promoted to Wing Commander and took charge of No 149, a Wellington squadron. He flew night operations from Mildenhall and bombed barges assembling for the invasion of Britain. He then joined the staff at Bomber Command's headquarters until, in May 1941, he was made station commander at Linton-on-Ouse.

Following his successful evasion of capture in France,

Whitley returned to station duties. He was awarded the DSO in 1943 and, still under 40, became an Air Vice-Marshal in 1944. As the war ended he took charge of Bomber Command's No 4 Group before moving to No 8, the Pathfinder Force.

In 1946, Whitley was posted to Air Headquarters, India, returning home as Director of Organisation (Establishments). From 1951 he was in charge of administration for British Air Forces of Occupation, Germany. In 1953 he took over Bomber Command's No 1 Group.

He was awarded a bar to his AFC in 1956, the same year that he was appointed KBE. In 1957 he joined the Air Council as Member for Personnel.

In 1959 Whitley became Inspector-General of the RAF. Three years later he was appointed Controller of the RAF Benevolent Fund and set it on course for pre-eminence among the Service charities.

Whitley left the fund in 1968 and retired to Lymington, where he indulged his love of sailing.

He was appointed CBE in 1945 and CB in 1946.

He married, in 1932, Barbara Liscombe; they had four sons, of whom one predeceased him. Barbara Whitley died in 1965 and he married secondly, in 1967, Alison Russell; she died in 1986.

SQUADRON LEADER
BOB NELSON
25 AUGUST 1999

Bob Nelson, who has died aged 84, evaded capture behind enemy lines in the Western Desert for 18 days, took part in the Great Escape, and subsequently established an international reputation as an air accident expert, representing the Government at each of the five de Havilland Comet jet passenger airliner accident inquiries of the 1950s.

Nelson's wartime journey through the desert began in darkness on September 18 1942, 50 miles south of Sollum on the Mediterranean border between Egypt and Libya, when he was forced to make a crash landing after losing one of the two engines on his Vickers Wellington bomber.

With the aircraft ablaze and the rest of his crew of five having baled out, he managed a juddering touch-down on the desert floor. Then, grabbing the bomber's dinghy emergency pack and the navigator's large compass, he scrambled through the pilot's escape hatch and was clear of the wrecked Wellington when its bomb load blew up.

Estimating that he was 100 miles west of the British 8th Army's positions at El Alamein, Nelson took stock of his supplies: four tins of tomato juice, some dried milk, a handful of benzedrine and water-purifying tablets, a torch, a .38 revolver with six rounds of ammunition, and a half-litre water bottle.

He abandoned the navigator's compass as too heavy, opting instead for a small pocket compass and the stars, and set out eastward in the cold desert night.

After four days, dropping with exhaustion and with all his liquid supplies gone, he came across a telegraph line which he pulled down in the hope that someone would be sent to investigate. No one came; but during the night, moisture condensed on the metal of some abandoned petrol tins nearby, and by licking them he obtained sufficient water to stay alive.

On the seventh day, Nelson saw movement on the horizon against the setting sun. After walking for two hours he encountered 50 camels driven by an Arab, who gave him water. Nelson staggered along behind the camel train until they reached a small camp alongside a well. There the Arabs supplied him with two extra water bottles and a haversack of British Army biscuits.

Leaving his Arab saviours with a note asking whomsoever it concerned to reward them, Nelson set off eastwards from a point some 20 miles south of the coast, agonised by blistered feet but determined to avoid German armoured cars.

Moving among abandoned camps, he came across two fighter aircraft, the remains of their pilots still in the cockpits. He took a long silk parachute cord and tin to obtain water from the occasional well, along with abandoned canvas to serve as a tent.

On the morning of October 6, Nelson reached the rear of the German lines at El Alamein. In plain daylight he walked unremarked through hospitals, cemeteries and tank repair depots, until in the afternoon British gunfire hastened him into a slit trench, where he hid until dark.

Moving forward into no-man's land on hands and knees, he knew that by morning he would be one of three things: dead, a prisoner or free. In the event, he was only a mile from British lines when a German patrol found him and took him prisoner.

Thomas Robert Nelson was born on March 10 1915 at Leeds, where he attended City of Leeds School and Leeds College of Technology and was apprenticed as a mechanical engineer.

He had a job with the Bristol Aeroplane Company

when in 1937 he was commissioned into the Reserve of Air Force Officers (RAFO). The next year he was posted to No 114, a Bristol Blenheim light-bomber squadron.

Shortly after the outbreak of war, Nelson trained as a flying instructor at the Central Flying School. From 1940 he served as an instructor in Rhodesia, until in 1942 he was posted to No 37, a Wellington bomber and transport squadron in Egypt.

He had completed 22 operational sorties by the time of his desert ordeal, after which he was despatched to Germany. In November 1942 he arrived at Stalag Luft III at Sagan in Silesia.

Very soon his engineering skills were employed on the construction of ventilation and transport systems for the tunnels Tom, Dick and Harry. His Mark 1 Nelson Trolley was a significant factor in enabling the Great Escape through tunnel Harry.

On the night of March 24 1944, Nelson was about 40th of the 76 Allied prisoners who escaped. Three of these were to reach Britain, 50 were murdered by the Gestapo on Hitler's orders, and the remainder, including Nelson, returned to captivity.

With snow on the ground, Nelson and Dick Churchill, with whom he had paired up, were cold, wet and hungry when after two days they were discovered in a barn and handed over. It appeared that the Gestapo had spared them on the assumption that they were related to their illustrious namesakes. They were returned to prison camps until the end of the war.

With the return of peace, Nelson was demobilised as a squadron leader and joined Transair, an air transport company based in Switzerland. He later moved to KLM.

In 1952 he joined the Air Accident Investigation Branch of the Ministry of Civil Aviation. Soon afterwards a Comet, the world's first passenger jet and a type which had recently joined BOAC's fleet, was damaged in an abortive take-off from Rome. There were no casualties.

Nelson attended the Italian inquiry as British representative. Next March he represented the Government at an inquiry into the loss of a Canadian Comet at Karachi in a repetition of the Rome accident that had fatal results.

Take-off procedures were modified. But the next year a BOAC Comet had almost reached its cruising altitude after taking off from Calcutta when it disintegrated in a high speed dive killing six crew and 37 passengers.

Travelling from London in a BOAC Comet Nelson again represented Britain at the Calcutta inquiry, which concluded that the accident was caused by structural failure owing to overstressing in the severe turbulence of monsoon conditions. "I was losing my confidence in fast jet aircraft," Nelson recalled, and returned to London in a Constellation.

In January 1954 a London-bound BOAC Comet, after climbing from Rome, exploded and fell into the sea killing six crew and 29 passengers.

While tests were carried out at the Royal Aircraft Establishment, Farnborough, all Comets were modified, and passenger flights were resumed. Then, on April 8, a BOAC Comet left Rome for Johannesburg. In a repetition of the Italian accident, it exploded while climbing; seven crew and 14 passengers died.

Eventually, water-tank tests and inspection of wreckage established metal fatigue as the cause of the accidents.

In 1957 Nelson was seconded to the International Civil Aviation Organisation (ICAO) at Montreal to write its manual on aircraft accident investigation.

In 1961 he was one of two observers appointed by the United Nations to the investigation of the air crash in which Dag Hammarskjöld was killed en route for the Congo.

In 1969 Nelson went to Afghanistan as civil aviation adviser and chief of the ICAO technical mission. He worked on a projected internal airline providing access to remote areas.

Nelson retired in 1975 and lived in Portugal until 1989, when he returned to London and was active in organising memorials at home and in Poland to his 50 murdered fellow escapers.

He is survived by his wife Anne, their son and two daughters.

WING COMMANDER
JOE KAYLL
3 MARCH 2000

Wing Commander Joe Kayll, who has died aged 85, had the exceptional distinction as a fighter pilot of being awarded the DSO and DFC on the same day.

Kayll was credited in the citation for his awards, dated May 31 1940, with having destroyed nine enemy aircraft since May 10, when Germany launched its invasion of the Low Countries and France.

His was an outstanding achievement for an Auxiliary Air Force weekend flier who had arrived in France in November 1939 as a flight commander. His squadron (No 607, County of Durham) was flying obsolete Gloster Gladiator biplane fighters. Based at Merville near Vitry en Artois, 607 was fortunate not to be seriously challenged during the phoney war of winter 1939–1940. In this sitting–duck biplane it was unnerving merely to overfly cemeteries from the Great War.

In March 1940, Kayll received command of No 615 (County of Surrey) Squadron and on May 2 led it to Le

Touquet to re-equip with Hawker Hurricane fighters in place of death-trap biplanes. But at dawn on May 10 the airfield was attacked and four of 607's spanking new Hurricanes were destroyed on the ground.

Back to strength again, the squadron returned to Merville. As enemy tanks supported by Ju87 dive-bombers advanced towards the Channel, Kayll led his gallant band of Auxiliaries – businessmen, farmers, lawyers and accountants against overwhelming fighter odds.

Forced to move from airfield to inadequate airfield as they were overrun, Kayll and his part-timers took off through curtains of falling bombs to fly six or seven combat sorties a day.

On May 20, as Belgian troops blew up the airfield, he flew to Abbeville, assembled a number of still serviceable Hurricanes, and strafed enemy forces on the Arras–Douai road. They lost three aircraft to ground fire.

The operational record book and pilots' logbooks of 615 were destroyed by a bomb, leaving no record of its exploits when Kayll's depleted and exhausted squadron was withdrawn to Kenley.

With replacement pilots and Hurricanes, 615 was kept busy all that June. One day, returning from a sortie over France, Kayll found King George VI waiting to pin on both a DSO and a DFC.

Shortly afterwards Kayll had another surprise when, landing back from France, he found Winston Churchill waiting to dine with the squadron and stay the night. The prime minister's visit provided a timely boost for 615. During the Battle of Britain it fought – with heavy losses – until the end of August, and again in October after a brief spell recuperating at Prestwick.

Joseph Robert Kayll was born in Sunderland on April 12 1914. He was educated at Stowe. But after failing all exams, he started work at 16 as a mill boy in the family business of Joseph Thompson, a sawmill in Sunderland.

From 1934 Kayll spent weekends and holidays learning to fly Westland Wapitis with No 607 Squadron. In 1939, called to full-time service, Kayll was posted with 607 to Drem in Scotland.

One Luftwaffe bomber pilot shot down over the sea by a 607 Gladiator pilot exclaimed in fluent English: "To be shot down by a bloody barrister in a bloody biplane is more than I can bloody well bear." Intelligence had led him to expect no more resistance than "a bunch of Auxiliary amateurs".

After the Battle of Britain, during which he notched up several further kills, Kayll was rested on Fighter Command's tactical staff until June 2 1941, when he received command of the celebrated Spitfire wing based at Hornchurch, Essex.

Kayll was dismayed on June 25 when the station commander, Group Captain Harry Broadhurst, decided to lead the wing in a daylight raid on France. Fearing this was a fateful decision, Kayll agreed to fly as No 2 to the Spitfire ace, and was shot down over St Omer.

Kayll crash landed in a pea field. He was taken prisoner and interrogated by a Captain Eberhart, who told him the Luftwaffe knew about his career from reports published in the *Sunderland Echo*.

"It was most disconcerting," Kayll recalled. "They knew I had performed aerobatics with 607 Squadron at Empire Air Days and had played rugger with 603 at Edinburgh.

"They even knew I had recently married Annette Nisbet of Harperley Hall."

As a PoW Kayll was involved from the first with escape plans. He was held at Spangenburg, 20 miles from Kassel, a 12th-century castle and former hunting lodge of the princes of Hesse. Here he assisted two successful escapes.

Further attempts were frustrated by a dry moat

inhabited by wild boar which made a commotion when disturbed. The animals proved impervious to potatoes stuck with razor blades, eating them with gusto and no ill effects.

In October 1941, Kayll was moved to Stalag VIB, a former Hitler Youth camp at Warburg. Most of the prisoners were Army officers. "I escaped from this camp," Kayll remembered, "with 10 RAF and 20 Army officers over the wire. The escape was organised by Captain Stallard, who was successful. I was out for seven days before being recaptured by a forester.

"I was escorted via a Berlin prison to Offlag XXIB at Schubin in Poland. After a period of solitary I helped with a tunnel which started from the lavatory. About 30 got out, but all were recaptured."

In 1943 Kayll was moved to Stalag Luft III at Sagan in eastern Silesia, where he was put in charge of escape attempts, with Squadron Leader Dudley Craig, a fellow 607 pilot, as his No 2 and Flight Lieutenant Aidan Crawley, the future broadcaster and MP, as intelligence officer.

This escape committee's greatest success was the Wooden Horse exploit, in which a makeshift gymnastic horse shielded tunnelling. This resulted in a "home run" made by Flight Lieutenants Eric Williams, Oliver Philpot and Lieutenant Mike Codner.

In the spring of 1945, as the Russians advanced, Kayll and his fellows marched westwards. They overcame their guards and camped at a farm near Hamburg, where Russian women slaveworkers, relieved of their forced labour, gladly cooked for them.

Kayll was demobilised in 1946 and returned to the family timber business. He re-formed 607 as a weekend fliers' Auxiliary fighter squadron at Ouston, Northumberland.

An enthusiastic yachtsman, Kayll founded the Sunderland Yacht Club. In 1981, aged 67, he sailed the family ketch *Wild Thyme* home after his sons Joseph and David had completed the *Observer* transatlantic two-handed yacht race.

In addition to his early war DSO and DFC Kayll was mentioned in despatches in 1941 and appointed OBE in 1945 when he also received the Air Efficiency award.

━━━━━━━

FLIGHT LIEUTENANT
JACK BEST
22 APRIL 2000

Jack Best, who has died aged 87, took part in one of the most audacious escape attempts of the Second World War, the plan to build and fly a glider out of Colditz.

The idea was dreamt up by Tony Rolt, a naval officer, who had noticed that the roof of the castle's chapel was hidden from sight of the guards below. He convinced Bill Goldfinch, a Sunderland flying boat pilot, to draw up a design for a glider which could be flown from the roof, and with Best erected a false-wall in an attic of the chapel to form a workshop.

In this, the glider was painstakingly constructed over nine months using tools improvised from bedsteads, iron window bars and gramophone springs, which were turned into makeshift saws.

Best made the wingspars from floorboards and parts of the fuselage from bed slats, while the control wires were electric cable torn from unused parts of the castle. The aircraft's skin was made from cotton sleeping bags stiffened with the prisoners' ration of boiled millet.

On the day of the flight, a hole was to have been made

in the wall of the attic and the glider hauled out on to the roof of the chapel. The wings, measuring 32 ft across, would then have been attached to the body, and the glider launched by a catapult system, the counterweight of which was an earth-filled bathtub dropping five storeys from the roof to the ground below.

The schematics were reviewed by Lorne Welch, a glider pilot, and Best and the others believed that the glider would have flown for about a mile across the River Mulde, enabling its two-man crew to get a head start on any pursuit.

Best, himself a bomber pilot, later played down suggestions that he would have been in the glider's cockpit. He had been recaptured after a previous escape in which he had shinned down a rope from a window of the castle, and he felt that it would have been right for someone else to have had the chance to make a bid for freedom.

In the event, however, the war ended too soon for them to discover whether the plan would have worked, and the glider is thought to have been broken up for firewood during the bitter winter of 1946 by occupying Russian troops.

But almost 50 years later, Best and his fellow PoWs did get the chance to see if their ingenuity would have been rewarded. In 1993, they returned to Colditz and successfully flew a one-third scale model from the chapel roof.

Then, in February 2000, Best was at RAF Odiham in Hampshire to see a full-size replica of the original glider – built for a Channel 4 series about Colditz – take to the skies.

Its maiden flight was almost half a century late, but there no longer could be any doubt that it would have made possible yet another break-out from the supposedly escape-proof fortress.

John William Best, known as Jack, was born on August 6 1912 at Vivod, near Llangollen in North Wales, and grew up on the family estate.

He was educated at Stowe, took part in a public schools' tour to Kenya, and in 1931 became an apprentice farmer there.

When war came in 1939, he was training for a civilian pilot's licence and accordingly joined the RAF, gaining his wings at No 4 Flying Training School, at Habbaniyah in Iraq. He then became a ferry pilot, flying aircraft from Takoradi in Ghana across Africa to Egypt.

He transferred to No 69, a Maryland bomber reconnaissance squadron, and on a flight in 1941 ran out of fuel over the Mediterranean. He was forced to land in the sea off southern Greece, where he was captured by the Germans.

He was sent to a camp at Biberach and in the winter of 1941–42 on to Stalag Luft I at Barth. Best was later moved to Stalag Luft III, at Sagan, near the Polish border.

Here he made several attempts to escape and in June 1942 he, Goldfinch and Henry Lamond tunnelled 80 ft out under the wire. They had pilot's notes for a Ju 52 transport and so headed for an airfield with the intention of stealing such an aircraft.

There they watched German air cadets undergoing glider training, but as they could not find a suitable aeroplane they walked instead by night to the banks of the Oder, staving off hunger with some potatoes which they had dug up.

There Best and the two other escapers found a skiff and so set off for the Baltic, intending to stow away on a ship bound for Sweden. But they made the mistake of failing to obey the rule of the sea and rowed up the wrong bank, against the river traffic. They were sleeping under the upturned boat when they were rumbled by the police, who gave them bread and cheese and beer before returning them to Sagan. From there they were dispatched to Colditz.

Best was liberated in May 1945 and demobbed as a flight lieutenant. He later farmed in Kenya and served with the reserve police during the Mau Mau troubles. Eventually he returned to Britain and farmed in Herefordshire.

He was awarded a military MBE in 1945.

Jack Best married first, in 1938 (dissolved 1959), Constance Otter. They had a son and a daughter. He married secondly, in 1959, Elisabeth Bunting.

FLIGHT LIEUTENANT DESMOND PLUNKETT
14 FEBRUARY 2002

Desmond Plunkett, who has died aged 86, was one of the Allied airmen who took part in what became known as "The Great Escape"; as the mapmaker for the escape committee at Stalag Luft III, he was one of several models for the character played by Donald Pleasence in the film made in 1963.

Of the 76 men who got away, 73 were recaptured – and 50 were executed on Hitler's orders. Plunkett the 13th man to crawl through the tunnel was among those retaken; but he was fortunate that he managed to remain on the run until the Germans had shot their quota of officers. Instead of being executed, he endured seven months at the Gestapo's headquarters at Prague; much of the time he was in solitary confinement, and subjected to frequent beatings.

Plunkett had served only eight days with No 218, his first operational squadron, when the four-engine Stirling heavy bomber he was co-piloting was shot down by an

Me 109 over enemy-occupied Holland in June 1942. He baled out, and landed in the midst of a herd of cattle. He was later arrested in a nearby village.

He was taken to Stalag Luft III at Sagan in Lower Silesia, 80 miles south-east of Berlin, where his fellow prisoners included Douglas Bader. The prison camp of prefabricated huts surrounded by high barbed wire fences was in a clearing in a thick pine forest.

Remembered by one fellow PoW as a "nuggety little man with a fierce moustache", Plunkett was charged by the men's escape leader, Roger Bushell, with leading the team of some 14 men who were employed in mapmaking. The aim was to produce local maps indicating the quietest routes leading away from the camp, as well as more extensive maps showing escape routes through Czechoslovakia to Switzerland and France, and through the Baltic to Sweden.

By bribing a guard, Plunkett obtained a large and detailed map of Europe which formed the basis of an eventual supply of some 2,500 maps in five colours. He abandoned tracing as being too time-consuming; instead, he conjured up an ingenious mimeograph using gelatine created from the crystal jelly sent in Red Cross parcels. The gelatine was poured into shallow trays made from old food tins bonded together by resin extracted from the ubiquitous fir trees. The ink was derived from the crushed lead of indelible pencils.

Plunkett and his team were able to run off not only maps, but also forged passes, permits and other "official" documents devised by Tim Walenn, the escape committee's master forger whose "department" was known as Dean & Dawson, after the travel business.

Between them Plunkett and Walenn came up with the essential kit for "The Great Escape", which took place on March 23 1944 after the tunnel diggers had made the most of Sagan's light sandy soil and forced an exit beyond the wire. The tunnel, which had been a year in the making, was 360 ft long and some 30 ft beneath the surface.

At his own request (no one else would volunteer for the unlucky number), Plunkett was the 13th man to crawl to freedom; and he had reached the safety of the woods before the Germans discovered the existence of "Harry" – the name the PoWs had given to their tunnel ("Tom" and "Dick" had been the less successful predecessors). With his companion, a Czech airman called Bedrich Dvorak, he went to the local railway station and boarded a train for Breslau.

The two men succeeded in getting into Czechoslovakia where, after several days in the relative luxury of a hotel, they hid in a barn. They eventually got as far as the Austrian border before being arrested. While Plunkett enjoyed the hospitality of the Gestapo (boiled blood was on the prisoners' menu every Tuesday and Thursday), Dvorak was sent to Colditz.

Plunkett was finally released by the Gestapo into the custody of Hradin prison at Prague. Later, in January 1945, he was sent to Stalag Luft I on the Baltic Sea, from where he was repatriated after VE Day. He returned home 50 lb below his normal body weight.

Desmond Launcelot Plunkett was born on February 21 1915 at Guntur in the Madras Presidency of India, where his father was a civil engineer. After the family had returned to England, Desmond was educated at King's College, Wimbledon. Years later, after he had been posted missing, the school inscribed his name on its roll of honour ("Desmond Plunkett, killed in action, 1942") where it remained for many years.

His first job was with the Hawker aircraft company at Kingston upon Thames, Surrey. In 1936 he found work with a company that designed and built gliders, and in the same year he had his first experience of flying, in a Gipsy 1 Moth at Redhill Flying Club. He then joined the RAF Volunteer Reserve, graduating as a flying instructor in 1939. Despite many requests for active service, he was retained as an instructor for the first two years of the war.

Finally, in 1941, Plunkett was posted for training as a bomber pilot with the rank of flight lieutenant, the notification coming only a few days before his wedding to Patricia Wildblood in November 1941. He was posted to RAF Marham in Norfolk, and his first bombing missions were in the raids on Cologne and Essen.

Before the escape from Stalag Luft III, Plunkett had been involved in earlier attempts to get away. His first plan had been to conceal himself in a cart which was removing ash from the camp. He and another airman duly climbed into the cart, and buried themselves in the ash; but because the coals lying underneath were still red hot, their trousers caught fire.

A second attempt, to escape via a tunnel, had been foiled by the German guard dogs. A third, to scale the perimeter fence by ladder, was also unsuccessful. And a further effort to dig a tunnel was abandoned after the excavators found themselves delving into the local sewage works. It was after this that Roger Bushell instructed Plunkett to concentrate on mapmaking.

After the war, Plunkett remained in the RAF for two years. He was posted to India with 10 Squadron, where he turned down the chance to become Lord Mountbatten's personal pilot. Instead, he left the RAF to join the Hindusthan Aircraft Company at Calcutta as sales manager. In 1949 he began a new career in India as a survey pilot, later moving to Africa. In 1965 he and his family settled in Rhodesia, where he continued to carry out air surveys.

In 1971 he was lucky to escape with his life when the de Havilland Dove aircraft in which he was instructing a young Canadian crashed at the airport at Salisbury (now Harare). He retired from flying in 1975, and decided to take up beekeeping.

He returned to England in the late 1990s, going to live at the Royal Air Forces Association home at Storrington, West Sussex.

In 2000 he co-wrote a book about his experiences, *The Man Who Would Not Die*.

Desmond Plunkett is survived by his wife and by their son and two daughters.

CLANDESTINE

GROUP CAPTAIN
RON HOCKEY
21 FEBRUARY 1992

Group Captain Ron Hockey, one of the RAF's most outstanding pilots, who has died aged 80, flew clandestine missions for the Special Operations Executive during the Second World War – notably, in 1941, a perilous round trip to Czechoslovakia, where he dropped the assassins of the Nazi *gauleiter* Reinhard Heydrich.

Already experienced in the task of dropping agents into German-occupied Europe, Hockey took off from Tangmere in Sussex at 2200 hrs on December 28 1941.

On board his four-engined Halifax bomber of No 158 Special Duties Squadron were seven agents – or "Joes", as SOE aircrew called their passengers – comprising two communications and training teams and "Anthropoid", the codename for the Czech assassins, Jozef Gabcik and Jan Kubis.

Despite a signal from the Czech resistance which cast doubt on the value of killing Heydrich (Himmler's deputy) and spoke of dire consequences, Dr Eduard Benes, head of the Czech government-in-exile, insisted on the murder. Mass arrests were to follow, and many thousands of Czechs died – including, in a direct reprisal, the entire populations of the villages of Lidice and Lezaky.

But Hockey, renowned for his imperturbability, would have known nothing of this. He was, in his own modest opinion, "just the bus driver".

This sortie, like so many others, required locating three separate dropping zones ("DZs") in snow and ever-decreasing visibility, defying flak and night fighters. But Hockey was unfazed.

In the event, when over Czechoslovakia, he was forced lower and lower by the weather, and obliged to make blind drops. It was remarkable that none turned out to be further than 10 miles from the DZ.

Nor did the nightmarish conditions abate on the return journey. As he crossed the French coast, his aircraft battered by flak, the escape hatch section of the canopy blew open and jammed. His second pilot, standing beside him, managed to hang on to it.

When Hockey finally landed at Tangmere at 0819 hrs the next morning he had been airborne for more than 10 hours.

In 1991 Hockey unveiled a 138 Squadron plaque in the crypt of St Cyril and Methodius church in Prague to mark the spot where the two hunted Czech agents, holed up with five other resistance fighters, had turned their guns on themselves after holding off 600 enemy troops for many hours.

Latterly Hockey also helped with arrangements for an exhibition to be staged at the Imperial War Museum to commemorate the 50th anniversary of Heydrich's assassination in May 1942.

A Devonian, Ronald Clifton Hockey was born on Aug 4 1911 and educated at Heles School, Exeter, and Imperial College, London, where he was a Kitchener Scholar and obtained an engineering degree.

He later joined the Royal Aircraft Establishment at Farnborough as a technical officer, and, in 1937, became an inspector of accidents at the Air Ministry. He also flew as a sergeant and instructor in the RAF Volunteer Reserve and by the outbreak of the war in 1939 he was a pilot officer in No 24, a communications squadron, flying an odd assortment of aircraft.

Shortly before and after the fall of France in the spring and early summer of 1940 this duty introduced him to the business of flying in and out of all manner of fields. He piloted Churchill to France and back on at least one occasion in 1940 and, during the Dunkirk period, picked up French VIPs and stragglers from the British Expeditionary Force.

In November 1940 Hockey joined a flight of two Whitley bombers and a Lysander light Army co-operation aircraft, which was committed to supporting Churchill's directive to SOE "to set Europe ablaze". Through carrying out a number of drops over France and Belgium, Hockey began to establish himself as one of the leading pilots in this moonlight speciality.

Initially he was based on the heath at Newmarket, where he lived in a hayloft and flew from the hallowed turf; the racecourse grandstand and its cellars provided the Flight's headquarters. In May 1941 the Flight grew into 138 and 161 Squadrons, and Hockey, by now a flying officer, flew 138's first operation, accompanied by Sqn Ldr Charles Pickard, celebrated in the film *Target for Tonight*.

It was typical of Hockey to learn to parachute at the SOE's jump school at Ringway so that as a pilot despatching "Joes" he could know something of their problems. One of the pilots there, bored with circuiting to train parachutists, was a certain Sqn Ldr Romanoff.

Hockey, shortly to command 138 Squadron as a wing commander, sympathised with Romanoff. After taking him unofficially on several sorties as second pilot in early 1942, he arranged his transfer to the squadron as a flight commander.

But as he took off on his first trip as captain, Romanoff crashed. Hockey, in the tower, dashed for a van and then ran across ploughed fields to the burning wreckage, only to arrive as ammunition grenades and other explosives went up.

Thrown some 40 yards, he returned to the blaze and managed to extract the rear gunner, who was the sole survivor. Hockey recovered, although he carried splinters all over his body for the rest of his life.

He experienced another close call shortly afterwards when he was despatched to Egypt with urgent supplies. He stopped over at Malta, where his Halifax was badly holed on the ground during enemy air attacks.

After this hazardous introduction to the Mediterranean theatre, Hockey was posted there in June 1943 to build up air support for SOE operations. He formed No 334 Wing for this purpose.

In early 1944 he returned to 38 Group, charged with assisting SOE's preparations for D-Day. He trained with 6th Airborne Division's tug-towing pilots.

In 1946 Hockey, by then a group captain, completed a test pilot's course at the Empire Test Pilots School. He remained in the reserve and maintained close links with aviation.

He was successively a departmental head at the Cranfield College of Aeronautics; divisional engineer with Smiths Aircraft Instruments; general manager of Blackburns (where he tested the Beverley transport); managing director of Arthur Low & Sons, engineers; and chief of mission at the International Labour Office in first Sudan and then Ghana.

Ron Hockey was a dedicated yachtsman and ocean racer; in his youth he had boxed as a heavyweight and played rugby for Wasps. He was a Fellow of the Royal Aeronautical and Royal Geographical Societies.

He was awarded the DFC in 1942, DSO in 1943 and was mentioned in despatches in 1945. He also held the Czech Military Cross and Cross of Valour, and received the Air Efficiency award in 1942 and clasp in 1951. He was a Deputy Lieutenant for Dunbartonshire.

Hockey married Winifred Holt; they had a son and a daughter.

VERA ATKINS
24 JUNE 2000

Vera Atkins, who has died aged 93, was the brilliant assistant to Colonel Maurice Buckmaster at the French section of the Special Operations Executive during the Second World War.

She was born Vera Maria Rosenberg in Romania on June 15 1907 and came with her parents to London in 1933, subsequently changing her surname. At the outbreak of the Second World War she joined the WAAF and soon went to work as a secretary at "F" Section, set up in 1940 to run covert operations and help the Resistance in German-occupied France. Buckmaster, the head of the section, spotted her flair and made her an intelligence officer and his deputy.

The two of them worked up to 18 hours a day at the section's headquarters at 64 Baker Street, and between them dispatched more than 400 agents – known as "Buckmasters" – across the Channel.

Vera Atkins helped to choose recruits – they had to be able to pass themselves off as French, as well as having guts and resourcefulness – briefed them on how to survive behind enemy lines, escorted them to the grass airstrip at Tempsford, Bedfordshire, and watched them leave at night in the cramped Lysander aircraft with their parachutes.

More than 100 agents never returned. A few were known to have been killed in action, but most were reported to have been arrested and some to have disappeared into Gestapo interrogation centres and concentration camps.

Their roll of honour was second to none in the story of British wartime undercover operations and their stories inspired a legion of books and films. They faced horrific dangers. In July 1944, four women members of F Section, who had been captured separately, were taken to Natzweiler concentration camp in Alsace, given a stupefying injection and plunged straight into an oven. Others, such as Violette Szabo, were shot, while a few, such as Odette Churchill, suffered at the hands of the Gestapo but survived.

Buckmaster was later rather unfairly accused of having run an "amateurish" operation and incurring unnecessary loss of life. But Eisenhower credited the French section with shortening the war by six months. "It was," he said, "the equivalent of 15 Divisions."

There was no doubt however that both Buckmaster and Vera Atkins felt keenly the responsibility of having sent some agents to their deaths. After the war, Vera Atkins determined to find out what happened to each one. "I could not just abandon their memory," she recalled. But her project led her into immediate confrontation with the military establishment.

After an early post-war trip to Germany, she was told that the SOE was to be disbanded and could no longer sponsor her search. But she used a personal contact to gain a semi-official attachment to MI6 and returned to Germany.

She spent most of the next year questioning concentration camp officials and going through records. "I was probably the only person who could do this," she explained. "You had to know every detail of the agents, names, code-names, every hair on their heads, to spot their tracks."

The confessions she obtained from Rudolf Hoess – the former commandant of Auschwitz – were later used as evidence during the Nuremberg Trials. She could later hardly bring herself to recall how Hoess had reacted to the suggestion that the deaths in the camp had perhaps amounted to 1,500,000. "Oh no," he retorted, as if he had been sadly misrepresented, "it was 2,345,000."

The results of her investigations would later form the basis of the roll of honour to the 104 dead (91 men and 13 women) of F Section on the memorial at Valençay in the Loire valley, which was opened in 1991.

The memorial helped to heal a division that went back to the formation of F Section. General de Gaulle, setting up his Free French in London, was bitterly opposed to the F section agents on the grounds that they were *Anglo-Saxons* attempting to take command of the French Resistance – he wanted complete control and all the credit for their successes. On their side SOE agents harboured suspicions that some of their comrades were betrayed to the Germans in the interests of politics.

In later life, Vera Atkins was much involved in fostering Anglo-French relations and in keeping alive the spirit of the Resistance. In 1987 she was appointed a Commandant of the Légion d'honneur. Latterly, she received a much overdue CBE. Vera Atkins had a tremendously warm personality. She was full of humour, indomitable courage and unstinting generosity.

GROUP CAPTAIN HUGH VERITY
14 NOVEMBER 2001

Group Captain Hugh Verity, who has died aged 83, was a member of the small group of RAF pilots who flew clandestine missions to support Special Operations Executive (SOE) agents and the French Resistance during the Second World War; they also picked up aircrew who had been shot down in Occupied France.

When Verity and his fellow pilots were picking up "Joes", as their unidentified passengers were known, the enemy's occupation forces were danger enough; but this was compounded by the preference for operating on moonlit nights.

Piloting a high-wing, single-engine Westland Lysander, Verity flew some 30 lonely and demanding missions. Apart from flying the aircraft without the benefit of advanced navigation aids, Verity had to find the small field where a reception party would be waiting for him.

On one sortie he was south of the Loire when he encountered impenetrable fog over his landing ground, forcing him to abort the mission. This was especially frustrating because he was to land Jean Moulin, the co-ordinator of General de Gaulle's Resistance networks in southern France.

Having decided to return to his base, Tangmere in Sussex, Verity first had to escape the attentions of enemy searchlights. When he finally found his home airfield, it too was blanketed in fog. Believing his wheels to be just above the runway, Verity cut the throttle; but he was 30 feet too high, and the Lysander smashed into the ground. Miraculously, it did not catch fire — and Verity, always the complete gentleman, apologised profusely in French. Moulin responded in kind, thanking his pilot for "a very agreeable flight".

Verity had come into this line of work in the fortuitous way of so many who became involved with SOE. He had long suffered from what he termed "a private shame" for his "physical cowardice" on the rugby field at school, and was determined to overcome it.

Consequently, in the winter of 1942 he arranged to get an introduction to Wing Commander P C Pickard, who commanded No 161 Squadron; this was designated to SOE and comprised Lysanders, Halifaxes, Wellingtons and one Hudson. Pickard in turn introduced Verity to his station commander, Group Captain "Mouse" Fielden, previously the Prince of Wales's personal pilot and captain of the King's Flight. Verity was soon accepted on to the team.

At the time, Verity's wife Audrey was expecting their second child, but he assured her that his new job would mean "very few operations and a lot of home life, which would be great fun". However, on the night of his first Lysander flight, November 6 1942, he was called to the telephone for the news that his second son had been born.

Verity soon became a hero to his French passengers and reception parties, sometimes flying a Hudson and picking up as many as eight people at a time. He was awarded the DFC and DSO in 1943. France awarded him the Legion d'honneur in 1946.

Hugh Beresford Verity was born in Jamaica on April 6 1918, and educated at Cheltenham and at Queen's College, Oxford. After a brief period teaching at a prep school in Northern Ireland, he was granted a short service commission in the RAF.

In September 1940, he was posted to No 608, an Avro Anson general reconnaissance squadron, and five months later to No 252, a Bristol Blenheim, later Beaufighter, squadron, stationed in Northern Ireland.

Having been detached briefly to Malta, he was on his way home when bad weather forced his plane to make a belly landing in Eire, where he was interned. MI9 – the War Office escape organisation – managed to free him in a secret operation in which Verity wore disguise.

He then moved to No 29, a Bristol Beaufighter night fighter squadron, in the autumn of 1941, serving afterwards on the night operations staff of Fighter Command's No 11 Group and also at Fighter Command headquarters.

After his exploits flying into France, he became an SOE

air operations manager organising drops and agent landings in Western Europe and Scandinavia.

In the autumn of 1944 Verity supervised clandestine air operations in South East Asia, then worked with the Recovery of Allied Prisoner-of-War and Internees organisation, arranging the dropping by parachute of medical staff into remote prison camps throughout South East Asia Command. Following a period in Singapore, Verity was posted to Quetta (then in India) as a member of the directing staff at the Army Staff College. Here he contracted polio and was invalided home.

He was later delighted to be passed fit to fly, and in early 1948 he received command of No 541, the photographic reconnaissance squadron equipped with the Spitfire XIX, at Benson, Oxfordshire.

The next year Verity was posted to the Central Fighter Establishment as wing commander weapons, but he seized the opportunity to learn to fly jets. After two years he went to the Joint Services Staff College.

From the spring of 1954, as wing commander flying at RAF Wahn, he was responsible for three Gloster Meteor jet night fighter squadrons. In 1955 he took over No 96, a Meteor squadron.

Verity's subsequent postings included spells on the bomber operations staff at the Air Ministry and at the CENTO headquarters in Turkey, and command of the RAF station at Akrotiri in Cyprus. Finally, he returned to the Air Ministry, charged with special and operations staff duties.

Verity retired in 1965 and joined the recently established Industrial Training Board. In 1978 he published a book about his wartime experiences, *We Landed by Moonlight*.

He married, in 1940, Audrey Stokes; they had two sons and three daughters.

ROYAL CONNECTIONS

WING COMMANDER
JOCK DALGLEISH
27 JANUARY 2000

Wing Commander Jock Dalgleish, who has died aged 80, saved the life of King Hussein of Jordan in November 1958 when the royal aircraft was attacked by two Syrian fighters above Damascus.

The summer of 1958 had been a testing one for the young monarch, who had been beset by conspiracies at home and by the hostility of Egypt, Iraq and Syria abroad. But by the autumn the situation seemed to have stabilised and Hussein decided to spend three weeks with his mother in Switzerland.

Syrian airspace was closed to Jordan but Signor Spinelli, the UN Special Representative in the Middle East, assured the King that his flight had been cleared with the Syrians. On November 11 1958 – three days before his 23rd birthday – Hussein took off for Geneva at the controls of a Royal Jordanian Air Force de Havilland Dove, a twin-engined light transport aircraft.

He was accompanied by his uncle, Sharif Nasser, and by Maurice Raynor, the king's English car mechanic. His co-pilot was Dalgleish, then in Jordan as Air Adviser to the government, having just relinquished command of the RAF contingent of the British force supplied to Hussein by Harold Macmillan earlier that summer as a deterrent against a coup d'état. Dalgleish had formerly been Hussein's flying instructor and later head of the fledgling RJAF.

Half an hour out of Amman, Hussein contacted Damascus air control and was given permission to proceed. Then, suddenly, Damascus called again and ordered the aircraft to land at the Syrian capital. Someone had realised that Hussein was within their grasp.

Dalgleish took the controls, turned the aircraft around and headed back for Amman at 200 mph, skimming the ground to evade the Syrians' radar. Then, two MiG-17 fighters appeared and began to swoop down repeatedly on the Dove. The Syrians seemed to balk at shooting down the aircraft, hoping instead to force it to crash, an event that could be passed off as an accident.

But Dalgleish was a highly skilled and experienced pilot, and he had charge of an aircraft which, while slower than its pursuers, could turn much more tightly than the MiGs. These overshot Hussein's aeroplane each time that they dived on it, almost colliding once as they pulled up. They only abandoned the chase after 20 minutes, by which time they were well inside Jordanian airspace.

Hussein later called the incident "the narrowest escape from death I have ever had"; he learned afterwards that a party of 200 Jordanian rebels had been waiting to lynch him at Damascus airport.

John Dalgleish, always known as Jock, was born in a shepherd's cottage in Peeblesshire on January 24 1919 and educated at Kingsland School. After serving in the Midlothian Constabulary he joined the RAF in 1941.

He was awarded his wings and commission in South Africa, where he remained as an instructor for the duration of the war in Europe. In 1946 he was posted home to No 6 Service Flying Training School, and later joined No 612 (County of Aberdeen), a Royal Auxiliary Air Force Spitfire fighter squadron.

In 1951 he was seconded to the air force of the Arab Legion in Jordan; and in July of that year began his friendship with Hussein when he flew the young prince back to Amman after he had escaped the assassin's bullets that had claimed the life of his grandfather, King Abdullah, in Jerusalem.

Dalgleish remained in Jordan for much of the 1950s, eventually rising to command what had become the Royal Jordanian Air Force. Hussein wanted his secondment to the RJAF to be extended, but Glubb Pasha, then leading the Arab Legion, demurred and in 1956 Dalgleish was posted home to No 603 (City of Edinburgh), a Royal Auxiliary Air Force Vampire squadron.

In March 1958, he joined Bomber Command for operational duties connected with H-Bomb tests on Christmas Island, but in July he was sent, at 30 minutes notice, to Cyprus to head the RAF detachment assigned to support 16 Parachute Brigade in Operation Fortitude, the mission to bolster Hussein during the difficult time that followed the assassination in Baghdad of his cousin King Faisal.

There was a peculiar coda to the attempted aerial assassination of Hussein. Six months after the event, Dalgleish was surprised to be visited at his base by two Syrians looking for political asylum – the pilots of the MiGs. They said that they had been told not to open fire without permission, and when they had requested this, Damascus had remained silent. On returning, they had been accused of allowing Hussein to escape, and ostracised.

They were given shelter by the Jordanians, but after a week one pleaded to return home to see his family. Dalgleish warned him of the probable consequences, but nonetheless he crossed the border at midnight. In the words of Dalgleish, "he never saw the sunrise".

Dalgleish retired from the RAF in 1960, but returned to Jordan the following year to help with the filming of David Lean's *Lawrence of Arabia*. From 1963 until 1981 he worked in the meat trade, and was President of the Edinburgh Meat Butchers' Association, 1975-77, and of the Scottish Federation of Meat Traders, 1979-81.

He was chief instructor for more than 25 years at Fife Aero Club.

Jock Dalgleish was appointed OBE in 1960. He was awarded the Star of Jordan in 1954 and the Orders of Istaqlal (Independence) and Al Nahda (Awakening) in 1959.

He was also made a Knight of the Holy Sepulchre by the Greek Orthodox Church, for protecting "the keeper of the holy places", one of Hussein's traditional titles.

He married, in 1941, Davina Steadman, who survives him together with a son and a daughter.

AIR COMMODORE
SIR DENNIS MITCHELL
25 DECEMBER 2001

Air Commodore Sir Dennis Mitchell, who has died aged 83, was awarded a DFC and Bar in 1944 for his courageous leadership of squadrons under his command in the north-west Europe campaign; from 1958 to 1959 he was Deputy Captain of the Queen's Flight and Captain from 1962 to 1984.

When Mitchell joined the Queen's Flight, the position of Deputy Captain was created to enable him to understudy the long-serving Air Commodore Sir Edward Fielden. Fielden had been the pre-war personal pilot to both the Prince of Wales and his brother King George VI and had formed, in 1942, No 161 Squadron, a unit designated for Special Operations Executive (SOE) clandestine missions.

He was a hard act to follow, but Mitchell was an exceptional and highly experienced pilot. In the late 1930s he had honed his flying skills over the unforgiving mountainous terrain of the North West Frontier of India. Flying a No 20 Squadron biplane Hawker Audax he provided air cover for trucks supplying the forts guarding the Khyber Pass. This involved several hours on patrol followed by overnighting at a fort with a lively evening guaranteed.

Returning from one such mission, Mitchell's Audax was brought down by a tribesman's lucky shot which hit the plane's radiator. Fortunately, he was rescued by a passing armoured car, and thus spared from presenting the tribesmen with the "goolie chit", which was carried by pilots patrolling dissident tribal areas and promised a handsome reward in gold for returning them with their private parts intact.

At the tail end of the Raj when rigid social rituals were observed at Mitchell's Peshawar base and elsewhere in the region, Mitchell was required to drop expensively printed and embossed calling cards on his seniors.

Once a young officer had been accepted invitations were received and he was also able to enjoy the many activities open to him among which Mitchell valued particularly opportunities for polo, jackal hunting and the hospitality of the Maharajah of Jaipur.

After two years of frontier flying, Mitchell became an instructor until December 1941 when he was posted No 146, an operational squadron still equipped with the obsolete Audax.

The fall of Singapore early in 1942, followed by the Japanese invasion of Burma, underlined the RAF's desperate need for modern aircraft, so some 100 Curtiss Mohawk American fighters were landed at Karachi. They were re-assembled at No 301 Maintenance Unit where

Mitchell tested them before their dispatch to operational squadrons. He was awarded the AFC in 1943.

Returning from India towards the end of 1943, Mitchell was dismayed to learn that the Air Ministry intended to send him on an extended flying course instead of posting him to an operational unit. However, after attracting the notice of Air Vice-Marshal Basil Embry, the leader of the 2nd Tactical Air Force's No 2 Group, he obtained a posting in February 1944 to the group's No 226 Douglas Mitchell squadron and received command in June.

Mitchell led perilous cross-Channel daylight attacks on enemy communications targets and airfields in preparation for the Normandy invasion. In 1944 he was awarded the DFC early in the north-west Europe campaign and received a Bar after its conclusion. In the final weeks of 1944, Embry employed Mitchell's experience at his No 2 Group headquarters and also in a special posting at the group's No 139 Wing, embracing Nos 98, 180 and 320 Mitchell squadrons.

A subsequent citation paid tribute to Mitchell's "inspiring leadership, untiring efforts, courage and high standards of operational efficiency in squadrons under his command". Referring to a period of intensive bombing operations prior to the final assault on the German Army, the citation praised his "constant supervision of the organisation on the ground and leadership of attacks on the more difficult targets [which] materially contributed to the effectiveness of a long series of operations".

Arthur Dennis Mitchell was born on May 26 1918, at Staplehurst in Kent. He was educated at Bloxham School, Banbury, in Oxfordshire, and the Nautical College at Pangbourne in Berkshire, before becoming a cadet at the RAF College, Cranwell.

During the post-war 1940s Mitchell served at No 2

Group headquarters, British Air Forces of Occupation, No 84 Group and the Air Ministry, before learning to fly the Gloster Meteor, the RAF's first jet fighter.

Following brief command of No 26, a Hawker Tempest squadron in Germany, he was posted to Brussels in 1948 as a member of an RAF delegation responsible for determining the needs of the future Belgian Air Force. In this period Mitchell met and married Comtesse Mireill Cornet de Ways Ruart.

His next posting was to the US Tactical Air Command headquarters where he volunteered for a tour with the United States Air Force in the Korean theatre which included difficult and dangerous operational flying.

To reassure his wife, Mitchell told her he was on a four-month flying course in Florida and arranged for a friend based there to send a weekly postcard describing the joys of golf and swimming. His next posting was to the training, plans and inspectorate division of Allied Forces Central Europe at Fontainebleau in France.

During Mitchell's first round of royal duties (beginning in 1956) the Queen's Flight retired its two-engine Vickers Viking transports – derived from the wartime Wellington bomber – in favour of four four-engine de Havilland Herons. Two helicopters were also added. It was a busy period for royal tours which included the Queen Mother's visit to Australia in 1958 and, later that year, Princess Margaret's tour of Canada, the West Indies, British Guiana and British Honduras.

The next year he toured South America and Nigeria before receiving command of RAF Cottesmore, Rutland. In 1962 he returned to the Queen's Flight, his captaincy coinciding with the replacement of Herons by two-engine turboprop Hawker Siddeley Andovers.

Initially, the Treasury resisted purchase of the Andovers but when Mitchell bluntly informed officials that in the absence of Andovers it would be better to hand the entire royal operation over to BOAC, funding was quickly made available.

Following retirement from the RAF in 1964, Mitchell launched Brussels Airways, an air taxi operation, and went on to develop Aero Distributors in Belgium. He founded Aero Systems there in 1972 and became the representative on the continent of leading British and American aviation companies.

In 1958 Mitchell was appointed ADC to the Queen; he was extra equerry from 1962. He was appointed KBE in 1977 and CVO in 1961. He was awarded the AFC in 1943, DFC in 1944 and Bar and French Croix de Guerre in 1945.

His wife died in 1999. He is survived by their son.

GROUP CAPTAIN JOHN GRINDON
9 JANUARY 2002

Group Captain John Grindon, who has died aged 84, won the DSO as a squadron commander during the Second World War, and later commanded the King's – and the Queen's – Flight.

Having survived numerous attacks on some of the most heavily defended targets in Germany and occupied Europe, Grindon took command of the King's Flight on March 1 1953, and the Queen's Flight on June 2 that year, holding the post until September 9 1956. (The title of Captain of the King's or Queen's Flight in this period remained that of Air Commodore Sir Edward Fielden.)

Grindon's command brought him into frequent contact with the young Queen, her husband and their children.

He took Prince Charles and Princess Anne on their first flight, from London to Scotland in 1955. Before take-off, the Prince and Princess, as Grindon recalled, argued as to who should sit next to him in the cockpit. When, some time later, he mentioned this to the Queen, she commented: "I bet Anne won."

Queen Elizabeth the Queen Mother, who was his most frequent passenger, also preferred to sit next to him. Once, in appalling weather, he was landing a two-engine Vickers Viking – developed after the war from the Wellington bomber – when an engine failed and the controls would not respond.

Glancing at the Queen Mother, Grindon noticed that her handbag was jamming the controls. There was no time for niceties. He reached across and removed the bag, his swift reaction ensuring a safe landing.

After leaving the Queen's Flight, Grindon was promoted group captain. Messages of congratulation included a telegram from officers of the Royal Yacht *Britannia*, with whom he had recently dined. The message was a gesture from wardroom officers who had ragged him for keeping his mess kit buttoned up during dinner (since naval officers leave their buttons undone, Grindon's hosts had snipped off his offending buttons and displayed them as a trophy in the wardroom cabinet).

John Evelyn Grindon was born at Newquay, Cornwall, on September 30 1917, 26 days before his father, a private in the Devons, was killed at Ypres. He was educated at Dulwich College and the RAF College, Cranwell, Lincolnshire, where he graduated in 1937 and joined No 98, a training squadron at Hucknall, Nottinghamshire, equipped with Hawker Hind single-engine light bombers.

Grindon was piloting a Hind when engine trouble forced an emergency landing in a field, where the aircraft buried its nose in the ground and damaged its undercarriage and a wing tip. He was lucky to escape only with superficial injuries.

In June 1939, he was posted to No 150, a Fairey Battle light bomber squadron. Shortly after the declaration of war on September 3, the squadron was despatched to support the British Expeditionary Force in France as part of the Advanced Air Striking Force.

All was quiet (this was the so–called "phoney war" of the winter of 1939-40) until May 10 1940 when Hitler launched his *blitzkrieg* drive to the Channel coast. As his squadron attacked advancing enemy columns, Grindon, after losing the toss with a fellow pilot, was ordered home for a navigation course. In his absence the squadron was all but wiped out.

Following two postings as an instructor in Canada and a spell on the navigation staff at Bomber Command, Grindon returned to operational flying in July 1944 when he replaced a No 106 Squadron flight commander who had been killed two days earlier in an Avro Lancaster heavy bomber.

Next morning Grindon chalked his name at the top of a list of Lancaster captains in the place where his predecessor's name had been rubbed out. He noted grimly that the name "Grindon" restored the number of captains to 13.

After five weeks during which he survived 13 operational sorties, including attacks on U-boat pens and V-1 flying bomb sites, Grindon received command of No 630, also a Lancaster squadron. Henceforth the figure 13 occurred regularly in his life, and he came to look upon it as his lucky number.

Shortly before the end of the war in Europe, Grindon took command of No 617, the Dambusters' squadron.

When, in 1945, Grindon was awarded the DSO, the

citation read: "In the course of numerous operational sorties, Wing Commander Grindon has established an excellent reputation for leadership, energy and courage. The worst weather or the heaviest opposition have never deterred him from the accurate completion of his allotted tasks.

"Over such heavily defended targets as Königsberg, Bremen and Bergen he has braved intense anti-aircraft fire and, despite damage to his aircraft on more than one occasion, has always fulfilled his mission.

"On one occasion, during a daylight attack on Hamburg, severe damage was sustained and his aircraft became difficult to control; but in spite of the damage he continued to lead his formation with skill and determination. He has at all times set an outstanding example."

After the war Grindon became chief instructor to the Long Range Transport Service until 1949; he remained in training appointments until beginning his Royal duties. In 1957 he received command of RAF Honington, which accommodated the Vickers Valiants, the RAF's first nuclear deterrent V-bombers.

Two years later, at the age of 41, Grindon retired at his own request and spent 10 years in printing and publishing, including five years as general manager of Thomas Skinner & Co's Dunstable offices, where he produced travel guides.

Later Grindon joined the Metropolitan Police, working in CID at New Scotland Yard as a civilian until 1981. In this period he discovered horse racing, and after his second retirement he frequented racecourses several times a week until prevented from doing so by ill health.

So long as he remained fit Grindon continued to enjoy visiting his native Cornwall where, he declared, there was nothing to beat surfing from Tolcarne beach and breathing the Cornish air. Later, music became a great solace, Puccini and Strauss being his particular favourites.

Grindon was appointed CVO in 1957. He won the AFC in 1948.

He is survived by a daughter and three sons.

PLANEMAKERS

SIR THOMAS SOPWITH
27 JANUARY 1989

Sir Thomas Sopwith, the early aviator and aeroplane maker who has died aged 101, had an extraordinary career. It encompassed the design and production of military machines for the Royal Flying Corps in the 1914–1918 War, the RAF's first modern monoplane eight-gun fighter in the 1930s and the world's first jump-jet in the 1960s.

The creator of the Sopwith Camel and Pup, he also had overall responsibility for the 1939–45 War Hurricane and the present-day Harrier.

As if those achievements were not enough, Tom Sopwith perkily confided to the television cameras in a documentary on his 100th birthday that he had also contested the America's Cup.

Thomas Octave Murdoch Sopwith was born on January 10, 1888, the eighth child and only son of a prosperous civil engineer.

After being privately educated as an engineer, young Tom indulged the pursuit of speed on water and land. Fascinated by the possibilities of the internal combustion engine, he also gratified a compulsive urge to fly.

In retrospect, the smooth progress of Sopwith's career gives the illusion that it was predestined early in the century and that to succeed he had merely to survive the perils of his pioneer flying exploits.

In reality, his success was the result of his personal vision, powers of concentration and talent for employing the right combination of apparently unremarkable men, who just happened to be there when he most needed them.

Under Sopwith's leadership Fred Sigrist, Harry Hawker, Sidney Camm and Frank Spriggs, recruited almost haphazardly, provided the engineering, design and managerial kills of Sopwith Aviation and its successor, Hawkers.

In 1910 Sigrist, hired as chauffeur and odd-job man, began to care for Sopwith's part-owned 166-ton schooner, *Neva*, six-cylinder 40 horsepower Napier motor-car, motor-boats and three aeroplanes.

By this time Sopwith had already crewed the winning yacht in the 1909 Royal Aero Club race and satisfied a teenage zest for ballooning.

His passion for flying dated from a day in 1910. Putting into Dover from sea he was told that a Blériot had just landed after crossing the Channel for the first time with a passenger.

On finding the pilot in a field seven miles away, he decided on the spot to turn from balloons to aeroplanes.

Within hours he arrived at Brooklands where, inside the concrete motor-racing circuit, flying lessons and joyrides were being offered in a Henry Farman machine. Producing a £5 note Sopwith booked two circuits.

From that moment he was "terribly bitten by the aviation bug", and paid £630 for a 40 horsepower Blériot-inspired Avis monoplane built under the railway arches at Battersea.

It was delivered to him at Brooklands on Oct 21, 1910, and he crashed it the same day.

Alarmed at the rate at which he was spending money, Sopwith decided to make flying pay by winning prizes.

Flourishing his flying certificate (the 31st issued in Britain) he contested the Michelin Cup for the longest non-stop flight by a British pilot in a British machine and, more rewardingly, the £4,000 Baron de Forest trophy for the longest non-stop flight from any point in England to anywhere on the Continent.

By the end of 1910 he had landed both, but not without the indispensable assistance of Sigrist. It was Sigrist who, on December 18, 1910, produced the engine-coaxing plan which enabled his employer to bank Baron de Forest's £4,000 after completing 177 miles in 3 hours and 40 minutes to land in Belgium.

Confident that he was now financially and technically equipped to compete in America, in 1911 Sopwith organised a tour of "air meets".

At first his arrival, accompanied by his sister, May, was far from welcome in the camp of the pioneer Wright brothers, Wilbur and Orville. They attempted to claim the patent on passenger carrying, which would have ruled out May and her picnic basket of thermos flasks.

But the Wrights were appeased when Sopwith, after wrecking his Blériot, purchased one of their biplanes.

Beginning to win prizes of as much as $14,000 and appearing before crowds of up to 300,000 spectators, he polished his performance in the popular quick start competitions until he could run and jump into the seat of his moving machine in nine seconds.

Having survived a crash into the sea off Manhattan Beach in the autumn of 1911, Sopwith returned to Brooklands where he opened a flying school. Among his earliest pupils were two men whose names were to become better known to the public than that of their instructor.

One was Harry Hawker. Still in his teens and a mechanic since running away from school in Australia he had hung around the Brooklands perimeter until hired by Sopwith to join Sigrist as another dogsbody.

The other was Major Hugh Trenchard, "Father" of the RAF, who urgently needed a certificate before taking up an appointment at the Services' recently established

Central Flying School.

As the 1914-18 War approached, the nascent Sopwith Aviation Company outgrew its Brooklands shed.

Soon Sigrist and Hawker (already Sopwith's test pilot), were chalking the outline of a biplane, known as the Hybrid, on the wooden floor of the disused roller-skating rink Sopwith had bought up-river at Kingston upon Thames.

Early in 1914, Hawker was in Australia demonstrating the Tabloid (a machine which would shortly distinguish itself as a Royal Flying Corps scout). In his absence Sopwith, who had roughed out modifications on the back of an envelope, selected Howard Pixton to fly one of the machines with floats in the Schneider Trophy competition held at Monte Carlo.

Sopwith had designed and built the airframe but selected his engine in France. It was a 100-horsepower Monosoupape Gnome, which he brought back "almost literally in my suitcase".

Shortly before the outbreak of the 1914-18 War Sopwith also designed a side-by-side two-seater modelled on the Tabloid, for Winston Churchill, First Lord of the Admiralty. Called the Sociable, it was popularly referred to as "Tweenie".

As the Tabloid went to war Sopwith stopped flying. It was not a conscious decision, as he later explained.

"I was so occupied with design and manufacture that I just didn't have the time to fly and did not pilot an aeroplane for about 16 years."

That, of course, was a characteristic understatement which overlooked the continual reinforcement of the RFC, the Royal Naval Air Service and, after April 1, 1918, the RAF on the Western Front with Pups, Camels, Triplanes and other machines destined to become museum celebrities.

By the end of the war two of Sopwith's factories were rolling out 90 fighters a week. Sopwith plants had built 16,000 machines in Britain and 10,000 in France. Camel pilots notched up the highest number of "kills" – 2,700.

After the Armistice the market for aircraft contracted almost as rapidly as it had expanded. But amid the gloom one beacon beckoned – the *Daily Mail* Atlantic Flight competition.

Sopwith entered the Sopwith B1, which boasted special features designed by Hawker. On May 18, 1919, Hawker took off from Newfoundland on the west-east crossing accompanied by Commander Kenneth Mackenzie-Grieve as navigator.

Less than half way Hawker was forced to put down in the sea and the pair were presumed lost. King George V sent a telegram of condolence to Mrs Hawker before it was learned that the *Mary*, a small Danish freighter, had rescued the airmen.

A month later John Alcock and Arthur Whitten Brown achieved the first Atlantic crossing in a Vickers Vimy and were knighted.

The following year, Sopwith put the company into voluntary liquidation while it remained solvent.

Hawker registered the HG Hawker Engineering Company and acquired a motor-cycle business.

Shortly afterwards "the gang", as Sopwith called his pioneering team, met up. Sopwith, Sigrist, Hawker and Spriggs were unanimous in their decision: "Let's make aeroplanes again".

In less than a year Hawker was dead. He had crashed his Nieuport Goshawk while testing it for entry in the 1921 Aerial Derby.

Sopwith put his heart and money into developing the Hawker Aircraft Company, totally eclipsing the name and achievements of the former Sopwith Aviation Company.

This meant that designs which might reasonably have been designated Sopwith's have entered history under the name of Hawker, though – to confuse the matter further – coming from the drawing board of Sidney Camm.

In the 1920s and 1930s Sopwith masterminded the gradual growth of the company as its military and civil designs found markets at home and abroad.

The Hawker Hart, Hind, Demon, Fury, Hornet, Audax and Hotspur are merely a few of the best remembered names. There was also the little Tomtit trainer for which Sopwith – and the Duke of Windsor – always had a soft spot.

Sopwith told a favourite anecdote about it. George Bulman, his chief test pilot, was about to fly the Tomtit to Martlesham Heath for assessment by the RAF when Sopwith climbed in and told Bulman: "Today you are my passenger".

Then, no longer the occasionally impetuous pilot of his youth, he reflected: "George, you had better take her off".

In 1930 Sopwith was elected to membership of the Royal Yacht Squadron. An outstanding helmsman he sailed *Shamrock V* (which he had bought from the executors of the tea merchant, Sir Thomas Lipton), to win the King's Cup at Cowes in 1932. In 1935 he won it again in *Endeavour I*.

Sopwith was ambitious to repair Lipton's failure to win the America's Cup, but *Endeavour I* was foiled in 1934. His professional crew walked out after a pay dispute and he lost 4–2 to Harold Vanderbilt's *Rainbow*.

Endeavour II, a new J-class boat, was defeated in four races by Vanderbilt's *Ranger* in 1937.

As *Endeavour* was being towed back to Newport a motor launch came alongside, and the helmsman called out: "You Sopwith? – I'm Fokker". Over a drink aboard *Endeavour* the former plane-making adversaries exchanged 1914–1918 reminiscences.

From 1935 Sopwith was chairman of the Hawker Siddeley group which he had put together with the help of the financier Philip Hill. The merger and reorganisation established Sopwith as Britain's foremost aircraft constructor.

After bringing Glosters, Armstrong Whitworth and A V Roe, builders of the Lancaster bomber, into the Hawker family Sopwith provided a foundation for the future British Aerospace. De Havilland was incorporated later.

Hawkers' consolidation and growth owed everything to Sopwith's good judgement and imperturbable coolness.

Enigmatic and rarely on the spot (he revelled in nautical and country pursuits) Sopwith maintained control by operating through an ubiquitous managing director, his former sweeper and office boy, Spriggs.

Meanwhile, Sigrist, dogsbody at the start, had become the hard man of Hawkers, troubleshooting and dealing with any unpleasantness.

As the business grew Sopwith encouraged each aircraft company to retain its individuality, enabling Camm and his associated designers to produce the fruits of their particular creative talents. His genius for knowing what was going on without interfering is best illustrated by his relationship with Camm.

If at times Sopwith recoiled at Camm's authoritarian manner in the drawing office, he bit on his pipe and remembered that fear of unemployment obliged Camm's men to put up with him. The end product was K 5083, the prototype of the Hawker Hurricane, financed by the company as a private venture.

In October 1935, George Bulman tested her at Brooklands. The Government dallied until the following summer before issuing a first contract for 600 Hurricanes.

Sopwith's investment and belief in the interceptor

monoplane, at a time when the Air Ministry still favoured biplane fighters and afforded priority to bombers, reaped its reward in the Battle of Britain. At that stage the Hurricane far outnumbered the Spitfire in RAF fighter squadrons.

As the war progressed and peace came other aircraft followed, the Typhoon, Tempest, Meteor and Hunter each being destined to become part of aviation archaeology in Sopwith's lifetime.

Even the revolutionary jumpjet Harrier, which Sopwith and Camm initiated, could be said to be anticipating obsolescence while Sopwith lived.

Always a man of few words, Sopwith observed the motto on his coat-of-arms, "work without talk" to the letter and to the end.

But on his 100th birthday, speaking sparingly on television from Compton Manor, his Hampshire estate near Winchester, he acknowledged the tributes of aviation's great and good as they banqueted at Brooklands in celebration.

Blind, and walking on the arm of a nurse in his garden, he lifted his head towards the sound of a replica Sopwith Pup as it circled overhead in salute. Repeating a favourite aside, he murmured: "You know, they were all done off the cuff".

Sopwith was appointed CBE in 1918 and knighted in 1953. He married first, in 1914, Beatrix Hore-Ruthven (who died in 1930), daughter of the 8th Lord Ruthven.

In 1932 he married secondly, Phyllis Brodie Gordon (who died in 1978). Their son, Tommy, also an adventurous all-rounder, survives him.

R E BISHOP
1 JUNE 1989

R E Bishop, who has died aged 86, was the designer of the de Havilland Mosquito (the "Wooden Wonder"), which was one of the most versatile military aircraft ever built and played a vital part in the 1939-45 War.

A quiet, unassuming man, he was nursed from apprenticeship to chief designer by Sir Geoffrey de Havilland and went on to design the Comet – the world's first commercial jet airliner and a series of military jets.

A day-fighter, a night-fighter, a bomber, torpedo-bomber and unarmed photographic reconnaissance aircraft – to name but some of its roles – Bishop's Mosquito, powered by twin Rolls-Royce Merlin engines, was a brilliant idea. But at first the aviation authorities were sceptical.

In the autumn of 1938 de Havilland took his idea for a "wooden speed bomber" to the Air Ministry and was rebuffed. He decided "to do it anyway" and packed Bishop and his design team off to Salisbury Hall, a moated manor house five miles from the company's works at Hatfield.

The project found one ally on the Air Staff, however: Air Chief Marshal Sir Wilfred Freeman. He gave the project his unofficial blessing and promised an order. The wooden aeroplane being created by Bishop and his team in the ballroom of Salisbury Hall was christened "Freeman's Folly."

Bishop's most cherished memory of the Mosquito's origins was of the stuffed pike in a glass case on the lavatory wall. His design began as a quick pencilled outline on the back of an envelope as he sat enthroned on the pedestal, and he drew inspiration from the contours of the fish – which happened to have been caught in the moat by Winston Churchill before the 1914-18 War.

Ronald Eric Bishop was born on Feb 27 1903 and joined de Havilland aged 18 as its second premium apprentice at Stag Lane, north London. He worked his way up through the sheet metal shop, fitting shop and engine shop before entering the drawing office in 1923.

The first design he worked on was the DH51 and he was also concerned with the DH42 Dormouse fighter-reconnaissance biplane and the little DH53 Humming Bird monoplane. In 1924 the Moth became the focus of effort.

But times were hard, and when the company could not afford heating Bishop and his colleagues kept warm by kicking a football about. Cutbacks took place and he left, nearly taking a job with Junkers in Germany; fortunately de Havilland recalled him after a few weeks.

The Mosquito owed much to an earlier de Havilland design, the Comet Racer, which had won the Mildenhall-Melbourne air race of 1934. Bishop had learned his craft under the Racer's designer, Arthur Hagg.

When Hagg left the company Bishop took charge of the design office and became responsible for the Albatross, a four-engined wooden airliner which might be termed the maiden aunt of the Mosquito.

Although a later Mosquito was flown from the neighbouring field at Salisbury Hall the prototype W4050 was transported to Hatfield, reassembled and flown for the first time at Hatfield by Sir Geoffrey's test pilot son and namesake. From the maiden flight to the conversion in 1945 of Mosquitos to carry Barnes Wallis's dambusting "bouncing bombs" to attack the Japanese fleet in the Pacific, the Mosquito carried all before it. Altogether more than 8,000 were built.

From the Mosquito, the fastest aircraft in the war for two-and-a-half years, Bishop went from strength to strength – through the Hornet to his first jet, the Vampire; the tailless DH108 study for high-speed flight; the Dove, Venom and Heron; and so to the Comet.

The world's first jet airliner was to test Bishop to the limit as he struggled to master the new fatigue phenomenon, which lay behind a series of disasters. He was also tackling the complex problems of military and naval fighter development from which the DH110 emerged as the Sea Vixen.

In 1946 Bishop became a director of the parent de Havilland company and six years later he also joined the board of de Havilland Propellers. In 1958 he was appointed deputy managing director of the aircraft company, by which time the design team was well advanced on the Trident airliner.

Beside his executive duties, Bishop was also design director of de Havilland Aircraft from 1946 to 1964, when he retired. He was appointed CBE in 1946, elected a Fellow of the Royal Aeronautical Society in 1948 and five years later received the British Gold Medal for Aeronautics.

He is survived by his wife, Nora, and two sons.

GEORGE MILES
19 SEPTEMBER 1999

George Miles, the aircraft designer and test pilot who has died aged 88, was a member of the remarkable Miles aviation family.

George Herbert Miles was born on July 28 1911 at Portslade, on the Sussex coast, where his father owned the Star Model Laundry. It was there, amid the clutter of wicker baskets, that George's elder brother Fred began to build the family's first aeroplane.

By 1929, at nearby Shoreham, Fred Miles had set up the Southern Aircraft Company in order to build a single-seat biplane, the Martlet. After leaving Hove College, George joined him to manage the fast-developing aircraft works, flying school and joyride business.

George Miles was quieter and more reflective than his extrovert brother, but he shared his flair for design. He complemented Fred's drive and impetuosity with a logical and incisive mind.

When the first Martlet was ready, it was bought by Maxine "Blossom" Freeman-Thomas, daughter of the actors Sir Johnston Forbes-Robertson and Gertrude Elliott. Blossom Freeman-Thomas adored her Martlet. She was also rather keen on Fred Miles, who taught her to fly it. In due course, Blossom divorced her husband, heir to the Marquess of Willingdon, and married Miles. She also became a director and designer of the aircraft company.

In the early 1950s, leaving George to mind the shop at Shoreham, Fred and Blossom Miles joined with Charles Powis – a Reading garage owner with aeronautical ambitions – to establish Phillips & Powis Aircraft at Woodley, Berks. In 1933, having identified a market for an affordable light aircraft to compete with de Havilland's Moths, Phillips & Powis produced the Hawk, a wooden, low-wing monoplane which would establish the Mileses' reputation in air races.

As new types of aircraft multiplied, the time came for George to join Fred and Blossom Miles as engine manager and test pilot. Among their new designs was a custom-built Mohawk for Charles Lindbergh, the American aviator, who commissioned this fast, long-range cabin tourer. In seeking to keep a record of their aircraft plans, the Mileses also invented an early photocopier – the "Copycat".

As war loomed, the Mileses' designs were much in

demand at the Air Ministry. The Hawk became an RAF trainer, and an Elementary Reserve Flying Training School was established at Woodley. The Miles trio also devised an early flight simulator, and in 1938 began to roll out the Miles Master, a two-seater tandem fighter trainer, more complex in design and operation than the Hawk. By September 1940, 500 of these aircraft had been built, and they had played a key role in the training of Hurricane and Spitfire pilots before the Battle of Britain.

The same team also designed the Miles Magister known as "Maggie" – the RAF's first monoplane trainer and one in which thousands of their pilots learnt to fly.

The family then set up Miles Aircraft, which came to incorporate Phillips & Powis; in 1941 Fred Miles became chairman and managing director. George, then aged 30, was appointed technical director and chief designer.

These duties, however, did not deter him from test flying. He had a lucky escape when the Observer Corps failed to recognise his aeroplane as a new type and an RAF fighter shot him down.

As chief designer, George Miles held ambitions beyond building the simple trainers which had laid the foundations of the company's success. In some instances, his unorthodox ideas so exasperated the authorities that he felt compelled to conceal new designs from them. One such secret project was the experimental Libellula canard-wing aircraft, which Miles saw as the answer to the problem of operating high performance fighters from aircraft carriers.

When the prototype Libellula was ready for its clandestine maiden flight, the company's chief test pilot refused to fly the strange-looking machine, whose main lifting surface was at the rear. "Very well," said Miles, "I'll take her up." It proved to be a hair-raising and hazardous experience, but despite its instability, the aeroplane's eccentric wing scheme provided many useful insights.

From 1943, George Miles helped his brother with the M-52, an experimental jet aircraft which promised to lead the world in supersonic flight. But in 1946 the government funded project was abruptly cancelled by Sir Stafford Cripps, Minister of Aircraft Production. Cripps compounded the blow by ordering the Mileses to hand over their designs to the American Bell Aircraft Company. On October 14 1947, Major Chuck Yeager, of the United States Air Force, made the world's first supersonic flight in a Bell-XI.

As military orders declined, Miles Aircraft sought to replace them with civil ones. George Miles was involved in the designs of the Messenger (one of which was used by Field Marshal Montgomery) Monitor, Gemini, Aerovan and Merchantman aircraft. He also helped with subsidiary activities, such as the contract to market the Biro ballpoint pen outside the United States. But the new ventures were not lucrative enough, and in 1948 the company collapsed.

George Miles moved to Airspeed, and in 1949 became chief designer there. Among the aircraft which he helped to build for them was the Ambassador, known to airline passengers as the British European Airways Elizabethan. Subsequently, Fred Miles re-established the Miles name in the aircraft business at Redhill, and in 1953 he returned to Shoreham, where George Miles rejoined him.

When, in 1960, Beagle Aircraft was set up to build light aeroplanes, George Miles, by then a Fellow of the Royal Aeronautical Society, became the company's technical director. Three years later he left to establish his own aircraft engineering business.

George Miles married, in 1939, Corinne Mackenzie; they had a daughter.

AIR COMMODORE
SIR FRANK WHITTLE
8 AUGUST 1996

Air Cdre Sir Frank Whittle, who has died in America aged 89, was the greatest aero-engineer of the century.

Whittle ensured that Britain was the first to enter the jet age when, on May 15 1941, the jet-propelled Gloster-Whittle E 28/39 flew successfully from Cranwell.

During 10 hours of flying over the next few days, the experimental aircraft – flown by the test pilot Gerry Sayer – achieved a top speed of 370 mph at 25,000 ft. This was faster than the Spitfire, or any other conventional propeller-driven machine.

Although this was a moment of triumph for Whittle, it was tinged with some bitterness, for he had had to overcome years of obstruction from the authorities. He felt, with justification, that if he had been taken seriously earlier, Britain would have been able to develop jets before the Second World War broke out.

He had been granted a patent for the first turbo-jet-engine in October 1932, but the Air Ministry's indifference had caused a long delay in realising his ideas. Thus it gave Whittle particular satisfaction when, days after the E28/39's maiden flight, Sir Archibald Sinclair, the Air Minister, and a gathering of officials stood stunned as Sayer put it through its paces over Cranwell.

As John Golley noted in his biography (*Airlife*, 1987): "Whittle – who had been the first man to get a turbo-jet running – had thrust Britain forward into the Jet Age and stood the aviation industry on its head."

Whittle's engineering genius led to the creation of several other aircraft: the RAF's Gloster Meteor, which saw action during the latter stages of the Second World War; the de Havilland Comet, the world's first passenger jet, and Concorde.

Frank Whittle was born on June 1 1907, in the Earlsdon district of Coventry, the son of a foreman in a machine tool factory.

When Frank was four his father, a skilful mechanic who spent Sundays at a drawing board, gave him a toy aeroplane with a clockwork propeller and suspended it from a gas mantle. During the First World War Frank's interest in aeroplanes grew when he saw aircraft being built at the local Standard works, and was excited when an aeroplane force-landed near his home.

In 1916 the family moved to Leamington Spa, where Frank's father had bought the Leamington Valve and Piston Ring Company, which comprised a few lathes and other tools, and a single cylinder gas engine. Frank became familiar with machine tools and did piece work for his father.

Frank won a scholarship to Leamington College, but had to leave when his father's business faltered. Instead he spent hours in the local library, learning about steam and gas turbines.

In January 1923, having passed the entrance examination, Whittle reported at RAF Halton as an aircraft apprentice. He lasted two days; five feet tall and with a small chest measurement, he failed the medical.

Six months later, after subjecting himself to an intense physical training programme supported by a special diet, he was rejected again. Undeterred, he applied using a different first name, passed the written examination again and was ordered to Cranwell where he was accepted.

In 1926, strongly recommended by his commanding officer, he passed a flying medical and was awarded one of five coveted cadetships at the RAF College. The cadetship meant that he would now train as a pilot. In his second term he went solo in an Avro 504N biplane after eight hours' instruction.

Whittle graduated to Bristol fighters and, after a temporary loss of confidence due to blacking out in a tight loop, developed into something of a daredevil. He was punished for hedge-hopping. But he shone in science subjects and in 1928 wrote a revolutionary thesis entitled *Future Developments in Aircraft Design.*

The paper discussed the possibilities of rocket propulsion and of gas turbines driving propellers, stopping short of proposing the use of the gas turbine for jet propulsion. However, Whittle launched his quest for a power plant capable of providing high speed at very high altitude.

In the summer of 1928 he passed out second and received the Andy Fellowes Memorial Prize for Aeronautical Sciences. He was rated "Exceptional to Above Average" as a pilot on Siskin operational fighters – but red-inked into his logbook were warnings about over confidence, an inclination to perform to the gallery and low flying.

At the end of August 1928, Pilot Officer Whittle joined No 111, an operational fighter squadron equipped with Siskins and based at Hornchurch, and was then posted to the Central Flying School, Wittering, for a flying instructor's course. In his spare time he conceived a gas turbine to produce a propelling jet, rather than driving a propeller. A sympathetic instructor, Flying Officer Pat Johnson, who had been a patent agent in civilian life, arranged an interview with the commandant.

This led to a call from the Air Ministry and an introduction to Dr A A Griffith at the ministry's South Kensington laboratory. Griffith was interested in gas turbines for driving propellers, and scorned Whittle's proposals. The Air Ministry told Whittle that successful development of his scheme was considered impracticable. Whittle nevertheless took out his jet patent, and qualified as a flying instructor.

Johnson, still convinced by Whittle's ideas, set up a meeting at British Thomson-Houston, near Rugby, with the company's chief turbine engineer. While not questioning the validity of Whittle's invention, BTH baulked at the prospect of spending £60,000 on development.

At the end of 1930 Whittle was posted to test floatplanes at the Marine Aircraft Experimental Establishment at Felixstowe. On leave he publicised his jet engine proposal, unsuccessfully. But a friend from Cranwell days, Rolf Dudley-Williams, was based at Felixstowe with a flying-boat squadron, and his efforts on Whittle's behalf soon bore fruit.

In the summer of 1932 Whittle was sent on an engineering course at RAF Henlow. He did so well that he was permitted to take a two-year engineering course as a member of Peterhouse College, Cambridge, where in 1936 he took a First in the Mechanical Sciences Tripos.

While he was at Cambridge his jet engine patent lapsed; the Air Ministry refused to pay the £5 renewal fee. But he had an inquiry from Dudley-Williams, who was by then a partner with another former RAF pilot, named Tinling, in General Enterprises Ltd.

The two men undertook to cover the expenses of further patents, to raise money, and to act as Whittle's agents. In the New Year of 1936 an agreement was signed between Dudley-Williams and Tinling, Whittle, the president of the Air Council, and OT Falk & Partners, a firm of City bankers.

A company, Power Jets, was incorporated and Whittle received permission from the Air Ministry to serve as honorary chief engineer and technical consultant for five years, providing there was no conflict with his official duties.

It was as well, because in July, turbo-jet experiments began at Junkers and Heinkel in Germany; at this stage, Whittle's ideas were not subject to the Official Secrets Act. It was a relief when the He 178, after some promise, was scrapped.

Whittle, seeking somewhere to develop his design on modest Power Jets' capital, returned to BTH at Rugby and the company contracted to build a "WU" (Whittle Unit), his first experimental jet engine. He tried to persuade companies to develop the specialised materials he needed.

First attempts to run Whittle's jet at Rugby in April 1937 caused alarm as it raced out of control and BTH hands bolted for cover. Money was needed for further development, but this was scarce. An Air Ministry contract provided a paltry £1,900.

In 1938 BTH moved the test-bed to its Ladywood works at Lutterworth where, in September, the engine, reconstructed for the third time, was assembled. A further £6,000 was pledged by the Air Ministry and engine tests resumed in December.

With the outbreak of war in September 1939, the project got a further lease of life. The Air Ministry commissioned a more powerful W 2 from Power Jets, and asked the Gloster Aircraft Company for an experimental aeroplane, specified as E28/39.

With finances more secure, Whittle faced a new threat. Relations with BTH, never easy, deteriorated as the company took the view that the jet engine would not compare favourably with conventional power plants. Whittle was further bedevilled by the politics of possible participation by the Rover motor-car company.

In the event, the Government cut the ground from under Whittle's feet in early 1940, bypassing Power Jets and offering shared production and development contracts direct to BTH and Rover. Power Jets was demoted to the level of a research organisation.

Then the Air Ministry, eager to obtain an operational jet fighter, side-stepped Whittle, ignoring the E28/39 and authorising Gloster to press ahead with a twin-engined jet interceptor specified as F9/40. This was to become the Meteor. In 1941 the ministry's director of engine production was to agree to Rover alterations to Whittle's design behind his back.

But fortunately, on July 9, Lord Beaverbrook, the Minister of Aircraft Production, personally assured Whittle that the jet fighter would go ahead.

Whittle was relieved by the reprieve, but agonised over the difficulties of, literally, getting his engine off the ground. He smoked and drank heavily, and the elbowing-out by BTH and Rover further depressed him.

But the events of April and May 1941, when he saw his E28 test-bed aeroplane flying successfully at Cranwell, lifted his gloom. When Johnson, who had long encouraged Whittle, patted him on the back and said, "Frank, it flies," he replied: "Well, that was what it was bloody well designed to do, wasn't it?".

Details of Whittle's inventions were made available both in Britain and America. Rolls-Royce, de Havilland and Metropolitan-Vickers became involved.

In June 1942, Whittle was flown to Boston to help General Electric to overcome problems. It built the engine under licence in America with the astonishing result that Bell Aircraft's experimental Airacomet flew in the autumn of 1942, beating the Meteor into the skies by five months.

Returning home, Whittle arrived at Power Jets' new factory at Whetstone and was astonished by its size after so many years of parsimony, although in practice it could not provide the capacity that would be needed.

Rolls-Royce stepped in and took over work on the

W 2B engine, which in 1943 cleared the way for Whittle to plan improvements which would evolve as later mark numbers. Then, with Rolls-Royce in almost total control of Power Jets, Whittle lost touch for three months while attending the RAF Staff College.

Fearing that private industry would harvest the pioneering work of Power Jets for nothing, he suggested it should be nationalised.

By the time Whittle had come to regret this proposal, he was taken up on it by Sir Stafford Cripps, the Minister of Aircraft Production. Cripps imposed a price of £135,563.10s, and re-named the company Power Jets (Research & Development). Whittle received nothing, having earlier handed over his shares worth £47,000 to the ministry.

But six months later Whittle was promoted air commodore and had the satisfaction of knowing that Meteors of No 616 Squadron were shooting down V1 flying-bombs.

In 1946 Whittle accepted a post as Technical Adviser on Engine Production and Design (Air) to the Controller (Air) at the Ministry of Supply. In 1948 he retired from the RAF on medical grounds. Soon after, he was awarded an ex-gratia sum of £100,000 by the Royal Commission on Awards to Inventors, and he was knighted.

Whittle was appointed CBE in 1944, CB in 1947, and KBE in 1948. He was made a Commander, the US Legion of Merit, in 1946. In 1986 he was appointed a member of the Order of Merit. He was a Fellow of the Royal Society, and of the Royal Aeronautical Society.

Whittle settled in America in 1976, and was a member of the Faculty of the Naval Academy, Annapolis, Maryland.

He published *Jet* (1953), and *Gas Turbine Aero-Thermodynamics* (1981).

Frank Whittle married, in 1930, Dorothy Mary Lee; they had two sons. The marriage was dissolved in 1976 and that year he married Hazel Hall.

HANS VON OHAIN
13 MARCH 1998

Hans Von Ohain, who has died aged 86, invented the jet engine that enabled the Heinkel 178, a German experimental aircraft, to fly 20 months before Frank Whittle's Gloster-Whittle E28/39 fighter, forebear of the RAF's Meteor.

While the He 178, Germany's first jet-powered aircraft, made its maiden flight on August 27 1939, the British fighter did not become airborne until May 15 1941. But although Ohain seemed to have given Germany the edge over Britain on the brink of the jet age, the He 178 was abandoned after only three flights.

Ohain had been convinced that there must be a faster, and less clumsy way of flying than by piston-engined aircraft, and since 1936 had been employed by the manufacturer Ernst Heinkel to carry out research at Rostock, on the Baltic.

"The Heinkel engineers considered me a crazy boy," Ohain recalled. "I was a physicist who really didn't know what nuts and bolts were."

By June 1939 Ohain's engine had been installed in the He 178 and was inspected by Hitler and Goering. Hitler, Ohain recalled, questioned the need for "a new engine to fly faster than the speed of sound", and seemed to think the approaching war would be won too soon for it to be of use.

Hans Joachim Pabst von Ohain was born at Dessau on

December 14 1911. His father prospered as a light-bulb distributor in Berlin.

As a student, Hans von Ohain was an enthusiastic glider pilot – until, as it seemed to him, the advent of the National Socialist Glider Club put more emphasis on marching than gliding. At Göttingen University, Ohain first worked on his theory of jet-propulsion, which came to the notice of Ernst Heinkel. Heinkel provided Ohain with company money and facilities, and subsequently employed him.

Following the demise of the He 178, Ohain's continued development of the gas-turbine engine resulted in the abandonment of the centrifugal flow concept and adoption of the axial flow, compressor type engine.

As the war continued, Ohain and Heinkel developed, with BMW and Junkers, the new 001 engine. Built despite increasing shortages of suitable materials, it was scheduled to be delivered around the time of VE day on May 8 1945. In the event, Ohain's prototype engines were buried before Allied troops arrived, but were very soon exhumed.

Ohain was interrogated by British and American experts, and the Americans snapped him up as an engineer for the US Air Force. In the early 1960s, he was appointed director of the US Air Force Aeronautical Research Laboratory.

Under American patronage, Ohain produced numerous new approaches in such fields as the colloid gas-core reactor for propulsion and power generation; electro-fluid dynamics; advanced diffusers and ejectors; dynamic energy transfer and Vertical/Short Take-off and Landing aircraft.

In America, Ohain added 19 patents to the 50 he had obtained in gas-turbine engine technology while at Heinkel's. When Sir Frank Whittle settled in America, he and Ohain became great friends.

Among many honours, Ohain received the Tom Sawyer Propulsion Award in 1990, and in 1992 was joint recipient, with Frank Whittle, of the Charles Draper Prize, a kind of Nobel prize for technology.

Hans von Ohain is survived by his wife, a son and two daughters.

SIR ARNOLD HALL
9 JANUARY 2000

Sir Arnold Hall, who has died aged 84, was one of the outstanding aeronautical engineers of his generation; later, as chairman of Hawker Siddeley Group from 1967 to 1986, he proved no less capable an industrialist.

In fact he had been managing director of the company from 1963. The mid-1960s were a difficult time for Hawker Siddeley, what with the cancellation of the TSR 2 fighter after the Government's preference for the American F111. Thousands of skilled workers were laid off. In the aftermath, all divisions of the firm were placed under one company, with Hall as chairman.

Over the next two decades, a period in which many engineering companies were suffering appalling reverses, Hawker Siddeley enjoyed strong, steady growth. Hall was closely associated with all the important aircraft developments, including the Harrier jump jet and the Hawk trainer. In 1966 he was the first chairman of the Anglo-French committee responsible for the development of engines for Concorde.

He steered the company through the nationalisation of its aerospace industries in 1977 by extending its engineering base, and proved equally successful in negotiating the severe recession of the early 1980s.

Hall's intellectual brilliance went with a tough, practical attitude to running the business. As far as possible he resisted state control, and was always careful to measure costs against the market. Thus in 1974, he did not hesitate, in spite of furious objections from the Labour Government, to suspend the HS 146 short haul airliner.

"Oil had gone up, while British inflation was heading towards 20 per cent," he explained. "We were accused of getting our sums wrong but in fact they were just suddenly going up by 20 per cent." Yet when the Government pulled out of the European co-operative to build the A300 Airbus, Hall ensured that Hawker Siddeley remained in to make the wings.

With Hall, common sense always prevailed. The story goes that John Banham – later Sir John and Director-General of the CBI, but then an eager young consultant to Hawker Siddeley – once came up with some bright idea for increasing efficiency. "My dear John," Hall replied, "to what problem could this possibly be the solution?"

Arnold Alexander Hall was born in Liverpool on April 23, St George's Day, 1915, the son of an upholsterer. From Alsop High School, he went up to Clare College Cambridge, intending to become an electrical engineer.

But he was attracted by the brilliant lectures of Sir Melville Jones, the Professor of Aeronautical Engineering, and subsequently took a First with special distinction in Applied Mechanics, Theory of Mechanical Structures, Heat Engines and Aeronautics. The achievement was the more remarkable in that he had fainted during the examinations and been treated for appendicitis.

Hall carried off three out of the four prizes attached to this tripos – the Rex Moir Prize for Mechanical Science, the Ricardo Prize for Thermo-Dynamics, and the Bernard Seeley Prize for Aeronautics.

Inevitably, research beckoned, and in 1936 Hall became

Resident Fellow in Aeronautics of the Company of Armourers and Brasiers, a post held at Cambridge. And in 1938, still only 23, he was appointed Principal Scientific Officer at the Royal Aircraft Establishment at Farnborough.

At Cambridge he worked with Frank Whittle on the first jet engine. Hall was responsible for stressing the compressor.

During the Second World War he remained at Farnborough, where he was at first concerned with aerodynamic research, and with building wind tunnels to take speeds up to 600 mph. He also helped develop a revolutionary gyro-electric gun-sight, which automatically worked out ranges and deflections; this enabled the RAF to double its rate of "kills". At Aberporth, in Wales, he worked on rockets and guided missiles.

After the war Hall became Zaharoff Professor of Aviation at London University. "It was nice being a Professor," he fondly recalled, though his appointment to the Air Safety Board in 1947 suggested that his talents were too valuable to be confined to theoretical research. And so it transpired; in 1951, during the Korean War, he gave up his Chair to become Director of the Royal Aircraft Establishment.

In this post he came for the first time into the public eye when he headed the investigation into the causes of the crash of the BOAC Comet which plunged into the Mediterranean off Elba in January 1954, with the loss of 35 lives.

Hall's explanation, which showed that the crash had been caused by metal fatigue, was a brilliant piece of detective work. At the same time, though, he insisted that the problem could be cured, and looked forward to an age of long-range civil aircraft which would cruise at between 500 and 600 mph. Indeed, he envisaged an aircraft capable of 1,300 mph, which would travel between London and New York in under three hours.

By now companies were bidding for his services, and it was Hawker Siddeley who won. He joined the board in 1955, and became vice-chairman in 1963. From the start, he was a notably relaxed businessman, with a talent for delegation and a preference for getting home by 7.00 in the evening. His secret was to issue clear instructions and delineate precisely the responsibilities of those who worked for him.

But though affable, Hall was never a man to underestimate. Appointed chairman of a transport working party of the CBI in 1966, he resigned within a fortnight when it was reported that the committee had been set up to oppose Barbara Castle's transport policy.

Hall was knighted in 1954. He had been elected a Fellow of the Royal Society the year before. From 1946, he was a Fellow of the Royal Aeronautical Society, which awarded him its Gold Medal in 1963; in 1958-59 he was President of the Society. He received the Gold Medal of the British Institute of Management in 1981.

He served as Pro-Chancellor of Warwick University from 1965-1970, and as Chancellor of Loughborough University of Technology from 1980 to 1989. He was chairman of the Board of Trustees of the Science Museum between 1983 and 1985.

Other appointments included the chairmanship of Fasco Industries (1980-81), and the presidency of the Federation of British Electrotechnical and Allied Manufacturers' Association (1966-67), and of the Society of British Aerospace Companies (1972-73).

He was a member of the Advisory Council on Scientific Policy (1962-64), and of the Advisory Council on Technology (1980-89).

He was a director of Lloyds Bank (1966-85), Phoenix

Assurance (1969-85) ICI (1970-85), Rolls-Royce (1983-86) and the Royal Ordnance (1984-86).

Sir Arnold Hall retired as chairman of the Hawker Siddeley Group in 1986. In his free time he liked reading and pottering about in boats. He was also an excellent handyman, who enjoyed trying his hand at his father's trade of upholstery.

After the death of his first wife Dione Sykes, whom he had married in 1946, he married secondly, in 1986, Iola Nealon. She survives him, together with three daughters of his first marriage, a step-son and a step-daughter.

TEST PILOTS

REGGIE BRIE
4 FEBRUARY 1989

Reggie Brie, pioneer of rotary-wing flying in Britain who has died aged 93, held the Royal Aero Club's No 1 Helicopter Aviator's certificate, issued on March 14, 1947.

Later that month he also obtained the Air Ministry's first certificate to land a helicopter – which he did at Hampden Park, Glasgow.

Brie had begun his romance with rotary flying in the inter-war years of autogiro experiments. Rotary flight, with its ability for almost vertical descent, was then so new that on one occasion in 1933 Brie's autogiro approach to land at Hook aerodrome alongside the Kingston by-pass resulted in a conviction for low and dangerous flying.

But the powers-that-be of the flying world supported a successful appeal against his £5 fine and costs.

Among Brie's many "firsts" as a test pilot were rotary-wing landings on a warship in 1935 and operating a rotary-wing machine from a merchant ship in 1942. The former adventure, when Brie made some spectacular take-offs and landings from the Italian cruiser *Fiume*, was achieved with the help of the Spanish autogiro designer, Juan la Cierva.

Brie hoped to interest the British Fleet Air Arm in the new technology but trials carried out in the Channel by two C.30s in the carrier *Furious* were unproductive, though in 1939 two C.40s were accepted by the Royal Navy. In the same period attempts to interest the War Office in the autogiro for artillery fire control and transport foundered.

It was not until 1940 that No 1448 Rotor Calibration

Flight was formed giving belated operational respectability to Brie's experimental work and the autogiro. In 1943 the Flight became No 529 Autogiro Squadron, the only RAF unit to be so equipped.

Thanks to Brie's pioneering work with Cierba's design 529 Squadron was available for the vital task of checking the accuracy of coastal radar stations, previously undertaken by balloons.

In early 1940 Brie personally calibrated for Fighter Command the seven main coastal radar stations from Ventnor in the Isle of Wight to Hatson in the Orkneys, a task which contributed significantly to the efficiency of the then rudimentary radar chain during the Battle of Britain.

Reginald Alfred Charles Brie was born in 1895 and educated at Uxbridge County School, the City and Guilds and then apprenticed to Submersible and J L Motors.

In the 1914–18 War he served first as a sergeant in the Royal Field Artillery and from 1918 as a lieutenant observer and pilot in No 104 Squadron of the Royal Flying Corps, being shot down and taken prisoner-of-war. Afterwards he joined the sales staff of Shell-Mex.

In 1930 he returned full-time to aviation with the Cierva Autogiro Company where he remained chief pilot and flying manager until 1939. The outbreak of war halted further development of autogiros in Britain and the company closed in 1940.

Brie returned to the RAF and in 1941 was posted to America to help further rotary-wing development. While there, he made test landings and takeoffs with the Pitcairn autogiro on the *Empire Mersey*, a British merchant ship.

He was also the first British pilot to fly the Sikorsky XR-4 helicopter. Early in 1945 he returned from America for duty with the Ministry of Aircraft Production. Shortly afterwards he produced a proposal for the Government and Post Office to sponsor an experimental mail service using three Sikorsky helicopters.

It was not until 1948 that the Post Office entered into a contract with British European Airways for an experimental service.

Having retired from the RAF in 1945 as a wing commander, Brie had joined Fairey Aviation, moving in 1947 to run British European Airways' helicopter experimental unit until 1954. In 1957 he joined Westland Aircraft, spending 12 years guiding their helicopter developments.

Brie was a Fellow of the Royal Aeronautical Society and was awarded the British Silver Medal for Aeronautics in 1954. He was appointed MBE in 1963.

He is survived by a daughter. His son was killed as an RAF Spitfire pilot in Malaya in 1948.

JEFFREY QUILL
20 FEBRUARY 1996

Jeffrey Quill, who has died aged 83, was a great test pilot who earned the title "Mr Spitfire".

Not only did he prepare the celebrated fighter for service, but, remarkably for a test pilot, saw action as a fighter pilot during the Battle of Britain. He shot down two enemy aircraft before returning to his own hazardous speciality.

It was in 1936 that Mutt Summers, then Vickers' chief test pilot, first flew the Spitfire. Quill, his assistant, was the second pilot to fly it.

Quill and his team put through their paces some 52 operational variants of a production total of 27,500 Spitfires.

Through hours of painstaking test-flying he helped the Spitfire – and many other aeroplanes – to perform as their designers had hoped they would.

In Quill's day, designers could not call upon computers or large wind tunnels to help them get it right, nor could test pilots use flight simulators; so he risked his life as he took prototypes off the ground for the first time.

By the summer of 1940 and the Battle of Britain, Quill had turned R J Mitchell's concept into an integrated fighting machine.

True, the sturdier Hurricane (designed by Hawker's Sydney Camm) far outnumbered the speedier Spitfire in the Battle of Britain. But Quill had brought the Vickers-Supermarine Spitfire to the point where it could tackle enemy Me 109 escorting fighters while Hurricanes took on the bombers.

As the fighting swayed across the south of England, Quill ached to join in. There was no problem about his qualifications. He had served as an RAF fighter pilot in the early 1930s. He feared, however, that an application to join a squadron would be opposed because of his unique value as a test pilot.

To meet this objection, he persuaded Vickers that he could do little more for the Spitfire without gaining firsthand experience of combat, or "a spot of practical" as he put it. After some string-pulling, the RAF went along with the scheme, and on August 5 1940 he was posted to No.65 Squadron at Hornchurch.

But, after he had shot down an Me 109 and a Heinkel 111 bomber, he was told to put his flying officer's uniform back in mothballs and return to the Supermarine works at Southampton.

As a result of his experience, a number of production changes were swiftly introduced. Vitally, aileron control at high speed was improved.

Combat had also taught Quill that pilots were getting shot down by an enemy they could not see. The optical qualities of the windscreen side panels were defective; worse, the lines of the rear fuselage and the canopy impeded rear vision. After his report, the design was changed.

Quill was an exceptionally articulate test pilot, and he gained a reputation as an outstanding troubleshooter. This helped him secure a second spell of Service flying when, in 1943, the Admiralty was confronted by problems with aircraft carrier operations.

He was commissioned as a lieutenant commander in the air branch of the RNVR, and so escaped from the works for another five months.

The Sea Spitfire, or Seafire as the Fleet Air Arm variant became known, was available from 1941, but ran into difficulties, particularly when operating from escort carriers whose decks were 30 per cent shorter than those of the big Fleet carriers.

Quill undertook innumerable deck landings which suggested ways to modify future production of Seafires and the training of their pilots. He enjoyed the Navy and was saddened when told to change out of uniform for a second time.

Jeffrey Kindersley Quill was born on February 1 1913. When he was five, an airplane landed and another crashed on the common between his Sussex home at Littlehampton and the sea. He always said that these events determined him to fly.

In 1931 he entered the RAF from Lancing College on a short service commission, being unable to afford a cadetship at the RAF College Cranwell because of the death of his father.

He went solo in an Avro Tutor after five hours' dual instruction. The next year he passed out with the rating "exceptional" and was posted to No. 17, a fighter squadron stationed at Upavon, equipped with Bristol Bulldogs.

Later he would reflect ruefully on what he saw as a scandal: that, seven years before the outbreak of the 1939-45 War, RAF fighters were little more than derivatives of RFC machines of the 1914-18 War.

At the end of 1933, Quill was posted to the Meteorological Flight at Duxford near Cambridge. He welcomed the challenge and occupational hazard of flying obsolescent Siskins in all weathers. He accomplished the astonishing feat of completing a year, irrespective of normally unflyable conditions, without missing one Met Flight daily climb. He was awarded the AFC.

Late in 1935, he was tipped off that Mutt Summers, the Vickers chief test pilot, was looking for a young assistant. He was disinclined at first to pass up the possibility of a permanent commission, but was persuaded to fly down to Brooklands for interviews by Summers and Sir Robert McLean, the chairman of Vickers Aviation.

He accepted the post at £500 year. The RAF released him, and from January 1 1936 he became busily employed testing aircraft produced by Vickers and its subsidiary, Supermarine.

These included the Vildebeeste torpedo-bomber, Valentia transport and a prototype Venom fighter (eventually abandoned in favour of the Spitfire, which performed better).

Mutt Summers first flew "The Fighter", as the prototype K5054 was known in the works, on March 6 1936. On March 26 he invited Quill to take her up.

The more Quill flew her, the more convinced he became, as he was to recall, that "this aeroplane was of immense importance". On June 18 that year, a recurring fear that he might crash the one and only Spitfire was almost realised on the day it was unveiled to the press.

At the last minute, it was found to have an untraceable engine oil leak. To fly or not to fly? Mitchell settled the matter. Tersely he told Quill: "Get in and fly it."

He was just airborne when, to his horror, he saw the oil pressure gauge drop to zero. There was no alternative but to climb sufficiently to turn, and land despite the very high risk of engine seizure and a crash.

The fault was traced, a new Rolls-Royce Merlin engine was substituted, and the Spitfire survived what might have been curtains.

Shortly after this incident, the RAF sought to attract Quill back with the offer of a permanent commission. He had hardly turned it down after "much heart aching" when his life was imperilled again.

He was giving a Wellesley geodetic bomber its production test when at 12,000 ft, the single-engined monoplane lurched into a right-handed spin and failed to respond to normal recovery action. At 3,000 ft he baled out.

After this escape, he was more certain than ever that his destiny lay entirely with the Spitfire and he moved from Vickers at Weybridge to Supermarine.

With the outbreak of war and the demand for more and more ever-improving Spitfires during and after the Battle of Britain, Quill was sorely stretched.

Yet from time to time there were moments of welcome relief as when, in the summer of 1940, Lord Beaverbrook, the Minister for Aircraft Production, who had invited him to dinner, failed to join Quill and his fellow guests.

At the cigar stage, the Beaver was discovered slumped in sleep over his desk in an adjoining room. The press baron was as much a casualty of the hour as were the fatigued fighter pilots for whom he was driving on fighter production.

There was also the bizarre plot – Operation Airthief – hatched by Captain Philip Pinkney of 12 Commando to paddle Quill ashore near a German airfield in France with the aim of stealing an Fw 190 fighter about which details were urgently required.

Quill mugged up every available piece of intelligence about the new fighter. He had also undergone a strenuous commando fitness and Folbot canoe paddling regime before the exploit was called off. The surrender at Pembrey in Wales by Oberleutenant Arnim Faber of a pristine Fw 190 had made such a perilous exploit unnecessary.

The end of the war brought Quill, now Supermarine's senior test pilot, no respite. The jet age had arrived and with it an experimental Supermarine design, the E.10/44, or Spiteful. Quill was climbing it on a June day in 1947 when he lost consciousness at about 40,000 ft. Coming to at 10,000 ft, he landed safely, but medical checks revealed the toll 16 years of hard flying had taken.

Three months' leave failed to restore his health fully. He had to accept he would never test high performance fighters again – though 30 years after his first flight in Mitchell's prototype, he flew a Spitfire for the last time in 1966.

"Flying a desk" did not come easily, but he made a great success of it with Vickers-Armstrongs, the British Aircraft Corporation and as a director of Sepecat, the company which administered the Jaguar programme.

He served also as marketing director of Panavia, the Anglo-German-Italian consortium which developed the Tornado multi-role combat aircraft.

In Munich on this programme, he shared an office with Willi Messerschmitt, creator of the Me 109, opponent of the Spitfire in the Battle of Britain.

Quill retired in 1978. In 1983 he published *Spitfire, A*

Test Pilot's Story.

Quill was awarded the AFC in 1936, appointed OBE in 1942 and elected Fellow of the Royal Aeronautical Society in 1980.

HARALD PENROSE

31 AUGUST 1996

Harald Penrose, who has died aged 92, was for 23 years chief test pilot for Westland Aircraft.

Penrose flew some 400 types and variants of British and foreign aircraft. His work involved many anxious moments and close escapes.

When in the New Year of 1933 a suitably modified aircraft was required for an RAF attempt to be first to overfly Mount Everest, Penrose undertook an altitude test on an open-cockpit Houston-Westland PV 3 biplane. Over Poole Bay, Dorset, he reached a record altitude of 38,000 ft indicated.

He recalled: "I flew on and on in serenity, enthralled by this new experience of unexplored heights and sun-blazed space, dreaming my thoughts, half guard and half robot while methodically recording the instruments and stopwatch reading."

An imaginative airman, Penrose knew how much could have gone wrong as he coaxed his supercharged 525 horsepower Bristol Pegasus engine ever upwards. The trial enabled Westland to prepare two Wallace aircraft for the conquest of Everest by Squadron Leader the Marquis of Clydesdale and Flight Lieutenant D F McIntyre on May 3 1933.

On another occasion Penrose became the first pilot to bale out of a closed cockpit. He was testing the PV7, a high wing braced monoplane, when the port wing broke off and carried the tail away with it. Trapped by enormous G forces, Penrose was unable to shift the cockpit cover and eventually escaped through a side window.

Penrose landed heavily, injuring his ankles, and was dragged into a hedge, over which an attractive girl was peering. Only then did he realise that his trouser buttons had been torn off.

Harald James Penrose was born on April 12 1904. When he was five his father showed him a newspaper picture of Blériot after he had flown the Channel. "Within an hour," Harald recalled, "I was nailing a wing-like piece of cardboard on to one of my oblong wooden building blocks to make my first model aeroplane."

A joyride in 1919 in a war-surplus Avro 504K, with the pioneer aviator Alan Cobham sealed his future. To the temporary dismay of his father, young Penrose determined to build a career in aviation. From Reading School he joined a four-year aeronautical course at Northampton Engineering College.

In 1925 he secured a post with Westland. The next year he was commissioned into the Reserve of Air Force Officers, where he learned to fly. He also obtained a commercial pilot's licence and by 1928 had been appointed to manage Westland's civil aircraft department.

His duties included demonstrating company aircraft, and he was dispatched on a tour of South America with a Wapiti. Briefing him, Sir Ernest Petter, Westland's autocratic chairman, said: "Do not forget, my boy, you represent a famous company. Keep up appearances. Find the finest hotel, but book a small room at the top. It will be cheaper."

Upon his return in 1931 Penrose, still only 27, slipped into the post of chief test pilot and soon took over the trials of the Pterodactyl, a futuristic tail-less and swept-back-wing prototype.

In this period he also flew the maiden flight of the monoplane Lysander. Its high wing owed something to the PV7 in which he had so nearly lost his life. Penrose enjoyed the "Lizzie", as it became known; he found it "noisy, smelly and heavy on the controls but able to bump in and out of ridiculously small spaces whatever the load." It made its name as a Special Operations Executive workhorse, flying agents to and from Britain and farm fields in occupied France.

With the coming of war and the search for a twin-engine fighter to outdo the German Me 110, Penrose introduced the Westland Whirlwind. It was, however, no match for the de Havilland Mosquito and was withdrawn in 1943.

But Penrose was inured to the ups and downs of test flying and found consolation in testing Vickers-Supermarine Spitfire and Seafire fighters built at the Westland works.

In l946 he introduced the Wyvern, Westland's last fixed-wing aircraft. A massive naval fighter, it presented endless problems. Before one flight he tossed up with his assistant Peter Garner to decide who would take the prototype up on a publicity picture-shoot. Garner won. He encountered propellor problems, crash landed and was killed.

Penrose persevered with the Wyvern for six years, diving 500 times from high altitude to overcome problems with propellor control. The aircraft killed three test pilots, and Penrose himself several times faced disaster. Once he was approaching Yeovil airfield when the machine turned on its back. Houses lay 500 feet ahead as he fought to recover control. Just in time he managed to roll level. "Few have escaped so close a call," he said afterwards.

Stepping out of his pilot's overalls in 1953, Penrose was appointed sales manager, responsible for the Westland, Bristol and Saunders–Roe helicopter group.

When he retired in 1968, Penrose kept a small Currie Wot biplane and continued to fly over his beloved Wessex countryside until he was well into his eighties.

Penrose was also an aeronautical engineer, a naval architect and a prolific writer. As a naval architect he designed sailing dinghies, yachts and power boats.

An entertaining writer, Penrose enriched aviation shelves with works including *I Flew with the Birds* (1949), *No Echo in the Sky* (1958), *Airymouse* (1967), and *Cloud Cuckoo Land* (1981). *Architect of Wings* (1985) was a biography of Roy Chadwick, the designer of the Lancaster bomber. He also published a renowned British aviation series in five volumes, covering the years 1902 to 1939.

Penrose was appointed OBE in 1946. He was made a Fellow of the Royal Aeronautical Society in 1936 and was also a Fellow of the Society of Experimental Test Pilots.

He married, in 1929, Nora Bailey. They lived, until her death in 1986, in the house at Nether Compton, Dorset, which he had designed 50 years before. They had a son and a daughter.

BILL BEDFORD
20 OCTOBER 1996

Bill Bedford, who has died aged 75, was the first man to fly a jump-jet.

Bedford was one of the best regarded post-war test pilots. Thirty-six years ago today he made the initial flight of P1127, the prototype of the Harrier, the world's first Vertical Take-Off and Landing jet.

Three years later, in 1963, he was the first pilot to land a jump-jet on the deck of an aircraft carrier, the *Ark Royal*. In 1966 he flew the inaugural flight of the first Harrier.

Bedford had his share of crashes, but the only time he was badly injured was as a passenger in somebody else's car. A few days before P1127's maiden flight in 1960, Bedford broke a leg in Germany when his driver ran into a tree.

The doctors allowed him to fly the prototype, or rather hover it, providing it was tethered. He took the controls with his leg in plaster.

Later Bedford had an alarming experience during flutter tests. At 5,000 ft and 400 knots there was a roughness and a roaring noise. Deciding to land, he was at 200 ft when the aircraft rolled uncontrollably to port. Bedford made a perfect ejection, his parachute opening just in time. But there was little left of P1127.

On Feb 8 1963 Bedford made his historic landing on *Ark Royal* off Portland Bill. This exercise was of the greatest significance because it led to the adoption of the aircraft for its current operational use in the Royal and US Navies, putting paid to early scepticism in naval circles.

Later that year Bedford gave a scintillating jump-jet demonstration to spectators at the Paris Air Show. But suddenly his aircraft seemed to fall out of the sky. It smashed itself up on a concrete platform used by its French Balzac VTOL competitor. Astonishingly Bedford stepped out of the wreckage uninjured.

Further Harrier development called for a sustained flight-test programme, entailing a prolonged period of risk for the pilot of a kind not experienced in test flying since the 1930s. Much of Bedford's work was exceptionally dangerous.

Alfred William Bedford was born on November 18 1920. He was educated at Loughborough College School and served an electrical engineering apprenticeship with the Blackburn Starling Company.

Commissioned into the RAF in 1940, he flew Hurricane fighters with 605 Squadron in 1941 until he was posted in that year to the Far East. There he survived the perilous circumstances of the Japanese invasion of Burma, where he flew Hurricanes with 135 Squadron. He also flew in India and Ceylon. In 1944 he returned home and joined 65 Squadron, which was equipped with Mustangs.

Bedford spent four years as an instructor after qualifying in 1945 at the Central Flying School. In 1949 he graduated from the Empire Test Pilots' School. For the next year he tested at the Royal Aircraft Establishment, Farnborough, but left the RAF as a Squadron Leader in 1951 to join the Hawker Aircraft Company as an experimental test pilot. He succeeded Neville Duke as chief test pilot in 1956.

As well as introducing jump-jet aviation Bedford put in more than 1,000 hours test-flying Hawker's highly successful Hunter fighter. He spent 11 arduous and active years as Hawker's chief test pilot.

Bedford was the thinking man's flyer: his learned contributions to Royal Aeronautical Society publications were much admired. Ever conscious of a test pilot's reliance on designers, scientists and engineers, he was the first to credit them for such achievements as the Hunter and the Harrier, aircraft with which he was so closely identified.

When Hawker Siddeley Aviation succeeded Hawker's, Bedford flew as its chief test pilot, at Dunsfold, from 1963 to 1967.

After giving up test flying he launched into a successful career as sales manager for the company. From 1978 to 1983 he was divisional marketing manager at British Aerospace.

As a speed record specialist Bedford was a sometime holder of the London-Rome, Rome-London records. He was also awarded the International Gold "C" with two diamonds for his gliding achievements.

Elected a Fellow of the Royal Aeronautical Society in 1963, Bedford was the Society's R P Alston Medallist in 1959 and the recipient of the Air League's Founder's Medal in 1967.

Among other honours were the Derry-Richards Memorial Medal in 1960, the Segrave Trophy in 1963, the Britannia Trophy in 1964 and the C P Robertson Memorial Trophy in 1987.

He was awarded the AFC in 1945 and appointed OBE in 1961.

He married in 1941 Mary Averill. They had a son.

SQUADRON LEADER
FRANK "SPUD" MURPHY
11 MAY 1997

Frank "Spud" Murphy, who has died, aged 80, was a wartime fighter ace and later a test pilot.

During the Second World War, Murphy notched up at least five "kills", the minimum qualification as an ace, and was awarded the DFC in less than two years. In early 1944, as a "rest" from operations, he was attached to the Hawker Aircraft Company for test flying.

This launched him on a series of test assignments, over 12 years, associated with the re-equipment of RAF fighters and the company's own research and development programmes.

Murphy – who was known as "The Flying Potato" – came to operational and test flying with a distinctly unpromising medical history.

At the age of 18 months he had been stricken with poliomyelitis, and doctors doubted that he would walk. But after two years on his back, he began to get on his feet; for the rest of his life he walked with an almost imperceptible limp.

At 15, when Murphy was experimenting with chemical powders in the back garden, an explosion deprived him of the use of a thumb, and blew away a piece of one finger.

As a test pilot, he also experienced his fair share of spills and close shaves. Shortly after the war, he had to belly-land a single-seat Hawker Fury on the Long Walk at Windsor Castle – to be confronted by a bellicose farmworker with a pitchfork.

On another occasion, an engine failed when he was taking off from Langley Airfield, and he was obliged to attempt a landing in a cabbage patch, from which he ploughed through some hedges and careered across the Bath Road.

"I came to rest near a lorry in the stream of traffic," Murphy recalled. "The driver leaned out and said: 'Women drivers, and now this! It's not safe on the roads anymore'."

Perhaps Murphy's most serious prang took place while he was carrying out tests on a Hunter fuel system. These necessitated turning off the booster pumps which risked stopping the engine; this happened, and a re-light proved impossible. Heavy cloud meant that he had to rely on guidance from the control tower at Ford, near Chichester – where he had already made four forced landings.

In the event, Murphy could not lower the flaps and landed at 230 mph with the undercarriage retracted. The Hunter jet developed an uncontrollable bounce, and Murphy almost blacked out. The aircraft then slewed sideways through a caravan park, where two people were killed. It hurtled on over the Clymping Road, and broke into three pieces.

The cockpit section rolled for another 100 yards. When Murphy was extracted, marks of the bolt ends in the cockpit canopy were found in the sides and top of his helmet, which was split from front to back.

This was the first time a new British "bone-dome" had been tested in a crash. The Institute of Aviation Medicine was well-satisfied, but Murphy spent many months in hospital recovering from his injuries.

Frank Murphy was born at Bolton, Lancashire, on January 19 1917. When he was five the family emigrated to New Zealand, where he went to school and university.

After working as a clerk he persuaded the Royal New Zealand Air Force to accept him for wartime training as a pilot, despite his medical record. In March 1942 he was posted as a sergeant-pilot to No 486, a New Zealand fighter squadron equipped with Hawker Hurricanes at Wittering.

Not long afterwards, the squadron was re-equipped with Hawker Typhoons, and later with Tempest Vs. In 1943, as Murphy began to claim successes, he was commissioned pilot officer, and later squadron leader.

Following his attachment in 1944 to Hawkers, Murphy tested a series of fighter aircraft, including the Fury, Tempest V, VI, and VII. He also helped to introduce the Hunter. At the end of this period of service he was appointed OBE.

From 1955 Murphy worked in technical sales for Hawker. He was foreign sales manager from 1959 to 1962, and until 1966 was responsible for international sales for Hawker Siddeley Aviation.

In 1956 Murphy navigated the Hunter on flights which established new London-Rome and Rome-London records. He also held the piston-engined British National 100 km close circuit record.

In 1971 he was elected a Fellow of the Royal Aeronautical Society.

Frank Murphy married, in 1945, Gloria Higgs; they had a son and a daughter.

BEN GUNN
22 SEPTEMBER 1999

Ben Gunn, who has died aged 76, survived an upside down ejection from a jet aircraft to pursue a notable career as a test pilot.

On August 6 1952, Gunn, then chief test pilot with the aircraft manufacturers Boulton Paul, was the first to test-fly a Boulton Paul P.120 delta-wing jet research aircraft.

Even though the black-painted aircraft was ominously known as the "Black Widow Maker" Gunn was not unduly worried as he was already familiar with the aircraft's eccentric predecessor, the P.111.

Yet after travelling down three quarters of the long runway at the Armament and Aircraft Experimental Establishment (A&AEE) at Boscombe Down, Gunn was dismayed to find the jet had still not left the ground.

"Things looked black indeed," he recalled. "If I closed the throttle a serious accident was inevitable. I decided on one last supreme effort and it paid dividends. Staggering, wallowing, dipping, the aircraft left the ground at the slowest rate of climb I have ever experienced.

"I shall never forget the startled amazement on the faces of a group of potato pickers at the end of the runway as this black shape scraped over their heads clawing frantically for altitude."

Despite this inauspicious start, three weeks later, on August 29, Gunn took the aircraft out again.

He was flying at 5,000 feet over the south coast when he heard a loud bang, whereupon the jet began rolling crazily before diving towards the ground. Managing to recover a level attitude, he was horrified to discover that the control column, rudder, nose and tailplane were all out of position.

As the aircraft approached 3,000 feet, Gunn jettisoned the hood before bumpy conditions made the aircraft unmanageable. But just as he ejected, the aircraft flipped over and he fell out upside down.

Spiralling and tumbling towards Salisbury Plain, Gunn found he was still sitting in his ejector seat. Struggling to get free, he pulled his parachute ripcord, though this was contrary to ejection drill. The ground was dangerously close when, with a final effort, he managed to release the seat, his parachute opening as he crashed through some trees.

"This," he noted, "made me the first pilot to eject from

a delta aircraft and the first to eject from an inverted position and survive."

Gunn's adventure with the short-lived Black Widow Maker provided much vital information. Investigation of the P.120's wreckage showed that intense flutter had caused a complete fracture of the hinges of the left elevon.

Alexander Ewen Gunn, inevitably known as "Ben", was born on June 24 1923 in Glasgow, where he attended Whitehill School and was inspired to fly after being taken up for a "five-bob flip" by the touring Sir Alan Cobham flying circus.

In 1941 he transferred from the Air Defence Cadet Corps to the newly formed Air Training Corps. Aged 17, he volunteered for the RAF. After getting his wings he was posted at the end of 1943 to No 501, a Spitfire Vb squadron at Hawkinge on the Kent coast.

After supporting the D-Day Normandy landings, Gunn was commissioned and moved to No 274, a Tempest V squadron in which he shot down the last V1 flying bomb over England in daylight.

On VE Day, May 8 1945, Gunn began test flying at the A&AEE, Boscombe Down, and in 1948 qualified for the coveted letters "tp" after his name at the Empire Test Pilots' School.

Shortly afterwards, he was seconded to the aircraft manufacturers Boulton Paul, to continue the test programme of their prototype advanced turbo–prop Balliol trainer, following the deaths of the company's two test pilots.

After leaving the RAF early in 1949, Gunn was appointed chief test pilot at Boulton Paul. As well as test flying the company's P.111 and P.120, in 1953 he also flew the vivid yellow P.111a, a modified version of the P.111, known as the "Yellow Peril".

In 1966 he joined Rover Gas Turbines as chief test

pilot, leaving the next year for Beagle Aircraft at Shoreham, Sussex, as marketing director for Africa and the Middle East.

After retiring from test flying in 1971, Gunn was appointed the manager of Shoreham Airport, which in 1988 was voted best airport of the year.

Gunn became a Master Pilot of the Guild of Air Pilots and Air Navigators (GAPAN) in 1966. He was appointed MBE in 1990.

He married, in 1946, Geraldine "Gerry" Phillips, whom he had met when she was an ATS ambulance driver. Their son is an RAF squadron leader.

―――

JACQUELINE AURIOL
12 FEBRUARY 2000

Jacqueline Auriol, who has died aged 82, was France's first woman test pilot and once the fastest woman in the air; in 1963 she flew at 1,261 mph in a Dassault Mirage IIIR, more than twice the speed at which she had first set the world record a decade earlier.

She was also the daughter-in-law of a President of France, Vincent Auriol, who was head of state from 1947 to 1954. Slim, blue-eyed and extremely pretty, Jacqueline Auriol acted as his hostess at many official functions, and at one dinner in 1948 found herself seated next to Raymond Guillaume, one of France's best-known pilots. He declared that flying was the closest thing to true freedom and offered her lessons.

She accepted and although, she later recalled, she was at first unenthusiastic about the experience, "all of a sudden I discovered a world where no matter what your name, the only things that count are merit, skill and courage." She set her heart on learning stunt flying, and eventually persuaded her father-in-law to give the necessary permission. "Jacqueline," sighed the President, "makes Demosthenes inarticulate."

Having qualified, Jacqueline Auriol showed off her skills at the Paris Air Show in July 1949 in front of 30,000 spectators. Three days later, an experimental seaplane in which she and Guillaume were passengers crashed into the Seine. Every bone in her face was broken, including both jaws; her skull was also fractured in three places. A leading French surgeon opined that little could be done for her.

But to this verdict Jacqueline Auriol reacted with characteristic tenacity. While she spent a year in hospital in France, undergoing 14 reconstructive operations, she studied the theoretical courses necessary to gain both military and commercial pilots' licences. Refusing to let her two young sons see her battered face, she then travelled to New York for another eight operations, drawing strength from her conviction that one day she would fly again.

In 1951, she returned to Paris. "The nose is American, but the smile is still French," wrote one newspaper bravely, but lifelong friends failed to recognise her, and soon she withdrew entirely from the social scene. Instead she spent every day supervising the building of the de Havilland Vampire jet in which she planned to assault the women's world record, then held by the American pilot Jacqueline Cochran.

When she landed after her first flight in the Vampire, Jacqueline Auriol burst into tears, the only time she had showed any emotion in two years. "That day I experienced a sense of power," she wrote later of having faced her fears and conquered them, "a sense of being in complete possession of myself."

On May 12 1951, she took off from Istres, near Marseilles, and flew around a 100 kilometre (62 mile) circuit at 509 mph, more than 40 mph faster than the previous world record. Her feat began a decade of competition between herself and Jacqueline Cochran, in which the record passed back and forth between them nine times, with Jacqueline Auriol wresting it from her rival on five occasions.

Later in 1951, Jacqueline Auriol made the first flight in a French Comet airliner, and she went on to test more than 100 different types of aircraft. Basing herself at the French test centre at Bretigny, in 1955 she flew at 715 mph in a Dassault-Breguet Mystère IVN fighter, and in 1959 went at Mach 2 – twice the speed of sound.

She had her fair share of narrow escapes. In 1956, while piloting a Mystère IV, the aircraft went into a tailspin as she attempted for a third time to break the sound barrier (a mark first passed by her American rival). Her oxygen mask became disconnected and she blacked out; but when she came round, she managed to re-connect the supply and then to correct the spin.

"Truth is with me when I fly," Jacqueline Auriol once wrote. "Now I know that only life and death are important."

She was born Jacqueline Marie-Thérèse Suzanne Douet at Challans, near the Bay of Biscay in the Vendée, on November 5 1917. Her father was a successful shipbuilder and importer of wood from Scandinavia, and her upbringing was firmly conventional, Roman Catholic and pro-monarchist.

She grew up mainly in Nantes, where she attended the Institution Blanche-de-Castille, before going to Paris to study art at the Ecole du Louvre in the mid-1930s.

At weekends, she went skiing in the Alps, and there met Paul Auriol, a political science student whose father,

Vincent, was then a leader of the Socialist Party. Both families deemed such a match inappropriate, and Jacqueline was packed off to Sweden on one of her father's cargo vessels while Auriol was sent to cool his heels in Italy. Nevertheless, in 1938 the pair were married and they soon had two sons.

During the Second World War, Paul Auriol became deeply involved in the Resistance movement and Jacqueline Auriol spent much of her time in hiding, avoiding the Gestapo. In 1947, her father-in-law was elected the first President of the Fourth Republic, and her husband became his press secretary. The young couple duly moved in with the President and lived in the Elysée Palace.

Jacqueline Auriol retired from competitive flying in 1963, although she continued to advance the cause of women pilots and worked as an ambassador for French aviation; in 1971, she became the first woman to pilot Concorde.

Away from flying, she enjoyed skiing, painting and meeting her few close friends, who included Edith Piaf. She published her autobiography *Vivre et Voleur* in 1968.

Jacqueline Auriol was three times awarded the Harmon Trophy, given to the world's leading flier. She was an officer of the Légion d'honneur and was also holder of France's Medaille de l'aéronautique.

Her husband predeceased her and she is survived by their two sons.

WING COMMANDER
JOHN DOWLING
14 JULY 2000

Wing Commander John Dowling, who has died aged 77, had the task as an RAF helicopter specialist of placing the spire on top of the rebuilt Coventry Cathedral, which had arisen from the ashes of the cathedral destroyed by German bombers in 1940.

Dowling was known universally as "Mr Helicopter", having pulled off a series of difficult and courageous operations during the Malayan emergency in the 1950s and the Borneo confrontation in the 1960s.

In 1961 Dowling was commanding No 72, a Belvedere helicopter squadron, at RAF Odiham in Hampshire, when he was asked to take on the tricky task of lifting the spire into place at Coventry. There was a 80 ft fleche and a surmounting sculpture; both had to be erected in the centre of the cathedral roof.

After a reconnaissance of the site Dowling realised that it was not the sort of task for which the Belvedere helicopter had been designed. He had to allow for the chance that one of the Belvedere's two engines might fail, and concluded that the fleche and its surmounting aluminium sculpture would have to be lifted separately.

Dowling also had to be sure he did not damage the delicate structure of the cathedral roof. Were it to be punctured the whole structure above the nave might collapse.

He would have to hover with great accuracy at about 200 ft above ground to lower the fleche and 300 ft to insert the sculpture. The very slow descent required would make normal flying control impractical. If he could hover steady, at six feet above the spot, human muscle power would be able to guide the pylon into place. The job would have to be done when wind speeds were less than five knots. It was imperative to avoid the loads developing a swing.

On April 22 1962 Dowling completed the operation in two lifts, totalling 45 minutes of airborne time. He was assisted by Flight Lieutenant R Salt (co-pilot) and Flight Lieutenant J Martin (crewman).

John Reginald Dowling was born on July 5 1923 in Manchester, where his father was a doctor. He was educated at Ampleforth College, and enlisted in 1941. He was commissioned as a pilot officer after training in Canada and the United States.

He was posted in 1944 to No 115, a Lancaster bomber squadron. He survived a tour of operations against Berlin and other heavily defended areas of Germany.

Dowling was a devoted Roman Catholic, and held rigid views about the rights and wrongs of attacking enemy targets. As captain of a Lancaster he regarded it as his duty to contribute to the devastation of Germany, but held that it was wrong to seek personal revenge for the bombing of such historic places as Coventry Cathedral. When he discovered that his tail gunner had been concealing a private stock of small incendiaries in his turret and indiscriminately dropping them by hand on Germany he was mightily displeased and issued a severe reprimand. Dowling was awarded a DFC in 1945.

Other than a spell in 1945 flying fighters at No 1688 Bomber Defence Training Flight, after the war Dowling experienced routine flying in the Middle East and at home. But in 1948 and 1949 he flew Yorks of Nos 242 and 40 Squadrons in the Berlin Airlift.

In 1950 Dowling began flying helicopters at the Royal Naval Air Station, Gosport, mastering the Sikorsky R4 and R6. As a promising performer Dowling moved on to the Westland Dragonfly, and flew this type from 1950 to

1953 on sorties to evacuate casualties during the Malayan Emergency.

Among Dowling's feats at this period, the most outstanding was his evacuation of a Cameronian patrol. Locating 17 sick and exhausted soldiers who had spent 29 days in a jungle swamp, Dowling lifted them from a small clearing. This had to be done in a series of sorties, since the Dragonfly could only carry three passengers, or two stretcher cases. It convincingly demonstrated the helicopter's suitability for jungle work. Dowling won a Bar to his DFC in 1952, in which year he was also mentioned in despatches.

In 1953 Dowling's flight provided the nucleus of the RAF's first helicopter squadron, No 194. Subsequently, Dowling furthered the development of helicopter operations as a flight and squadron commander at the Central Flying School. In 1960 he received command of the Belvedere trials unit, moving on in 1961 to introduce the Belvedere to squadron operational service as commander of No 72 Squadron.

Two years after the Coventry Cathedral operation Dowling was given an administrative post at RAF Seletar, Singapore, but soon escaped from this unwelcome desk work. Seizing the opportunity of the Brunei rebellion and Indonesian confrontation, Dowling made a request to command the helicopter wing. Thus he was strenuously involved in organising and flying jungle transport and evacuation operations.

During this period Dowling, keen since his Coventry exploits to obtain favourable publicity to promote the future of helicopter operations, put on two media performances.

When Edward Barnes, the producer of the children's programme *Blue Peter*, visited the Far East Air Force with the presenter Valerie Singleton, Dowling set up a film opportunity with Dyak tribesmen on the banks of a river in Sarawak. Valerie Singleton was the first white woman they had seen.

Towards the end of 1966 he repeated his Coventry success by mounting a 30 ft metal cross on the tall slender tower of the Hakka Methodist Church in Singapore.

Shortly afterwards Dowling returned home to a series of appointments, ending up as Wing Commander Helicopters at Headquarters Strike Command from 1972 to 1974. He then joined the RAF's Air Historical Branch. In 1992 he published *RAF Helicopters, The First 20 Years*.

Inclined to grumpiness, relieved by a wicked sense of humour, Dowling would always stick to his guns, and was prepared to defy conventions and authority in the cause of right.

Dowling was appointed MBE in 1959 and had received the AFC in 1957.

He married, in 1960, Anne d'Andria; they had a son and a daughter.

AIR MARSHAL
THE REV SIR PATERSON FRASER
4 AUGUST 2001

Air Marshal The Rev Sir Paterson Fraser, who has died aged 94, served as a test pilot and unit commander at the Royal Aircraft Establishment (RAE), Farnborough; he later developed planning techniques for the RAF, the logistics of the Normandy landings and in retirement entered Holy Orders.

As an Experimental Flying Department pilot from 1934, and from 1936 to 1938 as commander of the Aerodynamic Research Flight, Fraser was vital in efforts to prepare many aircraft types, including the Hawker Hurricane and Supermarine Spitfire, for war.

When eventually war came on September 3 1939, Fraser had completed a heavy programme of test flying and experimental work in addition to developing new test techniques and equipment.

In 1937 Fraser's overall contribution, not least his participation in hazardous spinning tests and catapult launches, was recognised with the award of an AFC. His catapult work paid dividends when, in the earlier stages of the Battle of the Atlantic, merchant ship losses led to the introduction of cargo boats equipped with a catapult-mounted Hurricane. With no aircraft carriers available and no planes with sufficient range to cover the mid-Atlantic gap at this stage, cata-fighters aimed to warn off Condor four-engine reconnaissance machines which were reporting convoy positions to U-boat packs.

After breaks at the RAF Staff College and the Air Ministry between 1938 and 1941, Fraser returned to Farnborough in command of RAE's Experimental Flying Section.

In the interim his 1937 paper for the Royal Aeronautical Society entitled *High wing loading and some of its problems* and award of the Society's Taylor Gold Medal had brought him some notice. While attending staff college in 1938, Fraser had also designed a mobile record office for control of postings and administrative functions. During 1939 Fraser moved to the Air Ministry's directorate of war organisation where he was responsible for preparing all documents dealing with RAF mobilisation and its move to France. He also wrote a revised edition of the RAF manual of war organisation and administration, for which he received an Air Council commendation.

During his second spell at Farnborough Fraser worked

out a system to measure RAE's work and its capacity to meet it in similar units, to secure maximum efficiency. In effect, this meant that Fraser introduced the concept of statistical control to RAE. The immediate result was that, while still a wing commander, he was appointed to the board of management.

In the course of his two spells at Farnborough, Fraser flew a remarkable total of 120 aircraft types, including the rare Rota autogyro, of which only 12 were supplied to the RAF.

Henry Paterson Fraser (always known as Pat) was born on July 15 1907, in Johannesburg, South Africa, and educated at Grahamstown. He went up to Pembroke College, Cambridge, taking a First in the mechanical science Tripos. After learning to fly with the University Air Squadron, of which he became president, he was granted a permanent commission in 1929 and joined No 16, an Army Co-operation squadron equipped with biplane Bristol Fighters at Old Sarum, Wilts.

In 1930 Fraser was posted to No 31 Squadron stationed at Quetta, and equipped since 1919 with Bristol Fighters – and, later, Westland Wapitis – for its task of co-operating with the Indian Army on the restless north west frontier.

Here Fraser honed his flying skills. In addition to normal flying duties, he was concurrently squadron engineer officer, parachute and supply dropping officer and accountant officer. He also found time to produce the first manual of supply dropping – a vital function on the frontier.

In 1933 Fraser returned home to take an engineering course at RAF Henlow. It stood him in good stead when, in 1942, he was posted to Washington as senior logistics planner and joint head of a working party on the allocation of United States aircraft for the RAF. He was also a member of the US and UK military transportation committee, responsible for provision and control of Allied shipping.

Now much admired as an organiser, Fraser returned to the Air Ministry in 1943 as deputy director war organisation with responsibility for co-ordinating RAF logistics and planning for the invasion of Sicily. He also produced early studies for the Normandy landings and submitted proposals for setting up RAF Transport Command.

Later that year, after becoming head of logistic and administrative planning at 2nd Tactical Air Force (2nd TAF), Fraser plunged into invasion preparations. Such was Fraser's logistical reputation that the Army brought some of its problems to him. For the invasion he worked out a method for timing supporting fire for the landings of waves of troops. He received a special commendation for this work from Lt-Gen H D G Crerar, the Canadian commander. Following the bridgehead breakout, Fraser was appointed deputy air officer responsible for RAF logistics and administration on the continent – a formidable brief.

It included the supply of everything required for the maintenance of the force, organisation of its personnel and equipment establishments, control of surface and air transport, legal, provost and financial matters and currency problems associated with a military force in occupied territory.

Fraser was relieved to be posted (on VE Day) to receive command of the Aircraft and Armament Establishment at Boscombe Down in Wiltshire. After two years he returned to Whitehall as Deputy Director Policy, and was heavily engaged in evolving a post-war RAF.

In 1948 Fraser was appointed air member of the defence research policy staff under Sir Henry Tizard and helped to devise a method of determining the relative importance of research and development for all three services.

Following a break in 1951 at the Imperial Defence College Fraser was appointed senior air staff officer (SASO) to Air Chief Marshal Sir Basil Embry, commander-in-chief, Fighter Command, on whose behalf he made a comprehensive study of the command's operational organisation and procedures.

In 1954 Fraser followed Embry to Allied Air Forces Central Europe as chief of staff, returning in 1956 to Fighter Command in charge of No 12 Group. Finally, he served as director RAF exercise manning in 1959, UK representative on the Central Europe Treaty Organisation (CENTO) permanent military deputies group and, from 1962 to 1964, as inspector general RAF.

While serving in No 12 Group and flying over the Isle of Man Fraser had noted the island as a beautiful place where he would like to retire. Settling there he took a number of computer courses and became a popular figure in Manx society.

Fraser was president of the Andreas Racing Association and as a lay reader took an increasing part in church affairs. In 1977 he was ordained as a non-stipendiary priest at Ramsey Deanery.

He was appointed KBE in 1961; CBE in 1945 and CB in 1953. Fraser was elected a Fellow of the Royal Aeronautical Society in 1951.

Fraser married, in 1933, Avis Gertrude Haswell. They had two sons.

SQUADRON LEADER
HEDLEY "HAZEL" HAZELDEN
27 AUGUST 2001

Squadron Leader Hedley "Hazel" Hazelden, who has died aged 86, survived a sustained period of bomber operations in the Second World War to attend the first course at Britain's Empire Test Pilots' School.

After the war, as chief test pilot of Handley Page, Hazelden saw many of the company's military and civil aircraft through the test stages. Notably, he carried out the flight test development of the Hastings military transport, the Victor four-jet nuclear bomber and tanker, and the Hermes and Herald airliners.

In the course of more than 25 years test flying, Hazelden several times saved his neck, if not always his aircraft, by dint of his superb airmanship. This enabled him to provide Handley Page with invaluable observations and reports, always immaculately presented.

On August 10 1958, he piloted a turbo-prop Herald, a small airliner designed to take the place of the Dakota, to Farnborough, where he was due to demonstrate its advantages at the Society of British Aircraft Companies' airshow. On the way, the aircraft's starboard engine caught fire.

Hazelden cut off the engine's fuel supply, feathered the propeller and applied the Herald's fire extinguishers, but the blaze continued. With eight passengers on board, including his wife, he had no alternative but to make an immediate forced landing.

All he could see ahead was heavily wooded countryside, so he throttled back the remaining engine and descended until an open field came into view. The starboard tailplane had already burned away, and now the Herald's starboard engine fell off, making the aircraft all but uncontrollable.

Approaching the field, Hazelden spotted an 80 ft tree in front of the only possible place to touch down. Worse, a farm roller was parked across the touch down area and high tension wires crossed the ground Hazelden needed for running on after landing.

In an astonishing manoeuvre, with his right wing now well on fire, Hazelden flew over the tree, belly-landed and slid under the wires. A concealed tree stump tore a hole in the fuselage in front of the burning wing, and this provided an escape route for all on board before the Herald burned out.

Hedley George Hazelden was born on June 7 1915 at Sevenoaks, Kent. His father had lost an arm in a sawmill accident and was frequently unemployed. Young Hedley won a scholarship to the Judd School at Tonbridge and then worked in London as a clerk at Standard Life Assurance.

After training with the RAFVR before the war, Hazelden qualified as a sergeant pilot and in September 1940 joined No 44, a Bomber Command squadron equipped with Handley Page Hampden twin-engine bombers and minelayers. He was lucky to survive a full operational tour, as well as a fogbound crash at Boscombe Down, Wiltshire, after returning from a mine-laying operation off the French harbour of St Nazaire.

Following a rest as an instructor on Hampdens, Hazelden joined No 83 Squadron, welcoming the chance to acquaint himself with the squadron's new twin-engined Avro Manchesters. But the Manchester turned out to be under-powered and liable to costly accident and operational losses.

Hazelden survived a series of mishaps: he coaxed a Manchester back from the Heligoland Bight on one engine, and in early March 1941 he was relieved to return in one piece from an attack on the Krupp works at Essen – so that he could marry the next day. When he returned to the squadron from a week's honeymoon, he was shocked to discover it had lost seven crews in three nights.

Shortly afterwards, No 83 re-equipped with four-engine Avro Lancasters, and in the spring of 1942 Hazelden piloted a Lancaster in the first of Sir Arthur "Bomber" Harris's 1,000-bomber raids, a mass attack on Cologne.

In the early summer, after taking part in a similar mass raid on Bremen, he was rested for a second time as chief flying instructor on twin-engine Vickers Wellingtons, and then posted to the newly formed Empire Test Pilots' School.

Shortly before reporting to the school, he fell off a motor-cycle injuring a leg, and fell out of a Wellington injuring an elbow. So it was wearing a sling and walking with a stick that he reported to join ETPS's No 1 course.

It is a measure of the hazards of test flying in that era that five of the 13 pilots on No 1 course subsequently lost their lives. Hazelden survived the course and passed out, entitling him to suffix his name with the hard-won letters "tp".

Posted to the heavy aircraft squadron at the Air and Armament Experimental Establishment, Hazelden next evaluated the handling requirements of a Lancaster-carrying a colossal 22,000 lb "Grand Slam" bomb. Later, as victory in Europe approached, he received command of the new Civil Aircraft Test Squadron, charged with the task of establishing airworthiness standards for the first generation of post-war airliners.

When Hazelden left the RAF in the spring of 1947 he was appointed chief test pilot at Handley Page. He prepared the four-engine Hastings to succeed the Avro York as the RAF's standard long-range military transport, and he test flew the Hermes, a civil version of the Hastings, recommending important modifications.

In the early 1950s, Handley Page's design team, led by Reginald Stafford, produced the highly unorthodox crescent-winged, four-jet Victor, which was to make an impressive debut as a sister to the Vickers Valiant and the Avro Vulcan in Britain's nuclear deterrent V-bomber force.

Hazelden took the Victor up for the first time on Christmas Eve 1952, and went on to conduct an exhaustive flight-testing programme until the bomber was ready for use by the RAF in 1957.

On one occasion, he was about to pilot the aircraft on a routine airspeed indicator test, when he was called away to have lunch with a Japanese admiral who was visiting Handley Page. During the lunch, the Victor crashed, killing Hazelden's No 2, Taffy Ecclestone.

After Handley Page had ceased trading in 1970, Hazelden spent several years flying for small airlines before retiring to Lincolnshire. He kept up a keen interest in aviation matters, and was a staunch supporter of the Handley Page Association, of which he became president in 1978.

Hazelden was awarded a DFC in 1941 and a Bar to it in 1942. He received the Air Efficiency Award in 1946, a King's Commendation in 1947, and a Queen's Commendation in 1959. The Royal Aeronautical Society awarded him its R P Alston Medal in 1965. He was a member of the Guild of Air Pilots and Air Navigators and a Freeman of the City of London.

He married first, in 1947, Esma Jones, who died in 1986. They had a daughter. He married secondly, in 1987, Jennie Valley, the widow of Flight Lieutenant Ralph Valley.

WING COMMANDER
ROLAND "BEE" BEAMONT
19 NOVEMBER 2001

Wing Commander Roland "Bee" Beamont, who has died aged 81, followed dazzling wartime service as a fighter pilot and wing leader with a long and sustained peacetime career as a test pilot.

Awarded a DSO and Bar and DFC and Bar, mentioned in dispatches and leading a fighter wing before he was 24, Beamont went on to lead the English Electric Canberra – the first RAF jet bomber – and English Electric Lightning flight test programmes.

Subsequently he was chief test pilot of the ill-fated British Aircraft Corporation (BAC) TSR2 supersonic bomber-reconnaissance programme until the aircraft's abrupt and brutal cancellation by the government.

Later Beamont directed British Aerospace and Panavia international flight operations of the multi-role combat Tornado until its introduction to RAF and other Nato operational squadrons.

Yet he would have achieved none of these distinctions but for combat and experimental skills acquired amid the pressures of war. Beamont had not long qualified for his wings – though graded "exceptional" – when, in November 1939, he joined No 87, a Hawker Hurricane fighter squadron in France.

After opening his account with a Dornier 17 bomber in May 1940, as France fell, Beamont remained with 87 Squadron and fought throughout the Battle of Britain. On August 15 he shot down two Me 110 fighters over Lyme Regis.

He recalled: "I was diving vertically while the Me 110 was climbing up at the same angle. At the crucial moment he stalled right across my bows and I squirted a good burst into his belly from such point blank range that the bullets could be seen striking and buckling the plating of its wings and fuselage.

"A flash of flame and a puff of smoke and I jammed the stick forward just in time to avoid colliding with him. I did not have to look for another target because straight ahead came another Me 110 firing as he came.

"He did not hit me but holding fire to the last minute as we flashed past each other less than 50 ft apart I caught a glimpse of a puff of white and there was the 110 on its back with a parachute opened behind it".

Roland Prosper Beamont – always known as "Bee" – was born at Enfield, north London, on August 10 1920, brought up at Chichester, Sussex, and educated at Eastbourne College.

From the moment as a child when the pilot of a silvery Hawker Fury waved to him, young Beamont was determined to join the RAF. A chance flip in a Fox Moth piloted by C W A Scott, the then solo-to-Australia record holder, clinched it.

In January 1939 he was granted a short service commission and as war came in September was completing his training. Somewhat unusually he accompanied his father, an Army lieutenant colonel, to the front.

Beamont's spell in Hawkers had given him a taste for test flying, particularly the powerful and punchy Typhoon. He was therefore delighted to be posted, in June 1942, from Hawkers to No 56, the first operational squadron to be re-equipped with Typhoons and after a month to No 609, the West Riding Auxiliary Air Force squadron.

Arriving at 609 as a flight commander, Beamont began to lead the "Tiffies" on low-level day and night intruder and ground attack operations across the Channel. It was largely due to Beamont's inventive employment of the

Typhoon as a fighter-bomber that he gained steadily increasing respect for himself and a type of aircraft then still regarded as decidedly dodgy.

When in June 1943 a second "test" spell was decreed, Beamont rejoined Hawkers where he tested the Tempest, a yet more powerful and efficient machine which was waiting to enforce forthcoming landings in Normandy.

In February 1944 Beamont returned to operational flying as leader of No 150, the first, Tempest wing comprising Nos 3, 56 and 486 squadrons.

On June 8, two days after D-Day, he shot down an Me 109 near Rouen, the first enemy aircraft to fall to a Tempest.

Almost immediately Beamont was faced with the new and desperate priority of countering V1 flying-bombs which had begun to terrorise Londoners.

After personally accounting for 31 V1 "doodlebugs" Beamont relocated his wing at Vokel in Holland and on October 2 shot down a FW 190 fighter. It was his last "kill" before his engine failed the wrong side of the lines and he became a prisoner-of-war.

Repatriated after VE Day, Beamont employed his flight test skills at the Central Fighter Establishment before refusing a permanent commission and joining Gloster Aircraft as an experimental test pilot.

Moving to de Havilland as a demonstration pilot he joined English Electric as chief test pilot in 1947 to lead the B3/45 jet bomber programme from which the Canberra emerged.

From May 1949, Beamont managed all prototype tests and also established two Atlantic speed records in the aircraft including, in 1952, the first two-way Atlantic crossing in one day – in fact in 10 hours and three minutes.

The journal *Flight* said that Beamont demonstrated the

Canberra which he was the first to fly – "like no aircraft has been demonstrated before or is ever likely to be demonstrated again".

In December 1949, Beamont burst the type on the world with an astonishing performance at the Farnborough Air Show. Beamont's mastery of the Canberra ensured sales of the plane to the American and 14 other air forces. Beamont went on to head the Lightning supersonic fighter test programme during which he became the first pilot to fly a British aircraft at the speed of sound in level flight; and later twice the speed of sound, Mach 2.

There followed the saddest and most frustrating period of Beamont's career. Involved with the concept, building and testing of the much advanced TSR2 supersonic bomber, he flew its maiden flight on September 29 1964.

When in April 1965, TSR2 – which in some respects was ahead of the later Tornados – was abandoned by Labour, the government rubbed salt in the wound by ordering the remaining planes to be broken up.

Beamont remained a director of the Warton division of BAC, later British Aerospace, until 1978 where he was director flight operations and a founder member of the team which set up the Saudi Arabian defence programme. From 1970 he was also responsible for international Tornado flight testing until he retired in 1979 and devoted himself to authorship and aviation journalism.

Beamont's publications included *Phoenix into Ashes*; *Testing Years*; *Typhoon and Tempest at War*; *English Electric Canberra*; *English Electric P1 Lightning*; *Fighter Test Pilot*; *My Part of the Sky*; *Testing Early Jets*; *Tempests over Europe* and *Flying to the Limit*.

Much honoured by the aviation community, Beamont was a Fellow of the Royal Aeronautic Society and

Honorary Fellow of the Society of Experimental Test Pilots (USA).

He was awarded the Britannia Trophy in 1953, Derry and Richards Medal in 1955, R P Alston Medal, 1960, Silver Medal for Aeronautics, 1965, and a Distinguished Achievement Award in 1992.

In addition to his wartime decorations Beamont received the US DFC in 1946. He was appointed OBE in 1954 and CBE in 1965.

In October 2001 the Guild of Air Pilots and Air Navigators presented Beamont with its Award of Honour.

Beamont married, in 1942, Shirley Adams, a WAAF, who died in 1945 while he was a prisoner of war. He married secondly, in 1947, Patricia Whitehead (née Raworth). He is survived by a daughter of his first marriage, two daughters by his second and a stepson.

DISTINGUISHED LEADERS

AIR CHIEF MARSHAL
SIR WALLACE "DIGGER" KYLE
31 JANUARY 1988

Air Chief Marshal Sir Wallace "Digger" Kyle, the former Governor of Western Australia, who has died aged 78, had an RAF career which began in Bristol Bulldog biplane fighters and ended with him heading Bomber Command's nuclear force.

An acknowledged low level attack specialist, he began the 1939-45 War as a bomber pilot in hazardous daylight operations, from 1940 to 1941, leading No 139, a Blenheim light-bomber squadron against targets in northern Europe.

In the action for which he was awarded the DFC, Kyle was briefed to attack Dutch iron and steel works at Ijmuiden. He led in his Blenheims at 50 ft in the face of intense anti-aircraft fire and attacks by Me 109 fighters. After they had dropped their bombs the squadron was followed out to sea by enemy fighters, which they shook off through skilful wave-hopping.

Wallace Hart Kyle was born in 1910 at Kalgoorlie, where his father was a gravedigger who had walked 300 miles from Perth during the gold rush. He was educated at Guildford Grammar School, Perth, and in 1928 entered RAF Cranwell, joining 17 Squadron.

In 1931 he was posted to what was then the Fleet Air Arm of the RAF – serving in 450 (Fleet Spotter Reconnaissance) Flight and 820 (Fleet Spotter Reconnaissance) Squadron – and becoming adept at landing on the aircraft carrier *Courageous*. Then he attended the Central Flying School, where he qualified as an instructor.

Kyle took over command of 139 ("Jamaica") Squadron in December, 1940. After distinguishing himself in the daylight raids with Blenheims, he was appointed commander of an operational training unit.

From 1942 he was commander of three East Anglian bomber stations, Marham, Downham Market, and Horsham St Faith, where he played an important part in the introduction of the "wooden wonder" – the versatile de Havilland Mosquito – in its bomber role.

A staff appointment followed at Bomber Command headquarters, and by the end of hostilities Kyle's inspiring leadership had been further recognised with awards of the DSO and CBE.

After Staff College, two years at HQ, Middle East, and a further two as Deputy Commandant, Cranwell, Kyle was appointed Director, Bomber Operational Requirements, at the Air Ministry.

While commanding the RAF in Malaya in 1955 he was responsible for strike operations against terrorists in the final phase of the Emergency. On his return to the Air Ministry as an Assistant Chief of Air Staff, Kyle worked on the provision of electronic counter-measures to enable nuclear V-bombers to penetrate Soviet defences.

He led Technical Training Command from 1959 to 1962 and served as Vice Chief of Air Staff from 1962 to 1965, then took over Bomber Command when the V-force was subject to a high degree of readiness.

On the merging of Bomber and Fighter Commands, Kyle stayed on to lead their successor, the new Strike Command, from its inception in 1968. Demonstrating that he had not lost his touch with fighters, he became at 58 the oldest member of the Ten Ton Club, flying at more than 1,000 mph in a Lightning fighter.

On his retirement Kyle became an extremely popular Governor of Western Australia, since he was seen as both an Imperial appointment and the first West Australian in the post since the war. His entrance into office was a moment to savour since it was the same room in which he had been interviewed for Cranwell.

During his five-year period of office he presided over a boom time, which coincided with the State's 150th anniversary, and was endeared for forming his own golf team. He developed a large vegetable garden to feed Government House in Perth.

Kyle, who returned home to Hampshire, was appointed CB in 1953, KCB in 1960, GCB 1966 and KCVO by the Queen during her Silver Jubilee visit to Australia in 1977.

He is survived by his wife, a daughter and three sons, one of whom is a serving Air Commodore.

AIR CHIEF MARSHAL
SIR DENIS BARNETT
5 JANUARY 1992

Air Chief Marshal Sir Denis Barnett, who has died aged 86, was the key air commander in the short-lived Suez campaign of 1956.

When Nasser nationalised the Universal Suez Canal Co in July 1956, Barnett was appointed Allied Air Task Force Commander with headquarters in London. He was the obvious choice as he had recently supervised, as Air Officer Commanding 205 Group, the RAF's evacuation of the Canal Zone to Cyprus.

Quiet and exceedingly modest, Barnett was ideal as a planner. Moreover, he knew where to find those he could work with and plundered the Imperial Defence College for "high-fliers" with Middle East experience.

The initial concept of Barnett's plan (codenamed

Musketeer) was to put the Egyptian Air Force out of business as an overture for landings from the sea at Alexandria, a drive on Cairo and an advance to the Suez Canal.

When this looked like producing large civilian casualties it was abandoned. Instead, the Egyptian Air Force was to be neutralised by air attack, with other key targets, before an assault on Port Said and a breakout down the line of the canal.

Once the RAF bomber force and French tactical squadrons had been deployed, Barnett transferred his team to Cyprus. This build-up was completed on Oct 30, at the same time as Israel's invasion of Sinai.

Barnett, surveying his order of battle, knew he could count on 115 bombers mustered on Malta and Cyprus, including 24 new Valiant V-bombers. Additionally there was a large mixed force of land and carrier-based fighters.

On Oct 31 Barnett was ordered to launch the Musketeer offensive at 16.15 GMT that day. Valiants and Canberras (the RAF's first jet bomber) attacked airfields, but their first bombs hit Cairo airport by mistake. As dawn broke on Nov 1 Barnett sent in his ground attack squadrons to destroy the Egyptian Air Force in the Nile Delta and around the canal. Within 48 hours he had all but eliminated it.

It was a disappointment for Barnett and his squadrons that with the canal already almost entirely under Allied control political decisions prevented them from finishing the job: they were called off on November 6.

The younger son of Sir Louis Barnett, an eminent surgeon, Denis Hensley Fulton Barnett was born at Dunedin, New Zealand on February 11, 1906, and educated at Christ's College, New Zealand, and Clare College, Cambridge, where he learnt to fly with the university air squadron. He was commissioned into the Reserve of Air Force Officers in 1927.

He joined No 13 Squadron, flying the biplane Armstrong Whitworth Atlas, the RAF's first operational aircraft specifically designed to co-operate with the Army. In 1937, after spells as an instructor, he was posted to No 84, a Vickers Vincent biplane bomber squadron stationed at Shaibah in Iraq. The next year he received its command.

Barnett returned home to the Central Flying School as flying examination officer. But when the Fall of France called for experienced bomber pilots he led No 40, a Bristol Blenheim IV squadron charged with perilous attacks on the German invasion build-up in the Channel ports.

While Fighter Command's Battle of Britain victory has been glamorised, Bomber Command's valiant contribution in the summer and autumn of 1940 to deterring Operation Sealion (the planned invasion) has been little noticed.

Barnett then went successively to Bomber Command's No 7 Group and HQ, where he was Group Captain Operations. He also commanded the bomber station at Swanton Morley.

In 1944 he was at the Air Ministry as deputy director of Bomber Operations. The next year he returned to Bomber Command as Bomber Ops director.

After stints on the staff in India and commanding British forces during their withdrawal from Pakistan, he became Commandant of the Central Bomber Establishment.

As director of Operations at the Air Ministry in the early 1950s Barnett was faced with problems posed by the Malayan Emergency and hampered by the lack of new aircraft.

These were supplied by America in the short term until

Canberras and V-bombers became operational in numbers.

From 1952 to 1954 he was in Tokyo, representing the British Chiefs of Staff at UN HQ during the Korean War.

Following his Middle East commands in 1956, Barnett was appointed Commandant at the RAF Staff College Bracknell. The next year he moved back to Whitehall as Air Secretary.

In 1959 he took over RAF Transport Command and had the satisfaction of introducing the military version of the Bristol Britannia, the RAF's first turbo-prop transport aircraft.

In 1962 Barnett returned to the region where he had built up much expertise, this time as Air Officer Commanding RAF Near East, with responsibility for the British Forces in Cyprus and the administration of the Sovereign base areas. He was in Cyprus in 1964, when the UN deployed its first peace-keeping force.

After retiring at the end of that year he sat on a Ministry of Defence committee to study the future of air power, and joined the Atomic Energy Authority as its member for Weapons Research and Development.

Barnett was awarded the DFC and mentioned in despatches in 1940. He was appointed CBE in 1945, CB in 1956, KCB in 1957 and GCB in 1964.

He married, in 1939, Pamela, youngest daughter of Sir Allan Grant; they had a son and two daughters.

MARSHAL OF THE ROYAL AIR FORCE
SIR DERMOT BOYLE

5 MAY 1993

Marshal of the Royal Air Force Sir Dermot Boyle, who has died aged 88, was the first Cranwell cadet to become Chief of the Air Staff.

A quarter of a century earlier Lord Trenchard, father of the RAF and founder of Cranwell, had boomed that Cranwell would not reach fruition until one of its cadets became CAS. Shortly after Boyle's appointment in 1956 Trenchard died, and Boyle attended his funeral at Westminster Abbey – his first official function as CAS.

Boyle had a "fine pair of hands" the accolade accorded the exceptional pilots of his generation – and an equal talent for driving a desk. Equipped, too, with Irish charm and wit and a deft political touch, he was a model CAS.

His qualities were never better displayed than during the Suez campaign in his first year in office, when he managed to stop Duncan Sandys, the Defence Secretary, from phasing out manned aircraft in favour of missiles.

Boyle achieved this by Operation Prospect, a public relations exercise in which the Air Staff presented the case for manned aircraft. This resulted in the continuation of the V-bomber nuclear deterrent and manned fighter aircraft, as well as Sandys's agreement to the development of the TSR2.

His counsel also prevailed to prevent Lord Mountbatten, Chief of the Defence Staff, from pirating the RAF's maritime role for the Fleet Air Arm.

Dermot Alexander Boyle was born on October 2 1904 at Rathdowney in Queen's County, where his father was agent to Lord Ashbrook.

The horse was the family's main means of transport, and young Dermot was hunting with the local harriers from an early age. He was educated at St Columba's, a Protestant school in the foothills of the Dublin mountains.

His father died when Dermot was 16. His mother asked him what he wanted to do: "To go into the new thing they have over in England called the Royal Air Force." After attending an aviation meeting on Leopardstown racecourse he had made a mock-up of a cockpit, in which he would sit for hours, imagining a range of manoeuvres. Some of the family opposed his choice of career, but his mother supported him.

Boyle duly went to Cranwell and was commissioned in 1924. He learned to fly solo in a 1918 Avro 504K biplane, before graduating to Bristol fighters and DH9As. He joined No 17, a Sopwith Snipe fighter squadron based at Hawkinge in Kent, and after a year answered a call for Snipe pilots to serve with No 1 at Hinaidi, outside Baghdad.

Delighted to discover that there were no low-flying regulations (though flying low over Baghdad was frowned upon), Boyle indulged himself at nought feet, skimming the surface of the Tigris. He also enjoyed bagging sand grouse, which provided a tasty alternative to the tinned food of the mess.

At the end of 1926 he was posted to No 6 Squadron based at Mosul with Bristol fighters. He volunteered for a flying instructors' course at the Central Flying School and was asked to stay on as an instructor. Boyle excelled at aerobatics, and in 1928 partnered Dick Atcherley (later Air Marshal Sir Richard) at the Hendon air display. Flying Genet Moths, they performed an inverted loop in public for the first time.

From CFS he was posted to No 601 (County of London), an auxiliary squadron at Hendon. Its commander was Squadron Leader Sir Philip Sassoon,

Parliamentary Under-Secretary of State for Air in the early to mid-1930s.

By now a flight lieutenant and adjutant of 601, Boyle met Una Carey, his future wife, on a skiing holiday. In 1931 Sassoon lent him his private aircraft to fly to Paris, where he had booked them into the Ritz.

On another occasion Sassoon asked Boyle to land the private plane at his house, Trent Park near Barnet, and for lunch. This meant bumping down in a small, ridged and furrowed field, surrounded by tall trees. Boyle often tried to persuade Sir Philip to cut some of them down, to be told: "Boylo, you fly beautifully, and trees are beautiful things".

On arrival he was greeted with the news that the Duke and Duchess of York were fellow guests, and that the Duchess (later the Queen Mother) wanted a joyride. With much trepidation he took off from "that appalling field", flew round, watched the Duke playing golf, took a look at London and landed back at Trent Park. When the Air Council learned of the jaunt it issued an instruction that flying members of the Royal Family should henceforth be cleared.

In 1933 Boyle was posted to Air Headquarters, India. It was a stroke of luck that the assistant purser of the P&O's *Rajputana* had served in No 601: the Boyles were moved to luxurious accommodation from a cabin below decks.

On his return to Britain he attended Staff College, and in 1937 received command of No 83, a Hawker Hind light bomber squadron in Scotland. After six months he was posted to Cranwell as chief flying instructor, and in 1939 was awarded the AFC.

His first war posting was a disappointment – a wing commander's administrative appointment with the Advance Air Striking Force in France, where he found himself organising a visit by Gracie Fields. After the Fall of

France, Boyle was astounded to be asked to arrange the evacuation of the entire Advanced Air Striking Force through the port of Brest.

After a brief stint as an ops staff officer at Bomber Command, he resumed command of No 83, flying Hampden bombers from Scampton. In January 1941 he flew his first operational sortie to Bremen.

Soon after he was summoned by the Chief of the Air Staff, who had earmarked him for a staff appointment. Thus Boyle found himself working for Winston Churchill, as Air Secretary in the Cabinet Offices.

Fresh from the sharp end of flak over German targets, he found the rarefied environment somewhat daunting, until a naval colleague reassured him: "Dermot, you are not meant to know anything – all you do is write down what the great men say."

Churchill chaired two of the Cabinet committees for which Boyle "wrote down" – Night Air Defence and Tube Alloys (the codename for development of the atom bomb).

Despite the fascination of the job Boyle was never really happy in it. He yearned for his squadron, and after a year in Whitehall took an operational step up as station commander of the Stirling and Wellington bomber base at Stradishall.

Although a group captain, Boyle flew three Stirling and two Wellington sorties. But he knew that his former Cabinet post would present the enemy with a valuable prisoner, and avoided asking permission to fly over Germany.

To his displeasure his operational command was cut short, and at the end of 1942 he was promoted air commodore and moved to No 91, a training group, as senior air staff officer. It later transpired that his Bomber Group commander, with whom he had not hit it off, had reported him as a defeatist.

By spring 1943 he was back at the sharp end, though, as Senior Air Staff Officer to No 83, already preparing to support an invasion of Europe. On the evening of D-Day (June 6 1944) Boyle waded on to a Normandy beach from a landing craft.

In April 1945, after 83 had been highly effective in supporting the Allies from the beaches and into Germany, he was promoted air vice-marshal. He briefly commanded No 85 Group at Ghent before returning home to take over No 11, the renowned fighter group, at Uxbridge.

He then moved to the Imperial Defence College, before a spell as assistant commandant of the Staff College, Bracknell. He later returned to Bomber Command as leader of No 1 Group, then introducing the English Electric Canberra into operational service.

Boyle learned to fly the jet and led a goodwill mission of four Canberras round South America; he was knighted after the tour.

Appointed Commander-in-Chief, Fighter Command, in 1953, he felt slightly out of place – not having had any part in the Battle of Britain. But he was very much at home on a frisky horse in the Coronation procession. He also took responsibility for the Queen's Coronation Review of the RAF at Odiham, with 650 aircraft in the flypast. After lunch that day the Queen appointed him KCVO.

In 1956 he succeeded Marshal of the RAF Sir William Dickson as CAS. He worried senior officers by flying a Canberra on overseas visits, which he argued kept him more alert than drinking and dozing in transport aircraft.

Boyle was released from full-time duty in 1959, but a Marshal never retires. The next year he joined the board of the British Aircraft Corporation (now part of British Aerospace). He was vice-chairman from 1962 to 1971, but felt his lack of experience strongly; it concerned him that he did not feel at one with the shop floor, as he had done with airmen on a station.

He had some distressing moments with BAC, not least in difficult negotiations in Saudi Arabia as chairman of the Saudi Arabian Defence Consortium. But the most unhappy event was the cancellation of the TSR2 a few days after the perfect first flight of its prototype. The jigs and tools on the production-line were destroyed, so that it could never be reinstated.

Meanwhile Boyle retained strong contacts with the RAF. He was a patron of the Old Cranwellian Association, president of the RAF Club and deputy chairman of the RAF Benevolent Fund.

But by far the most satisfying of his post-CAS activities was his part in the creation of the RAF Museum at Hendon; he was chairman of the Board of Trustees from 1965 to 1974.

Sailing, holidays in the Caribbean (where for some years he owned a property in the British Virgin Islands), and carpentry were among his pastimes.

Boyle was appointed CBE in 1945, CB in 1946, KBE and KCVO in 1953, and GCB in 1957. He married, in 1931, Una Carey; they had three sons (one of whom predeceased him) and a daughter.

AIR COMMODORE
IAN BRODIE
22 JULY 1993

Air Commodore Ian Brodie, who has died aged 94, was closely associated with Lawrence of Arabia in that enigmatic figure's subsequent incarnation as Aircraftman T E Shaw.

In 1926 Brodie was posted to India to join No 5, an Army co-operation squadron; aboard the troop ship *Derbyshire*, he found that Shaw *alias* Lawrence was in the draft under his command.

Two years later he again came upon Lawrence when he was posted as 27 Squadron's C Flight commander at Miramshah Fort on the North-West Frontier, surrounded by unruly Waziri and Afghan tribes.

Lawrence served there as Brodie's clerk. "A very good one too", Brodie recalled. "He almost always produced a typed reply before presenting me with the original incoming letter or signal."

Air HQ India was considering withdrawing the flight from the fort but Brodie was eager to retain his first command, and Lawrence to remain in the wilderness. Between them, they persuaded the authorities to leave the flight at Miramshah.

Lawrence wrote from Miramshah that "we have had an idyllic two and a half months here under the best and kindest CO of my experience". He repaid Brodie's kindness by using his influence in Whitehall and elsewhere to obtain perks for the fort. He even persuaded George Bernard Shaw to offer to pay for a swimming pool, though this project eventually had to be abandoned.

Flying in India in the 1920s was seldom without incident. Once Brodie lost sight of a train carrying the King of Afghanistan, which his flight was escorting. Two hours later, after a frantic aerial search, the train was found in a tunnel. It emerged that the King had mistaken an emergency cord for a lavatory chain, and pulled it.

The happy collaboration between Brodie and Lawrence came to an end when a high-grade signal from Air Officer Commanding India was received ordering Lawrence's recall to Britain; although the message was addressed to Brodie, he was confounded by the cipher, and it was Lawrence who decrypted it.

Ian Eustace Brodie was born in Sept 1898 at San Remo, Italy, where his father was installing an electrical system. Young Ian was educated at Oundle and entered the Royal Navy (his second choice to the Sappers) in 1916 as a cadet at Keyham College, Devonport. He later attended a sub-lieutenants' course at St John's College, Cambridge.

In 1917 he served in *Marlborough* in the 1st Battle Squadron. The next year he was in *Canterbury* of the elite Light Cruiser Squadron and proceeded to the Dardanelles to shadow the German cruiser *Goebens*.

Subsequently he was navigation officer in *Bramble* in the Persian Gulf, but in 1923 he fell victim to the service cuts known as the "Geddes Axe". Fortunately, his father knew Sir Samuel Hoare, Minister for Air, and the next year Brodie was commissioned in the RAF. He joined the "Tadpole Flight" of the "Suicide Club" – otherwise No 406 Fleet Fighter Flight – to learn deck-landing on aircraft carriers.

One of his early duties was to look after a temporary landing ground at Lossiemouth used by the Prime Minister, Ramsay MacDonald, who invited him for a round of golf. Brodie was surprised to find that the Prime Minister was barred from the Lossiemouth Golf Club; the committee nursed doubts about his patriotism. Consequently, MacDonald was obliged to use an inferior course some miles away.

After his years in India, Brodie joined No 43 Squadron (the "Fighting Cocks") at Tangmere in 1930. Flying a Siskin III A, he was selected for the aerobatic team in the 1931 Hendon and Croydon air displays.

Later in the 1930s, as an armament specialist, Brodie served in Iraq. He joined the Royal Exodus Hunt and also hunted with the Baghdad Boar Hunt.

On the outbreak of war in 1939 he was an armament and navigation officer at the Air Ministry's gunnery and navigational schools. He set up the new Central Gunnery School and in August 1940 became its first commander at Warmwell in Dorset.

As Senior Air Staff Officer in No 25 and 29 (Armament) Groups, Brodie was much envied for owning and flying his own Gladiator, an obsolescent biplane which he had retrieved from a maintenance unit. He caused a sensation when he flew his Gladiator into Aldergrove, in Northern Ireland, when assuming command of that station in September 1942.

The next year he was posed to Iceland as SASO for operations, and between 1945 and 1947 was acting Air Vice-Marshal advising the Italian Air Force.

Later in 1947 he was appointed deputy director of Intelligence (Security) at the Air Ministry. This led, after his retirement in 1951, to a civilian post as intelligence security officer with NAAFI.

Brodie worked strenuously for the Boy Scout movement. He was a keen yachtsman, boxed, skied, rowed and played golf, rugby, squash and tennis.

Brodie was appointed OBE in 1941 and mentioned in despatches in 1945. He was a Deputy Lieutenant for Buckinghamshire.

He married, in 1925, Mary Gonville Coates; they had three daughters.

AIR CHIEF MARSHAL
SIR EDMUND HUDLESTON
14 DECEMBER 1994

Air Chief Marshal Sir Edmund Hudleston, who has died aged 85, was a former Vice-Chief of the Air Staff and Commander-in-Chief Allied Forces Central Europe.

Hudleston's promotion before and after the Second World War was exceptionally rapid. With characteristic modesty he always attributed this to cricket, insisting that his selection for the RAF XI had enabled him to field in the slips alongside more senior officers, who took him up the ladder with them.

In fact, Hudleston was marked down early in his career as a brilliant staff officer, and quickly earned a reputation as a troubleshooter. In 1956, for instance, he was plucked from the Imperial Defence College, where he was instructing, and flown to Cyprus as Chief of Staff of Air Operations in the Suez campaign.

His staff duties during the war – mostly in the Middle East – were onerous, although not always strictly operational. On one occasion King George VI visited British units on the Italian front and Hudleston found himself charged with setting up a dinner and providing an orchestra.

He hastily assembled a collection of servicemen with some musical ability, whose rendition of the Afrika Corps melody *Lili Marlene* delighted the King; he requested several encores and stood up to sing along in German.

Edmund Cuthbert Hudleston was born on December 30 1908 at the gold-rush town of Kalgoorlie in Western Australia. His father, the archdeacon of Perth, had emigrated from Northumberland.

Young Edmund was educated at Guildford Grammar School, Western Australia, and was then encouraged by a schoolfriend, the future Air Chief Marshal Sir Wallace "Digger" Kyle, to follow him to the RAF College, Cranwell. Hudleston's application was endorsed by the state governor and in 1927 he arrived at Cranwell with a cadetship.

Hudleston was commissioned in 1928 as a pilot officer and joined No 25, a fighter squadron based at Hawkinge on the Kent coast. It flew the Gloster Grebe, the first of a new generation of bi-plane fighters ordered to replace obsolete machines from the First World War.

The squadron was commanded by Sqn Ldr "Lousy" Payne, a retired air commodore who was later to serve with distinction as *The Daily Telegraph*'s air correspondent.

After qualifying as an instructor at the Central Flying School, Hudleston returned to Cranwell to help to teach a generation of cadets; they were to form the nucleus of operational leaders in the Second World War.

From 1935 to 1937 he was group armaments officer at Peshawar and served operationally on the North-West Frontier, where he was mentioned in despatches.

Hudleston returned to Britain in 1938 and attended the RAF Staff College. He hoped for a squadron and was disappointed when at the end of the year he was lent to Turkey to teach its air force.

Although unhappy to be still there at the outbreak of war he found consolation in flying the Turks' German-built Heinkel 111 bombers.

He was posted to Cairo in 1941, and a series of crucial staff appointments followed as the Italians and Germans were defeated in the desert, Sicily and Italy. Hudleston was mentioned three more times in despatches.

Throughout this period he was one of the few senior officers authorised to read Ultra decrypts of enemy Enigma cipher signals. To his disappointment, he was barred from flying lest he should fall into enemy hands with such knowledge.

In 1944, as a 36-year-old air vice-marshal, he received command of 84 Group in 2nd Tactical Air Force, with the task of supporting the First Canadian Army in Holland.

After a spell at the Imperial Defence College during Gen Slim's tenure as commandant, Hudleston played an important part in preparing a review of British post-war strategy for the Chiefs of Staff. In 1948 he was dispatched to Europe as leader of the British delegation to the Western Union Military Staff Committee, and helped to shape Nato.

In 1950 he was called back to Britain to lead Bomber Command's 1 Group. The next year he returned to France as deputy chief of staff at the new Supreme Headquarters, Allied Powers, Europe.

Bomber Command reclaimed him in 1953, and he ushered its 3 Group into the nuclear deterrent era as the Valiant, first of the RAF's V-bombers, entered operational service.

In 1956 he was instructing at the Imperial Defence College when Marshal of the RAF Sir William Dickson ordered him to Cyprus as the air chief of staff to Operation Musketeer, the assault on Egypt after Nasser's seizure of the Suez Canal.

He was next appointed vice chief of the air staff, with overall responsibility for RAF operations. He held this post for five years, an exceptionally long period.

Appointed commander-in-chief of Transport Command in 1962, Hudleston left Britain a year later to serve as commander-in-chief Allied Air Forces Central Europe.

He retired in 1967 and from 1971 to 1979 was a director of the optical division of Pilkington Brothers.

Hudleston was appointed CBE in 1943, CB in 1945, KCB in 1958 and GCB in 1963.

He married first Nancye Davis, who died in 1980; they had a son and a daughter. He married secondly Mrs Brenda Withrington.

███████████

MARSHAL OF THE ROYAL AIR FORCE
THE LORD ELWORTHY, KG
4 APRIL 1993

Marshal of the Royal Air Force The Lord Elworthy, KG, the former Chief of the Defence Staff, who has died at Christchurch, New Zealand, aged 82, exercised immense influence during the late 1960s, when Denis Healey, the Labour Defence Minister, re-shaped the Armed Forces.

A genial New Zealander, "Sam" Elworthy had hit it off with Healey from his days as Chief of the Air Staff earlier in the decade. Their rapport was helped by Elworthy's acceptance of the cancellation of TSR2, on the understanding that the Labour Government intended to order the F-111 from America instead.

As Chief of the Air Staff from 1963 to 1967, Elworthy had to deal with a series of cutbacks. It was a difficult period, marking the end of the RAF policy of buying British aircraft in peacetime.

He found himself juggling with resources to meet commitments east of Suez, including the Indonesia confrontation, and facing Army criticism of inadequate helicopter support.

As Chief of the Defence Staff from 1967 to 1971 – first under Healey and then under Lord Carrington – Elworthy was faced with such contrasting issues as Soviet expansion (including the Czech crisis of 1968) and the need for Nato to develop its policy of flexible response. Northern Ireland posed reinforcement problems for the

Army in Germany; and, to his bitter disappointment, the pledged F–111 was cancelled. At the same time the RAF lost its V-bomber deterrent role to the Navy's Polaris submarine.

Elworthy's principal achievements as CDS included masterminding the main withdrawal from the Far East and implementing a defence policy which concentrated on support of Nato in Europe and the North Atlantic. His efforts were recognised by the creation of the first "RAF peerage" since the Second World War.

Samuel Charles Elworthy was born in New Zealand on March 23 1911 and came to England for his education. He attended Marlborough and Trinity College, Cambridge, where he read law and rowed (he became a member of Leander at Henley).

Although he did not join the University Air Squadron, he subsequently became a pilot officer in No 600, an Auxiliary Air Force squadron, flying biplane Hawker Harts.

Elworthy was called to the Bar by Lincoln's Inn in 1935, but his heart was in flying and later that year he was granted a permanent commission in the RAF. He joined No 15 Squadron, flying Harts and Hinds, and was soon selected to take part in dive-bombing trials.

After two years he was appointed ADC to Sir Edgar Ludlow-Hewitt, C-in-C at Bomber Command. Thus at an early stage of his career Elworthy absorbed the atmosphere of High Command, while also obtaining an insight into the RAF's pre-war weakness.

By the outbreak of war in 1939 he was back with a bomber squadron, although No 108's Blenheims were switched to a training role as part of No 13 Operational Training Unit with Elworthy as chief flying instructor.

Subsequently he was fortunate to survive a perilous period of unescorted day bomber operations. When he joined No 82, a Blenheim light bomber squadron, in August 1940, the posting had looked like a death sentence: losses were horrendous.

On his arrival at Watton in Norfolk to command the squadron's "A" Flight, Elworthy learned that of 12 aircraft – the entire serviceable squadron – recently ordered to attack a German air base at Aalborg in northern Denmark, only one Blenheim had returned, and that was because its pilot had turned back, fearing he had insufficient fuel to reach the target and get home. The pilot's excuse was not accepted. He was court-martialled, but acquitted.

It was against this unpromising background that Elworthy and his fellows were hurled at low level against the German "Operation Sealion" invasion vessels assembling in Channel ports and against enemy coastal convoys.

There were further heavy losses but Elworthy's excellence as a flight commander – and good fortune in defying the odds – helped to ensure his promotion to command the squadron.

In early April 1941, together with an inexperienced sergeant, he attacked two 3,000-ton tankers in daylight off the German coast. Inevitably, Me 109 fighters swept in. An air gunner was killed and one of the Blenheim's two propellers fell off, but he shepherded the novice pilot home.

Halfway through that month the squadron was posted to Lossiemouth on the north-east coast of Scotland to enable it to attack shipping off Norway. Even more dangerous, Elworthy reckoned, was an order to attack Krupps at Essen in daylight. He wrote a last letter to his wife, then, to his enormous relief, the raid was cancelled. Fruitless losses across the North Sea in the face of Me 109s – against which the Blenheim stood little chance – caused terrible grief to 82 Squadron's leader. When, that

May, Elworthy was posted for staff duties at Bomber Command's No 2 Group HQ, he gave vent to his feelings and took issue with Air Vice-Marshal Donald Stevenson, the Group Commander.

Elworthy argued that heavy losses were being incurred to no purpose on the anti-shipping operations. When his fellow pilot, the 5th Earl of Bandon, added his disquiet at the senseless attrition, "Butcher" Stevenson threw an ink-well at the wall, shouting: "Churchill wants it!"

In fact, the Prime Minister minuted that, while eclipsing the Charge of the Light Brigade, such deeds produced losses disproportionate to results.

In the early summer of 1942, Elworthy was posted to join the recently appointed C-in-C, "Bomber" Harris, at Bomber Command as his Group Captain Operations. This was a critical point in the Command's fortunes and there could have been no more appropriate choice for this post as Harris began to question the rationale of the bomber offensive, and to introduce new techniques.

On the night of May 30 1942, Elworthy played his part in planning and executing the RAF's first 1,000-bomber raid on Cologne – in fact, after scraping operational training units, there were 1,046 aircraft.

After a hard year working with Harris, Elworthy was rewarded with his own command, RAF Waddington, a Lincolnshire bomber base accommodating Nos 9, 44 and 50 Lancaster Squadrons.

At first Elworthy's squadrons operated from satellite airfields, while concrete runways were built, but that November, when the work was finished, he welcomed two Australian Lancaster squadrons, Nos 463 and 467.

For a year Elworthy presided over a crescendo of bombing – including many notable attacks on Hamburg, Berlin, Nuremberg and the flying-bomb and rocket V-weapon development station at Peenemunde.

In the spring of 1944, anticipating the June landings in Normandy, Harris entrusted Elworthy with the delicate duty of representing him at the HQ of the Supreme Commander, Gen Eisenhower.

With Bomber Command committed to the direct support of "Operation Overlord", it was Elworthy's task to ensure that heavy bomber operations were integrated. It fell to him specifically to prepare a blitz on enemy rail communications, sparing, where possible, French casualties.

As the Allies began their advance through North-West Europe, Elworthy was posted as Senior Air Staff Officer to Bomber Command's No 5 Group, where, under Sir Ralph Cochrane, he oversaw numerous operations, including the sinking of the *Tirpitz*.

When the war ended in Europe Elworthy was not yet 35 and had held the rank of Air Commodore for a year. But that Christmas he was obliged to revert to Group Captain on joining the Central Bombing Establishment at Marham in Norfolk to plan for the eventual operational use of the Canberra, the RAF's first jet bomber.

In 1947 he experienced a change of scene and pace when he arrived in India as SASO of its No 2 Group. After Partition he transferred to the Pakistan Air Force. During this tropical interlude Elworthy reflected that, thanks to the war, he had come a long way without any formal staff training and that if he was to go further this should be remedied.

Dropping rank again to Wing Commander, he attended the Joint Services Staff College at Latimer. This led, in 1950, to an Air Ministry desk as Deputy Director of Personnel.

He enlivened this dreary task ("the kiss of death") with an outspoken argument against Fighter Command's refusal to employ senior officers without a fighter background.

The Air Marshals responded by sending this career bomber officer off to command the fighter station at Tangmere in Sussex in 1951. On encountering fighter squadrons for the first time he seized the opportunity to fly with his Meteor Squadrons, Nos 1 and 29.

Two years later Elworthy took over the Meteor station at Odiham in Hampshire. Later he moved up to command Fighter Command's Metropolitan Sector, responsible for guarding London and the south-east against Soviet air attack.

In 1956 he was plucked from the Imperial Defence College to head the Planning Staff for the Suez Crisis. During the campaign he was taken ill and rushed to hospital. But by the end of the year he was fit enough to take up the post of Commandant of the Staff College at Bracknell.

In 1959 he joined the Air Council as Deputy Chief of the Air Staff. Almost immediately he was selected by Mountbatten, then Chief of the Defence Staff, to command British forces in the Aden peninsula, the first post-war tri-service integrated command.

When, in 1961, Iraq threatened to invade Kuwait, a well-prepared plan, named "Vantage" – to which Elworthy had contributed significantly – was implemented. Its success as a deterrent owed much to Elworthy's talent for achieving co-operation between the three services and civilians, particularly in Aden.

On his retirement as Chief of the Defence Staff, Elworthy became Constable and Governor of Windsor Castle for seven years. He also served as Lord Lieutenant of Greater London from 1973 to 1978.

The combination of these illustrious offices gave rise to some diverting incidents.

During the State Visit of the President of Italy, Elworthy greeted the visitor on arrival at Tilbury as Lord Lieutenant and then dashed by helicopter to Windsor to perform the same duty as Governor of the Castle. The Queen, when presenting Elworthy on that occasion, remarked that the President must be beginning to think that she was rather short of functionaries.

Among his numerous other appointments, he was chairman of the Royal Over-Seas League and of the King Edward VII Hospital for Officers; Master of the Skinners' Company; a director of British Petroleum, Plessey and the National Bank of New Zealand; and a governor of Wellington, Marlborough and Bradfield Colleges.

Sam Elworthy was an extraordinarily handsome man and, despite his gallant war record and distinguished career, a modest one. He remained at heart a serving officer and was happiest in the company of his fellow officers.

His courage and physical prowess were legendary and until Whitehall swallowed him up, he took part in all the exercises and endurance tests which the troops under his command underwent, often lasting the course far better than much younger men.

He had a keen sense of humour and greatly enjoyed jokes in the Mess, especially when they were at his own expense. When he reached the higher ranks he was equally fearless in fighting for what he believed was right – his arguments with Mountbatten as CDS, and at Cabinet level when he, himself succeeded "Uncle Dickie" were celebrated in their day.

Elworthy was awarded the DSO, DFC and AFC in 1941 and mentioned three times in despatches between 1941 and 1944. He was appointed CBE in 1946, LVO in 1953, CB in 1960, KCB in 1961 and GCB in 1962. He was created a Life Peer as Baron Elworthy in 1972 and in 1977 became the first New Zealander to be installed as a Knight of the Garter. He was also a Knight of the Order of St John of Jerusalem.

In 1978, after he left Windsor, he returned to New Zealand, to live in the valley where he had been born. But he continued to make annual trips to Britain to attend the Garter Ceremony and to see his many devoted friends in the old country.

Elworthy married, in 1936, Audrey Hutchinson, who died in 1986. They had three sons and a daughter.

AIR CHIEF MARSHAL
SIR HARRY BROADHURST
29 AUGUST 1995

Air Chief Marshal Sir Harry Broadhurst, who has died aged 89, was an outstanding leader of Bomber Command in the 1950s and ended his career as Commander of Allied Air Forces, Central Europe.

During the Second World War he had been an exceptional fighter pilot with a score of 12 enemy aircraft destroyed and four probables. He won the DFC in 1940, a Bar to it in 1942 and a DSO and Bar in 1941.

"Broady" Broadhurst always remained an aviator at heart. In 1956, when the new Vulcan bomber was flying home from Australia and New Zealand, Broadhurst, then a 51-year-old air marshal, insisted on taking the second pilot's seat.

Visibility was poor, with low cloud and driving rain, as the Vulcan approached Heathrow Airport. In the murk the bomber's 33-year-old captain, Squadron Leader Donald Howard, decided he was unlikely to get in and attempted to overshoot. At that moment the Vulcan's wheels stuck in a field of Brussels sprouts short of the runway.

Howard ejected and Broadhurst, after a desperate effort to regain control, followed him. Three other crew and a representative of A V Roe were not equipped with ejector seats and perished when the aircraft exploded.

Broadhurst escaped with injured feet and legs. His skill had always been matched by luck, from the time he made an opportunistic escape from an embattled airfield during the fall of France.

On May 20 1940 his Hurricane fighter, one of the last out of France, was shot up and harried home across the Channel by four Me 109 fighters. Though the aircraft was assumed to be lost, Broadhurst landed it, riddled with holes, at Northolt. A week later he heard that it had been repaired.

Broadhurst collected the fighter and had it painted black, with the initials "H B" monogrammed on the fuselage. He then persuaded Rolls-Royce to install the latest two-stage Mark XX Merlin engine, so his Hurricane performed like a Spitfire.

In June 1940, on the eve of the Battle of Britain, he was appointed to command the fighter sector at Wittering. That summer he also flew operational sorties with No 1, a Hurricane squadron in his sector.

When he was posted on Christmas Eve to command RAF Hornchurch, he caused a stir among its Spitfire wing by arriving in his Hurricane. He flew a Spitfire by day and his Hurricane by night, until a spoilsport senior officer questioned the Hurricane's origins, proclaimed it illegal and ordered its removal.

Early in 1941, Broadhurst led his wing on numerous aggressive sweeps over France. In June he was wounded during a heavy engagement over Béthune.

A cannon shell tore a large hole in the port wing of his aircraft, wrecked his port guns and damaged the controls. A second shell hit the side of the fuselage, causing havoc in the cockpit.

In May 1942 Broadhurst was appointed Deputy Senior

Air Staff Officer at No 11, the fighter group which was defending much of the south of England. Though a staff officer, he provided eight hours of air cover during the ill-fated Dieppe raid of August 19, and shot down at least one enemy fighter.

Later that year he was posted to Egypt, where he found the 8th Army and Western Desert Air Force in triumphant mood after the Battle of Alamein. He was soon appointed Air Officer Commanding.

When, on March 20, General Montgomery's assault on the Mareth Line in southern Tunisia ran into trouble, vigorous action by Broadhurst's squadrons prevented a crisis. After that he was Monty's favourite airman and regarded by the Army as an air leader who understood the needs of infantry and armour. He continued to support the 8th Army in Sicily and in Italy.

Broadhurst's rapport with the Army assured him a key role as the Allied Air Expeditionary Force prepared for and took part in the D-Day invasion of Normandy in 1944. He was commander of No 83 Group in the 2nd Tactical Air Force.

Largely due to his masterly control of the Group's 22 squadrons of Spitfires and Typhoons during the fierce fighting for the Falaise Gap, the remnants of 16 German divisions were driven into headlong retreat. It was an impressive end to a brilliant war.

Harry Broadhurst was born on October 28 1905 at Frimley in Surrey and educated at Portsmouth Grammar School. After a spell as an artillery officer in the Territorial Army he was granted a short service commission in the RAF at the age of 21.

Posted to India in 1928, he served on the North-West Frontier with No 11, a Wapiti bomber squadron, and was mentioned in despatches for punitive action against rebel tribes.

In 1932 Broadhurst joined No 41, a Bristol Bulldog fighter squadron based at Northolt, and the next year moved to No 19, also equipped with Bulldogs, at Duxford.

In this period his daredevilry as an aerobatic pilot made him a star attraction at air displays. He led the Air Force's formation team with wingtips tied together and was awarded the AFC.

After a stint as chief instructor at the RAF's No 4 Flying Training School in Egypt, Broadhurst attended a Staff College course in 1938. In the New Year of 1939 he received command of No 111, the first squadron to be equipped with the Hurricane.

He led "Treble One" in the defence of the fleet at Scapa Flow at the beginning of the Second World War. This was followed by a brief spell as Wing Commander Training in No 11 Group. In May 1940 Broadhurst was posted to command No 60 Fighter Wing in France.

After the war he had a staff job at Administrative Fighter Command, commanded No 61 Group and, after further staff posts at home and in Germany, was in 1956 appointed Air Officer Commanding-in-Chief, Bomber Command. When he first arrived at High Wycombe he met with raised eyebrows on account of his fighter background.

For his part Broadhurst was profoundly unimpressed. "To be utterly frank," he observed, "I was appalled at the tedious way they were still behaving. Bomber Command is still back in the Second World War".

Bombers were taking up to six hours to get airborne. Broadhurst decided to "put a jerk into Bomber Command by bringing in a few fighter people like myself". Before long the Quick Reaction Alert procedure of the fighters had been introduced to bring techniques in line with the jet age.

Later in 1956 Broadhurst had to provide bombers for the Suez campaign. His characteristically outspoken and irreverent reception of the plan presented to him by Antony Head, the Minister of Defence, inspired a not entirely jocular threat of arrest. "Don't worry," consoled Sir Dermot Boyle, the Chief of Air Staff, "it happens to me before breakfast every morning."

"We didn't get it all wrong," Broadhurst later reflected. "For example the Canberras blew off the wall of Cairo prison and released most of the inmates, who may have caused a few problems."

From 1959 until his retirement in 1961 Broadhurst was Commander Allied Air Forces Central Europe. Thereafter he was in immediate demand in the aviation industry, where A V Roe employed him on the Blue Steel missile project.

He was managing director of A V Roe from 1961 to 1966, deputy managing director of Hawker Siddeley Aviation from 1965 to 1976, and director of Hawker Siddeley Group from 1968 to 1976.

Broadhurst was disappointed by the cancellations of the P1154 and HS 681 projects, but encouraged by the success of the Harrier programme. He helped to lay the foundations for two outstandingly successful civil aircraft, the European Airbus and the HS 125 executive jet.

His contribution to the aircraft industry was recognised by the Society of British Aerospace Companies; between 1973 and 1976 he was successively vice-president, president and deputy president.

Broadhurst was appointed CB in 1944, KBE in 1945, KCB in 1955 and GCB in 1960.

He married first, in 1929 Doris Kathleen French and secondly, in 1946, Jean Elizabeth Townley. He had a daughter by each marriage.

AIR VICE-MARSHAL ROBERT DEACON-ELLIOTT

5 JUNE 1997

Air Vice-Marshal Robert Deacon-Elliott, who has died aged 82, shot down at least one enemy aircraft a day over four of the most critical days of the Battle of Britain in the late summer of 1940.

On September 6 in the same week he was himself shot down over Kent after making a head-on attack on an enemy Me 109 fighter with his Spitfire, as part of the defensive action of No 72 Squadron.

"The Deac", as he was popularly known, baled out and returned that same day to his squadron at Croydon, immediately resuming operations. He bagged a 109 and evened the score.

Up to that moment in the Battle of Britain, Deacon-Elliott seemed to have led a charmed life. He was scrambled with 72 Squadron from Acklington in Northumberland on Aug 15, two days after Hermann Goering, the head of the Luftwaffe, had launched his Eagle Offensive, which was intended to destroy Fighter Command within four days.

When Deacon-Elliott took off on Aug 15, radar had inaccurately suggested about 20 enemy aircraft heading in over the North Sea. In the event, the Deac, with no more than 11 of his fellows, encountered beyond the Fame Islands some 100 enemy aircraft — 30 He 111 bombers escorted by 70 Me 110 fighters.

Despite these heavy odds, it took an equipment failure to give Deacon-Elliott his narrowest shave that summer. He was flying at 20,000 feet over the north of England when his oxygen supply failed. He blacked out and his Spitfire nosed into a dive. He did not come round until he was at 1,000 feet — too low to bale out — over the Cheviots.

Deacon-Elliott, fit from squash and extremely strong, managed to heave the Spitfire out of its dive. Although he succeeded in landing at Acklington, his Spitfire was declared a write-off. The aircraft was subsequently restored and retired to the Science Museum where it is still exhibited.

At the end of August, 72 Squadron was ordered south to reinforce No 11 Group, which was reeling from the Eagle Offensive's sustained assault on its fighter airfields.

On the afternoon of the last day in August, Deacon-Elliott landed at Biggin Hill, or "The Bump" as pilots knew it, the Kent fighter base. He was appalled by the mayhem he found there.

The only runway in use was pockmarked with bomb craters. Enemy bombers, heavily escorted by fighters, had paid yet another visit at lunchtime. Even so Deacon-Elliott's squadron was in action late that afternoon; it lost two Spitfires.

Robert Deacon-Elliott was born on November 20 1914 at Church Brampton, Northampton, where he was educated. He seemed destined to become an accountant but in 1938 volunteered for pilot training in the Royal Air Force Volunteer Reserve.

In December 1939 Deacon-Elliott was posted to No 72 Squadron whose Gladiator biplane fighters had been replaced by Spitfires. In January 1940 the squadron flew south from Drem, in East Lothian, to Church Fenton, North Yorkshire. On June 1 it was transferred to Gravesend, Kent, so that, though greatly outnumbered, its presence helped to raise the morale of troops on the Dunkirk beaches during the British Expeditionary Force's evacuation of France.

In the New Year of 1941, as Fighter Command went on the offensive, Deacon-Elliott took part in fighter sweeps across the Channel and over France. By July he had survived many months of intensive fighter operations and was rested on courses until October 1942, when he joined the staff at HQ Fighter Command to report on its pilot morale and battle fatigue problems.

Deacon-Elliott attended the RAF Staff College in 1943, an indication that he was already regarded as a candidate for higher command. The next year he joined No 84 Group in 2nd Tactical Air Force to help prepare this highly successful fighter group to support the invasion of Normandy in June 1944 and the subsequent Allied advance through north-west Europe.

He remained with 84 Group until victory had been achieved in Europe in May 1945. Later he was posted to Cyprus to command a flying wing and the armament practice camp.

Although a wing commander and somewhat more restrained than in his heady days as a young fighter pilot, Deacon-Elliott was none the less still ready to participate in air crew officers' traditionally boisterous mess games. As agile as his youngest officers at the high-spirited late-night high jinks of "Highcockalorum" he was also reputed for his skill at carrying out a particularly difficult manoeuvre with a beer glass.

Flying Tempest fighter-bombers on Cyprus was supposedly less hazardous than Highcockalorum, at which he broke a leg, but Deacon-Elliott also survived a near-fatal beach crash-landing after a ricochet on the rocket range had disabled his aircraft.

Throughout the 1950s Deacon-Elliott climbed the ladder towards air rank. This involved staff appointments, a spell at the Army Staff College as a member of the directing staff, and station commands at Leconfield and Driffield. There was a particularly enjoyable exchange posting to the Air University of the United States Air Force at Maxwell Air Force Base.

In 1962, he returned home as the first Commandant of the Officers and Aircrew Selection Centre at Biggin Hill. He moved on to Gibraltar in 1965 as Air Officer Commanding both RAF Gibraltar and RAF Malta, in addition to being Deputy Commander-in-Chief (Air) Allied Forces Mediterranean.

Following his retirement in 1968, Deacon-Elliott was appointed Bursar at the Civil Service College. There the sensitive and introspective side of his nature balanced his press-on reputation as a fighter pilot and assured 11 years of much appreciated service.

He was awarded the DFC and mentioned in despatches in 1941. In 1944 he was again mentioned in despatches and gained the Air Efficiency Award. He was appointed OBE in 1954 and CB in 1967.

Deacon-Elliott married Grace Joan Willes in 1948. She survives him, together with two sons and a daughter.

He was proud that both his sons graduated from the RAF College, Cranwell, as pilots and that one of them led a flight of RAF Tornadoes over Buckingham Palace on the 50th anniversary of the Battle of Britain.

AIR CHIEF MARSHAL
SIR DENIS "SPLINTERS" SMALLWOOD
26 JULY 1997

Air Chief Marshal Sir Denis "Splinters" Smallwood, who has died aged 78, was a superb fighter pilot and ended his career as C-in-C, RAF Strike Command.

Smallwood's career prospered despite a period of intense frustration during the Suez crisis in 1956, when he was responsible for planning the action of the Air Task Force. His sunny disposition, charm, sense of humour and strong powers of leadership helped him to perform what seemed an impossible task.

Later Smallwood, with characteristic forthrightness, called the basis on which he and fellow planners were expected to work "a monumental political cock-up".

"As far as the planners' perspective was concerned," he told an RAF Historical Society seminar, "I would liken this to one of Roald Dahl's *Tales of the Unexpected*. It certainly had all the ingredients – intrigue, high drama – difficulties of all sorts."

Nevertheless, the RAF bombing operations, which neutralised the Egyptian Air Force, were completely successful from the military point of view.

Following initial planning in Britain, Smallwood boarded a Comet to fly out with Air Marshal Sir Denis Barnett, the Allied Air Force Task Force commander to headquarters in Cyprus. There was a moment when he thought he might never reach the island.

"At roughly 45,000 feet," he recalled, "the aircraft went quite astonishingly quiet. Barnett was reading a novel when the captain, dressed in his best blue, appeared and reported to him that he had lost all four engines."

Barnett merely murmured: "Well, tell me how you get on," and resumed reading. Fortunately the engines re-started after the Comet had lost sufficient height to escape the very low temperature which had caused the problem.

Denis Graham Smallwood was born on August 13 1918 at King's Norton and educated at King Edward VI School, Birmingham.

He joined the RAF in 1938 and after getting his wings was posted to No 605 (County of Warwick), an Auxiliary Air Force squadron.

In 1940 he was moved to No 87, a Hurricane night fighter and intruder squadron, but he did not fight in the Battle of Britain that summer and autumn.

But he saw plenty of action later, in command of 87 – not least a heavy day of fighting and low-level attack during the ill-fated Operation Jubilee on Aug 19 1942. This was a Combined Operations assault on Dieppe, during which the RAF lost more than 100 aircraft.

In the first of three sorties Smallwood led 12 Hurricanes in an attack on the east headland, strafing gun emplacements and setting fire to a tower on the cliffs. For his action that day he was awarded the DFC.

After a spell in command of No 286, another Hurricane squadron, Smallwood took over a Spitfire wing in the far south-west of England. He was in his element there, operating principally from Pradannack, before, during and after the D-Day landings. Smallwood led 131 and 165 Squadrons, equipped with the latest Spitfire IX, in aggressive support of the invasion forces.

Smallwood was rated a highly competent leader, whose briefings were meticulous, but he was too often denied opportunities to engage enemy fighters. Nevertheless he was awarded the DSO in 1944.

He then joined HQ, Air Defence of Great Britain, and took the RAF staff college course at Haifa. From there he went to HQ British Air Forces of Occupation Germany. In 1948 he received command of No 33, a Tempest fighter squadron, in Germany.

Between 1948 and 1952 he was an Air Ministry planner and a member of the directing staff of the Joint Services Staff College.

On June 2 1953, while commanding RAF Biggin Hill, Smallwood led a seven-wing salute by jets for the Queen's Coronation.

After the Suez crisis, he took command for two years of the guided missiles at North Coates, and in 1961 became Commandant of the College of Air Warfare at Manby. He became assistant Chief of Staff (Operations) in 1963.

Smallwood the renowned fighter pilot built a new reputation as a bomber leader on his appointment in 1965 to No 3 Group, Bomber Command. This was in the testing era of the Cold War when nuclear deterrent V-bombers were on quick-reaction alert. Smallwood soon found himself at home.

In 1967 he was appointed Senior Air Staff Officer at Bomber Command, moving up the next year to deputy Commander-in-Chief Strike Command.

From 1969 to 1970 he was Air Officer Commanding the Near East Air Force and at the same time administrator of the Sovereign Base Area in Cyprus. On returning to Britain, Smallwood became Vice Chief of the Air Staff in 1970 and then, from 1974 to 1976, C-in-C Strike Command. Additionally, from 1975, he commanded Nato's UK Air Forces.

Smallwood was inclined to be outspoken, and in the House of Commons in 1975 the Labour MP Frank Allaun told him to keep "his mouth shut" about sensitive issues. This was in response to Smallwood's expressing concern on television about the Soviet arms build-up at a time of cutbacks in the RAF.

Smallwood also campaigned in the letters column of *The Daily Telegraph* when he felt action was called for. Shortly after he left the service, *World in Action* criticised the RAF's future front-line aircraft, the Tornado. Smallwood energetically defended the multi-role combat aircraft.

When other correspondents to the *Telegraph* queried the feasibility of a future for the RAF, Smallwood returned to the fray, his instincts as a fighter rekindled.

On retiring from the RAF in 1976 Smallwood spent six years as a military adviser to British Aerospace. In later years he was able to indulge his interest in horses, and became the organiser of the Tythrop Horse Trials near

Thame, Oxon.

Smallwood was appointed MBE in 1951, CBE in 1961, CB in 1966 and KCB in 1969.

He was President of the Friends of St Clement Dane, the RAF Central Church, in the Strand.

Denis Smallwood married in 1940 Frances Jeanne Needham, who died in 1992; they had a son and a daughter.

AIR CHIEF MARSHAL
SIR FREDERICK ROSIER
10 SEPTEMBER 1998

Air Chief Marshal Sir Frederick Rosier, who has died aged 82, ended his career as Deputy Commander-in-Chief Allied Forces Central Europe, but he made his mark as an exceptional fighter commander in the Desert War.

In the spring of 1941, No 229, a Hurricane squadron, embarked for North Africa in the aircraft carrier *Furious*. Neither Rosier, then a Squadron Leader, nor his pilots had ever taken off from the deck of a carrier, but when *Furious* steamed within range of Malta he led the squadron to it.

The next day he flew on to Egypt to reinforce the Desert Air Force. On hearing that several Italian-crewed Ju 87 "Stuka" divebombers had force-landed in a forward area, Rosier determined to bag one.

Accompanied by his Wing Commander, and helped by an Army patrol, he duly located a Stuka. As the Wing Commander saw to refuelling, Rosier fiddled with the switches in the cockpit. Suddenly there was a thud, a shout and everyone scattered. Rosier had released the bombs. Fortunately, they had to fall rather further than they had before they were armed.

Rosier and his companion then took off, but after 20 minutes the engine spluttered, forcing them to land. "The outlook was bleak," Rosier recalled. "We were far away from any established route. That night we slept in the folds of our parachutes. At dawn, after leaving a message in stones, we walked due north."

For hours they saw no sign of life. Then, after streaming a parachute in the wind, they were spotted by some Allied trucks. The Stuka was repaired and the pair flew their prize back to base.

Rosier both loved and hated the desert. He cursed its extremes of heat and cold, the sandstorms, flies and shortage of water, but he was fascinated by the desert's beauty at night, its sunrises, and its silences, which he took every opportunity to break with his violin.

In 1941, aged just 25, Rosier was promoted Wing Commander and took charge of the newly formed No 262 Wing. With Group Captain "Bing" Cross, in command of 258 Wing, Rosier was responsible for the operational control of the Desert Air Force's fighter squadrons.

In November 1941 Operation Crusader Defensive began; Rosier stuffed his kit and prized silver tankard into his Hurricane and headed for the airfield at Tobruk to organise fighter support. He was escorted by two Australian Tomahawk squadrons, and soon encountered a force of Me 109 fighters. Rosier spotted a Tomahawk being forced to crash land and touched down alonngside.

In order to squeeze the Tomahawk's pilot, Sergeant Burney, into the single seat of his Hurricane, Rosier took off his parachute, sat on Burney and attempted to take off. But a tyre burst, and for the second time in two months Rosier faced the prospect of a long walk, this time through enemy territory.

He hid the precious tankard, his wife's photograph and a few other possessions in brushwood; then, as he was about to set off, truckloads of Italian troops appeared and found his belongings. Rosier and Burney hid in a wadi.

They began to walk across the desert, navigating by the Pole Star and coming within a whisker of German tanks. On the fourth day, with shells passing overhead, they ran towards the sound of gunfire and found a Guards unit.

Rosier went to Cairo for a short leave soon afterwards and fell into conversation with a South African officer over a drink. He began to tell how he had lost his much-prized tankard when the major suddenly produced it like a rabbit from a hat. His men had found it in a captured Italian truck.

Rosier went on to assume further responsibility as second-in-command of No 211 Fighter Group and made important contributions to the 8th Army's victory at El Alamein and to the eventual capture of Tripoli. For his leadership in the desert theatre, he was awarded the DSO in 1942.

Frederick Ernest Rosier, the son of a railway engineer on the Great Western Railway, was born at Wrexham on October 13 1915. He went to Grove Park School and played for North Wales Schoolboys at rugby.

In 1935 he was granted a short service commission. The next year he joined No 43, a Fury biplane fighter squadron stationed at Tangmere, Sussex. By May 1940, he was a Flight Commander in No 229, which he had helped to form and convert from Blenheims to Hurricanes. During the fall of France he led a detachment to Vitry, near Arras.

Two days later he was shot down over the airfield by an Me 109. Though badly burned about the face, Rosier managed to bale out before his Hurricane plunged into the ground. As he got to his feet, he was fired on by

French troops until a fellow pilot intervened.

By October he had returned to active service, and led 229 from Northolt for the last 12 days of the Battle of Britain after its squadron commander had been shot down.

After his desert exploits, Rosier returned home in 1943 to take charge of No 52 Operational Training Unit and then the fighter stations at Northolt and Horsham St Faith.

Rosier subsequently served as Group Captain Operations at the Central Flying Establishment, and then, under Lord Mountbatten, was the first director of the Joint Planning Staff. From 1956 to 1958 he was an ADC to the Queen.

In 1961 he was posted to Aden as Air Officer Commanding Air Forces, Middle East – an appointment for which his wartime desert experience suited him well. He arrived in the wake of the Kuwait crisis, and was confronted by tribal unrest in the Aden protectorates and hostile moves from Yemen.

In 1964, he returned home as Senior Air Staff Officer at Transport Command, moving over in 1966 to Fighter Command as Commander-in-Chief. He was its last C-in-C before it was amalgamated with Bomber Command to form Strike Command.

From 1968 Rosier served on the Permanent Military Deputies Group and then at Allied Forces, Central Europe, Ankara. He was promoted to Air Chief Marshal in 1970, and became Deputy Commander-in-Chief Allied Forces Central Europe.

Rosier retired in 1973 and was appointed Military Adviser and Director of the British Aircraft Corporation at Preston. He later served on the board of BAC in Saudi Arabia, paving the way for the Al Yamamah arms deal.

Rosier was appointed OBE in 1943, CBE in 1955, CB

in 1961, KCB in 1966 and GCB in 1972. At Northolt he had been much impressed by the spirit shown by Polish pilots and later became chairman of their benevolent fund. He was appointed to the Polish Order of Merit this year.

He married, in 1939, Hettie Blackwell; they had three sons and a daughter.

AIR CHIEF MARSHAL
SIR PETER FLETCHER
2 JANUARY 1999

Air Chief Marshal Sir Peter Fletcher, who has died aged 82, led a Hurricane fighter squadron against overwhelming Japanese air attacks in the desperate and costly defence of Ceylon in 1942.

Early that year, Fletcher arrived in Karachi from the Middle East expecting to be sent on to reinforce Singapore. But in late February, as the situation there deteriorated, posing an imminent threat to Ceylon, he was detached from 135 Squadron and despatched to Colombo in command of a flight of eight Hurricanes.

Fletcher arrived at Ratmalana, a small flying club airfield, to discover that facilities were minimal. The squadron's Hurricanes were parked under palm trees some distance away from the mess, and Fletcher had to borrow motorcycles to speed his pilots out to their aircraft.

Having acquired six more Hurricanes, Fletcher was promoted squadron leader. His unit, designated as the re-formed 258 Squadron, was then moved to Colombo's racecourse.

On Easter Sunday, Fletcher was having his breakfast when a mass of Japanese bombers and fighters suddenly appeared overhead, bound for Colombo's harbour. Fletcher scrambled the squadron and, having climbed to a height from which to attack the bombers, shouted "Tally-ho".

"From then," he recalled, "it was every man for himself." He opened fire on an aircraft diving on the harbour and saw it go into the sea. He had just "knocked a few bits off another Jap" when he felt a heavy thud underneath his Hurricane. Oil and fumes came into the cockpit and to his fury he realised he had been hit by friendly ground fire.

Fletcher then felt bangs against the back of his seat and pain in his shoulder. This time he had been hit by a pair of Zeros who were on his tail. As oil began to gush on to his face, he baled out.

As he drifted down on his parachute, the Zero pilots took turns to fire bursts at him. Although Fletcher feigned death by hanging his head limply to one side, they continued to shoot at him even after he had landed near a small temple next to a coconut plantation. A Buddhist priest took him to hospital. Fletcher was later awarded the DFC.

A total of 30 Hurricanes from 258 and 30 Squadrons and six Fleet Air Arm fighters had engaged the enemy. Heavily outnumbered, and at a tactical disadvantage, only 15 Hurricanes and two Fulmars survived the air battle. Moreover, six Fleet Air Arm Swordfish torpedo bombers preparing to attack the Japanese fleet were shot down.

Although at the time many successes were claimed, it was later estimated that of a force of 126 Japanese aircraft only a handful were destroyed. But had Fletcher, a Rhodesian, and his mixed bag of pilots – among them an American and an Argentinian volunteer – not given such a good account of themselves, the Eastern Fleet might have suffered a similar fate to that of their American counterparts at Pearl Harbor.

Peter Carteret Fletcher was born on October 7 1916 in Durban, South Africa, and brought up in Southern Rhodesia, where his father built up a large tobacco farm.

He was educated at St George's College, Rhodesia, and at Rhodes University in South Africa. When war broke out in 1939, he joined the Southern Rhodesia Air Force and qualified as a pilot. In 1941 he transferred to the RAF.

Following his exploit in Ceylon, and on account of his wounds, Fletcher returned to Rhodesia, where he served as a flying instructor. At the age of 27, he was promoted wing commander and received command of Belvedere, the RAF's station at Salisbury racecourse.

Having received a permanent commission in the RAF, in 1946 Fletcher joined the directing staff at the Joint Services Staff College and in 1948 was appointed Chief Flying Instructor at RAF Feltwell. Following a spell on the joint planning staff at the Air Ministry, in 1953 he became Air Attaché at the British Embassy in Oslo.

Fletcher's instinctive grasp of strategy had already marked him out for promotion and, after a spell on the staff at the Imperial Defence College, in 1960 he became Deputy Director Joint Plans (Air) in Whitehall. The next year, as Director Operational Requirements at the Ministry of Defence, he began negotiations to buy from the Americans the C-130 Hercules, to this day the workhorse of the RAF.

In 1964, Fletcher was promoted Assistant Chief of Air Staff (Policy and Plans), a post in which he weathered a long struggle with the Royal Navy over the future of aircraft carriers, and emerged the victor. Then, in 1967, having briefly returned to operational duties in charge of No 38 Group Transport Command, he went back to Whitehall as Vice Chief of Air Staff.

In this capacity, Fletcher was given responsibility for the

operational efficiency of the RAF and, together with the Air Member for Personnel, he changed the pattern of flying training. He also introduced into service the Buccaneer low-flying bomber.

In 1971 Fletcher, following a year as Controller of Aircraft, Ministry of Aviation Supply, took a leading role in the restructuring of defence procurement. He took his turn as rotating chairman of the Concorde directing committee, and of the Panavia multi-role combat aircraft (the future Tornado) group.

He also selected the Hawk, the advanced trainer which still equips the Red Arrows, and was responsible for the programme which produced the Anglo-French Jaguar, which remains in operational service as a strike aircraft.

Fletcher retired in 1974, but remained much in demand; he was soon welcomed on to the board at Hawker Siddeley Aviation (HSA). When, in 1977, HSA became part of the newly-formed and state-owned British Aerospace, Fletcher was appointed director responsible for Corporate Strategy and Planning. He was much involved in the development of the successful Airbus programme.

He retired in 1982 and thereafter worked as a consultant to several aviation companies. He was elected a Fellow of the Royal Aeronautical Society in 1986.

Fletcher was awarded the AFC in 1951, and was appointed OBE in 1945 and CB in 1965. He was advanced to KCB in 1968.

He married, in 1940, Marjorie Kotze, a South African. They had two daughters.

AIR MARSHAL
SIR HAROLD MAGUIRE
1 FEBRUARY 2001

Air Marshal Sir Harold Maguire, who has died aged 88, led RAF resistance to the Japanese invasions of Sumatra and Java in 1942, and subsequently endured great privation during three years in a Far Eastern prison camp; he was awarded the DSO in 1946 for the gallant example he had set to his fellow captives.

Early in February 1942, Maguire arrived in Batavia (now Jakarta) to assume command of No 266 Fighter Wing. This consisted of some 40 Hurricane pilots, for the most part inexperienced recruits from the Dominions, although Maguire himself was a veteran of the Battle of Britain and seven other pilots had had some taste of combat.

On Friday February 13, Maguire led these seven to P 1, an airfield at Palembang, Sumatra. They arrived overhead as the strip was under heavy attack by Japanese fighters, and Maguire claimed a Zero before landing.

P 1 was shortly afterwards cut off and surrounded by Japanese paratroops, and Maguire took charge of its ground defence. Aircraft were stripped of their Browning machine-guns, and Bofors anti-aircraft guns were depressed to give a horizontal line of fire. Even so, Maguire found himself with only 20 men, scant food and water and little ammunition with which to take on the advancing Japanese.

He took up a position in a slit trench and found himself facing several Japanese soldiers who were similarly dug in. When, unexpectedly, they climbed out and began to run towards the jungle, he and another officer managed to kill a number of them.

He was then told that some Dutch troops had arrived

to reinforce his garrison. He made for the main gate to greet them, only to discover that the new force in fact comprised 70 enemy paratroops. Maguire resorted to bluff. Laying down his tommy-gun, he marched purposefully up to the nearest Japanese soldier and demanded to see his commanding officer. When he was duly produced, Maguire informed him that he was vastly outnumbered and advised him to surrender.

The Japanese officer, however, who spoke English, countered with a promise to give safe conduct to Maguire and his men if they left their positions. On the pretext of consulting a non-existent superior officer, Maguire returned to the airfield and organised the destruction of all remaining aircraft and equipment.

He and his men then trekked for a week to the west coast of Sumatra, where they found a small coaster to take them back to Batavia. There Maguire took command of what remained of its air defences.

By early March, further resistance proved impossible and Maguire was allocated a seat in one of the last aircraft to leave Java. He gave his spot up for a wounded pilot, however, and so was taken prisoner when the island eventually fell.

He was sent to the Boei Gledale camp, Java, where he exhibited great devotion to those under his command in conditions of tremendous hardship. He was remembered by many prisoners for the way in which he stood up to the bullying treatment of the Japanese. After the return of peace, Maguire compiled a detailed dossier on the war crimes perpetrated by his captors, but otherwise succeeded in putting the experience behind him. If asked, he would only describe his life in the camp as "a bad time".

Harold John Maguire was born at Kilkishen, Co Clare, Ireland, on April 12 1912. He was educated at Wesley

College and then at Trinity College, Dublin.

After working briefly as a travelling salesman for Smith's Premier Typewriters, he was commissioned into the Royal Air Force in 1933 and in late 1934 joined No 230, a Coastal Command squadron at Pembroke Dock in Wales. The next year the squadron was ordered to Egypt during the Abyssinian crisis and Maguire piloted a Short Singapore twin-engined flying boat out to Alexandria.

In September 1939, he took command of No 229, a fighter squadron flying Bristol Blenheims on convoy patrols and night-fighter radar trials. In March 1940 it was re-equipped with Hurricanes, and Maguire led it first from Biggin Hill, Kent, to cover the retreat of the BEF and then from Digby, Yorkshire, during the Battle of Britain.

On his release from captivity, Maguire resumed his career in Fighter Command. Initially he took charge of the station at Linton-on-Ouse, North Yorkshire, flying the new piston-engined de Havilland Hornet.

From 1950 to 1952 he commanded RAF Odiham, Hampshire, which was home to a wing of de Havilland Vampire jets. He then moved on to Malta in 1955 as Senior Air Staff Officer, returning to the Air Ministry the next year to direct tactical and air transport operations.

In 1959 Maguire, by now an air vice-marshal, was forced to land a Spitfire on a cricket pitch in Bromley only 10 minutes after flying over Whitehall in a display commemorating the Battle of Britain.

As his engine failed, he spotted the company sports ground of Oxo and managed to put the aircraft down on the square, breaking the stumps at one end while the teams were off having tea. When he entered the pavilion, nursing an injured back, he was welcomed by the players with a strong cup of Darjeeling.

In 1962 Maguire returned to the Far East to take part

in the Indonesian Confrontation as Senior Air Staff Officer. He then became Assistant Chief of Air Staff (Intelligence), and in 1965 Deputy Chief of Defence Staff (Intelligence). He retired in 1968, but was then called back to become the Ministry of Defence's Director-General of Intelligence for four more years.

From 1975 until 1982 he was a director of Commercial Union, the insurance group, and he was also its political and economic adviser from 1972 to 1979. In final retirement, he lived at Brantham, Suffolk, where he was an active churchgoer. He was chairman of the local Conservative Association and of the branch of the British Legion, and was a keen member of the Royal Harwich Yacht Club. He also enjoyed fishing and swimming.

Harold Maguire was appointed OBE in 1949 and CB in 1958. He was advanced to KCB in 1966. He was also mentioned in despatches three times, in 1940, 1942 and 1946.

He married, in 1940, Mary Elisabeth Wild. She died in 1991. They had a son and a daughter.

AIR MARSHAL
SIR KENNETH HAYR
2 JUNE 2001

Air Marshal Sir Kenneth Hayr, who has died in a flying accident at the Biggin Hill air show aged 66, held senior positions in the RAF during both the Falklands campaign and the Gulf War; his abiding passion, however, was piloting fighter aircraft.

Since retirement, Hayr had divided his life between his homes in New Zealand and Britain in order that he would get the best of two summers and could fly throughout the year. He was particularly enthusiastic about undertaking aerobatics in either of two Russian Yak 52 aircraft which he kept near Whangaparoa, his house in New Zealand.

Kenneth William Hayr was born on April 13 1935 at St Helier, New Zealand and educated at Auckland Grammar School before attending RAF College, Cranwell.

After honing his fighter skills with Hawker Hunter and English Electric Lightning jet squadrons in the Middle East between 1957 and 1964, Hayr transferred to the Central Fighter Establishment/Fighter Command Trials Unit. He served there from 1964 to 1967, before becoming Phantom OCU Squadron Commander at Coningsby, Lincolnshire, the following year. Thereafter he concentrated on piloting the Hawker-Siddeley Harrier.

Hayr, who made a priority of keeping flying whatever posting he received, had been dismayed in 1969 when he was told that he was to be sent to the RAF staff college at Bracknell, Berks.

In the event, however, at the last moment he received a transfer from his post at the Phantom fighter operational conversion unit to take command of No 1 (Fighter) Squadron at Wittering, Cambridgeshire.

During his time there, "Boss" (as Hayr's squadron crews knew their commander) quickly appreciated the unique operational value of the Harrier and its vertical take-off and landing capability (VTOL), and was an early exponent and employer of the aircraft in a highly mobile role.

In *No 1 in War and Peace*, a history of the squadron, Hayr recalled this period warmly: "Every dog has its day and this was the time of my life because it was the most exhilarating, interesting and fantastic period in the peacetime life of a squadron commander.

"It was all totally new and nobody could tell us what to

do because nobody knew. We, therefore, broke new ground both literally and figuratively. We wrote our own book."

Hayr owned that in the earlier stages flying a Harrier was difficult. He spent five hours in a helicopter to familiarise himself with straight ascent and descent because there was no two-seat version of the Harrier for training. Although the Harrier's VTOL feature, enabling simpler take-offs and landings on aircraft carriers, has since become standard, it was a novelty when Hayr made his first landing on *Ark Royal* in 1972.

Hayr finally attended staff college that year, and after leaving Bracknell became station commander at Binbrook in 1973. The Lincolnshire base, home of the RAF's Lightning fighters, presented him with as many flying opportunities as he could accommodate.

His next posting, as the RAF's inspector of flight safety from 1976 to 1979, could not have suited him better; the nature of his role provided him with opportunities to fly as frequently as desk duties permitted.

In 1980 Hayr attended the Royal College of Defence Studies before his appointment as Assistant Chief of Air Staff (Operations), a post he held for the next two years. During this period he was instrumental in planning the RAF's role in the Falklands War.

Hayr then took command, in 1982, as AOC No 11 Group before being appointed, in 1985, commander of British Forces in Cyprus and administrator of the sovereign base areas on the Mediterranean island. He returned after two years as Chief of Staff UK air forces and deputy C-in-C, Strike Command, until 1988.

Finally, in 1989, Hayr was appointed Deputy Chief of Defence Staff (commitments) which involved preparing and implementing Operation Granby – the MoD's code-name for the RAF's role in the Desert Shield and Desert

Storm Arabian Gulf operations. He retired in 1993.

Hayr was appointed chairman of the New Zealand Aviation Heritage Trust in 1993. He was awarded the AFC in 1963 and Bar in 1972. He was appointed CBE in 1976, CB in 1982, KCB in 1988 and KBE in 1991. He was awarded the Kuwait Liberation Order (1st Grade) in 1991.

Hayr, a courteous and popular man, with a slightly old-fashioned air, was respected as one of the best pilots in the RAF. He was always eager to get his hands on any airborne craft, and counted paragliding and parachuting, as well as display aerobatics, amongst his hobbies. He was flying a de Havilland Vampire on the Saturday, when, after executing four passes, it spiralled out of control and crashed.

He married, in 1971, Joyce Gardiner, who predeceased him in 1987. They had three sons.

INDEX OF PERSONALITIES

(Italics denotes main entry)